# GOD, GOVERNANCE, AND "ECONOMIC MAN"

*The Lessons of the Founders as Derived from Economic History*

Gene W. Heck

University Press of America,® Inc.
Lanham · Boulder · New York · Toronto · Plymouth, UK

Copyright © 2009 by
University Press of America,® Inc.
4501 Forbes Boulevard
Suite 200
Lanham, Maryland 20706
UPA Acquisitions Department (301) 459-3366

Estover Road
Plymouth PL6 7PY
United Kingdom

All rights reserved
Printed in the United States of America
British Library Cataloging in Publication Information Available

Library of Congress Control Number: 2009929898
ISBN: 978-0-7618-4816-5 (clothbound : alk. paper)
eISBN: 978-0-7618-4817-2

⊖™ The paper used in this publication meets the minimum
requirements of American National Standard for Information
Sciences—Permanence of Paper for Printed Library Materials,
ANSI Z39.48-1992

# THE FIFTH COMMANDMENT

"Honor thy Father and thy Mother"

To Bill and Stena Heck, whom, I am proud to say, were my parents – who loved and believed in a God and in an America that we are losing – and raised my brother Ed and me in a home filled with magnanimity, faith, love, and compassion in the 1950s, the nation's greatest decade!

# TESTIMONIES OF THE FOUNDERS

I have always believed that there was a Divine Plan that caused people to uproot their lives to come to this continent to pursue their dreams in America.

—President Ronald Reagan

If angels were to govern men, neither external nor internal controls on government would be necessary. In framing a government which is to be administered by men over men, the greatest difficulty lies in this: you must first enable the government to control the governed; and in the next place, oblige it to control itself.

—James Madison

The God who gave us life gave us liberty. Can the liberties of a nation be secure when we have removed their only firm basis, the conviction that these liberties are the gift of God? I tremble for my country's future when I reflect that God is just, and that His justice cannot sleep forever.

—Thomas Jefferson

The longer I live, the more convincing proof I have that God governs the affairs of men. If a sparrow cannot fall to the ground without His notice, is it probable that an empire can rise without His aid? . . . He who shall introduce into public affairs the principles of primitive Christianity will change the face of the world!

—Benjamin Franklin

Liberty has never come from government. The history of liberty is the limitation of governmental power, not the increase of it.

—Woodrow Wilson

What government is best? That which teaches us to govern ourselves.

—Johann Goethe

# Contents

| | |
|---|---|
| Acknowledgments | vii |
| Introduction: Manifest Destiny: God's Hand in the Building of America | ix |

Part I: The Creed
| | |
|---|---|
| 1. The Faith of the Founders | 3 |
| 2. Sorting Through the Founders' Faiths | 33 |

Part II: The Cause
| | |
|---|---|
| 3. Portents of the Precipitous Death of God | 67 |
| 4. The Ideology of the Counter-Culture | 101 |

Part III: The Challenge
| | |
|---|---|
| 5. God's "Invisible Economic Hand" | 133 |
| 6. Education in the Founders' Vision for America | 161 |
| Epilogue: God, Governance, and "Deicide" | 185 |

Part IV: The Cure
| | |
|---|---|
| Appendix A: Civic Governance: "Covenantial Change" | 195 |
| Appendix B: Financial Meltdown: Crisis of Capitalism or Failure of Federalism? | 219 |

| | |
|---|---|
| Notes | 231 |
| Bibliography | 275 |
| Index | 293 |

# Acknowledgments

The author acknowledges his debt and gratitude to many for making publication of this book possible. Foremost among them are the publisher, University Press of America, and its superb editor, Brooke Bascietto, for making its publication not only possible but enjoyable; to Tiffany Migliore, as always, for her wit and wisdom; and last, but certainly not least, my wife Adrienne whose counsel and support have been a source of strength for many years. Thank you all.

# INTRODUCTION
# Manifest Destiny: God's Hand in the Building of America

*The Lord your God will set you high above all the nations of the earth. And all of those blessings shall come onto you and overtake you if you obey the voice of the Lord, your God.*

(Deuteronomy 28: 1-2)

## I. THE FOUNDERS AND FAITH

The American financial meltdown that commenced with devastating impact in mid-2008 – bred, in large part, of mounting decades of vain attempts to employ the tools of government to safeguard society against the workings of free enterprise– has proven as tragically transformational to her fiscal well-being as "9/11" was to her security well-being, In the quest for remedy, it is illuminating to contemplate how America got from "there" to "here." More specifically, it is critical to examine how those structural factors that once were the incipient sources of her economic strength have been increasingly corrupted to now threaten her demise.[1]

Throughout history, fiscal fidelity bred of prudent stewardship and imbued by profit motive has been a winning economic formula inexorably linked to faith– to faith in markets, faith in political systems, but overarchingly to faith in God, irrespective of how the concept of "Supreme Being" has been defined by various civilizations over time. This inquiry explores that phenomenon—the enduring role of religion in instilling work ethic and diligent commitment in the economic rise and fall of nation states – exploring how America got from "then" to "now." It is a story of the Founders' vision, God and the so-called "Protestant Ethic," and the building of America.

"Never was a state founded," the eighteenth century French political philosopher Jean Jacques Rousseau said, "that did not have religion as its basis."[2] In a more modern context, Harvard social historian Samuel Huntington has determined that: "those countries that are more religious tend to be more nationalist."[3] The corollary to these findings is that most civilizations that do not succumb to *force majeure*, ultimately perish, as in the case of ancient Rome, from socioeconomic exhaustion subsequent to abandoning their fundamental cultural and moral bearings. America was founded upon the cresting waves of eighteenth century religious revival. Today, her classic faith-based values are in peril. This inquiry explores what such findings posit for her future.

Religion is the fulcrum of American history – the engine of a destiny powered by strong historic precedent. Ronald Reagan's vision for America was framed within the prism of seventeenth century Puritan preacher John Winthrop's "shining city on a hill." In his words: "Without God, democracy cannot and will not long endure. If we forget that we are 'one nation Under God,' he said, then "we will be a nation gone under."[4] In a 1984 speech, Reagan further said:

> Think for a moment how special it is to be an American. Can we doubt that only a Divine Providence placed this land, this island of freedom, here as a refuge for all those people in the world who yearn to breathe free?[5]

President Reagan's global view was thus forged within an overarching sense of "Divine destiny." Speaking to the "National Association of Evangelicals" in 1983, he castigated the Soviet Union as the Evil Empire, "the focus of evil in the modern world." Viewing history as a Manichean struggle between the forces of good and evil, he continued: "I have always maintained that the struggle for the world now going on will never be decided by bombs or rockets, armies or military might."[6] Reagan did not operate in isolation. Three centuries before, in an address to the British Parliament in 1656, Oliver Cromwell decried the "wicked of the world . . . (who hate us) "from that very enmity that is within them."[7]

Great empires have, in fact, invariably risen imbued by a sense of divine destiny and confidence in their abilities to succeed. Contrarily, Harvard historian Niall Ferguson's span of the causes of imperial decline concludes that a loss of faith in Empire has often gone hand-in-hand with a loss of faith in God."[8] Thus, Virgil's Aeneid, with supreme confidence in Rome's war god, Mars, proclaimed:

> O Rome, tis thine alone, with awesome sway,
> To rule mankind and make the world obey,
> Disposing peace and war in thy majestic way;
> To tame the proud, the fettered slave to free,
> These are imperial arts and worthy thee.[9]

Thus, the 18th century British Anglican empire also proceeded on the mantra:

Tis Britain's care to watch o'er Europe's fate;
And hold in balance each contending state;
To threaten bold presumptuous kings with war;
And answer her afflicted neighbors's prayer.[10]

In launching WWI, Kaiser Wilhelm likewise pronounced:

Remember that the German people are the chosen of God. . . . On me, on me as the German emperor, the spirit of God has descended. I am His weapon, His sword, and His Viceregent. Woe to the disobedient! Death to cowards and unbelievers![11]

America was similarly born to be a religious nation. In the oft-quoted phrase of G.K. Chesterton, she is "a nation with the soul of a church."[12] Alternately put by America's aristocratic French visitor Alexis de Tocqueville in 1831: "In the United States, religion . . . is mingled with all the habits of the nation and all of the feelings of patriotism from whence it derives a peculiar force."[13] Yet such conclusions come as no surprise, as they are precisely what the Founders intended — and that is what they worked to work. As appraised by her sixth president who presided in the 1820s, John Quincy Adams:

"From the day of the Declaration of Independence, the people of the North American Union and of its constituent states were associated bodies of civilized men and Christians. . . . They were bound by the laws of God, which they all, and by the laws of the Gospel, which they nearly all, acknowledged as the rules of their conduct. . . ."[14] "The Declaration cast off all of the shackles off this dependency. The United States of America were no longer colonies. They were an independent nation of Christians."[15]

Accordingly, from her inception, confident aspiration has been the theme of America's sense of distinct calling – a conviction that the nascent nation's future was God's hand working history – that through diligent commitment, a "manifest destiny" would issue from the unique virtue of the "American experiment. " She was virgin territory waiting to be molded, as clearly recognized by John Locke in his retrospective reflection that: "In the beginning, the whole world was America."[16] Her Founders believed, in fact, that her birth was a reincarnation of God's covenant with ancient Israel as expressed in the Scriptures:

I will make of thee a great nation, and I will bless thee and make thy name great; and thou shalt be a blessing.
And I will bless them that bless thee and curse them that curse thee; and in thee shall all of the families of the earth be blessed.[17]

As later articulately captured by 19th century U.S. clergyman Josiah Strong in 1885:

When Napoleon drew up his troops under the shadow of the Pyramids, pointing to the latter, he said to his soldiers: "Remember that from yonder heights, forty centuries look down on you."
Men of this generation, from the pyramid top of opportunity on which God has set us, we too look down on forty centuries! We stretch our hand into the future with power to mold the destinies of unborn millions . . .
We of this generation and nation occupy the Gibralter of the ages which com-

mands the heights of the world's future.[18]

The Founders thus were driven by the exceptional nature of their polity's founding – a Divinely-inspired mandate – a mission in fulfilment of "God's cause." Accordingly, Thomas Jefferson, the nation's third president, proposed in 1785 that the seal of the nascent nation should be the Children of Israel led by a pillar of light. Even Thomas Paine, often Deist if not agnostic in conviction, marveling that "we have it within our power to build the world over again," wrote that the Supreme Being was "visibly on our side."[19]

In short, America was to be "the Creator's Crucible," "liberty's melting pot," wherein, from the strengths of the God-given abilities of people from every corner of the earth, a republic imbued with democratic capitalism offering equal opportunity to all would be forged. As John Adams eloquently expressed in an early letter to Thomas Jefferson: "Many hundred of years must roll away before we shall be corrupted. Our pure, virtuous, public-spirited federated republic will last forever, govern the globe, and introduce the perfection of man."[20]

In this quest, the Founding Fathers' founding documents were cast – drafted as embodiments of God's covenant with humankind in Holy Writ. They were to be the Lord's architecture for governance revealed to man — documents drafted, designed, and deemed to be timelessly valid. To this end, future judges were to do exacting exegesis on the Constitution – "manifest destiny hermeneutics" – as framed by the Declaration of Independence and the Bill of Rights – in the same manner that men of faith today search the Scriptures for Divine Truth.[21] Accordingly, finding an "ostensible respect for Christian morality and virtue" pervading the nation, de Tocqueville in 1831, assessed:[22]

> Religion in America takes no direct part in the government of society, but it must be regarded as the first of their political institutions; for if it does not impart a taste for freedom, it facilitates the use of it. Indeed, it is in this same point of view that the inhabitants of the United States themselves look upon religious belief. I do not know if all Americans have a sincere faith in their religion – for who can search the human heart? — but I am certain that they hold it to be indispensable to the maintenance of republican institutions.[23]

Hence, a half century after the nation's creation, it was evident that, at that stage at least, religion remained central to its cultural creed.

## II. THE FOUNDERS AND CLASSIC HISTORY

The Founders, in their deliberations, did not function in a vacuum. Indeed, their intellectual sustenance issued from the Scriptures as well as the great later scholars of the Enlightenment, most notably Montesquieu, Blackstone, and Locke, as Chapter 2 reveals. But they all likewise derived ideological inspiration from classic historians and philosophers of antiquity – Aristotle, Plutarch, Herodotus, Thucydides, and Virgil – while foremost of their sources was the *Bible*.[24]

For they firmly believed that historical memory is essential in perpetuating civil community; that ideas have consequences and serve as the conceptual architecture for forging society; that sound governance is more than a manner of process, it is about ideals and moral commitments; and conversely, that trees cut from their historic roots die – all classic ideas that provided the basis for their theories of government, sense of social responsibility, perception of the essence of human nature, and the nature of virtue itself.[25] To these ends, they consulted the ancient *philosophes* for their unique wits and wisdoms:

- Cicero for his rhetoric and valiant defense of the Roman republic against empire;
- Tacitus also for his defense of the republic and condemnation of public corruption;
- Both Catos as conservatives who fought for morality and republican principles;
- Polybius for his original historical research and narrative impartiality;
- Plutarch for his accounts of heroes who overthrew tyrants; and
- Plato for his philosophy of idealism.[26]

From each, then, they gleaned universal truths. Most importantly, however, the classics gave the Founders the ideological substance with which to take on the political challenges of their age – most noteworthily at the Constitutional Convention of 1787 and the early sessions of the First Congress that issued from it. These affinities for the lessons of ancient history likewise likely flowed, in no small part, from the early American school system which focused upon the classics as a prime mode of education. Speaking of them, the great American historian Henry Commager wrote:

> Intellectually, the Founding Fathers knew the ancient world better perhaps than they knew the European or even British world; better, in all likelihood than they knew the America beyond their sector.[27]

The Founders thus were not illiterate men. To the contrary, they were schooled in the classics. John Adams – who wrote that "except for my Wife and Children, I want to see my books"– reportedly as a child was seldom seen without a copy of Cicero's *Orations*. He often quoted Polybius, whom he greatly admired; and once sailed to Europe with Molière's *Amphitryon* as his traveling companion. Among the more modern philosophers, Machiavelli and Montesquieu were his favorites. Accordingly, he was able to write to Thomas Jefferson that he had carefully studied Plato using two Latin translations, one French and one English, as well as the original Greek.[28]

Jefferson similarly referred to his books as his "mental furniture,"and would complain when the manifest "enormities of the times" would take him away from "the delightful pursuit of knowledge." Assessing select speeches of Scipio Africanus and Cato as classics, he correctly then proceeded to credit the historians Livy and Sallust as their actual sources. The Roman political historian Tacitus he deemed to be the foremost writer in the world. Indeed, even on his deathbed, Jefferson was found to be reading the assembled works of Aeschylus, Sophocles, and Euripides, in addition to the *Bible*.[29]

James Madison, who succeeded Jefferson as president, was also well acquainted with Aristotle and Demosthenes, John Locke and David Hume, John Milton and Jonathan Swift; whereas Alexander Hamilton is said to have read the philosophies of Plutarch, Cicero, Bacon, Hobbes, Pope, and Hume, and had a keen affinity for Greek, Prussian, and French history.[30]

Benjamin Franklin, in turn, was reportedly so well read, and found reading stimulating to such an extent, that he was determined to instill the same spirit in others, organizing America's first subscription library in Philadelphia. Relishing *Plutarch's Lives*, he proved he had learned his lessons well when he presciently predicted for the nation that he was helping to build: "When a future Xenophon or Thucydides shall arise to do justice to their virtues and their actions, then the glory of America will rival — it will outshine — the glory of Greece."[31]

The writings of the Founders thus make clear that they learned much from history – and that they diligently employed their learning in their daily lives both in developing models for debate and as symbols employed to persuade. For theirs was, as demonstrated, a world view eclectic and diverse – being equally conversant in Aristotle, Herodotus, Plutarch, Thucydides, and Virgil and the Greek version of the New Testament. Indeed, the cover title on Jefferson's commentary on the *Bible*, euphemistically called the *Jefferson Bible*, makes clear that he extracted it "from the Gospels in Greek, Latin, French, and English."[32]

From the Spartans, they learned the importance of individual liberty to a republic. From the Persian wars, they learned that a republic must defend itself against strong monarchies. From the demise of Athens, they learned that majority democratic rule must be tempered by checks and balances operating within a strong central government committed to a clear separation of powers. From the early Roman republic, they learned the importance of "virtue," both social and individual, in building a nascent state.[33]

Indeed, predicated upon the Athenian experience, they came to prefer mixed republican government to unadulterated mass democracy. For this reason, writing in Federalist No. 63, Madison, citing Aristotle, Polybius, and Cicero, warned:

> Wherever the real power in Government lies, there is the danger of oppression. In our Governments, the real power lies in the majority of the Community, and the invasion of private rights is chiefly to be apprehended not from the acts of Government contrary to the sense of its constituents, but from acts in which Government is the mere instrument of the major number of constituents.[34]

In thus arguing for a structured bicameral republican form of government, Madison concluded: "History informs us of no long-lived republic which had not a Senate." For this reason also, it was no accident that the Founders carefully selected both the Roman concept and name of "senate" when establishing the upper house of their nascent congress. In like manner, the Great Seal of the United States would over time bear two Latin mottos: *E Pluribus Unum* ("Out of many, one") and *Novus ordo saeclorum* ("New Order of the Ages").[35]

On the criticality of a strong central republican government governed by the separation of powers, John Adams – reflecting that "we shall learn to prize the checks and balances of free government when we recall the miseries of Greece that arose because of its ignorance of them"[36] – would similarly assert:

> If there is one certain truth to be collected from the history of all ages, it is this: that people's rights and liberties, and the democratic mixture in a constitution, can never be preserved without a strong executive; or, in other words, without separating the executive power from the legislative. If the executive power, or any considerable part of it, is left in the hands of either an aristocratic or democratic assembly, it will corrupt the legislature as necessarily as rust corrupts iron, or as arsenic poisons the human body; and when the legislature is thus corrupted, the people are undone.[37]

Like Polybius, therefore, Adams concluded that democracy was a mere way station on the road to tyranny[38] — as reflected in his admonition: "'Remember, democracy never lasts long. It soon wastes, exhausts, and murders itself. There never was a democracy yet that did not commit suicide."[39] To which Alexander Hamilton concurred: "The ancient democracies, in which the people themselves deliberated, never possessed one feature of good government. Their very character was tyranny; their figure deformity. When they assembled, the field of debate presented an ungovernable mob, not only incapable of deliberation, but unprepared for every enormity."[40]

In this manner, from *Plutarch's Lives*, the orations of Demosthenes and Cicero, and the *Histories* of Polybius, Tacitus, and Livy, the Founders forged their views on the proper role of governance within a free society. In Federalist No. 56, Hamilton cites the failure of the Greeks to rally around a strong central government as the prime reason for the fall of Greece to Macedon and Rome. In Federalist No. 18, Madison concurringly responds: "Had Greece, says a judicious observer on her fate, been united by a stricter confederation, and persevered in her union, she would have never worn the chains of Macedon; and might have proven a barrier to the vast projects of Rome." Citing the Achaean League as their model, then, the Founders made their case for a federal government strong in its delineated powers, but limited in the range of those enumerated.[41]

Accordingly, the Founders chose the early Roman Republic, not the more democratic Athens or Sparta, as their model for America. Athens was *too* democratic and unstable, whereas Sparta was too collectivistic, to serve as political exemplars. Republican Rome, however, ceded to the masses enough power to avoid tyranny, yet without yielding so much as to create anarchy.[42]

To this end, they valued Cicero, who once declared: "Whereas our ancestors respected tradition when they were at peace, they were invariably guided by expediency in times of war."[43] Because of this propensity for the pragmatic, the historian Livy wrote: "It was as natural for the Romans to win battles as for water to flow downhill."[44]

At the same time, they despised Julius Caesar, as well as Marc Anthony and Sulla, for turning the republic into a dictatorship. Thus, in Patrick Henry's famed "Stamp Act Speech" of 1765, the great American patriot would compare the British monarch to Caesar, declaring: "Caesar had his Brutus, Charles the First his Cromwell . . . and George III may profit by their example."[45]

In like manner, likening the tyranny of the British empire to that of later Rome — while asserting that: "Rome never introduced the term 'Roman empire' until the tragedy of her freedom was complete"[46] — John Adams said of the Stamp Act: "The Stamp Act was like the sword that Nero wished for to have decollated the Roman People at a stroke."[47] Building upon this theme, Pennsylvania Founder John Dickinson, the "Penman of the Revolution," in turn, would write:

> We ought to firmly believe what is an undoubted truth, confirmed by the unhappy experience of many states heretofore free, that unless the most watchful attention be exerted, a new servitude may be slipped upon us under the sanction of usual and respectable terms. Thus, the Caesars ruined the Roman liberty under the titles of tribunals and dictatorial authorities, old and venerable dignities, known in the most flourishing times of freedom.[48]

Echoing these sentiments, Thomas Jefferson in 1774 observed: "History has informed us that bodies of men as well as individuals are susceptible to the spirit of tyranny."[49] Quoting Tacitus, he concluded: "The more corrupt the commonwealth, the more numerous its laws."[50]

In this assertion, Jefferson was powerfully supported by James Madison when he wrote: "The accumulation of all powers . . . in the same hands may justly be pronounced as the very definition of tyranny." He went on to observe: "What is government itself but the greatest of all reflections upon human nature? . . . In framing a government which is to be administered by men over men, the great difficulty lies in this: you must first enable the Government to control the governed; and in the next place oblige it to control itself."[51]

Concerned with what they perceived to be the imperial tendencies of Alexander Hamilton – who had called Julius Caesar "the greatest man who ever lived" – both John Adams and Thomas Jefferson compared him with Caesar. Of him, Adams, who had studied the classics at Harvard, wrote: "When Burr shot Hamilton, it was not Brutus killing Caesar in the Senate-House, but killing him before he crossed the Rubicon (!)"[52] In 1812, when certain New Englanders opposed to the nascent nation's war measures spoke of succession, Adams, citing Sallust, counseled: "Small communities grow great through harmony; great ones fall to pieces from discord."[53]

Focused on the dangers that tyranny poses to a republic, Adams – called by some the "Cato of the American Revolution" – in 1775, describing the coming imperative for the colonies to revolt against perceived British monarchic tyranny, would explain: "These are what are called 'revolution principles.' They are the principles of Aristotle and Plato, of Livy and Cicero, of Sidney, Harrington, and Locke — the principles of nature and eternal reason."[54] In this sense, then, relying upon the wisdom of the ancients to justify their current course of action, their strategy was, in fact, a paradox: a revolution fueled by tradition.[55]

Jefferson, like Adams, as noted, was concerned about the threat of tyranny – while believing that the purpose of history was to ensure its prevention. Accordingly, in 1779, he wrote:

> The most effectual means of preventing this would be to illuminate, as far as is

practicable, the minds of the people at large, and more especially to give them knowledge of those facts which history exhibiteth, that possessed thereby of the experience of other ages and countries, they may be able to know ambition in all its shapes, and prompted to exert their natural powers to defeat its purposes.[56]

Accordingly, the future president commended the Greek, Roman, British, and American histories as those best suited to effect this purpose – as in aggregate, the Founders viewed constraining the discretionary powers of government as central to the rule of law and essential to forging the free society that they were aspiring to create.[57]

Further reflecting their fondness for the historians of classic antiquity, the Founders frequently took recourse to using them as pseudonyms in their correspondence. In this spirit, James Madison took the name "Publius" in authoring his contributions to the *Federalist Papers*, and George Washington was deemed by some to be a "modern Cincinnatus." John Dickinson, in turn, would adopt the name "Fabius" in his series of essays endorsing the Constitution, and Hamilton frequently compared contemporary Washington to the historic Fabius as well.[58]

Given this warm affinity for the classicists, then, it is not surprising that John Adams would lecture his son John Quincy Adams: "I wish to hear of your beginning Sallust, who is one of the most polished and perfect of Roman historians, every period of whom, and I had almost said every syllable and every letter, is worth studying. In company with Sallust, Cicero, Tacitus, and Livy, you will learn Wisdom and Virtue."[59]

Later, he would follow with the admonition: "I would have upon you Demosthenes. The plainer authors you may learn yourself at any time. I absolutely insist upon it that you begin upon Demosthenes and Cicero. You may learn Greek from Demosthenes and Homer as well as from Isocrates and Lucian – and Latin from Virgil and Cicero as well as from Phaedros and Nepos."[60]

The Founders thus made clear that they were not an aggregate of unlearned and unwashed barbaric Indian-murdering, river-polluting, plantation-possessing slave owners, as "New Wave" counter-culturalist historical revisionists often now contend. Indeed, in the Constitution's framing, as analysis will show, they drew heavily upon Greek and Roman models – making their careful choice of the words "senate," "congress," and "republic" – all latinate appellations – to describe the nation's governance no accident.[61]

Thus Thomas Jefferson would say of the luminaries assembled at the 1787 Constitutional Convention at Philadelphia: "A more able assembly never sat in America . . . . It is really an assembly of demigods."[62] James Madison would add that: "It is impossible to perceive the degree of concord that prevailed, no less than a miracle. . . . . It is impossible for a man of pious reflection not to perceive in it a finger of the Almighty hand."[63]

Hence, John Adams in 1776 would rejoice: "It has been the will of Heaven that we should be thrown into existence at a period when the greatest philosophers and lawgivers of antiquity would have wished to live. . . . How few of the human race have ever had the opportunity of choosing a system of government for themselves and for their children?"[64]

xviii    *Introduction*

Similarly, Benjamin Franklin would assert: "We have gone back to ancient history for models of Government and examined the different forms of those Republics which have been formed. . . . and we have viewed modern states all around Europe."[65] It was in this spirit, then, that colonial founder Charles Lee would say to Patrick Henry: "I much regret not being thrown into the glamorous fourth century (B.C.) of the Romans, but now I am thoroughly reconciled to my lot."[66]

The Founders thus were as equally astute as they were articulate. Nonetheless, the challenge raised to anyone who would predicate a vision for America on the consummate wisdom of the Founders invariably confronts the question: "Why should an aspiring 21st century nation pursue a future course based on architecture framed by "dead white men" two centuries ago?

The ready response, of course, is that the Founders were far more than a random aggregate of dead white men. Indeed, they were perhaps the most remarkable assembly of intellects ever joined in common cause. President John Kennedy, addressing a White House dinner for Noble Prize winners in 1962, hailed them as "probably the greatest concentration of talent and genius in this house except for perhaps those times when Thomas Jefferson ate here alone."[67]

Nineteenth century Harvard Professor James Lowell Russell was once asked by French historian François Guizot: "How long will the American Republican endure?" To which he then replied: "So long as the ideas of the men who founded it continue dominant." They were, in fact, the modern repository of all of humankind's great learning – in Jefferson's compelling metaphor, they were the "keepers of the vestal flame."[68]

## III. THE FOUNDERS AND "MANIFEST DESTINY"

Like the pioneers themselves, as stated in the preface, the Founders' faith issued from a notion of "exceptionalism" – the precept that God, in forging this new nation, had somehow it set apart from the ranks of others through its commitment to republican democratic capitalistic ideals – and upon the foundations of this ideology, it would stand as an exemplar to the world.[69]

Often such expectations were cast in millennial predestination terms, such as those of William Penn in 1682: "God will plan America, and it shall have its day."[70] As equally elegantly asserted by the nation's second president, John Adams:

> I always consider the settlement of America with reverence and wonder, as the opening of a grand scene and design in Providence for the illumination of the ignorant and the emancipation of the slavish part of mankind all over the earth.[71]

Whereas John Adams' cousin and fellow Founder, Samuel Adams, predicted that "Providence will erect a mighty empire in America" just as Britain is "sunk into obscurity and contempt."[72]

To which America's First Chief Justice John Jay would contribute in Federalist # 2:

*Manifest Destiny: God's Hand in the Building of America* xix

> As a nation, we have made peace and war; as a nation, we have vanquished our common enemies; as a nation, we have forged alliances and made treaties, and entered into conventions with foreign states.[73]

The reality is that they succeeded, as the French-born Alexis de Tocqueville marveled as he passed through the nascent nation in 1831. "Everything in America," he exclaimed, "is extraordinary.... Upon my arrival to the United States, the religious aspect of the country was the first thing that struck my attention.... America is great because she is good, and if America ever ceases to be good, then America then will also cease to be great."[74]

Two centuries ago, at the close of the U.S. Constitutional Convention in 1787, when asked: "What kind of government will we have" — Benjamin Franklin responded: "A republic if we can keep it" – an answer doubtless reflecting equally his knowledge of the underlying causes precipitating the demise of the Roman republic, and the contemporary thinking of his French friend Voltaire who believed that all republics eventually end in tyranny.[75] To which Thomas Jefferson nonetheless assessed somewhat more optimistically: "I believe that our government will remain virtuous."[76]

Succinctly put, America was to be the global lantern – the "shining city on a hill" – that would illuminate an otherwise dismal world.[77] Speaking precisely to this point, however, Reverend Winthrop's famed "City on a Hill" speech itself concurrently cautioned that:

> If we shall deal falsely with our God in this work that we have undertaken, and so cause Him to withdraw His present help from us, we shall be made a story and a byword to the world, we shall open the mouths of enemies to speak evil of that which was of God and all professors for God's sake; we shall shame the faces of many of God's worthy servants, and cause their prayers to be turned into curses upon us till we be consumed out of the good land whither we are going.[78]

Predicated on such prescient proclamations, the Philadelphia's noted Reverend George Duffield in 1873 would preach: "Here hath our God ... prepared an asylum for the oppressed in every part of the earth."[79] Echoing Oliver Cromwell's dictum that religion and civil liberty are "the two greatest concernments that God hath in this world," President George W. Bush, in his address to a joint session of Congress nine days after "9/11," asserted: "Freedom and fear, justice and cruelty, have always been at war, and we know that God is not neutral between them."[80]

Hence, like ancient Israel, America came to be a select people delivered from bondage into a promised land — "God's chosen people" reincarnate — and thus, the nation has proceeded on the conviction that its liberty is God's special gift – as evidenced in the closing verse to *America*, the classic patriotic hymn written by Samuel Francis Smith in 1832:

> Long may our land be bright.
> With freedom's holy light,
> Protect us by Thy might,
> Great God, our King.[81]

Accordingly, in rededicating the nation to preserving government of, by, and for the people, President Lincoln prayed at Gettysburg that:"this nation, under God, shall have a new birth of freedom"[82] – a supplication that again comes as no surprise, as to again invoke de Tocqueville:

> Americans combine the notions of Christianity and liberty so intimately in their minds that it is impossible to make them conceive the one without the other.[83]

And thus it was that, America, from her inception, proudly proclaimed God, not George III, to be her sovereign – and as such, throughout her history, driven by her intrinsic faith, has met and overcome great challenges. Her pioneers braved the North Atlantic in pursuit of a manifest destiny. She won a War of Independence against near insurmountable odds.

Her Founders forged a unifying constitution at a time when her original thirteen colonies lacked both political and economic cohesion. She prevailed in a bitter and divisive Civil War. She survived the Great Depression and two Great World Wars. She endured the social chaos of the 1960s and won the Cold War in the 1980s.

After Japan attacked Pearl Harbor in 1941, Franklin Roosevelt commissioned a then disarmed America to build 50,000 airplanes – a seemingly impossible challenge, but one that America met and exceeded. Starting from a theoretical "Ground Zero" in 1941, the Manhattan Project at Oak Ridge and Los Alamos then designed, built, and detonated the devastating bombs that ended WWII in 1945.[84]

This is the American legacy – a faith-imbued commitment to succeed. Indeed, throughout her history, America's leaders have dared to dream great dreams. In 1961, moved by his perception of a mounting U.S. technological gap vis-â-vis the Soviet Union, President Kennedy mounted a massive, ultimately successful, educational campaign designed to restore America's traditional industrial strengths.

His goal culminated in his vision to place a man on the moon within the 1960s decade — a dream posthumously fulfilled on July 20, 1969. His initiative precipitated the greatest peacetime mobilization of resources ever undertaken — as the "Apollo Project" took ten years to implement and ultimately wound up costing the nation over $25 billion! But for an entire generation, America's technological pre-eminence and economic prosperity were restored.[85]

Yet well over century and a half before, in January, 1803, President Thomas Jefferson entertained a similar vision — asking Congress for the then considerable sum of $2,500 for an expedition west of the Mississippi River "for the purpose of extending the foreign commerce of the United States." Like President Kennedy's dreams of space conquest, President Jefferson's ends were equally noble and futuristic — and culminated in the successful westward expedition of Meriwether Lewis and William Clark in 1805.[86]

Magnificent achievements both — but could either of these, America's two boldest "expeditions of discovery," have ever occurred without a committed, dedicated, determined leadership and a faith-driven will to succeed.

In sum, "America's story" is framed in her personal belief that she was predestined to be unique – the knowledge that hers was the first revolution of a people breaking off from a colonial power to establish a free nation – and upon the residual strength of her historic values and her sense of "manifest destiny," she has aspired to the mantle of global leadership.[87] It was in this spirit that John Quincy Adams, in his July Fourth address in 1821, proclaimed:

> America does not go abroad in search of monsters to destroy. She is the well-wisher to the freedom and independence of all. She is the champion only of her own. She will recommend the general cause by the countenance of her voice and the benign sympathy of her example.[88]

To which Colin Powell has recently eloquently appended:

> Far from being the Great Satan, I would say that we are the Great Protector. We have only sent men and women from the Armed Forces of the United States to other parts of the world throughout the past century to put down oppression. We defeated Fascism. We defeated Communism. We saved Europe in World War I and World War II. We were willing to do it. We were glad to do it. We went to Korea. We went to Vietnam. All in the interest of preserving the rights of people. And when those conflicts were over, what did we do? Did we stay and conquer? Did we say: "O.K., we defeated Germany; now Germany belongs to us? We have defeated Japan; so Japan belongs to us?"
> No. What did we do? We built them up. We gave them democratic systems which they have embraced totally to their soul. Did we ask for any land? No. The only land that we ever asked for was enough land to bury our dead. For that is the kind of nation that we are.[89]

No eloquence has better cast the U.S. national creed. America is not an imperial power. Like Rome, she could have ruled the world. Unlike Rome, she has contented herself within defensible borders framed by two great oceans – and for that reason, she is indeed special in history. After more than two centuries, America, therefore, need not apologize – her record speaks for itself.[90]

She is today oft misunderstood – yet misunderstanding in the quest to do the good is nothing new – but merely a manifestation of the frustration that the Apostle John likewise doubtless felt when he wrote: "The light shineth in the darkness, but the darkness comprehended it not."[91]

Today she stands threatened – not only by terrorists who aspire to the leadership of an avenging alien god – but internally by secular counter-culturalists who would deny the very God she has. She is a nation at peril, and the question is: how long can she hold on? At a time when her hard-won role of global preeminence is threatened, the issues at stake, as Samuel Huntington has aptly asserted, are who she is and what type of nation she aspires to be.[92]

The answers will forge the republic's future. In its pursuit, therefore, analysis proceeds with a determined quest for definitive responses to those questions. As such, this work completes a trilogy of analyses addressing the impact of the Founders in the forging of America. The first volume, *Building Prosperity: Why Ronald Reagan and the Founding Fathers Were Right on the Economy* spoke to what America did right – in the forms of tax and regulatory moderation and building an amenable entrepreneurial climate – that made the twentieth century "the American Century."

The second volume, *The Eclipse of the American Century*, in turn, describes what the nation is now doing wrong that will likely preclude its twenty-first century from a repeat performance. Predicated upon the Roman model of decline, and focused upon the callous campaign of counter-culturalism within the last half century that directly assaults those historic values that built the nation's incipient greatness, it concentrates upon the decline of educational quality, the rise of blatant media bias, and a massive infiltration of illegal immigrants – and the attendant massive tax and regulatory costs that those disparate socioeconomic phenomena have engendered – as the greatest internal threats impacting upon its future today.[93]

Analysis further demonstrate that the nation's current cultural dissonance traces its provenance to the handiwork of a left wing "professoriat" launched from a 1960s academic bridgehead that has now seeped out into society at large to create a parochially-biased "mainstream" press that it has carefully cultivated — effective now to the degree that what was called "yellow journalism" a mere century ago today is simply called "journalism;" and which – through the rigidly enforced dogma of an extremist sexist, racist "political correctness" agenda that it has constructed – is increasingly corrupting the core of America's traditional socioeconomic values.

Reflected in the 2008 U.S. presidential election campaign, wherein the sincere pursuit of such constitutionally-guaranteed liberties as freedom of religious expression and the right to bear arms were decried as sheer sub-cultural "bitterness," America's current counter-cultural movement thus epitomizes the philosophy of its 1960 founding guru, Herbert Marcuse, in his discourse on "Repressive Tolerance," wherein he passionately queried: "Is there any alternative other than the dictatorship of an 'elite' over the people?"[94]

The present work – *God, Governance, and Economic Man* – in turn, reverts to the lessons of the Founding Fathers for policy guidance in restoring the erstwhile greatness of America. Mindful of the cogent lessons of economic history, it commences by examining the critical role of the Founders' vision for the role of religion in the nation's architecture for governance — and concludes with an assessment of what those determinations posit for shaping meaningful economic governance in America today. Focused upon their faith-based approach to honest, prudent stewardship, it then advances an agenda of development and attendant requisite education that can once again ensure that the twenty-first century can again be "the American Century."

***
### "The Founding Fathers"

The term – "Founding Fathers" – herein is employed to define those who provided prominent leadership in the birth, development, and establishment of America as an independent, self-governing nation. Such individuals include the fifty six-signers of the Declaration of Independence; the fourteen presidents of the Continental Congress during the Revolution of 1776; the two dozen generals who won the War of Independence; and the fifty-five delegates to the federal Constitutional Convention of 1787.[95]

This august group also includes the earliest state governors responsible for the ratification and adoption of the Constitution; the ninety members of the First Congress who drafted the Bill of Rights; the first members of the U.S. Supreme Court who shaped the nation's nascent judiciary; and the earliest members of the Executive Branch who helped to establish it – a total of some 250 American patriots.[96]

Some would argue that the Founders should not be deemed moral exemplars – that they were, in fact, mere mortals whose views on governance were focused upon the challenges of another time. Yet while the observation may be nominally true, they were nonetheless remarkable leaders – a unique body of intellect firmly grounded in the classics, decisive in its aspirations, and determined to make America a singularly distinguished polity – a "shining city on a hill" – thereby reducing those who would look to others as role models to studying the likes of Albert Fall and the Harding Administration and Bob Haldeman and that of Richard Nixon.

The fifty-five active participants in the Constitutional Convention of 1787 were a particularly distinguished group. Statesmen, patriots, and *illuminati* all, thirty-six had been members of the Continental Congress; twenty were at one time governors of states; twenty were United States senators; eight were federal judges; and thirteen were members of the House of Representatives. Among them, Washington and Madison would serve as future presidents of the United States and Elbridge Gerry as vice president. Several had served as U.S. diplomats overseas and others held senior Cabinet posts. They were indeed, in Halberstamian terms, America's "best and brightest."[97]

***

# PART I
# The Creed

The liberties of our country, the freedom of our civil constitution, are worthy of defending at all hazards; and it is our duty to defend them against all attacks. We have received them as a fair inheritance from our worthy ancestors; they have purchased them for us with toil and danger and expense of treasure and blood, and transmitted them to us with care and diligence. It will bring an ever-lasting mark of infamy upon our present generation, enlightened as it is, if we should suffer them to be wrestled from us by violence or without a struggle, or to be cheated out of them by artifices of false and designing men.

—American Founder-Statesman Samuel Adams

# Chapter One
# The Faith of the Founders

> Faith of our fathers, living still
> In spite of dungeon, fire, and sword!
>
> —Classic American Hymn

## I. The Blueprint of the Nation's Architects

### A. Present at the Creation

As analysis has shown, America was built upon a religious foundation forged within a framework that has characterized the of the rise of great societies– with history replete with stirring tales of civilizations whose gods forged life from primordial mass – affirming 18th century French political philosopher Jean-Jacques Rousseau's determination that: "never was a state founded that did not have religion as its basis."[1]

Many, if not most, ancient cultures owned their very provenance, in fact, to a concept of a "Supreme Being." Minos, who gave Crete its creed, was reputed to be the son of Zeus and Europa. Sparta was given its laws by Lycurgus, who is said to have received them from the god Apollo. Marduk, the Babylonians' God, was believed by them to have created the world out of a cosmos of chaos. The Roman poet Virgil informs that Aeneas, son of Venus, led the Trojans to Italy. Romulus, progenitor of Rome, reportedly was the son of Mars, the god of war. In like manner, the ancient Israelis founded their commonwealth upon a theocracy of a righteous God overseeing national affairs.[2]

Most of the *civil institutions* of the ancient world themselves were likewise outgrowths of religious belief, as nations governed as the gods directed. Kings ruled, judges judged, and generals planned their campaigns under the patronage and guidance of revered deities. This clear reality was, in fact, a universal truth already known by the Greek historian-philosopher Plutarch, a disciple of Plato in his time:

> There never was a state of atheists. You may travel all over the world, and you may find cities without walls, without a king, without a mint, without a theater of gymnasium; but you will never find a city without a god, without prayer, without oracle, without sacrifice. Sooner may a city stand without foundations than a state without a belief in the gods. This is the bond of all society and the pillar of all civilization.[3]

Indeed, all of civilization – whether in Carthage, China, India, or Central America – has risen upon the cornerstones of intrinsic religious ideals, and whenever those beliefs have eroded, that society has commenced to die.

Thus it was that when Europe's Dark Ages resulted from the collapse of the Roman Empire, destroying that continent's erstwhile civic stability and balance for a thousand years, only the Church was positioned to lend meaning to human lives— and it became the task of Charlemagne, Louis the Pious, Otto the Great, and their successors to implement godly discipline and ecclesiastic order in a decimated secular world. These were, in fact, rulers who would not dream of executing their administrative functions without a foundation in divinity.[4]

When the West finally did emerge from its Dark Ages and transitioned into renaissance, moreover, that development, and the Reformation that accompanied it commencing in 1517, would become the cultural vehicles that transported the Christian religion throughout all of Europe and beyond to the planet's furthest corners.[5] And thus it is that to this day, every king or queen of England rules "by the Grace of God" – (*Dei gracia, rex*; *Dei gracia, regina*) – founding precepts that remain engraved on every British coin.[6]

The lessons of history, therefore, could not be more clear. Never in the annals of humankind is it recorded that any society has been able to establish standards for decency and social order without a moral code. Indeed, "there is no significant example in history before our time," the eminent historian Will Durant has written, "of a society successfully maintaining moral life without religion."[7] It is this sense of innate values, in turn, that leads to those cultural traits of patriotism and work ethic that produce prosperity for all.

Today, there is a flawed counter-cultural notion to the contrary — that much of the problem of world poverty has stemmed instead from sheer Euro-Christian imperial exploitation of lesser colonial nations. But the proponents of this postulate must address the tripartite question: "Why is it that some of the world's most affluent nations, such as Sweden and Switzerland, never had colonies at all – while others, such as Germany and Japan, became wealthy only after losing their colonies—

whereas some of the most chronically economically underdeveloped nations, among them Nepal, Afghanistan, and Liberia, were never colonies at all.[8]

Some may deem the late Soviet Union to be the exception to this process. But that is why that erstwhile nation is precisely that – defunct, as Communism was a valueless ideology. Her gods were those of atavistic statism — godlessness was, in effect, their god – bringing poverty, not prosperity, starvation, not salvation. When the fraud of its false promise finally became undeniable in the 1980s, therefore, the Soviet people lost faith in their false gods – and the USSR fell.[9]

For at the bottom line, in that process of acculturalization that determines societal success or failure, values, particularly religious values, are quintessentially important. To argue that religion should now play no role in America's society, an established tenet that was intrinsic to her founding, then, is patent nonsense. For one cannot span the panorama of civilizational evidence and deny the linkage of religion and nation-building either in the course of socioeconomic history or in the vision of the country's architects.

Indeed, the inculcation of America's core values started at the nation's discovery. Christopher Columbus, now written off by counter-culturalists as no more than an Indian-killing imperialist, in his *Book of Prophecies*, explicitly attributes his keen motivation to explore to Divine Inspiration: "Our Lord opened to my understanding (I could sense His hand upon me) so it became clear to me that the voyage was feasible. Who doubts this illumination was from the Holy Spirit?" [10]

America was thus first discovered by Spanish Catholics and then built by predominantly British Protestants upon the foundation of a firm commitment to "civil religion" – created with a mission of carrying out God's will on earth – a nation wherein the churches first made the people; and the people then made the laws. In the words of Noah Webster: "God's word, contained in the *Bible*, has given us all of the necessary rules to direct our conduct."[11]

Accordingly, America's Declaration of Independence – with 52 of whose 56 signers professing Christians, called by some a promissory note cosigned by God, contains four explicit references to the Providential Being – "Divine Creator," "Lawmaker," "Supreme Judge," and "Protector" – and similar articulations of religious expression permeate their other seminal writing as well. But though they spoke with clarity in employing such terms, their documents reveal that they were not referring to a particular Christian denomination but rather to the more ecumenical conviction that a Sacred Force was foreordained to guide the nation's political and economic destiny.[12]

Onward through her history, America has thus sought to imbue a firm commitment to behavior based on traditional values of honor, mutual respect, and duty – based equally upon the rule of law and a reverence for the omniscient omnipotence of a Supreme Being – a reality noted by de Tocqueville when he observed of the nascent nation that democracy cannot survive in the absence of religion: "Despotism may govern without faith," he said, "but liberty cannot. . . . When a people's religion is destroyed, not only will they let their freedom be taken away, they will hand it over themselves."[13]

## B. God and the Colonies

"Behold, how pleasant it is for brethren to dwell together in unity," the 133rd Psalm proclaims," and that clearly was the conviction of the Founders who, in addressing the relationship between Church and State in the First Amendment – "Congress shall make no law respecting an establishment of religion, nor prohibiting the free exercise thereof" – nonetheless did not intend for America to be a "godless" nation. To the contrary, their manifest intent was to create a distinctly religious commonwealth, with the net result that the state they ultimately formed was an outgrowth of the church and not conversely.[14]

Indeed, the concept of a "Divine Being" forging the destiny of the new nation was intrinsic to their precepts from the Pilgrims' first landing at Jamestown, Virginia, in May, 1607, over four centuries ago.[15] In the words of Supreme Court Chief Justice John Marshall: "One of the great objects of the colonial charters was avowedly the propagation of the Christian faith." Fleeing perceived religious persecution then rampant in England to an extent that moved one contemporary to observe that absent it, there would never have been a "New England," the colonists came to North America in common purpose, impelled by common impulse, and sustained by common hope.[16]

Accordingly, in the First Charter of Virginia, dated April 10, 1606, contracted while still en route, the colonists' express goal was to: "by the providence of the Almighty God, hereafter tend to the glory of His Divine Majesty in the propagating of the Christian religion to such peoples as yet live in darkness and miserable ignorance of the true knowledge and worship of God."[17]

Pursuant to this mandate, the colony's first legislative assembly enacted in 1619 stipulated that clergymen were to be retained at an annual salary of 1,500 pounds of tobacco and sixteen barrels of corn, then estimated to be worth in proximate value to two hundred English sterling pounds. To fund such undertakings, each male inhabitant over sixteen years of age within the colony was to be assessed an annual tax of ten pounds of tobacco and one bushel of corn — and the assembly further enacted in 1624 that on every plantation "a house or room" shall be provided for Sunday worship, attendance at which was made mandatory.[18]

Given this outward commitment to devoted piety, therefore, it is not surprising to learn that immediately upon his arrival in May, 1607, Captain John Smith knelt and planted a Christian flag at Camp McHenry, port of Jamestown. In 1609, a follow-on charter enacted for Virginia read: "The principal effect that we can desire or expect of this action is the conversion . . . of the peoples of these parts unto the true worship of God and the Christian religion."[19]

To these ends also, the Virginia Assembly in 1625 ordered that every plantation erect "some decent howse or sitting roome" for worship[20] — whereas the Massachusetts Charter of 1629, proclaimed: "Our said people . . . being so religiously and civilly governed that their good life and orderly conversation may win and incite the natives of . . . the country to the knowledge and obedience of the only true God and Savior of mankind and the Christian faith which is. . . the principal end of this plantation."[21]

Similarly, the "Mayflower Compact," signed on November 11, 1620, which would become the governing constitution of the Plymouth Colony – marking the first time in recorded history that a free, commonly-enfranchised community created a new civil government by means of a social contract – also affirmed that the settlement's prime purpose was to promote the Christian creed, its first six words reading: "In the name of God, Amen" – then proceeding: "by the grace of God . . . having undertaken for the glory of God and the advancement of the Christian faith – committed to government for the common good executed with the consent of the governed – whereupon, landing at Plymouth Rock, Miles Standish and John Alden placed a cross upon the beach to dedicate "New England" to God's cause.[22]

Thus Calvinist Puritan Governor John Winthrop's famed, oft-quoted "City on a Hill" sermon, delivered to the Puritans destined to create the Massachusetts Bay Colony while still on the ship Arabella in 1630, likewise invoked God's calling for a new covenant for the people to be domiciled in the "Holy Commonwealth of Massachusetts:"

> For our persons, we are a Company expressing ourselves as fellow members of Christ . . . For the work we have at hand, it is by a mutual consent through a special over-ruling Providence, and a more than ordinary approbation of the Church of Christ to seek a place of Cohabitation and Consortship under a due form of government both civil and ecclesiastic. . . We are a company professing ourselves fellow members of Christ . . . knit together by this bond of love . . . We are entered into covenant with Him for this work. . . . For we must consider that we shall be as a city upon a hill, the eyes of all people are upon us . . .[23]

This compact, like those of the other earliest colonies, thus was "a covenant of governance with consent of the governed" as it proudly proclaimed itself to be. Theirs was not to be a theocracy but a "civill bodie politic" formed to serve the glory of a Christian God. Drawing upon the scriptural "city set upon a hill that shall not be hid," it was aimed to create a nation destined to become the world's beacon of democratic freedom – part and parcel of a Divine mandate.[24]

The New Hampshire Province, created in 1631, and later to be united with the Massachusetts Bay Colony, likewise adopted among its prime missions that: "the infidel may be incited and desire to partake of the Christian religion." With the same purpose, the Maryland Colony, was chartered in 1632 to those fleeing perceived religious persecution by the state Anglican Church in England.[25]

Similarly, the Fundamental Orders of Connecticut – promulgated on January 14, 1639 and deemed by many to be the "first full-fledged written constitution in history"[26] – declared that:

> The word of God requires that to maintain the peace and union of such a people, there should be orderly and decent government established according to God . . . to preserve the liberty and purity of the Gospel of our Lord Jesus Christ which we now profess. . . ."[27]

The "New England Confederation," implemented on May 19, 1643, also articulated as its express goal: "to advance the Kingdom of our Lord Jesus Christ and to enjoy the liberties of the Gospel with purity and peace."[28]

These individual colonial pacts would be followed on September 30, 1649 by a proclamation of the "Synod of New England Churches" convened at Cambridge, Massachusetts, that was the first formal attempt to forge America's church-state architecture for civil governance. To wit:

> I. God, our Supreme Lord and King of the world, hath ordained civil magistrates to be under him, over the people and for his own glory and for the public good; and to this end, hath armed them with the power of the sword for the defense and encouragement of them that do well and for the punishment of evildoers.
> II. It is lawful for Christians to accept and execute an office of magistrate when called thereto. In the management whereof, as they ought to especially maintain piety, justice, and peace according to the laws of each Commonwealth.
> IV. It is the duty of the people to pray for magistrates, to honor their persons, to pay them tribute and other dues, to obey their lawful commands, and to be subject to their authority for conscience's sake.[29]

In 1653, as Quakers and other Christian groups commenced to settle North Carolina, their founding charter likewise affirmed:

> Excited with a laudable and pious zeal for the propagation of the Christian faith . . in those parts of America not yet cultivated or planted, and inhabited only by . . . peoples who have no knowledge of the Almighty God. . . .[30]

South Carolina, initially chartered by English immigrants in 1662 and then re-charted in 1669, similarly was to be administered in accordance with a constitution personally drafted by the English philosopher-statesman John Locke who declared that it "had God for its author, salvation for its end, and truth without any mixture of error for its matter."[31]

The 1663 Charter for Rhode Island also explicitly set forth its colonists' godly intent: "Pursuing with peace and loyal minds their sober, serious, and religious intentions of Godly edifying themselves and one another within the holy Christian faith."[32]

The Massachusetts Constitution of 1680, in turn, proclaimed that good order and civil government "depend upon piety, religion, and morality." In explaining their confederation, the colony's founders determined that: "We all came into these parts of America with one and the same end and aim: namely, to advance the Kingdom of our Lord Jesus Christ."[33]

The Pennsylvania Charter of Privileges," concluded on October 28, 1701, in like manner, acknowledged "the Almighty God being the only Lord of Conscience, Father of Light and Spirit, and Author as well as Object of all divine Knowledge, Faith, and Worship, who doth enlighten the Minds, and persuade and convince the Understandings of People . . . who shall confess and acknowledge One Almighty God, the Creator, Upholder, and Ruler of the world ." And the charters of Connecticut, New York, New Jersey, and other colonies contained nearly identical restatements of their Christian goals.[34]

Indeed, to such ends, every colony without exception ordered fines, and sometimes even death, for those convicted of the crime of blasphemy, and most demanded some public confession of Christian belief as among the rights of passage for entering colonial politics.[35]

It is not surprising, then, that in 1777, with the Revolutionary War threatening the continuing import of *Bibles* from England, the Congress authorized the purchase of 20,000 *Bibles* from Holland to distribute amongst the states. Four years later, it then authorized the printing of 'the *Bible* of the Revolution' in Philadelphia. In consequence, John Adams, reflecting upon the widespread Christian colonization of the North American continent, would assert:

"I always considered the settlement of America with reverence and wonder, as the opening of the grand scheme of Providence for the illumination of the ignorant and the emancipation of the slavish part of mankind all over the earth."[36]

---

\*\*\*

### ACKNOWLEDGMENTS OF THE FOUNDING FATHERS OF THE EXISTENCE OF A SUPREME BEING [37]

The power and goodness of the Almighty were strongly manifested in the events of our late glorious revolution – and his kind intervention on our behalf has been no less visible in the establishment of our present equal government. In war, He directed the sword, and in peace, He has ruled in our councils

– GEORGE WASHINGTON, America's First President.

The Christian religion, as I understand it, is best

–JOHN ADAMS, America's Second President.

Rendering thanks to my Creator for my existence and station among His works, for my birth in a country enlightened by the Gospel and enjoying freedom, and for all His other kindnesses, to Him, I resign myself, humbly confiding in His goodness, and in His mercy through Jesus Christ through the events of eternity

– JOHN DICKINSON, Signer of the Constitution.

> The law dictated by God Himself is, of course, superior in obligation to any other. It is binding all over the globe, in all countries, and at all times
>
> – ALEXANDER HAMILTON, Signer of the Constitution.

> To the eternal and only true God be all honor and glory now and forever
>
> – CHARLES PINCKNEY, Signer of the Constitution.

> Principally, and first of all, I commend my soul to the Almighty Being who gave it and my body which I commit to the dust, relying on the merits of Jesus Christ for the pardon of my sins
>
> – SAMUEL ADAMS, Signer of the Declaration of Independence.

> I am constrained to express my adoration of the Supreme Being, the Author of my existence, in full belief of His Providential goodness and His forgiving mercy revealed to the world through Jesus Christ, through whom I hope for never-ending happiness in a future state
>
> — ROBERT PAINE, Signer of the Declaration of Independence.

> With an awesome reverence to the Great Almighty God, Creator of all mankind, being sick and weak in body but of sound mind and memory, thanks be given to the Almighty God for the same
>
> – JOHN MORTON, Signer of the Declaration of Independence.

> My soul I resign into the hands of my Almighty Creator whose tender mercies stand over His works, who hateth nothing that he hath made, and to the justice and wisdom of whose dispensations I willingly and cheerfully submit, humbly hoping from His unbounded mercy and benevolence, through the merits of my blessed Savior, a remission of my sins
>
> – GEORGE MASON, Drafter of the Bill of Rights.

> My hopes of a future life are all founded on the Gospel of Christ
>
> – JOHN QUINCY ADAMS, Future President of the United States.
>
> Unto Him, who is the author and giver of all good, I render sincere and humble thanks for His manifold and unmerited blessings, and especially for our redemption and salvation by His beloved Son
>
> – JOHN JAY, First Chief Justice of the United States Supreme Court.
>
> This is all of the inheritance that I can give to my dear family. The religion of Christ can give them one that will make them rich indeed
>
> – PATRICK HENRY, American Patriot and Three-Term Governor of Virginia.
>
> Religion is the only solid basis of Morals and Morals are the only possible support of free governments
>
> – GOUVERNEUR MORRIS
>
> \*\*\*

## C. GOD AND THE FOUNDING OF AMERICA

Religion in America thus enjoyed an auspicious and inspired beginning. In a resolution reflecting that reality to the inhabitants of Massachusetts Bay, the Massachusetts Provincial Congress proudly enjoined its citizens to:"nobly defend those rights that God gave us and no one can take from us!"[38] As encapsulated by America's second president John Adams: "The general principles on which the Fathers achieved independence . . . were the general principles of Christianity."[39]

Such precepts were perpetuated in the convictions of other Founders as well – as perhaps first articulated on June 7, 1776 by Richard Henry Lee within the Congress when he boldly asserted "that these united colonies are and ought to be free and independent states, and that all political connection between them and Great Britain is and ought to be dissolved." These were fighting words — and would prove to be precisely the inspiration that Thomas Jefferson needed to write the Declaration of Independence of July 4, 1776.[40]

Pursuant to her spiritual covenant, then, America's Declaration of Independence unabashedly made reference to God – "appealing to the Supreme Judge of the World" – "with a firm reliance on the protection of Divine Providence" – adding the proclamation that Americans are "endowed by their Creator with certain unalienable rights" — in essence, making the Declaration "America's Creed." Indeed, when Abraham Lincoln referred to the vision of the Founders in his reference to "four score and seven years ago" in his November 19, 1863 Gettysburg address, it was to these historic values to which he was referring.[41]

These, then, were indeed "unalienable" rights – granted by God and vested in the nation's founding documents – that no man, court, or government had a right to take away. Foremost among them was the First Amendment's guarantee of free exercise of religion" – while concluding with the invocation of the "protection of Divine Providence" – as well as with the designation by Article 1, Section 7 of the Constitution – consonant with the Fourth Commandment as articulated in Exodus 20: 8-10 – of Sunday as a day of rest — a day wherein no federal legal or judicial process may take place – and with the document's dating ending "in the year of our Lord" (*Anno Domini*).[42]

Thus, speaking to the absolute rights of the American people to life, liberty, the pursuit of happiness, and freedom of religion, Thomas Jefferson wrote:

> Whenever any form of government becomes destructive to these ends, it is the right of the people to alter or abolish it, and to institute new government, laying its foundation on such principles, and organizing its power in such form as to them shall seem most likely to affect their safety and their happiness.[43]

To these ends also, the Northwest Ordinance passed in 1787 explicitly identified religion as one of the quintessential values within the territory that the schools would explicitly advance, with its Article III opening: "Religion, morality, and knowledge being necessary to government and the happiness of mankind." In like manner, the Continental Congress – whose opening session in 1774 featured a prayer offered by the Reverend Jacob Duché based on *Psalm* 35 – routinely designated days of fasting and prayer, appointed governmentally-funded chaplains, and appropriated monies to pay for Christian missionaries to convert the Indians. These were practices pursued by the post-Declaration, formally constituted First Congress as well, which passed a resolution calling for a "National Day of Prayer" on September 25, 1787, the very day that the Bill of Rights, and its controversial First Amendment mandating religious freedom, were enacted.[44]

On September 8, 1783, moreover, the armistice signed with Britain concluding the Revolutionary War opened with the line: "In the name of the most Holy and undivided Trinity . . .," and a proclamation of the Congress voted on October 18, 1783 declaring a national day of prayer and thanksgiving on the occasion commenced: "Whereas it has pleased the Supreme Ruler of all human events to dispose the hearts of the belligerent powers to put an end to the effusion of human blood by proclaiming a cessation of hostilities by sea and land . . . ."[45]

Resolutions introduced into the Congress in 1777 and 1778 similarly had called for proclamation of a national "Day of Thanksgiving onto God," with the former, introduced by Samuel Adams amongst others, commencing:

> Forasmuch as it is the indispensable duty of all men to adore the superintending providence of the Almighty God, to acknowledge with gratitude their obligations

to Him for benefits received, and to implore such further benefits as they stand in need of; and it having pleased Him to . . . smile upon us in the prosecution of a just and necessary war for the defense of our unalienable rights and liberties . . . and to crown our arms with most signal success . . .[46]

On the day preceding George Washington's inauguration as America's first president on 30 April, 1789, a Congressional resolution likewise proclaimed:

Resolved that after the oath shall be administered to the President, the Vice President, and members of the Senate, the Speaker and members of the House of Representatives shall accompany him to St. Paul's Chapel to hear divine service performed by the Chaplains.[47]

## D. God in the Words of the Founders

Religious expression permeated Washington's presidential proclamations as well. Pursuant to his conviction that "religion and morality are the essential pillars of civil society,"[48] his First Inaugural Address on April 30, 1789 – opening with homage to "the Great Author of every public and private good" – commenced:

"It would be particularly improper to omit in this first official act my fervent supplication to that Almighty Being who rules over the universe, who presides in the councils of nations, and whose providential aid can remedy every human defect, and that His benediction may consecrate to the liberties and happiness of the people of the United States a Government instituted by themselves, and may enable each instrument employed in its administration to execute with success the functions allotted to His charge."[49]

A response to Washington by the Senate eight days later, on May 7, 1789, read: "We commend you, sir, to the protection of the Almighty God, earnestly beseeching Him long to preserve a life so valuable and dear to the people of the United States."[50]

Declaring November 26, 1789 to be a "national day of thanksgiving" proclaimed pursuant to a resolution transmitted by Congress, Washington responded by calling upon Americans to "unite in most humble offering of our prayers and supplications to the great Lord and Ruler of Nations, and beseech Him to pardon our national and other transgressions."[51]

He further counseled in his 1795 thanksgiving declaration that: "It is the duty of all nations to acknowledge the providence of Almighty God, to obey His will, to be grateful for His benefits, and to humbly implore His protection and favor"[52]— continuing that: "True religion affords to government its surest support."[53] A contemporary, Supreme Court Chief Justice John Marshall, would thus say of him: "He is a sincere believer in the Christian faith and a truly devout man."[54]

"Do not indulge the supposition that morality can be maintained without religion,"America's first president further admonished in his Farewell Address. "Of all the dispositions and habits which lead to prosperity, religion and morality are indispensable supports" – a belief predicated upon his conviction that: "Reason and experience forbid us to expect that national morality can prevail in exclusion of religious principles." Later he would append in a letter to the nation's Baptist leaders:

> Had I the slightest apprehension that the Constitution framed in the Convention wherein I had the honor to preside might possibly endanger the religious rights of any ecclesiastical society, I would have never placed my signature to it.[55]

To all of which John Adams, the nation's second president, in his first year as vice president, concurred: "We have no government capable of contending with human passions unbridled by morality and religion. Our constitution was made only for a moral and religious people. . . . It is wholly inadequate to any other."[56] He would add that: "a Republic can only be supported by religion or austere morals," and that "these cannot generally be diffused throughout a community but by the institution of the public worship of God;" adding that the *Bible* offers "the only system that ever did or ever can support a Republic in the world;"[57] then querying:

> Is it not that the Declaration of Independence organized its social compact on the foundation of the Redeemer's mission on earth? That it laid the cornerstone of human government upon the precepts of Christianity?" . . . On the Fourth of July, the Founders simply took the precepts of Christ, which came into the world through His birth, and incorporated them into civil government.[58]

Explicitly linking constitutional liberties to religious values, then – to wit: "the right to freedom being the gift of God Almighty, which is not in the power of man to alienate" – Adams assessed that:

> Statesmen . . . may plan and speculate for liberty, but it is religion and morality alone which can establish those principles upon which freedom can securely stand. The only foundation of a free Constitution is pure virtue, and this cannot be inspired into our people in greater measure than we have it now. They may change their rulers and forms of government, but they will not obtain a lasting liberty.[59]

Fervently believing that "it is the duty of all men in society, publicly and in stated seasons, to worship the Supreme Being, the Creator, and Preserver of the Universe," in his own Inaugural Address as George Washington's successor to the presidency, delivered on March 4, 1797, Adams thus beseeched:

> May that Being who reigns supreme over all, the Patron of Order, the Fountain of Justice, and the Protector in all ages of the world of liberty, continue His blessing upon this nation and its Government and give it all possible success and duration consistent with the ends of His providence.[60]

In three sequential letters to Thomas Jefferson, Adams would write: "The Ten Commandments and the Sermon on the Mount contain my religion;" "Without religion, this world would be something not fit to be mentioned in polite company;" and "The question before the human race is whether the God of nature shall govern the world by His own laws" — and in a letter to fellow Founding Father and signer of the Declaration of Independence Benjamin Rush, he would add: "Religion and virtue are the only foundations not only of republicanism and of all free government, but of social felicity under all governments and in all combinations of human society."[61]

Thus, he would ultimately proudly proclaim: "The highest story of the American Revolution is this. It connected in one indissoluble bond the principles of civil government with the principles of Christianity."[62]

Thomas Jefferson, the third U.S. president, also focused extensively on religious affairs, affirming – "I am a real Christian, that is to say, a disciple of the doctrine of Jesus"[63] – and in his retirement even produced two works: in 1804, a monograph, "The Philosophy of Jesus," and in 1818 a book titled: *The Life and Morals of Jesus*, delving into Latin, Greek, French, and English versions of the New Testament in his research.[64] In his own words: "The precepts of philosophy, and of the Hebrew Code, laid hold of actions only. (Jesus) pushed his scrutinies into the hearts of man, erected his tribunal in the region of his thoughts, and purified the waters at the fountain head."[65]

His view on the role of Church vis-à-vis State, however, was perhaps best articulated in his assertion:

> The liberty to worship our Creator in the way we think most agreeable to His will is a liberty in other countries deemed compatible with good government and proved by our experience to be its best support.[66]

Earlier, in his 1777 *Bill for Establishing Religious Freedom*, advocating the formal religious disestablishment of the Anglican Church in Virginia, Jefferson commenced:

> Well aware that the opinions and beliefs of men depend not on their own wills, but follow involuntarily evidence proposed to their minds; that Almighty God hath created the mind free, and manifested his supreme will that free it shall remain by making it insusceptible of restraint . . ."[67]

Shortly thereafter, in his "Notes on the State of Virginia," Jefferson, in 1781, avowing that the God who gave us life gave us liberty,[68] asked: "Can the liberties of a nation be thought secure when we have removed their only firm basis, the conviction in the minds of the people that these liberties are a gift of God? That they are not to be violated but with His wrath? I tremble for my country's future when I reflect that God is just; and that His justice cannot sleep forever." [69]

In like manner, predicated upon his belief that — "to suppose that any form of government will secure liberty or happiness without any form of virtue in the people is a chimeric idea" —James Madison, "Father of the Constitution" and fourth U.S. president – who had studied under the tutelage of Presbyterian-preacher-turned-Princeton-president John Witherspoon and early on had himself considered a career in ministry before opting for politics – powerfully expressed his commitment: "to the same Divine Author of every good and perfect gift we are indebted for all of those privileges and advantages, religious as well as civil, which are so richly enjoyed in this favored land."[70]

The clearest expression of his application of these mutually sustaining precepts to civil governance doubtless came in *Federalist No. 51* when he wrote: "What is government itself but the greatest of all reflections upon human nature? If men were angels, no government would be necessary. If angels were to govern men, neither external nor internal controls on government would be necessary."[71] In his *Memorial and Remonstrance* of 1785, Madison continued that "religion is the basis and foundation of government.... Before any man can be considered a member of civil society, he must be considered as a subject of the Governor of the Universe."[72]

Madison's religious convictions thus had been forged early on. In his *Memorial and Remonstrance*, he likewise proclaimed: "We hold it for a fundamental and undeniable truth that religion, or the duty that we owe to our Creator and the manner of discharging it, can be directed only by religion and conviction, not by force or violence."[73]

Accordingly, in his First Inaugural Address delivered more than three decades later, Madison invoked "that Almighty Being whose power regulates the destines of nations, whose blessings have been so conspicuously dispensed to this rising Republic, and to whom we are bound to express our devout gratitude for the past, as well as our fervent supplications and best hopes for the future."[74]

An abiding faith in an Almighty God permeated the souls of other contemporary statesmen as well. "The longer I live, the more convincing proof I have that God governs the affairs of men," Benjamin Franklin asserted at the Constitutional Convention in Philadelphia in the summer of 1787. Proposing that each session commence with prayer, he cited the biblical verse from the gospel of Jesus, Matthew 10:29: "If a sparrow cannot fall to the ground without His notice, is it probable that an empire can rise without His aid?" — continuing with Psalm 127:1: "We are assured in the sacred writings that 'except the Lord build this house, they who build it labor in vain.'"[75]

Though deemed less religious than many of the other Founders, Franklin nonetheless affirmed his faith as:

> Here is my Creed. I believe in one God, the Creator of the universe; that He governs the world by his Providence; that he ought to be worshipped; that the most acceptable Service that we render to him is doing good to his other children; that the Soul of Man is immortal and will be treated with Justice in another Life, respecting its Conduct in this. These I take to be the fundamental Principles of sound Religion.[76]

Later, Franklin would write in his *Maxims and Morals*: "Freedom is not a gift bestowed upon us by other men, but a right that belongs to us by the laws of God."[77]

John Jay, first Chief Justice of the Supreme Court likewise directly linked public well-being to faith, steadfastly maintaining: "National prosperity can neither be attained nor preserved without the favor of Providence:"[78]

> Providence has given to our people the choice of their rulers, and it is the duty as well as the privilege and interest of our Christian nation to select and prefer Christians for their rulers.[79]

Whereas "America's first Treasurer," Alexander Hamilton, as early as 1775, would state:

> The sacred rights of mankind are written by the Hand of Divinity itself and can never be erased or obscured by mortal power... (They) are not to be rummaged for among old parchment or musty records. They are written, as with a sunbeam, in the whole volume of human nature, by the Hand of the Divinity itself, and can never be erased or obscured by mortal power.[80]

It likely is no accident then that, contending that "only a virtuous people are capable of freedom,"his proposal for America's first motto was the words: "Rebellion to tyrants is obedience to God."[81]

Indeed, even the rabble-rousing revolutionary pamphleteer Thomas Paine – often cited by the ACLU as one of its heroes– wrote that he was "not so much of an infidel as to believe that the Almighty God could abandon a people committed to that liberty to which He had called them."[82] Explicitly for these reasons, then, for four centuries, people have flocked to America's shores to be free to practice the faith of their choosing.

For when Thomas Jefferson penned the Declaration of Independence, as observed, he explicitly used the words "God" and the "Creator" to produce: "All men are endowed by their Creator with certain unalienable Rights . . . and that to secure these Rights, Governments are instituted among Men." When George Washington took his oath of office as America's first president," his hand laid on a *Bible* opened to *Deuteronomy* 28, he ended with the words: "So help me God!" – a phrase adopted by every incoming U.S. president ever since.[83]

---

\*\*\*

## THE SUPREME BEING INVOKED IN EARLY INAUGURAL ADDRESSES [84]

Each president of the United States has assumed office with his hand upon a *Bible* and an oath that concludes "So help me God!" — and each has, without fail, invoked God in his follow-on Inaugural Address. The first ten of such inaugural invocations are as follows:

1st President George Washington: "that Almighty Being who rules over the universe. . ."

2nd President John Adams: "that Being who is supreme over all, the Patron of Order, the Fountain of Justice . . ."

> 3rd President Thomas Jefferson: "that Being, in whose hands we are, who led our forefathers, as Israel of old . . ."
> 4th President James Madison: "that Almighty Being whose power regulates the destiny of nations . . ."
> 5th President James Monroe: "with a firm reliance on the protection of the Almighty God . . ."
> 6th President John Quincy Adams: "knowing that 'Except the Lord keep the city, the watchman waketh but in vain' . . ."
> 7th President Andrew Jackson: "my fervent prayer to that Almighty Being before whom I now stand . . ."
> 8th President Martin Van Buren: "that Divine Being whose strengthening support I humbly solicit . . ."
> 9th President William Henry Harrison: "the Beneficent Creator hath made no distinction among men . . ."
> 10th President John Tyler: "the all-wise and all-powerful Being who made me . . ."
> (etc.)

\*\*\*

Indeed, predicated on their faith in the existence of a Supreme Being guiding the destiny of man, the Founders chose as the nation's logo: *Annuit Coeptis* – "God smiles on our undertakings" – an expression characteristically derived from the Roman poet Virgil. To John Adams' "Let the mind loose," Thomas Jefferson's rejoinder was: "Almighty God hath made the mind free." It may be more than mere coincidence, then, that Adams and Jefferson, concluding their earthly missions, both died on July 4, 1826, the date of the fiftieth anniversary of the Declaration of Independence.[85]

**Number of Churches in the Thirteen Colonies, 1776:**[88]

| Denomination: | Number of Churches: | Percent of Total: |
| --- | --- | --- |
| Congregational | 668 | 21.0 |
| Presbyterian | 588 | 18.5 |
| Baptist | 497 | 15.6 |
| Anglican | 495 | 15.6 |
| Quaker | 310 | 9.8 |
| German Reformed | 159 | 5.0 |
| Lutheran | 150 | 4.8 |
| Dutch Reformed | 120 | 3.8 |
| German Sectarian | 71 | 2.2 |
| Methodist | 65 | 2.1 |
| Roman Catholic | 56 | 1.8 |
| TOTAL | 3,179 | 100.0 |

Though the Constitution's explicit focus on religion itself was cursory – having been designed with very limited civil objectives, among them safeguarding the free exercise of religion through its First Amendment — "Congress shall make no law respecting an establishment of religion nor prohibiting the free exercise thereof" — banning religious tests for holding federal office — while putting Sunday off limits for federal activity – the states soon rapidly moved in to fill the theocratic void – exercising the powers vested in them by Tenth Amendment which stipulated that public functions not designated as federal were remanded to their jurisdictions.[86]

## E. Fulfilment of the Founders' Vision

Indeed, by the onset of Revolutionary War, nine of the thirteen original colonies – building upon the precepts of John Winthrop's covenant contracted on the Arabella – had established state-supported churches — and all refused to ratify the Constitution until it contained a prohibition of federal meddling in their establishments of religion. Most had Sabbath observance and blasphemy laws as well. In some, there was a spiritual qualification on suffrage, as only church members were allowed to vote.[87]

Acting accordingly, each of the original thirteen colonies' constitutions, without exception, also designated Christianity as the state-recognized religion – and many, among them Massachusetts, Maryland, Delaware, Pennsylvania, and North Carolina subsequently likewise established adherence to Christianity as a litmus test for legislative office. The 1776 Delaware Constitution, for instance, required state-wide officer-holders to affirm the following oath attesting to the Trinity:

> I, (name), do profess faith in God the Father, and in Jesus Christ, His only Son, and in the Holy Ghost, one God, blessed for evermore; and I acknowledge the Holy Scriptures of the Old and New Testament to be given by divine inspiration.[89]

The 1776 Pennsylvania Constitution – clearly heeding the admonition of William Penn that: "If we will not be governed by God, then we must be governed by tyrants" – likewise required that each legislative member subscribe to the conviction that:

> I believe in one God, the Creator and Governor of the Universe, the Rewarder of the good and the Punisher of the wicked; and I acknowledge the Scriptures of the Old and New Testaments to be given by Divine inspiration.[90]

In analogous provisions, the 1776 Maryland Constitution, in Article XXXIV, explicitly required a "declaration of a belief in the Christian religion" as a condition for office-holding — the 1778 South Carolina Constitution, in addition to designating the "Christian Protestant religion as the established religion of this State," also provided that:"No person who denies the existence of the Supreme Being shall hold any office under this constitution" — and the 1780 Massachusetts Constitution mandated in its gubernatorial oath the affirmation: "(I, (name), do declare that I believe in the Christian religion and have firm persuasion of its truth." Tennessee and Vermont imposed similar requirements for holding public office.[91]

Some states even specified that its Christian officeholders must be Protestant. The aforesaid South Carolina requirement, Article XXXII of the 1776 North Carolina Constitution, for instance, stipulated among its qualifications for state public officers that "No person who shall deny the being of God or the truth of the Protestant religion, or the divine authority of the Old or New Testaments, or shall hold religious principles incompatible with the freedom and safety of the State, shall be capable of holding any office or place of trust or profit in the civil department within this state."[92]

Article VI of the 1777 Georgia Constitution, in turn, mandated of its elected legislators that: "The representatives shall be chosen out of the representatives in each county . . . and they shall be of the Protestant religion." Other erstwhile colonies incorporating analogous provisions included New Jersey in 1776 and New Hampshire in 1784.[93]

The 1776 Maryland Constitution, in fact, levied a general statewide tax for "support of the Christian religion" to meet the financial needs of its in-state clergy; whereas Massachusetts invested its legislature with the authority to require all municipalities "to make suitable provision, at their own expence, for the institution of the public worship of God, and for the support and maintenance of public Protestant teachers of piety, religion, and morality."[94] In 1777, the New Jersey Legislature likewise formally exhorted its delegates to the Congress that:

> We hope that you habitually bear in mind that the success of the great cause in which the United States are engaged depends upon the favor and the blessings of the Almighty God; and therefore you will neglect nothing competent to the Assembly of the States for promoting piety and good morals among the people at large.[95]

It is doubtless no accident, then, that every U.S. state constitution, without exception, today invokes God in its preamble — as there can be no doubt of the intent of the nation's architects at both the federal and state levels respecting the role of religion in American life. Accordingly, in his 1831 visit to America, the French social philosopher Alexis de Tocqueville found what he called "an ostensible respect for Christian morality and virtue."[96]

## F. The Faiths of the Nation's Later Molders

This religious commitment was subsequent affirmed by many of the nation's follow-on leaders. In the midst of the Civil War, Abraham Lincoln described Americans as "a Christian people" — and asserted that "the only assurance of our nation's safety is to lay our foundation in morality and religion."[97] On March 30, 1863, in announcing a "National Day of Fasting," he proclaimed:"

> (I)t is the duty of nations, as well as of men, to owe their dependence upon the overruling power of God, to confess their sins and transgressions in humble sorrow, yet with the assured hope that genuine repentance will lead to mercy and pardon, and to recognize the sublime truth announced in the Holy Scriptures, and

proven by history, that those nations only are blessed whose God is the Lord.[98]

Later that same year, on October 3, 1863, in calling for a national day of thanksgiving, he would express similar sentiments, adding: "No human counsel hath devised nor hath any mortal hand worked out these great things. They are the gracious gifts of the most high God who, while dealing with us in anger for our sins, nevertheless remembered mercy."[99] His philosophy of governance was however perhaps best encapsulated in his response to a Civil War clergyman's quip that he hoped: "the Lord is on the Union's side:"

> I am not at all concerned about that, for I know that the Lord is always on the side of the right. But it is my constant anxiety and prayer that I and this nation should be on the Lord's side.[100]

In so affirming, Lincoln thus built upon his assertion in his First Inaugural that:

> Intelligence, patriotism, Christianity, and firm reliance upon Him, who has never forsaken yet this favored land, are still competent to adjust, in the best way, all our present difficulty.[101]

Lincoln, it is well known, devoutly read the *Bible*. From it, he got many of his defining metaphors, among them:

— "a house divided against itself cannot stand" (Mark 3:25);
— "woe to that man by whom the offense cometh" (Matthew 18:7);
— "the judgements of the Lord are true and righteous." (Psalm:19:9; and
— "blessed are those nations whose god is the Lord." (Psalm 33:12).[102]

"But for the *Bible*," he would thus continue, "we could not know right from wrong. All things most desirable for man's welfare . . . are contained in it."[103] Pursuant to his motto:"With malice toward none; with charity for all; with firmness in the right, as God gives us to see the right," Lincoln's Gettysburg Address, delivered on November 19, 1863, concluded with the supplication that: . . "this nation, under God, shall have a new birth of freedom — and that government of the people, by the people, and for the people shall not perish from this earth."And his Second Inaugural Address likewise cited two *Bible* verses leavened with fourteen other references to God.[104]

Accordingly at the onset of the Civil War, President Lincoln, by Executive Order issued on November 15, 1862, directed the Union Army to circumspectly observe the Sabbath[105] — thereby rendering it, in the considered opinion of eminent historian James McPherson to be: "arguably the most religious army in American history."[106]

Concurrently, consistent with the spirit of the age, the Union Army marching song in the Civil War, "The Battle Hymn of the Republic," penned by Julia Ward Howe, contained the immortal words: "As Christ died to make men holy, let us die to make men free"– lines later amended to proclaim: "let us *live* to make men free." Reflecting the religious calling of the Union cause, it proclaimed:

> In the beauty of the lilies, Christ was born across the sea; With a glory in his

bosom that transfigures you and me. As he died to make men holy, let us die to make men free; While God is marching on! [107]

In like manner, President Grover Cleveland's Second Inaugural Address, delivered on March 4, 1893, affirmed: "Above all, I know that there is a Supreme Being who rules the affairs of men and whose goodness and mercy have always followed the American people; and I know that He will not turn from us now if we humbly and reverently seek His powerful aid."[108]

Woodrow Wilson's Second Inaugural Address, delivered on March 5, 1917, in turn acknowledging the "full responsibility that (the presidency) involves, pray to God that I may be given the wisdom to do my duty in the true spirit of this great people."[109] Reflecting upon the religious spirit manifest in America's early heritage in a speech delivered in Denver, he also said: "America was born to be a Christian nation, born to exemplify that devotion to the elements of righteousness which are derived from of the Holy Scriptures."[110] To these ends, he expounded:

> The *Bible* . . . is the one supreme source of the meaning of life, the nature of God, and . . . the nature and needs of men. It is the only guide of life which really leads the spirit in the way of peace and salvation.[111]

Franklin Roosevelt, in turn, asserted: "We cannot read the history of our development as a nation without recognizing the place that the *Bible* occupies in shaping the advances of the Republic."[112] Accordingly, his sole statement on "D-Day," 1944 was to read a supplication for Divine assistance that he had written drawn from the "Episcopal Book of Common Prayer." [113]

In a 1947 letter to Pope Pius XII, Harry Truman affirmed as well: "This is a Christian nation" – and in a speech in Columbus Ohio asserted: "No problem on this earth is tough enough to withstand the flame of a genuine renewal of religious faith." "Without it," he continued, "we are lost."[114] Relating these sentiments to his philosophy for governance, Truman prophetically asserted:

> The basis of our Bill of Rights comes from the teachings that we get from Exodus and St. Matthew, from Isaiah and St. Paul. I don't think that we emphasize that enough these days. If we don't have a proper fundamental moral background, we will finally end up with a . . . government which does not believe in rights for anybody except the State.[115]

To which John Kennedy appended: "The rights of man come not from the generosity of the state but from the hand of God."[116] — concluding his Inaugural Address with the assertion: "Let us then go forth to lead the land we love, asking His blessing and His help, but knowing that here on earth God's work must truly be our own."[118] In like manner, George W. Bush, in his January 28, 2003 State of the Union address stated: "Liberty is not America's gift to the world; it is God's gift to humanity."[119]

Later, Jimmy Carter would state: "We have a responsibility to try to shape government so that it exemplifies the will of God."[120] Ronald Reagan similarly concluded: that "Without religion, there is no virtue because there is no prompting of of conscience. . . . Without God, democracy cannot and will not long endure. If we forget that we are 'One Nation Under God,' then we will be a nation gone under."[121] In a 1984 speech, he continued:

> Think for a moment how special it is to be an American. Can we doubt that only a Divine Providence placed this land, this island of freedom, here as a refuge for all those people in the world who yearn to breathe free? [122]

On the legislative side, in 1854, the U.S. House Judiciary Committee, in a formal report transmitted to the Congress on March 27, 1854, also unconditionally affirmed that: "We are a Christian people" — appending that: "Had the people, during the Revolution, had a suspicion of any attempt to war against Christianity, that revolution would have been strangled in its cradle. At the time of the adoption of the Constitution and the amendments, the universal sentiment was that Christianity should be encouraged . . . That was the religion of the founders of the republic, and they expected it to remain the religion of their descendants."[123]

Responding to the report by formal resolution, the House, in its capacity as "Committee of the Whole," then proclaimed: "The great vital and conservative element in our system is the belief of our people of the pure doctrines and divine truths of the gospel of Jesus Christ."[124]

In 1908, another House of Representative Committee likewise reaffirmed by resolution the United States to be a "Christian nation," and that "the best and only reliance for the perpetuation of the republican institution is upon Christian patriotism." In 1917, Congress passed a resolution declaring a "day of prayer" in support of the WW-I war effort and reinvoking America's status as a Christian nation.[125]

Such convictions were historically sustained by the nation's courts as well."We are a Christian people, and the morality of the country is deeply engrafted upon Christianity," the Supreme Court ruled in 1811. In 1892, in *Church of the Holy Trinity v. the United States*, building upon a lengthy body of jurisprudential precedence, the Supreme Court proclaimed: "This is a Christian nation"— a ruling reaffirmed by the court in 1931 and again in 1952 in *Zorach v. Clauson*.[126]

Indeed, after vindicating the Holy Trinity Church for violating a ban on hiring foreign workers by employing an English clergyman as its pastor, the Court in *Church of the Holy Trinity*, citing *Updegraph v. the Commonwealth* (1894) as legal precedent, further ruled that it would be repugnant to the spirit of the Constitution to in any way hinder, whether directly or indirectly, the spread or propagation of Christianity by legislative act. Writing the majority opinion, Justice David Brewer held that the federal government could not interfere in the free exercise of religion; in effect, denying to Caesar those things that belong to God.[127]

The decision built upon a consistent longstanding court record. *Updegraph*, the cited 1824 precedent, had been unequivocal, holding that: "No free government now exists in the world unless where Christianity is acknowledged and is the religion of the country . . . . Christianity, general Christianity, is and always has been, part of the common law. . . not Christianity founded upon any particular religious tenets; not Christianity with an established church . . . but Christianity with liberty

24                                    *Chapter One*

of conscience to all men. . . . Its foundations are broad and strong and deep. . . . It is the purest system of morality, and the only stable support of all human laws." [128]

The 1931 U.S. Supreme Court ruling, in turn, declared: "Our law and institutions must necessarily be based upon and embody the teachings of the Redeemer of mankind. . . . Our civilization and our institutions are emphatically Christian. . . . We are a Christian people, according to one another the right of religious freedom, acknowledging with reverence the duty of obedience to the will of God."[129]

In the 1952 decision, Justice William O. Douglas, in *Zorach v. Clausen*, in like manner, wrote: "We are a religious people, and our institutions presuppose the existence of a Supreme Being."[130] To which, Chief Justice Earl Warren, in 1954, appended:

> I believe that no one can read the history of our country without realizing that the Good Book and the spirit of our Savior have, from the very beginning, been our guiding geniuses . . .
> Whether we look to the First Charter of Virginia . . . or to the Charter of New England . . . or to the Charter of Massachusetts Bay . . . or to the Fundamental Orders of Connecticut . . . the same objective is present, a Christian land governed by Christian principles.
> I believe that the entire Bill of Rights came into being because of the knowledge that our Forefathers had of the *Bible* and their belief in it: freedom of belief, expression, assembly, petition, the dignity of the individual, the sanctity of home, equal justice under law, and reservation of powers to the people.[131]

---

\*\*\*

## PROOF CITED BY THE SUPREME COURT THAT AMERICA WAS BORN TO BE A CHRISTIAN NATION[132]

From the Majority Opinion: *Church of the Holy Trinity v. United States (1892):* From the discovery of this continent to the present hour, there is a single voice making this affirmation. The commission of Christopher Columbus . . . (recited) that: "It is hoped by God's assistance that some of the continents and islands in the ocean will be discovered." The first colonial grant – that made to Sir Walter Raleigh in 1574 – and the grant authorizing him to enact statutes for the government of the proposed colony provided that "they not be against the true Christian faith . . . ." The First Charter of Virginia, granted by King James I in 1606 . . . commenced the grant in these words: ". . . in propagating of the Christian Religion to such People as yet live in Darkness . . ."

> Language of similar import may be found in . . . the various charters granted to the other colonies in language more or less emphatic in the establishment of the Christian religion, declaring it to be one of the purposes of the grant. The celebrated compact made by the Pilgrims on the Mayflower, 1620, recites:"Having undertaken for the Glory of God, and the advancement of the Christian faith a voyage to plant the first colony in the northern parts . . ."
> 
> The Fundamental Orders of Connecticut, under which a provisional government was instituted in 1638-1639, commence with this declaration: "Well-knowing where a people are gathered together in the word of God requires to maintain the peace and union . . . that there should be an orderly and decent government established according to God . . . to maintain and preserve the liberty and purity of the Gospel of our Lord Jesus Christ which we now profess, and of the said Gospel which is practiced amongst us. . . ."
> 
> In the Charter of Privileges granted by William Penn to the province of Pennsylvania, in 1701, it is recited: ". . . no people can be truly happy, though under the great enjoyment of civil liberties, if there is abridgement of their religious profession and worship . . ."
> 
> Coming nearer to the present time, the Declaration of Independence recognized the presence of the Divine in human affairs with these words: "We hold these truths to be self-evident, that all men are created equal and that they are endowed by their Creator with certain unalienable Rights . . . ". . . appealing to the Supreme Judge of the world for the rectitude of our intentions . . . ;" "And for the support of this Declaration, with a firm reliance on the Protection of Divine Providence, we mutually pledge to each other Our Lives, our Fortunes, and our sacred Honor."

*\*\**

In 1879, moreover, the Supreme Court affirmed the constitutionality of the national motto: "In God we trust;" and in 1883, it upheld the longstanding practice of paying chaplains by the Congress.[133]

These determinations enjoyed powerful historic precedent. In the words of Patrick Henry: "It cannot be emphasized too strongly or too often that this great nation was founded not by religionists but by Christians, not on religions but on the Gospel of Jesus Christ. For this very reason, peoples of other faiths have been afforded asylum, prosperity, and freedom of worship here."[134] As similarly assessed by early twentieth century Supreme Court Justice David Brewer: "The American nation, from its first settlement at Jamestown to this hour, is based upon and permeated by precepts of the *Bible*."[135]

It is no accident, then, that Part I, Article II of the Massachusetts Constitution of 1780 reads — "Every denomination of Christians denouncing themselves peaceably, and as good subjects of the commonwealth, shall be equally under the protection of the law: and no subordination of any one sect or denomination to another shall ever be established by law" — language replicated in the New Hampshire

shire Constitution of 1783 and other state constitutions of the era — and Article VI of the U.S. Constitution affirming that: "No religious test shall ever be required as a qualification to any office or public trust under the United States."[136]

Accordingly, the Founders clearly understood that sanctioning and encouraging religious practices was not the same as establishing a national religion. Indeed, a formal report of the U.S. Congress in 1854, resolving to open its daily sessions with prayer, by resolution affirmed "the belief of our people in the pure doctrines and divine truths of the gospel of Jesus Christ."[137]

## II. AMERICA: "ONE NATION UNDER GOD"

In light of such powerful attestations, then, it is particularly noteworthy that neither the Constitution nor its subsequent amendments, formally refer to a "separation of church and state" — and though one of its principal architects, James Madison, does refer to both in passing, it is explicitly in a context not to establish freedom *from* religion but rather freedom *for* religion – as in the view of the Founders, as noted in the Introduction, they fervently believed that America was "God's great plan" enacted on earth.[138]

It is in this spirit, therefore, that the Declaration of Independence invoked the "Creator," "Divine Providence," and the "Supreme Judge of the World" — and that well into the nineteenth century, Sunday church services were held in the chambers of the House of Representatives as well as in those of the Supreme Court.[139]

It was in this spirit, therefore, that Thomas Jefferson in 1785, together with Benjamin Franklin, proposed that the seal of the United States be an encapsulation of Moses, lifting his wand to divide the Red Sea with the Pharaoh in his chariot overwhelmed with water – encircled by the banner: "Rebellion to Tyrants is Obedience to God." It was in this spirit that the Congress also authorized that the words: "In God we trust" initially be inscribed on certain coins in the Civil War era; and that the mandate was extended to all coins in 1908 and to paper money in 1955.[140]

When the seat of the U.S. federal government relocated from New York to Washington in 1800, the Congress authorized the Capitol Building to serve also as a church – a fact recorded in the diary of John Quincy Adams who attended services there, as well as at the Treasury Building. For all of these reasons, a full half century after the Constitution's adoption, Alexis de Tocqueville observed that Americans hold religion "to be indispensable to the maintenance of republican institutions."[141]

Central to the country's founding, then, was the premise that the American system of government presupposed a Divine Being reigning supreme over the republic. For the Constitution's framers believed that the nation that they were creating could only survive if it was imbued with bedrock religious values – a conviction that, as shown, would find endorsement by subsequent generations of American leaders at federal, state, and local levels alike. Indeed, as noted following the precedent set by the original thirteen colonies, even today, each of the fifty state constitutions invoke

God for their preservation.[142]

As a consequence, as also noted, American presidents take their oaths of office with one hand on a *Bible*, and conclude their oaths with: "So help me God!" – and end their major addresses to the nation with "God Bless America." Since 1923, each president annually lights the national Christmas tree. Each day, when the U.S. Supreme Court convenes, all justices stand as the court crier calls out: "May God save the United States and this honorable court." Throughout the nation, court witnesses also swear on a *Bible* with an oath that concludes: "So help me God!" [143]

Indeed, ever since the Continental Congress met on September 7, 1774, each daily convention of the Congress opens with a prayer of supplication delivered by public chaplains employed by the federal government – and all annual sessions of Congress and state legislatures invariably commence and end with prayer. In 1952, Congress instructed the President to declare a "National Day of Prayer" annually, and the concept of a "National Prayer Breakfast" was also born during this era.[144]

In like manner, tax-funded chaplains are employed in the armed services, military members are sworn in with an oath that ends: "So help me God!" and religious institutions are tax-exempt nationwide, as are their clergy, who are also exempt from military conscription. The president is authorized by law to proclaim at least two annual "National Days of Prayer;" indeed, until the presidency of Barack Obama, the president has publicly celebrated a "National Day of Prayer" — and each year, the president proclaims the fourth Thursday of November as a "National Day of Thanksgiving."[145]

Since 1954, Americans pledge their allegiance to: "one nation under God" – each session of each House of Congress opens with the Pledge of Allegiance – and the phrase: "In God We Trust," which became America's official motto in 1956, is inscribed on all of the nation's currency and has appeared on federal postage stamps as well. Indeed, the Post Office for a time even cancelled stamps with the phrase: "Pray for Peace." In 1983, Congress proclaimed that year to be the "Year of the *Bible*."[146]

America's profound religious legacy is further reflected upon many monuments reposing in the U.S. capital. The national motto: "In God We Trust" is inscribed in gold lettering behind the rostrums of both the House and Senate chambers. The bronzed Senate doors likewise depict George Washington taking the presidential oath with his hand on a *Bible*. A relief of Moses, surrounded by twenty-two other great lawgivers, hangs in the House chamber, and the phrase "In God We Trust" appears prominently engraved in bronze both on the House Speaker's rostrum and the Dirksen Senate Office Building.[147]

The words: "The New Testament according to our Lord and Savior Jesus Christ" appear on the Capitol Dome, and a painting of the crucified Christ appears in its Rotunda – as do those of the baptism of Pocahontas, the *Pilgrims at Prayer*, and Christopher Columbus holding a cross while praying with his crew.[148]

In the Cox Corridor in the House wing of the Capitol, a line from "America the Beautiful" — "God shed His grace on thee" — is engraved into the wall. Within the cornerstones for the new House and Senate wings, set in place fifty eight-years after

28                           *Chapter One*

the first Capitol cornerstone was embedded, reposes a manuscript prepared by then Secretary of State Daniel Webster that invokes the blessings of God to preserve the Union and its Capitol, concluding: "with hearts devotedly thankful to Almighty God for the preservation of the liberty and the happiness of the country . . . God save the United States."[149]

The Capitol prayer room features a stained glass window that bears the verse Psalms 16:1: "Preserve me, O God, for in Thee do I put my trust." Through the top of its stained glass window, a subdued light reveals the figure of George Washington in somber prayer for his soldiers and his country at Valley Forge – a scene known as "Washington's Gethsemane"– which is captioned "In God We Trust," and is also inscribed with the words: "This nation under God." Both Thomas Jefferson and James Madison attended church services in the Capitol building, and during Jefferson's presidency, as noted, church services were held in the Treasury building and the Supreme Court chambers as well.[150]

In the White House, in the West Wing, carved into the marble of the fireplace in the State Dining Room are the famed words of John Adams: "I pray Heaven to bestow the best of Blessings upon this White House and on all that shall hereinafter inhabit it. May none other than Honest and Wise men ever rule under this roof."[151]

The walls of the Library of Congress, in turn, proclaim the verse Psalm 19:1: "The heavens declare the glory of God, and the firmament showeth His handiwork." They likewise display the verses: Micah 6:8: "He has shown thee, O man, what is good; and what God doth require of thee, but to do justly, and to love mercy, and to walk humbly with thy God;" and Proverbs 4:7: "Wisdom is the principal goal; therefore get wisdom; and with all of thy getting, get understanding." The Library's "Main Reading Room" also includes a statue of Moses holding the Ten Commandments, and its ceiling portrays a painting called *"Judea"* depicting a young Jewish woman in prayer."[152]

The Supreme Court building is similarly adorned with four *bas-relief* sculptures replicating the Ten Commandments. Amongst them is including one featuring the "Majesty of Law" that depicts Moses receiving the twin stone pillars upon which they were inscribed. Another on the building's portal portrays Moses, standing amidst other noted lawgivers, holding the Ten Commandments inscribed in Hebrew; whereas the commandments likewise are carved into each oak door opening into the courthouse and are again displayed within it above the seated judges.[153]

Atop the Washington monument on the east side of its capstone are the words: *Laus Deo* ("Praise be to God") and lining its spiraling ascending stairwell are inscribed such biblical verses as:[154]

    "Search the Scriptures" (John 5:39);
    "The memory of the just is blessed" (Proverbs 10:7);
    "Holiness is to the Lord" (Zechariah 14:20);
    "Train up a child in the way he should go, and when he is old, he will not depart from it" (Proverbs 22:6); and
    "Suffer the little children to come unto me, and forbid them not, for of such is the Kingdom of God (Luke 18:6).

In the Lincoln Memorial are inscribed phrases from the sixteenth president's Second Inaugural Address alluding to "God," "the Bible," "Providence," "the Almighty," and "Divine attributes." Another scriptural excerpt from his Second Inaugural Address is inscribed on the wall of its north chamber: "The Almighty has His purposes. Woe be unto the world because of offenses; for it must needs be that offenses come, but woe to that man by whom the offense cometh" (Matthew 18:7).[155]

The Jefferson Memorial similarly bears the third president's words: "God who gave us life gave us liberty. Can the liberties of a nation be secure when we have removed their only firm basis, the conviction that these liberties are the gift of God? I tremble for my country's future when I reflect that God is just, and that His justice cannot sleep forever." Another quote asserts: "I have sworn upon the altar of God eternal hostility against every form of tyranny over the mind of man."[156]

Carved on the portal of the lobby of the U.S. CIA headquarters are words from John 8:32. signifying that agency's vital mission: "You shall know the truth and the truth will make you free" — a proclamation also carved on the arch of the entrance to Union Station in Washington, together with the verse: "The desert shall rejoice and blossom like the rose" (Isaiah 35:1).[157]

The nation's initial logo: *Annuit Coeptis* – "God smiles on our undertakings" – is inscribed upon the Great Seal of the United States and below it is the phrase from Lincoln's Gettysburg address: "This nation under God." The Liberty Bell prominently displays Leviticus 25:10 encircling its top: "Proclaim liberty throughout all of the land unto the inhabitants thereof." The rear panel of the "Tomb of the Unknown Soldier" bears the inscription: "Here rests in honored glory an American soldier known only to God."[158] And the fourth refrain of the national anthem proudly proclaims:

> "And this be our motto: 'In God we trust.'"[159]

All issued in the fulfilment of the Founding Fathers's scripturally-based patriotic vision embedded in the biblical Book of Proverbs (16:12) that "a throne is established by righteousness." Such legacies thus powerfully affirm the commitment of the nation's architects to make America "God's nation" – a polity inspired by religious values; precepts which, as a consequence, for nearly two centuries, guided its political thought through the prism of a religious world view.

For such noble cause, the sublime status of America as a Christian nation was deemed "wise and virtuous" by John Jay; "rational" by John Adams; and "civilized" by John Quincy Adams — with the elder Adams adding: "The general principles upon which the fathers achieved independence were . . . the principles of Christianity."[160]

For as was succinctly asserted by Founder Samuel Adams: "Divine Revelation assures us that 'Righteousness exalteth a nation.'"[161] Again, in the words of Alexis de Tocqueville in 1831:

> There is no country in the whole world in which the Christian religion retains a greater influence over the souls of men than in America. . . . Upon my arrival in the United States, the religious aspect of the country was the first thing that struck

my attention, and the longer I stayed there, the more that I perceived the great political consequence resulting from this state of affairs to which I was unaccustomed.....

Americans combine the notions of Christianity and of liberty so intimately within their minds that they cannot conceive the one without the other.... Religion in America takes no direct part in the government of society but it must be regarded as the first of their political institutions; for if it does not impart a taste for freedom, it facilitates the use of it....

Two distinct elements that elsewhere have often made war with each other, in America... have succeeded somehow in incorporating one into the other and combining marvelously. I speak of the spirit of religion and the spirit of freedom."[162]

The testimonies of the Founders themselves stand in affirmation of these commitments.

***

### AFFIRMATIONS BY THE NATION'S LEADERS THAT AMERICA WAS BORN A FREE CHRISTIAN NATION[163]

Freedom is not a gift bestowed upon by other men; rather it is a right that belongs to us by the laws of God

–Benjamin Franklin in *Maxims and Morals.* [164]

God who gave us life gave us liberty. And can the liberties of a nation be thought secure when we have removed their only firm basis, a conviction in the minds of the people that these liberties are indeed the Gift of God

–Thomas Jefferson, 1781, in his "Notes on the State of Virginia."[165]

Natural liberty is a gift of the beneficent Creator to the whole human race; and civil liberty is founded in that; and cannot be wrestled from any people without the most manifest violation of justice

–Alexander Hamilton, "In Defense of Liberty."[166]

A Christian cannot fail of being a republican. . . . for every precept of the Gospel inculcates those degrees of humility, self-denial, and brotherly kindness

– Benjamin Rush, Signer of the Declaration of Independence.[167]

Bad men cannot make good citizens. It is impossible that a nation of infidels or idolaters should be a nation of free-men. It is when a people forget God that tyrants forge their chains

– Patrick Henry, Three-Term Governor of Virginia. [168]

The right to freedom, being the Gift of God Almighty . . . may best be understood by reading and studying the institutions of the Great Lawgiver and the Head of the Christian Church

– Samuel Adams, 1772, in "The Rights of the Colonists."[169]

It seems perfectly plain that the right to equality has for its foundation reverence for God. If we could imagine that swept away, our American government could not long survive

– Calvin Coolidge, 1924, Address to the "Holy Name Society."[170]

America is dedicated to the conviction that all people are entitled by the gift of God to equal rights and freedoms

– Harry S. Truman, 1949. [171]

History comes and goes, but principles endure and ensure future generations to defend liberty not as a gift from government but a blessing from Our Creator

– Ronald Reagan, 1993, "Medal of Freedom Ceremony."[172]

Liberty is not America's gift to the world; it is God's gift to humanity

–President George W. Bush, "Third State of the Union Address."[173]

\*\*\*

# Chapter Two
# Sorting Through the Founders' Faiths

> Religion and virtue are the only Foundations not only of Republicanism and of all free Government, but of social felicity under all Governments.
>
> —John Adams

## I. THE CRUCIBLE WHEREIN AMERICA'S RELIGIOUS HERITAGE WAS FORGED

### A. The Piety of the Puritans

The religious propensities of the Founding Fathers thus are clear. But precisely what was the religious provenance of America herself? At her inception, as shown, she aspired to be a nation that accommodated all religious faiths, as the Founders were as determinedly opposed to the absolutism of the Anglican Church – which even then had become the established religion in nine of the thirteen colonies – as they were appalled by the authoritarianism of the King of England.[1]

Notwithstanding what some have called striking "Deist" propensities amongst many of the nation's early leaders, most of America's average citizens were Protestants whose creed embraced a rich admixture of Christian virtues: a powerful work ethic, limited government, the English language, British traditions of law and justice, and an appreciation for classic European literature and philosophy.

As the religious foundations of America were laid in the old world — Spain, Portugal, Holland, Germany and France – but most particularly in England. From them came values that have shaped the nation's special and unique character. Indeed, the country would be quite different today had it been settled not largely by British Protestants but instead by the French, Spanish, or Portuguese – perhaps then becoming a Catholic nation more resembling Quebec, Mexico, or Brazil.

Instead, on strong and durable Anglo-Saxon foundations, what is today known as the "American Creed" was forged. In the assessment of Arthur Schlesinger: "The language of the new nation, its laws, its institutions, its political ideas, its literature, its customs, its precepts, and its prayers, primarily derived from Britain." As a result, America's citizens have been integrally a part of a "nation of immigrants" possessing distinct Anglo-Protestant values — with such values comprising the essence of the American Creed.[2]

Thus, the colonial newcomers were somewhat of an homogenous mix – people coming to the nation's hospitable shores in common cause seeking explicitly to be free to practice their religious freedoms and beliefs. It brought the Pilgrims to Virginia in 1607 to create a settlement of indentured colonists at Jamestown; The Puritans, arriving in 1620, were another group not long to follow in a fervent quest to create that "City on a Hill" that would serve as a beacon of religious piety to the world.[3]

Many of the earliest Protestant colonists to New England were, in fact, Calvinists who subscribed to "covenant theology" as their foundation of civil governance. To wit: that rulers derive their authority from God as prescribed in Romans 13: 1-4, delegating to them authority to preside through that election over a religious commonwealth created and voted by the people.[4]

This "covenantial view of government" would soon find vivid expression in English parliamentarian philosopher John Locke's "social compact theory" – a proposition holding that men in a state of nature form a government by mutual consent and give it limited authority to act in order to protect their basic rights to life, liberty, and property.[5]

This concept would manifest itself in the Preamble to the U.S. Constitution: "We the People of the United States, in order to form a more perfect Union . . . do ordain and establish this Constitution of the United States of America"[6] — and the Declaration of Independence, which states that governments exist to secure human rights and "derive their powers from the consent of the governed." On this, the Declaration was explicit:

> All men . . . are endowed by their Creator with certain unalienable rights. . . . That to secure these rights, Governments are instituted among Men.

Hence, in the eyes of the Founders, the Constitution was supreme law issuing from a social contract that Americans pledged to honor in its ratification and continually reaffirmed in their oaths to uphold — a *corpus* of sacred precepts to be upheld, not undermined, by judges who would be legislators.[7]

Yet this again was by design – as James Madison, "Father of the Constitution," believed that "government with the consent of the governed" was comprised of five components:

- First, that public power must derive from the people;
- Second, that government has only such powers as the people delegate to it through their political covenant, the Constitution;
- Third, that the covenant cannot contravene "the law of Nature and of Nature's God;"
- Fourth, that there must be a separation of powers amongst the executive, legislative, and judicial branches; and finally
- Fifth, that the separate branches must serve each other as an independent branch.[8]

Recourse to the precepts of the British political philosopher John Locke and others thus comes as no surprise — given that America's Founding Fathers themselves were largely English settlers – and the ancestors of all her citizens, in one way or another, with the exception of Rhode Island and Pennsylvania, initially came as predominantly European immigrants protesting perceived religious persecution at home. For the same reason that Israel is Jewish and Pakistan is Muslim, then, in the words of the 19th century Swiss-German visitor Phillip Schaff: "everything here had a Protestant beginning" – a phenomenon that would generally prevail for the first two centuries of the Republic.[9]

The nation's economic preeminence was built, in fact, directly upon the success of those intrepid souls who, imbued by the so-called "Protestant ethic," came in equal status – entrepreneurs, factory workers, merchants, and farmers – dedicated to the premise of diligent endeavor seeking a fair return. As described by the aristocratic young French social philosopher Alexander de Tocqueville who arrived in America on May 11, 1831: "they were born equal, and didn't have to become so."[10]

Equally so, most were born Protestant, – staunchly Calvinistic and firmly believing that God had foreordained their purpose to establish His Kingdom on earth– as recognized by Edmund Burke, himself a puritan in precept:

> (The Americans) are Protestant, and of that kind which is the most averse to all implicit submission of mind and opinion. All forms of Protestantism, even at its most cold and passive, are a form of dissent. But the religion most prevalent in our northern colonies is no mere refinement on the principle of resistance; it is instead the dissidence of dissent, and the protestantism of the Protestant religion.[11]

Thus, speaking of what Max Weber called "the Protestant ethic" a century later, F.J. Grund observed of America in 1837: "Protestantism, republicanism, and individualism are all one."[12]

In short, Protestant culture made Americans the most individualistic and enterprising people in the world. Indeed, the notion of the "self-made man" made explicit in the Constitution, the nation's social contract with its people, came strikingly to the fore in the presidency of Andrew Jackson, and Henry Clay was the first

36                    Chapter Two

to employ that very phrase on the floor of the U.S. Senate in 1832. The concept continues to this day, as observed by President Bill Clinton:

> The American Dream upon which we were all raised is a simple but powerful one — if you work hard, and play by the rules, you should be given a chance to go as far as your God-given ability will take you.[13]

## B. The Founder's Gods: Kaleidoscopic in Focus, Diverse in Provenance

Defining the faiths of the Founders may be a task as complex as discerning the nature of their constitutional goals. In the latter, they were called to craft a creed for all citizens – Jews as well as Gentiles; Catholics as well as Calvinists; Muslims as well as Methodists – as the Kingdom of God on Earth could not be denominationally-defined. The challenge was theologically compounded by the realities that many were fleeing perceived theocratic imposition within their erstwhile homelands; and that Christ himself admonished: "My Kingdom is not of this world;"[14] and "Render unto Caesar the things that are Caesar's; and unto God the things that are God's."[15]

Indeed, in 1920, the early twentieth century Baptist theologian George W. Truett would proclaim from the steps of the U.S. Capitol that: "the utterance of Jesus 'Render unto Caesar the things that are Caesar's and unto God the things that are God's' is one of the most revolutionary and history-making utterances that ever fell from those lips divine. That utterance, once and for all, marked the divorcement of church and state."[16]

Such a confluence of conviction and fact thus created a fervent, yet fertile, intellectual milieu wherein, while the Founders resoundingly opposed the establishment of a single national denomination, they equally vigorously opposed governmental attempts to separate biblical principles and values from the public arena.

It was in this spirit of religious neutrality, then, that the Constitution's First Amendment was crafted to open: "Congress shall make no law respecting an establishment of religion, or prohibiting the free exercise thereof . . ." That it was a controversial determination is reflected in the reality that the amendment was the subject of multiple iterations and intense debate within the First Congress over the summer of 1789, with James Madison, as lead architect, receiving final Conference Committee approval on September 25, 1789.[17]

It was in this spirit that Justice Hugo Black, in *Everson v. Board of Education*, writing for the majority in a landmark 1947 parochial school busing case, asserted: "The "establishment of religion" clause of the First Amendment means at least this: Neither a state nor the Federal Government can set up a church. Neither can pass laws which aid one religion, aid all religions, or prefer one religion over another."[18] This ruling, in essence, thus established that:

> (1) Congress cannot give nondiscriminatory aid to religion; and
> (2) That this prohibition to the Congress applied to the individual states as well.[19]

Yet however virtuous its intent, with this ruling, the Court concurrently used the First Amendment to prohibit the very religious activities that the Founders had intended to encourage in promulgating it. This reality, as Chapter 3 describes, is the fundamental premise over which the issue of "separation of church and state" is debated today.

For though America was founded primarily by Protestant Calvinists, the religious views of many of her principal Founders — George Washington, Thomas Jefferson, James Madison, Benjamin Franklin, and Thomas Paine foremost among them — were kaleidoscopic – convictions held by leaders who believed in a Supreme Being but had differing visions of what that concept meant – while being nonetheless statesmen who rightly concurred that the nation's governing documents had to transcend the convictions of particular sects.

Indeed the prismatic views of the nature of "God" held by the Founders have led to intense modern exegesis and debate. A conventional contention held that a significant number of the principal Founders were "Deists" – professors of a existential belief in a Supreme Being without necessarily accepting an underlying "three-in-one" Trinitarian premise.

The issue centered on an illusion, perpetuated by modern secularists, that the religious die cast by the Founders was the handiwork of disciples of an effete, ephemeral, remote, and abstract "Supreme Being," if such an entity existed at all. The question becomes: does this supposition stand the test of evidence?

Contemporary eighteenth century Deism, which evolved out of the Renaissance "Age of Enlightenment," and thereby lent its doctrine a distinctly European flavor, undeniably attracted believers more comfortable with the notion of deriving the Creator's handiwork from nature than from biblical documentation.

The foremost professing American Deist at the nation's founding was Thomas Paine, who described the creed's fundamental precepts in his work *The Age of Reason* thusly: "I believe in one God and no more; and I hope for happiness beyond this life. I believe in the equality of man and I believe that religious duties consist of doing justice, loving mercy, and endeavoring to make fellow creatures happy."[20]

Generically, the doctrine traced its origins to the medieval rationalism of French philosopher René Descartes (1596-1650) as interpreted in the seventeenth century through the scientific method of British philosopher-scholar Sir Isaac Newton (1642-1727) and the empiricism of the aforesaid late seventeenth century English philosopher John Locke (1632-1704), all of whom were carefully studied by the Founders in a period of great patriotic intellectual awakening – the "Great Awakening of 1740-1760" – regarding religious freedom that commenced midway through the eighteenth century.[21]

Thomas Jefferson, in particular, who drew heavily upon Aristotle and Cicero from antiquity, concurrently derived much from Locke, Joseph Priestly, and Lord Bolinbroke, all Enlightenment thinkers. It was from them that he discerned that the Creator had invested mankind with certain inherent rights that no human power had the authority to take away.[22]

The rationalism of the *Two Treatises on Government* of Locke – who, in his own words, was deeply impressed by the colonists' "fierce spirit of liberty" – was thus widely influential in the development of contemporary political thought. Indeed, Jefferson, Franklin, Paine, and others looked to him for guidance in addressing the political problems of their age, and without his intellectual framework, the Declaration of Independence would have likely been improbable.[23]

The phrase within the Declaration: "the Laws of Nature and Nature's God," which had been used by such contemporary jurists as Locke and William Blackstone in their expositions, was, in fact a precept to which all of the Founders subscribed – reflecting a universal belief in a form of higher law to which mankind's law should conform and by which mankind should be judged [24] – adhering fervently to the teachings of the Scriptures as articulated in Romans 2:14: that "the Gentiles... having not the law, are a law unto themselves, which shew the work of the law written in their hearts."[25]

As in rejecting the Calvinistic concept of predestination, the Founders believed that rational man, with God as architect, was capable of forging his own destiny — including, in the present instance, building a republican capitalistic nation governed by the workings of natural law and right reason.

The latter challenge was not easy. As defined by Jefferson in his defense of the nation's legal architecture — reflecting the reality that the Founders had to weigh in delicate balance the interests of prevailing mainline Protestant sects with a multitude of other diverse religious interests, including Catholics, Quakers, Jews, and Muslims — it "was meant to comprehend, within the mantle of its protection, the Jew and the Gentile, the Christian and the Mahometan, the Hindu, and infidels of every denomination."[26]

As he also somewhat indelicately put it in speaking to the need to preserve religious freedom for all: "The legitimate powers of government extend to such acts only as are injurious to others. It does me no injury for my neighbor to say there are twenty gods or no God. It neither picks my pocket nor breaks my leg."[27]

His assurance thus echoed that of George Washington to the Hebrew Congregation of Newport News, Rhode Island in 1790 that "America gives bigotry no sanction"[28] — as the Founders clearly perceived their mission to be that of linking the cause of religious liberty to the concept of avoiding sectarian imagery or denominational dominance.[29]

The critical question arises, however, whether such convictions issued from a Deistic rejection of the precepts of Christianity, or were instead no more than an ecumenism that transcended parochial sectarian beliefs – in so doing, proving that the Founders enjoyed greater intellectual depth than do their modern day exegetes. As it was the Christian *Bible* that the Founders quoted and to which they turned for their theological reference and intellectual sustenance.

The conundrum of the logic algorithm was founded on these improbable premises: John Locke was a Deist; the Founding Fathers followed the teachings of John Locke; *ipso facto*, the Founders were Deists. This syllogism merits further contemplation in all of its dimensions – as in a quest for answers, a reread of both their cogent political pronouncements in conjunction with the philosophical doctrine of

John Locke is illuminating.

For contrary to contemporary contention, throughout his treatises, Locke, born into a Puritan family as the son of a Calvinist lawyer, was actually a staunch Christian who, in his writings, invoked the *Bible*, Jesus Christ, the Apostle Paul's message to the Romans, Divine miracles, and many other elements of orthodox Christianity.[30]

Indeed, Locke opens his *Essay Concerning Human Understanding* by quoting the Apostle Peter that God has given humanity all things pertaining to life and goodness and causes all men to have a knowledge of their Maker and their duties to Him.[31] His faith-based convictions are readily evident in his other writings as well. Yet predicated upon an admixture of semantic sophistry and simple misunderstanding, his concepts of the "Laws of Nature and of Nature's God," later incorporated into the preamble of the Declaration of Independence, have often come to be misinterpreted in modern legal exegesis.[32]

The issue at stake drew from deep historic roots – as early on, the Christian practice of speaking of the "Law of Nature" and the "Law of God" stemmed from the Church's reading of the New Testament as expressed in Romans 1 and 2 wherein the Apostle Paul maintained that the biblical "Law of God" was not at variance with His general revelations in nature and creation.

For as scripturally defined, humankind instinctively does what God's law requires (Romans 2: 14) because God writes the requirements of the law on their hearts and affirms it through the voices of their conscience.[33] Based on these determinations, Locke's writings, to which the Founders all took counsel, as noted, make clear that he was no Deist. To wit:

> The Holy Scripture is to me, and always will be, the constant guide of my belief; and I shall always hearken to it as containing infallible truth. . . .[34] Not that any to whom the gospel has been preached shall be saved without believing Jesus to be the Messiah; for all being sinners and transgressors of the law, and so unjust, are all liable to condemnation.[35]

Locke likewise relied heavily upon the *Bible* in his legal exegesis in which he equated the Law of Nature and the Law of God. Indeed, in his first treatise on government, he cited the *Bible* eighty times; whereas twenty-two biblical references are cited in his second. His basic doctrines on private property and social compact, subscribed to by both Jefferson and Adams, also derived from Scriptural provenance.[36] In his words:

> The Law of Nature stands as an eternal rule to all men, legislators as well as others. The rules that they make for other men's actions must . . . be conformable to the Law of Nature, *i.e.* to the will of God. . . . No human sanction can be good or valid against it.[37]

Locke concluded that if man-made laws did not conform to both the Law of Nature and the Law of Scripture, then "they are ill-made."[38] Accordingly, he explicitly argued that the source of natural law was God Himself and commanded absolute obedience to "the Law of Nature, that we should obey the Law of God, whenever he should be pleased to make addition to the Law . . . of Nature. Alternately put, the Law of Nature requires humankind to obey the morality of the *Bible* and conversely, as each was an expression of the other – the Law of Nature being the natural revelation of God's Law.[39]

Indeed, when Locke wrote his *Second Treatise of Government*, the "Law of Nature" argument had long been fundamental to both Puritan and Calvinistic-Presbyterian political thought. Hence, if Jefferson was indeed following Locke in crafting the phrase "laws of nature and of God" into the Declaration of Independence, he was drawing upon biblical precepts in his draft.[40]

John Adams, who was also on the Declaration's draft committee, in articulating a position consistent with Calvinistic doctrine then prevailing in New England, in fact, explicitly linked the Law of Nature both with the Old Testament (Galatians 5:14) and the New Testament (Matthew 7:12) when he wrote: "One great advantage of the Christian Religion is that it brings the great principle of the Law of Nature and Nations. Love your Neighbor as yourself, and do unto others as you would that others do to you."[41]

Thus it was that Locke's paradigms describing the interactions of natural and Divine law came to be woven into the fabric of America' Declaration of Independence – to wit: acting in concert, they regulate the lives of men and nations; that all persons are created equal and endowed with "unalienable rights," which he defined as "life liberty, and property" – a phrase found both in the Fifth and Fourteenth Amendments which had been earlier embellished by Jefferson into the "pursuit of happiness" in the Declaration –that it is the purpose and obligation of government to secure those rights; and that such government, exercising just power, is established by a binding contract affirmed by the consent of the governed. Such precepts thus issued not from the handiwork of an ephemeral, secular Deist god, but rather from biblically-defined religious precepts.[42]

William Blackstone (1723-1780), another Founder favorite who wrote more than a half century after Locke, likewise was a Christian concerned with the interaction of Divine and Natural Law – believing that Natural Law was prescribed by God Himself: "Man, considered as a creature, must necessarily be subject to the laws of his Creator, for he is entirely a dependent being. . . . And consequently, as man depends entirely upon his Maker for everything, it is necessary that he should in all points conform to his Maker's will. This will of his Maker is called Natural Law."[43]

In Blackstone's view,"Natural Law" consisted of two interchangeable components (1) the revealed Divine Law of the Scriptures; and (2) its emanations in human natural law: In his words: "The Law of Nature . . . as dictated by God Himself, is, of course, superior in obligation to any other. . . . No human laws are of any validity if contrary to this. . . . The revealed or Divine law. . . found only in the Holy Scriptures is found upon comparison to be a part of the original Law of Nature."[44]

As such, in Blackstone's "natural law philosophy," civil law was clearly subordinate to Divine law and must not conflict with the Law of God. But in areas where neither natural law nor Divine law provided guidance, mankind is freed to create its own law through a process of structured governance.[45] That such tenets are not mere secular interpretations, but scriptural, will be shown presently. [46]

That this philosophy greatly influenced the Founders, moreover, is evidenced in the statement of George Mason, author of Virginia's "Bill of Rights, that: "The Laws of Nature are the Laws of God, whose authority can be superceded by no power on earth." It was in this context, in fact, that the phrase "the laws of nature and of nature's God" were subsequently incorporated into the Declaration of Independence.[47]

In like manner, the Baron Montesquieu of France (1689-1755), a lifetime practicing Catholic, who chronologically bridged the intellectual gap between Locke and Blackstone and shared their fervent zeal for doctrinally-driven governance, was a powerful advocate for the contention that "society, notwithstanding all of its revolutions, must repose on principles that do not change,"[48] holding that Christianity fostered good laws and good government:

> The Christian religion, which ordains that men should love each other, would, without doubt, have every nation blest with the best civil, the best political laws; because these, next to this religion, are the greatest good that these men can give and receive.[49]

Thus, the Founders were not mono-focused in their quest for guidance in forging their nascent nation. Indeed, as Benjamin Franklin explained the eclectic process: "We have gone back to ancient history for models of Government and examined the different forms of those Republics which have been formed. . . . and we have viewed modern states all around Europe."[50]

Instead, the Founders were remarkably ecumenical in divining their governing doctrine. In their deliberations, however, there was one source they consulted above all others – four times more than Montesquieu or Blackstone, twelve times more than Locke – the *Bible*. In one scholarly survey of their writings, which studied 3,154 references gleaned from more than 15,000 publications surveyed, the *Bible* accounted for 34 percent of all of the Founders' quotes; whereas another 60 percent were drawn from authors who derived their ideas from the *Bible* – for a total of 94 percent of their quotes attributable to biblical provenance, as follows:[51]

| Source:[52] | Percentage of Quotes: |
|---|---|
| Bible | 34.0% |
| Montesquieu | 8.3% |
| Blackstone | 7.9% |
| Locke | 2.9% |

This concentration of foundation sources was no accident. In the words of the colonial minister Dr. Lyman Beecher: "Our Republic, in its Constitution and its laws, are of heavenly origin. It was not borrowed from Greece and Rome but from the *Bible*. Where we borrowed a ray from Greece or Rome, its stars and suns were borrowed from another source — the *Bible*.[53]

As was likewise assessed by Founder Noah Webster: "The principles of all genuine liberty and of wise laws and administrations are to be drawn from the *Bible* and sustained by its authority. The man therefore who weakens or destroys the divine authority of that book may be accessory to all the public disorders which society is doomed to suffer."[54]

Such realities also underlie a second reality embedded within the Declaration likewise of concern to Locke, Blackstone, and Montesquieu that belies its biblical inspiration; that is its affirmation of the interaction of Natural and Divine Law to produce "governance with the consent of this governed" characterized by a concurrent firm commitment to the "separation of powers"[55] — in the aforesaid words of Jesus Christ: "Render unto Caesar the things that are Caesar's; and unto God the things that are God's."[56] At the same time, it held that there must be structured governance: "And Moses chose able men out of all of Israel, and made them heads over the people, rulers of thousands, rulers of hundreds, rulers of fifties and rulers of tens. And they judged the people at all seasons."[57]

On this ten-fold mandate, the *Bible* itself is indelibly explicit:

| Mandate: | Verse(s): | Provisions: |
|---|---|---|
| 1. Good government is ordained by God: | Isaiah 33:22 | For the Lord is our judge; the Lord is our law-giver; the Lord is our king; he will save us. |
| | Romans 13:1 | Let every soul be subject unto the higher powers. For there is no power but of God: the powers that be are ordained of God. |
| 2. Yet it is a human creation: | I Peter: 2:13 | Submit yourself to every ordinance of man for the Lord's sake: whether it be to the king, as supreme. |
| | II Samuel 3:21 | And Abner said unto David: I will arise and go and gather my lord the king that they may make a league with thee, and that thou mayest reign over all that thine heart desireth. |

| Mandate: | Verse(s): | Provisions: |
|---|---|---|
| 3. Its leaders must be elected: | Deuteronomy 1:13 | Take ye wise men with understanding and known among your tribes, and I will make them rulers over you. |
| | Deuteronomy 17:15 | Thou shalt in any wise set him king over thee whom the Lord thy shall choose; one from among thy brethren shalt thou set king over thee. |
| | II Samuel 5: 3 | So all of the elders of Israel. . . anointed David king over Israel. |
| 4. The elected leaders have a compact with the governed: | I Chronicles 11:3 | Therefore came of the elders of Israel to the king in Hebron; and David made a covenant with them in Hebron before the Lord. |
| | II Kings 11:17 | And Jehoi'ada made a covenant between the Lord and the king and the people: that they should be the Lord's people; between the king also and the people. |
| 5. Their mandate is to govern strictly on behalf of the people. If they fail to do so, they lose their right to rule: | Psalms 72: 1-2 | Give the king thy judgements, O God, and thy righteousness unto the king's son. He shall judge the people with righteousness and thy poor with judgement. |
| | Psalm 17:13 | Arise, O Lord: disappoint him, cast him down: deliver my soul from the wicked, which is thy sword. |
| 6. As such, secular leaders enjoy no absolute or divine right to rule: | I Samuel 13: 13-14 | And Samuel said to Saul: Thou hast done foolishly; thou hast not kept the commandment of the Lord thy God, which he hath commanded thee: for so would the Lord have established thy kingdom over Israel forever. |
| | | But now, thy kingdom shall not continue: the Lord hath sought him a man after his own heart, and the Lord hath commanded him to be captain over his people, because thou hast not kept that which the Lord commanded thee. |
| | Jeremiah 22: 3,5 | Thus sayeth the Lord: Execute ye judgement and righteousness and deliver the spoiled out of the hands of the oppressor . . . |
| | | But if ye not hear these words, I swear by myself, sayeth the Lord, that this house shall become a desolation. |

| Mandate: | Verse(s): | Provisions: |
|---|---|---|
| 7. As righteous rulers are sent by God to protect His people: | Romans 13:3-4 | For rulers are not a terror to good works but to evil. Wilt thou then not be afraid of power? Do that which is good and thou shalt have the praise of the same. |
| | | For he is minister of God to thee for good. But if thou do that which is evil, be afraid; for he beareth not the sword in vain. |
| | I Corinthians 4:2 | It is required of stewards that men be found faithful. |
| | I Peter 4:10 | As every man hath received the gift, even so minister the same one to another, as good stewards of the manifold grace of God. |
| | Joshua 24:15 | Choose you this day whom you will serve; As for me and my house, we will serve the Lord. |
| | Psalm 144:15 | Happy is that people whose God is the Lord. |
| 8. With their mission to do justice through natural law which issues from Divine law as a Divine mandate: | II Samuel 23:3 | He that ruleth over men must be just, ruling in the fear of God. |
| | Exodus 18:20 | And thou shalt teach them ordinances and laws, and shalt show them the way wherein they must walk, and the work that they must do. |
| | Deuteronomy 17: 18-19 | And it shall be, when he sitteth upon the throne of his kingdom, they shall write him a copy of this law out of that which is before the priests the Levites. |
| | | And it shall be with him and he shall read therein all the days of his life: that he may learn the fear of God, to all of the words of this law and these statutes and to do them. |
| | Titus 1:7 | For a bishop must be blameless as the steward of God.[58] |
| 9. As those who do right are honored; while those who do wrong are punished: | Proverbs 14:34 | Righteousness exalteth a nation but a sin is a reproach unto any people. |
| | I Peter 2:13-14 | Submit yourselves . . . unto governors as unto them that are sent by him for the punishment of evildoers and for the praise of them that do well. |

| Mandate: | Verse(s): | Provisions: |
|---|---|---|
| 10. Yet in the course of rule, the separation of powers must be explicitly observed. | Matthew 22:21 | (In the words of Christ:) Render unto Caesar that which is Caesar's and give unto God that which is God's. |
| | Ezra 7:25-26 | And thou, Ezra, after the wisdom that is thy God, that is in thine hand, set magistrates and judges which may judge all the people that are beyond the river, such as know the laws of God, and teach ye them who know them not. |
| | | And whosoever will not do the law of thy God, and the law of the king, let judgement be executed speedily upon him, whether it be unto death or banishment, or confiscation of goods, or to imprisonment. |

Accordingly, there is no question that the Founders understood the interaction of natural and divine law as biblically set forth – as four fundamental biblical principles derived from the phrase "laws of nature and of Nature's God" that formed the basis for America's legal system defined in the Declaration of Independence that: (i) God is the ultimate source of law; (ii) God's law is universal and unchanging; (iii) only laws . . . consistent with God's laws are legitimate; and (iv) law contrary to God's law is void or invalid.

In this spirit, one of the ultimate signers of the Constitution, later to become a Supreme Court Justice, James Wilson, advocated that God "is the promulgator as well as author of Natural Law;" whereas another, Rufus King, speaking to the legality of slavery, would assert in a speech in the U.S. Senate: "I hold that all laws or compacts imposing any such conditions upon any human being are void because they are contrary to the Law of Nature which is the Law of God."[59] Indeed, George Washington himself said: "The propitious smiles of Heaven can never be expected on a nation that disregards the eternal rules of order which Heaven has ordained."[60]

Such divine-inspired doctrine, of course, comports fully with the aforesaid governing philosophies of Blackstone and Montesquieu, as well as John Locke's concept of a compact of "governance with the consent of the governed" expressed in his *Second Treatise of Government*, asserting that: "That which begins and constitutes any political society is nothing but the consent of freemen capable of a majority to unite and incorporate into such a society; and thus is that which did or could give beginning to any lawful governance in the world."[61] As Locke further explained: "The body politic is formed by a voluntary association of individuals. It is a social compact by which the whole people covenants with each citizen, and each citizen with the whole people, that all should be governed by certain laws for the common good.[62]

The concept of "governments with the consent of the governed" thus had deep historic roots — having been espoused by the "Philosophers of the Enlightenment" as articulated by Locke in his concept of a "social compact," which was, in turn, itself deeply rooted in the Calvinist concept of "compact" whereby people, in the presence of God, join together to form a body politic.[63]

In the quest for such self-determination, in his counsel to the colonies, Locke, citing the *Bible*, Judges 11, further contended that it is morally right to throw off tyranny, calling upon the aid of the "Supreme Judge" to support their revolution. Again, he phrased his argument in biblical, not Deistic, terms — and again, the Declaration of Independence reflects this spirit in calling for the American people to form a compact to combat the litany of tyrannical acts that it explicitly attributes to the King of England; hence, its phrase: describing the American people as "deriving their just powers from the consent of the governed."[64]

Like the Magna Carta before it, then, the Declaration drew sustenance from the "unalienable rights of the people" — invoking biblical precedent to such extent that it is safe to assert that absent the Scriptures and the body of Judeo-Christian values that they embodied, the document itself would have been improbable.[65] Accordingly, in its quest to ensure those "unalienable rights, the prescription of the Preamble to the Constitution for biblical governance was founded on five precepts that rendered the document both pioneering and unique:[66]

| Precept in the Preamble: | Biblical Verse: | Provision: |
|---|---|---|
| 1. Establish justice: | I Peter 2:13-14 | Submit yourselves to every ordinance of man for the Lord's sake; whether it be to the king, as supreme. Or unto governors, as unto them that have been sent by him for the punishment of evildoers and for the praise of them that do well. |
| | Genesis 9:6 | Whoso sheddeth blood, by man shall his blood be shed: for in the image of God made He man. |
| 2. Ensure the domestic tranquility: | I Timothy 2:1-2 | I exhort, therefore, that, first of all, supplications, prayers, intercessions, and giving of thanks be made for all men. For kings, and for all that are in authority; that we may lead a quiet and peaceable life in all godliness and honesty. |

*Sorting Through the Founders' Faiths*

| Precept in the Preamble: | Biblical Verse: | Provision: |
|---|---|---|
| 3. Provide for the common defense: | Romans 13:4 | If thou do that which is evil, be afraid for he beareth not the sword in vain; he is the minister of God: a revenger to execute wrath upon him that doeth evil. |
| | Luke 22:36 | He that hath no sword, let him sell his garment and buy one. |
| 4. Promote the general welfare; and | Romans 13:3 | For rulers are not a terror to good works but to evil. Wilt thou then not be afraid of power? Do that which is good and thou shalt have praise of the same. |
| 5. Secure the blessings of liberty: | Leviticus 25:10 | Proclaim liberty unto all the land unto all the inhabitants thereof. |
| | II Corinthians 3:17 | Where the Spirit of the Lord is, there is liberty. |
| | Galatians 5: | Stand fast, therefore, in the liberty wherewith Christ hath made us free. |

Other governing precepts asserted in the Constitution itself having biblical provenance include:[67]

| Constitutional Precept: | Biblical Verse: | Provision: |
|---|---|---|
| Government with consent of the governed: | I Chronicles 29:22 | And they did eat and drink before the Lord that day with great gladness. And they made Solomon son of David king the second time, and anointed him unto the Lord to be the chief governor, and Za'dok to be priest. |
| | II Chronicles 23:11 | And they brought out the king's son, and put upon him the crown, and gave him the testimony, and made him king. And Ja-hoi'a-da and his sons anointed him and made him king. |

| Constitutional Precept: | Biblical Verse: | Provision: |
|---|---|---|
| Freely elected representatives within a separation of powers: | Deuteronomy 1:13 | Take you wise men, with understanding, and known among your tribes, and I will make them rulers over you. |
| | Exodus 18: 21-22 | And thou shalt provide out of all the people able men, such as fear God, hate covetousness; and place such over them, to be rulers of thousands, to be rulers of hundreds, and rulers of tens: |
| | | And let them judge the people at all seasons: and it shall be that every great matter they shall bring unto thee, but every small matter they shall judge so it be easier for thyself, and they shall bear the burden with thee. |
| | Isaiah 33:22 | For the Lord is our judge, the Lord is our lawgiver, the Lord is our king, He will save us. |
| And equality before the law: | Exodus 12:49 | One law shall be to him that is home-born and unto the stranger that sojourneth among you. |
| | Leviticus 24:22 | You shall have one manner of law; as well for the stranger as well as for one of your own country: for I am the Lord your God. One ordinance shall be both for you of the congregation, and also for the stranger that sojourneth with you; an ordinance forever in your generations. |

Consonant with these biblical precepts, then, as demonstrated in Chapter 1, in asserting that America is a "Christian nation," the Supreme Court, in *Church of the Holy Trinity v. the United States* in 1892, invoked "organic utterances" as prima face evidence; to wit: "they are organic utterances that speak the voice of the entire people."[68]

For this reason also, in setting upon his great voyage of exploration, Christopher Columbus would determine: "Our Lord opened . . . my understanding (I could feel his hand upon me) so it became clear to me that it was feasible to navigate from here . . . Who doubts that this illumination was from the Holy Spirit? I attest that He, with marvelous rays of light, consoled me through the holy and sacred Scriptures. . . . They inflame me with a sense of great urgency. . . . And I say that the sign which convinces me . . . is the preaching of the Gospel recently in so many lands."[69]

It is consistent with this spirit, then, that one also better understands that religion was the express reason for the founding of America. Religion is why the Pilgrims and the Puritans originally came. Indeed, the 1606 charter that the former obtained from British King James I to establish a permanent settlement in Virginia expressed as its objective: "to make Habitation . . , and to deduce a colony of sundry of our People into that part of America commonly called Virginia. . . . in propagating of Christian religion to such people as yet live in Darkness . . ."[70]

The 1662 royal charter granting the Quakers a right to settle in North Carolina similarly indicates that they were: "Excited with a laudable and pious zeal for the propagation of the Christian faith . . . in parts of America not yet cultivated or planted, and only inhabited by . . . people who have no knowledge of Almighty God"[71] — whereas the follow-on 1663 charter granted by King Charles II expresses that they were "pursing with peace and loyal minds, their sober, serious, and religious intentions . . . in the holy Christian faith (so that) . . . a most flourishing civil state may stand. . . grounded on gospel principles."[72] The founding charters of Connecticut, New Hampshire, New Jersey, and Georgia, amongst others, as noted, expressed similar ambitions.[73]

It is in this spirit also that the Massachusetts Puritans who arrived more than a decade after the Virginia Pilgrims in November, 1620, expressed in their "Mayflower Compact" that: "Having undertaken for the Glory of God and Advancement of the Christian faith. . . a voyage to plant the first colony  . . ., (we) combine ourselves together in a civil Body Politick for. . . Furtherance of the Ends aforesaid."[74] Indeed, the spiritual leader in a companion mission, John Winthrop was explicit in their goal: "We are a Company ourselves fellow members of Christ. . . knit together by this bond of love . . . We are entered into a Covenant with Him for this work."[75]

Similarly, the 1632 "Charter of Maryland" issued by King Charles to Lord Baltimore asserts that the latter "being animated with a laudable and pious Zeal for extending the Christian Religion . . . hath humbly besought Leave of Us that he may transport . . . a numerous colony of the English Nation to a certain Region . . . having no knowledge of the Divine Being."[76]

It was in the same spirit, moreover, that the initial state constitutions affirmed their mandates. Hence, the very first state constitution, the 1639 "Fundamental Orders of Connecticut," adopted as its preamble: "Well knowing that when a people are gathered together, the word of God requires that to maintain the peace and union of such a people, there should be a decent and orderly government established according to the laws of God."[77]

When the colonists of New Hampshire established their own government seven months later, they attested to the rationale that: "Considering with ourselves the Holy Will of God, and our own necessity that we should not live without wholesome laws and civil government among us of which we are altogether destitute, do in the name of Christ and in the Sign of God combine ourselves together to erect and set up amongst us such Government as shall be to our best discerning, agreeable to the will of God."[78]

Similarly, when Massachusetts and Connecticut joined to form the New England Confederation in 1643, the amalgamated government proclaimed as its purpose: "We all came into these parts of America with one end and aim, namely to advance the kingdom of our Lord Jesus Christ;"[79] whereas when the eminent Quaker minister William Penn drafted his "Frame of Government" for his new territory, Pennsylvania, in 1682, he made its mandate to: "Make and establish laws as shall best preserve Christian and civil liberty, in all opposition to unchristian ... practices."[80]

It is within the context of such consensual religiously-inspired governance, then, that one more properly perceives John Adams' aforesaid assertions that a nation that takes the *Bible* for its lawbook will be amongst the best of nations, and that "the Christian religion is the best;" contending that:

> The great and Almighty author of nature; who first established the rules which regulate the world, can as easily suspend those laws whenever His Providence sees sufficient reason for such suspension. There can be no objection, then, to the miracles of Jesus Christ[81]

— and that Thomas Jefferson, though he railed against the excesses of organized religion, never sought to contravene Christian principles and believed that those found in the Gospels were the guideposts to an exemplary life — even fastidiously reworked the New Testament to glean a better understanding of the nature of Christ. For what he opposed was not the religious precepts themselves but instead what he perceived to be their institutional abuse.[82]

## II. Faith of the Founders: the Deist Mythology

Given this apparent legacy of Christian inspiration, then, who exactly were the exemplars of the so-called "Deist Founders"? The quest for definition becomes one of seeking to clarify a prismatic phantasmagoria of ideas that are, in fact, kaleidoscopic – as each person's individual religious views of God are, of course, precisely a function of how they are developed or defined.

What was the colonists' concept of faith? Was it that of the Continental Congress which proclaimed: "Our cause is just ... and it is our Christian duty to defend it?"[83] Was it the official "Committees of Correspondence" within the colonies whose slogan was: "No King but King Jesus?"[84] Was it the armistice signed on September 8, 1783 with Britain concluding the Revolutionary War which opened with the line: "In the name of the most Holy and undivided Trinity?"[85]

Was it an accident that the Constitution, in Article 1, Section 7, singled out Sunday, the Christian Sabbath, as the day exempted from official federal deliberations and activities?[86] Was it sheer Deist happenstance that the U.S. Senate by resolution decreed after President Washington's First Inaugural Address and oath of office that he, "attended by the Vice President, and members of the Senate and House of Representatives, proceed to St. Paul's Chapel to hear divine service to be

*Sorting Through the Founders' Faiths* 51

performed by the Chaplain of the Congress appointed"[87] — and that the Annals of Congress show that is precisely what they did?[88]

Who, then, was the first Deist Founder? Was it Samuel Adams, called by many the "Father of the American Revolution," who quoted Proverbs 14: 24 that: "Righteousness exalteth a nation" — who praised "all who love the Lord Jesus Christ in sincerity" and prayed for "that happy period when the Kingdom of our Lord and Savior Jesus Christ may everywhere be established"[89] — who asserted that: "The right to freedom being the gift of God Almighty. . . may best be understood by reading and carefully studying the institutions of the Great Law Giver and Head of the Christian Church" — and who, in defending religious rights inherent in the colonists' aspirations to Christianity, declared:

> The right to freedom being the gift of God Almighty, the rights of the colonists as Christians may best be understood by reading and carefully studying the institutions of the Great Law Giver and Head of the Christian Church, which are to be found clearly written and promulgated in the New Testament."[90]

Was it George Washington, America's first president, who served as a church warden in the Episcopal Church, regularly took communion, and scrupulously observed its fast days – who, while he worried about the "horrors of spiritual tyranny," nonetheless believed in God as the supreme architect of governance – and whom Supreme Court Chief Justice John Marshall called: "a sincere believer in the Christian faith and a truly devout man."[91]

Was it the George Washington who told his troops at Valley Forge: "To the distinguished character of Patriot, it should be to our highest Glory to add the more distinguished character of Christian"[92]— who equipped their regiments with chaplains and insisted that they attend Sunday services; and whose first "General Order" to his troops on July 9, 1776 called upon them "to live and act as becomes a Christian soldier defending the Rights and Liberties of his country" [93] — and who declared in a speech to the Dutch Reformed Church in New York that: "It is impossible to rightly govern . . . without God and the Bible?"[94]

— the George Washington who admonished the Delaware Indian chiefs: "You would do well to wish to learn our arts and ways, and most of all, the religion of Jesus Christ?"[95] — who sanctioned a treaty providing federal funding to build a church for the Oneida Indians[96] – who would proclaim that: "It is impossible to rightly govern the world without God and the *Bible*[97] — and that: "The propitious smiles of Heaven can never be expected on a nation that disregards the eternal rules of order and right which Heaven itself has ordained" — and whose dying words before an open *Bible* were: "Tis well, Father of Mercies, take me to thyself? "[98]

Was it John Adams, the nation's second president, who professed a firm belief in the divinity and resurrection of Christ — who invoked "the Redeemer" and the 'Holy Spirit" in multiple proclamations — who asserted that "the general principles upon which the Fathers achieved independence . . . were the general principles of Christianity"— who, in conceding that "for fifty years I have neglected all sciences except government and religion,"concluded that: "My religion is founded on the love of God and my neighbor" — and "the Christian religion, as I understand it, is the best?"[99]

Was it the same John Adams who who claimed that "the Ten Commandments and the Sermon on the Mount contain my religion"[100] — who proclaimed national days of fasting honoring God's compact with His chosen people[101] — and who queried:

> Is it not that the Declaration of Independence organized its social compact on the foundation of the Redeemer's mission on earth? That it laid the cornerstone of human government upon the precepts of Christianity . . . On the Fourth of July, the Founders simply took the precepts of Christ, which came into the world through His birth, and incorporated them into civil government?[102]

— who would add that: "The Christian religion is, above all of the religions that ever prevailed or existed in ancient or modern times, the religion of wisdom, virtue, equity, and humanity" [103] — and, in contending that "our Constitution was made only for a moral and religious people,"[104] would conclude: "The highest story of the American Revolution is this. It connected in one indissoluble bond the principles of civil government with the principles of Christianity?"[105]

Was it Thomas Jefferson, the third U.S. president, a nominal Episcopalian whose life focused extensively on religious affairs, affirming that: "I am a real Christian, that is to say, a disciple of the doctrine of Jesus, very different from the Platonists;"that "Religion is the Alpha and Omega of moral law;" and "It is in our lives and not from our words that our religion must be read?"[106]

The Thomas Jefferson who opened his 1777 Virginia *Bill for Establishing Religious Freedom* with the preamble: "Whereas Almighty God has created the mind free"[107] – approved federal funding to spread Christianity to the Indians[108] – declared that "the Bible is the cornerstone of liberty"[109] – and in his retirement, even produced two works: in 1804, one monograph, "The Philosophy of Jesus," and in 1818 a book titled: *The Life and Morals of Jesus*, delving into Latin, Greek, French, and English versions of the New Testament in his work[110] – who said of Jesus that he "pushed his scrutinies into the hearts of man, erected his tribunal in the region of his thoughts, and purified the waters at the fountain head;"[111] and concluded that:

> Of all of the systems of morality ancient and modern which have come under my observation, none appear so pure as that of Jesus. . . . His system of morality was the most benevolent and sublime that probably has ever been taught, consequently more perfect than those of the ancient philosophers.[112]

That Jefferson – in editing his own version of the "New Testament" – was a religious visionary is nearly universally admitted. American Historian Daniel Boorstin who maintains that Jefferson accomplished for American civilization what St. Augustine provided for the early Middle Ages, replicating the notion of a heavenly"City of God" as an earthly polity epitomizing the "American Dream" – and observed that Jefferson thus "put God at the service of their early American task."[113]

Undeniably, Jefferson questioned the traditional Christian "three-gods-in one" concept of the Trinity, calling it "Platonic mysticism" and the "hocus-pocus phantasm of a god-like Cerberus with one body and three heads."[114] To this extent, then, his posture puts him in agreement with the Deists and Unitarians of his day — arguing in defense of their beliefs, that: "I have sworn on the altar of liberty eternal hostility against every form of tyranny over the mind of man.[115]

However, he concurrently rejected the prevalent Deist belief that God merely created the universe, established certain scientific laws and principles by which it works, and now takes no active role in the affairs of humankind, save possibly through the continuing effects of the Laws of Nature which He set into motion.[116] So again, those who have frequently labeled Thomas Jefferson a "Deist" might due well to listen to the Founder himself, as Jefferson may well be the best interpreter of Jefferson.[117]

Was it, then, James Madison, the fourth American president – who had studied under the precise tutelage of Presbyterian-preacher-turned-Princeton-president John Witherspoon and had considered a career in ministry before opting for politics – who attended a college whose logo proclaimed: "Cursed be all learning contrary to the Cross of Christ"[118] — who powerfully expressed his conviction that: "to the same Divine Author of every good and perfect gift we are indebted for all of those privileges and advantages, religious as well as civil, which are so richly enjoyed in this favored land" — and asserted that "It is the mutual duty of all to practice Christian forbearance, love, and charity toward each other?"[119]

Was it James Monroe, America's fifth president, who attended, and was ultimately buried by, the Episcopalian Church, whose First Inaugural Address, promised to proceed with "with a firm reliance on the protection of Almighty God?" [120] Or John Quincy Adams, her sixth president, who, in his own First Inaugural Address delivered on March 4, 1925, quoted Psalm 121:1: "knowing that 'Except the Lord keep the city, the watchman waketh but in vain" — who made it an annual practice to read the *Bible* fully through every year — and who believed that "the birthday of the nation is indissolubly linked with the birthday of the Savior and forms a leading event in the progress of the Gospel dispensation. . . . The Declaration of Independence first organized the social compact upon the foundation of the Redeemer's mission upon earth and laid the cornerstone of human government upon the first precepts of Christianity?"[121]

Was it Benjamin Franklin, called by some an "avowed Deist," — but who, born and raised a Puritan Calvinist, financially supported the local Presbyterian Church and maintained a pew within it — who referred to "we zealous Presbyterians" in a 1760 personal letter — who rearranged the "Book of Common Prayer"— and who, in proposing that each session of the 1787 Constitutional Convention commence with a religious invocation seeking Divine guidance, cited in argument the New Testament biblical verse, Matthew 10:29: "If a sparrow cannot fall to the ground without His notice, is it probable that an empire can rise without His aid?" — continuing with Psalm 127:1: "We are assured in the sacred writings that 'except the Lord build this house, they who build it labor in vain'"[122] — and who, upon the Convention's close, assessed that it had been guided by the Hand of God in producing the Constitution?[123]

In a separate instance, Franklin would contend that "whoever shall introduce into public affairs the principles of primitive Christianity will change the face of the world"[124] — and "as to Jesus of Nazareth, my opinion of whom you particularly desire, I think that his system of morals and his religion, as he left them to us, (are) the best the world ever saw or is likely to see"[125] — and amongst the twelve virtues cited in his "Plan for Attaining Moral Perfection," counseled that one should strive to imitate the humility of Jesus.[126]

In asserting at the Convention that "God governs in the affairs of men, "Franklin likewise ruled himself out of the Deistic category, as for a Deist, God does not interfere in the daily activities of humankind.[127] Accordingly, of him, the noted biblical scholar John Orr observes:

> Franklin's view on providence and prayer were quite inconsistent with the Deistic conception of an absentee God who does not, and who could not, in consistency with the perfection of his work of creation and his impartial nature, interfere in the affairs of men.[128]

As Franklin admonished fellow Founder and organized religion critic Thomas Paine, in fact, if societies "are so wicked with religion, what would they be without it?"[129]

Was it therefore John Jay, First Chief Justice of the Supreme Court and founder of the "American Bible Society," who directly linked public well-being to faith, steadfastly maintaining that: "national prosperity can neither be attained nor preserved without the favor of Providence:"[130]

> Providence has given to our people the choice of their rulers, and it is the duty as well as the privilege and interest of our Christian nation to select and prefer Christians for their rulers?[131]

In personal testament, Jay would add: "Unto Him who is the author and giver of all good, I render sincere and humble thanks for His manifold and unmerited blessings, and especially for our redemption and salvation by His beloved Son."[132]

Was it America's first Treasurer, Alexander Hamilton, who, in 1802, proposed creation of an "American Constitutional Society" to promote the two factors most influential in forging America: "1$^{st}$: The Support of the Christian religion; 2$^{nd}$: The Support of the Constitution of the United States"[133] — who on his deathbed, requested communion[134] — and who said: "The sacred rights of mankind are not to be rummaged for amongst old parchments or musty records. They are written, as with a sunbeam, in the whole volume of human nature, by the hand of Divinity itself, and can never be erased or obscured by mortal power?"[135]

Was it Dr. Benjamin Rush, signer of the Declaration of Independence and Keeper of the U.S. Mint, who wrote: "I have always considered Christianity as the strong ground of republicanism . . . . Republican forms of government are the best repositories of the Gospel . . . . A Christian cannot fail of being a republican, for every precept of the Gospel inculcates those degrees of humility, self denial, and brotherly kindness which are directly opposed to the pride of monarchy. . . ." A Christian cannot fail of being useful to the republic, for his religion teaches him that no man 'liveth onto himself'"[136] — and who then added:

> I have alternately been called an aristocrat and a democrat. I am now neither. I am a "Christocrat." I believe that all power . . . will always fail of producing order and happiness in the hands of man. He alone who created and redeemed man is qualified to govern him.[137]

Was it Virginia Governor Patrick Henry, a driving force behind promulgating the First Amendment — who delivered a sharp rebuttal in defense of Christianity in response to perceived deism in Thomas Paine's *Age of Reason* [138]— whose last will and testimony affirmed that: "This is all the inheritance that I can give to my dear family. The religion of Christ can give them one which will make them rich indeed" [139] — and asserted:

> It cannot be emphasize too strongly or too often that this great nation was founded not by religionists, but by Christians; not on religions, but on the gospel of Jesus Christ. For this very reason, peoples of other faiths have been afforded asylum, prosperity, and freedom of worship here. . . .[140] Bad men cannot make good citizens. It is impossible that a nation of infidels or idolaters should be a nation of free men. It is when a people forget God that tyrants forge their chains?"[141]

Was it George Mason, father of the Bill of Rights, whose personal testimony was: "My soul, I render into the hands of my Almighty Creator, whose tender mercies are over all His works, who hateth nothing that he has made, and to the justice and wisdom of whose dispensations I willingly and cheerfully submit, humbly hoping from His unbounded mercy and benevolence, through the merits of my blessed Savior, the remission of my sins?"[142]

Was it Roger Sherman, the only Founder distinguished by having signed all four major founding documents — "The Articles of Association" (1774); "The Declaration of Independence" (1776);"The Articles of Confederation" (1777); and "The Constitution of the United States" (1787) — who said: "I believe that there is only one living and true God, existing in three persons, the Father, the Son, and the Holy Spirit, the same in substance and equal in power and glory"[143] — and who cited faith in Jesus Christ as "one of the five tenets whereby a true believer should examine himself?"[144] Was it John Dickinson, Pennsylvanian and signer of the Constitution, who maintained that: "The rights essential to happiness. . . . We claim them from a higher source – from the King of Kings and Lord of all the earth?"[145]

Was it Noah Webster who avowed: "The religion which has introduced civil liberty is the religion of Christ and his apostles which enjoins humility, piety, and benevolence; which acknowledges in every person a brother or a sister and a citizen with equal rights. This is genuine Christianity, and to this we owe our free constitutions of government"[146] . . . .; that:

> The moral principles and precepts contained in the Scriptures ought to form the basis of all of our civil constitutions and laws. All the miseries and evil which men

suffer from vice, crime, ambition, injustice, oppression, slavery, and war, proceed from their despising or neglecting the precepts contained in the *Bible*"[147] —

and that: "No truth is more evident to my mind than that the Christian religion must be the basis of any government intending to secure the rights and privileges of a free people?"[148]

Or was it Daniel Webster who, in a December, 1820 speech at Plymouth, Massachusetts commemorating the arrival of the Pilgrims, described their legacy as having left the nation with the conviction that the "cultivated mind was to act upon uncultivated nature; and more than all, a government and a country must commence with the very first foundations laid under the divine light of the Christian religion."[149] And who then added: "The *Bible* is our only safe guide. So long as we take it as our instructor for conduct and character, we will go on prospering in the future as in the past?"[150]

Indeed, even Thomas Paine, nearly universally conceded to be a Deist (if not an atheist), and openly professed to be such, at the nation's creation would assert that the Supreme Being was "visibly on our side;"[151] and would even ultimately confess that: that he was "not so much of an infidel as to believe that the Almighty God could abandon a people committed to that liberty to which He had called them."[152]

In sum, the Founders were far from being religiously inert or remotely acting in thrall with some absent and distant Supreme Being — no Deists these. They were instead students of the *Bible*, and with few exceptions, proclaimed a deep faith in God. In one scholarly analysis: "With no more than three exceptions, most – fifty two out of the fifty five most prominent – of the founders were members of one of the established Christian orthodox communions: consisting of approximately twenty-nine Anglicans, sixteen to eighteen Calvinists, two Methodists, two Lutherans, two Roman Catholics, one lapsed Quaker and sometime Anglican, and one open Deist."[153]

Acting in concert, then, they produced the Declaration of Independence, the Constitution, the Bill of Rights, and *the Federalist Papers*, the latter called by some "the most important work in political science that has ever been written, or is likely to be ever written, in the United States.[154] Again, as Alexis de Tocqueville asserted: "The Americans combine the notions of Christianity and of liberty so intimately in their minds that it is impossible to make them conceive one without the other."[155]

The reality that the Founders may have chosen such terms as "Divine Providence" and "Supreme Being" in their writings, rather than "Our Lord and Savior Jesus Christ" in their founding documents, therefore, may well be irrelevant to the quest to determine the nature of their religious convictions – as linguistic analysis reveals that George Washington used 54, Abraham Lincoln 49, and Robert E. Lee 45 separate synonyms for "God."[156]

The Mayflower Compact does not invoke the name of Jesus Christ either, yet no one would conspicuously advance the argument that the Pilgrims were Deists. To the contrary, when lofty and sublime terms were substituted for the name of

God in the Declaration of Independence, they were clearly within the historic Christian mainstream tradition – and were fully consonant with their goal to recreate God's "Kingdom on Earth."[157]

For in their quest, the colonists shared a transcendent vision. They viewed America as the heir to England as mankind's conservator of liberty. North America was the "promised land." They, as emigrés, were Israel, escaping bondage, crossing a forbidding sea, living in the wilderness until, by the grace of God, that wilderness would become the fulfilment of their covenant with God that commissioned them to build a mighty nation as part and parcel of His master plan for human redemption, irrespective of creed.[158] As expressed by Justice John Marshall, as noted: "One of the great objects of the colonial charters was avowedly the propagation of the Christian faith."[159]

Hence, the Reverend John Winthrop, writing in transit on the *Arabella* when crossing the Atlantic en route to America in 1630, expressed the aspiration:

> We shall be a City on a Hill. The eyes of all people are upon us. So that if we shall deal falsely with our God in this work that we have undertaken, and so cause Him to withdraw His present help from us . . . we shall open the mouths of enemies to speak evil of God and all professors for God's sake.[160]

As alternately expressed in a noted, oft-quoted Independence Day oration of Doctor David Ramsay at Charleston, South Carolina in 1778:

> We bid fair to be the happiest and freest people in the world for ages yet to come. Generations yet unborn will bless us for the blood-bought inheritance that we are about to bequeath to them. O happy times! O glorious days! O kind, indulgent, bountiful Providence that we would live in this highly honored period, and have the honor of helping forward these great events, and join in suffering in a cause of such infinite importance![161]

That they succeeded is attested by de Tocqueville in *Democracy in America* as he passed through the nascent nation in 1831:

> There is no country in the whole world in which the Christian religion retains a greater influence over the souls of men than in America – and there can be no greater proof of its utility, and of its conformity to human nature, than that its influence is most powerfully felt over the most enlightened and free nation of the earth.[162]

Indeed, de Tocqueville may have assessed best America's faith-based foundations when he said of the nation's still nascent experiment in its unique form of democratic republican "capitalism;" "Despotism may govern without faith, but liberty cannot. Religion is needed more in democratic societies than in any other."[163]

It comes as no surprise, then, that when asked by the French historian Francois Guizot: "How long will the American Republic endure?" – James Lowell readily replied: "As long as the ideas of the men who founded it continue dominant!"[164] This too was the conclusion of Benjamin Franklin immediately in the aftermath of the 1787 Constitutional Convention – when asked "What form of governance have

58                                Chapter Two

you given us" – responded: "a republic if you can keep it!"[165] The Founders thus did do their part. They gave America a constitution for the ages. It is her challenge now to keep it.[166]

### III. THE FAITH OF THE FOUNDERS: THE TRINITARIAN CONUNDRUM

The question of whether the Founders deemed themselves Christians, Theists, Deists, or "Christian Deists," however, may center around whether "Unitarians" and "Trinitarians" view each other to be "Christians," and how a "Unitarian Christian" dualistic hybrid might fit into that equation. Thus, John Adams, already in his time, would assert: "For more than sixty years, I have been attentive to this great subject. Controversies between Calvinists and Arminians (Methodists), Trinitarians and Unitarians, Desists and Christians, Atheists and both, have attracted my attention."[167]

Alternately, however, the possibility cannot be dismissed that because a people's religious beliefs tend to be complex and prismatic – and as such, cannot be neatly categorized or compartmentalized — God for them comes as an amalgam of qualities and characteristics that they perceive Him or Her to be. Given that prospect, who knows whom Heaven has predestined for its halls, save for the predestined divinely enfranchised Calvinistic Trinitarians, of course?

Part of the confusion in this historical context, as noted, likewise arises because the Founders frequently referred to the Supreme Being as "Providence" rather than "God." The reality is, however, that the word "Providence" was more than frequently used by Christian theologians of the time – in the sense of "the care of God over created beings" as defined by Samuel Johnson's 1755 *Dictionary of the English Language* – and as such, it was a term then more compatible with Christianity than with contemporary Deism.[168]

For there can be no question that it was the consensus vision and expressed mission of most of the Founders to build "God's Kingdom" on earth – a phenomenon in which a Deist god would never indulge because of a policy of non–daily-interference in the affairs of His creations. As such, for most of the Founders, the term "Theist" rather than "Deists" may be more appropriate[169] — in acknowledgment of the reality that the same fundamentalist religious faith that initially imbued the early colonies also guided America's establishment as an independent nation, as the professed Unitarian John Adams acknowledged:

> The principles upon which the Fathers achieved independence were . . . the general principles of Christianity."[170]

This, then, was the Founding Fathers' mission and intent. But theirs was not a simple task – for as Jefferson asserted, the nation's civilizing mission required ideological breadth sufficient to reconcile the views of Trinitarians with those of Unitarians, Muslims, and Jews; and those of evangelicals with those of the more orthodox. The *Zeitgeist* was perhaps best exemplified by an early colonial legislator, an opponent of the Constitution in the New Hampshire ratification process, who justified his opposition on the basis that "a Turk, A Jew, a Roman Catholic, and what is worse than all, a Universalist, may become President of the United States."[171]

Such realities impact dramatically upon the public sector status of religion in America today — as modern secularists have concurrently often attempted to make the case for an absolute wall of separation between church and state using negative evidence argumentation: to wit, that it must be a reality because God is mentioned only passingly in the Constitution. But in reality, this was explicitly by design, not merely because "Doctor, we forgot," as Alexander Hamilton jokingly replied to the Reverend John Rogers of the New York Presbyterian Church after the 1787 Philadelphia Constitutional Convention had adjourned.[172]

For the Constitution's legal construct in its purpose was, in large part, for political, not religious, objectives, in order to govern the affairs of an entire diverse nation. As such, it had to be neutral in prescription as to afford equal treatment to that broad mosaic of faiths and creeds – Protestant and Catholic, Jew and Muslim, atheist and agnostic – that was contemporary America.

No small part of the modern debate either, as this analysis makes vividly clear, is one of semantic sophistry centered upon whether many of the Founders were Christians who subscribed to the Divinity of Christ or Deists who believed, without embellishment, that a "Providential Entity" reigned and ruled over the affairs of men – or was instead an amalgamated hybrid that might properly be euphemistically described "Christian Deists" – or "a theistic Unitarian Christian dualistic hybrid," as John Adams and others have sometimes been labeled.[173]

For operating more as a question of theological degree than of sectarian kind, most Founders clearly believed in a "Supreme Being" or God – with varying degrees of understanding regarding the relationship of that Supreme Being to Jesus Christ – notwithstanding that the issue invoked the very clashes of denominational doctrine that the Founders had deliberately sought to avoid in their early deliberations.[174]

As aptly assessed by Alexis de Tocqueville in 1831: "Each sect adores the Deity in its peculiar manner, but all sects preach the same moral law in the name of God. . . . Moreover, all of the sects of the United States are comprised within the great unity of Christianity, and Christian morality is everywhere the same."[175]

The fulcrum of the controversy nonetheless for decades continued to center on the issue of "Unitarianism" versus "Trinitarianism" – a debate that has plagued Christendom from its inception through its first four millennia of existence. For though colonial Deism found its embodiment in contemporary Unitarianism — a commitment to the concept of a single Supreme Being in renunciation of the Trinitarian creedal statements of the Church of England which had blossomed to full flower within the colonies at the nation's creation in 1776 — debate over the issue of the "Unity of God" dated back a full two millennia further still to the very onset of the Christian era.[176]

The crux of the theological question has focused on the precept: how does the Trinitarian who fervently believes in the Father-Son-Holy Ghost symbiosis described by the Apostle John: "As the Father knoweth me, so I know the Father " and the command of Jesus in Matthew 28:19: "Go ye, therefore, and teach all nations, baptizing them in the name of the Father, and of the Son, and of the Holy Ghost" – reconcile with the New Testament verse I Timothy 2:5: "For there is one God, and one mediator between God and men, the man Christ Jesus"— or the biblical depiction in Matthew 27:46 of Christ's supplication on the Cross: "My God, my God, why hast thou forsaken me?"[177]

The debate is longstanding in gestation. Indeed, many of the very earliest so-called "Christians," the *gnostikoi*, "knowing ones," Arias of Alexandria foremost among them, did not believe in the doctrine of the Trinity. Citing such verses as Colossians 1:15:in which Jesus is described as "the image of the invisible God, the firstborn of every creature" — and John 14: 28, wherein Jesus states: "I go unto the Father because the Father is greater than I" — they believed that God was a uni-personality to whom Jesus was subordinate.[178]

Certainly, the issue is not unequivocal. For in the *Bible,* there is no single reference wherein the "Three Divine Personages" are denoted collectively. Indeed, the term *"trias"*(of which the Latin *"trinitas"* is a translation) can first be found in a slightly different connotation in Theophilus of Antioch circa 180 A.D. wherein he speaks of "the Trinity of God, His Word, and his Wisdom." It subsequently reappears as *"trinitas"* on a *passim* basis in both Tertullian and Origen over the next two centuries.

The *spiritual* basis for the concept, as noted, derives from "Matthew 28:19," wherein Jesus, after his Resurrection, exhorts his disciples to baptize all nations "in the name of the Father, and of the Son, and of the Holy Ghost;" and I John 5:7, wherein the "Word," but not the Lord, is curiously specified:

> For there are three who bear record in heaven, the Father, the Word, and the Holy Ghost, and these three are one.

This latter verse, of course, comports perfectly with the message of John 1:1:

> In the beginning was the Word and the Word was with God, and the Word was God.[179]

Adherence, however, was not universally subscribed – as intense debate raged throughout the early Christian centuries as to the "true nature" of Jesus – leading to several major Church councils that attempted to establish a firm theological view on the essence of "God's Trinity."

Indeed, the issue of the alleged non-Divinity of Christ was embedded in an eastern orthodox view which Rome had earlier denounced as the "monophysite heresy" — a singular "unity of god" perspective that then prevailed throughout much of the Near East, including in Judaism and Islam. The great popularity of the view, in fact, may significantly help to explain the theological readiness of much of the region to accept the Judeo-Islamic portrayal of Jesus as a mere prophet, not a God.[180]

Over time, however, the 'Trinitarian view" came to be affirmed as an article of faith in a number of rescripts – the most noteworthy of which came in the proclamation issued at the "Council of Nicaea" convened by the newly converted Christian Byzantine Emperor Constantine in Nicaea, in what is now Turkey, on May 20, 325 A.D., which ruled – [181]

---

\*\*\*

### "The Proclamation at Nicaea"

"We believe in one God, the Father Almighty, maker of all things visible and invisible; and in one Lord, Jesus Christ, the Son of God, the only begotten of the Father – that is, of the substance (Gr. = "*ousia*") of the Father – God from God, light from light, true God from true God, begotten not made, of one substance (Gr. = "*homoousion*") with the Father, through whom all things were made – those things that are in heaven and those things that are on earth – Who for us men and our salvation came down and was made man, suffered, rose again on the third day, ascended into heaven, and will come to judge the living and the dead. And we believe in the Holy Spirit. . . ."

\*\*\*

---

— and the 'Athanasian Creed' ( 350 A.D.), promulgated by Athanasius, bishop of Alexandria, shortly thereafter — which attempted to necessarily reassure and standardize belief in the face of disagreement, particularly in light of the "Old Testament" admonitions:

> Hear, O Israel: the Lord our God is One Lord
> (Deuteronomy 6:4);
> Thou shalt have no other gods before Me
> (Deuteronomy 5:7); and
> I am the first and I am the last; and beside Me there is no god.
> (Isaiah 44:6).

Indeed, even the "New Testament" is not without equivocation, with Christ himself referring to himself as the "Son of Man." Accordingly, the Apostle Paul tells the Corinthians:

> We know that an idol is nothing in the world and that there is no other God but one. (I Corinthians: 8:4).

And therein lies the great theological debate – with the formal Church itself, at times, simply writing it off as just another one of those "unfathomable mysteries." But irrespective of whether, on the Christian side, "God found out about the Trinity only in 325 A.D.," as noted Aramaic biblical scholar Rocco Errico has asserted, the question of whether Deists are Christians continues to semantically haunt the debate of the Founders' precise intent for the role of religion in the founding of America.[182]

Early on, within the colonies, it appears to have occasioned no small amount of acrimonious, often satirical *anti-clerical* debate, as evidenced in the following ballad — titled "The Beauties of Predestination" — which seems to have characterized the spirit of the age:[183]

> No wonder to me,
> When we often see,
> Deism prevail in our nation:
> Since Calvins declare;
> That God everywhere
> Is working out Predestination. . . .
>
> Could the Author of all,
> Condemn men at all,
> Who work all in all through creation,
> When no praise or blame,
> On the good or profane,
> Can be found in our Predestination.[184]

That said, there was unquestionably a concurrent contemporary popular backlash to the some of the *political Founders'* alleged Deism as well. Thomas Jefferson's run for the presidency in 1800, for instance, bought on an anti-Deist campaign, as the opposing Federalists sought to link Jefferson to the Jacobin anti-clericalism and atheism that characterized the by then notorious French Revolution. Ministers denounced Jefferson from their pulpits and lamented the prospect that the reins of the nation might fall into the hands of a deistic agent of the Devil.[185]

Indeed, Timothy White, president of Yale and prominent Congregationalist minister, warned that "we may see the holy *Bible* cast into a bonfire and the vessels of the sacramental supper borne by an ass in public procession;" whereas New York's Dutch Reformed leading clergyman charged the future president with "Disbelief in the Scriptures . . . and rejection of the Christian religion and open progression of Deism" – adding in editorial comment that "no professed Deist ought to be promoted to this place by the suffrages of a Christian nation."[186]

Yet Jefferson prevailed. And thus it is that "civil religion," albeit controversial, came to insinuate itself into the American polity and became a transcendent goal in her political society — a view that prevails still, as articulated by President Kennedy in his Inaugural Address on January 20, 1961 that "the rights of man come not from the generosity of the State but from the hand of God" — and encapsulated in his conclusion acknowledging that "here on earth God's work must truly be our own"[187] — words then echoed in President George W. Bush's 2003 State of the Union address: "The liberty that we prize is not America's gift to the world, it is God's gift to humanity"[188] — both views reflecting faith in the premise of the promise articulated in the Scriptures:[189]

"Where the Spirit of the Lord is, there is liberty."

(II Corinthians 3:17)

# PART II
# The Cause

Because Roman civilization perished through barbarian invasions, we are perhaps too much inclined to think that is the only way that a civilization can die. If the lights that guide us ever do go out, they will fade little by little, as if of their own accord.... We therefore should not console ourselves into thinking that the barbarians are still a long way off. Some people may let the torch be snatched from their hands, but others may stamp it out themselves.

—Alexis de Tocqueville. *Democracy in America*, 1831

# Chapter Three
# Portents of the Precipitous Death of God

> When Christ drew near the city,
> He wept over it.
>
> —*Bible*, Luke 19:41

### I. THE MYTH OF SEPARATION [1]

Preceding analysis makes clear that America's Founders framed a model for governance that they intended to be an exemplar to the world. The fact that they succeded is manifest in the reality that despite her relative youth among nations, hers is the oldest written Constitution in effect today. It is the governing document that other nations seeking liberty and freedom seek to emulate and follow.[2]

The Founders forged their vision for religious liberty upon the twin cornerstones of two provisions embedded within the Constitution and the Bill of Rights:[3]

> FIRST AMENDMENT: Congress shall make no law respecting an establishment of religion, or prohibiting the free exercise thereof; and
> ARTICLE VI: No religious test shall every be required as a qualification to any office or public trust under the United States.[4]

Upon the completion of the Constitution itself, Benjamin Franklin said: "Our General Convention . . . when it formed the new Federal Constitution (was) . . .

influenced and guided and governed by that omnipotent and beneficent Ruler in whom all . . . live and move and have their being."[5] James Madison asserted: "It is not possible for a man of pious reflection to not perceive in it a finger of that Almighty Hand."[6] In like manner, Alexander Hamilton would assert: "I sincerely esteem it a system which, without the finger of God, could never have been suggested and agreed upon by such a diversity of interests."[7]

The libertarian spirit of the age was perhaps best captured by George Washington in a letter to the Marquis de Lafayette in ushering in the new U.S. Constitution on February 8, 1788:

> It appears to me little short of a miracle that the delegates from so many States, differing from each other, as you know, in their manners, circumstances, and prejudices, should unite in forming a system of national government so little liable to well-founded objections. . . . We are not to expect perfection in this world; but mankind in modern times have apparently made some progress in the science of government. . . .[8]

Later, in an address to the people of Philadelphia, he would add:

> When I contemplate the interposition of Providence, as it has been visibly manifest in guiding us through this Revolution, in preparing us for General Government, and in conciliating the good people of America toward one another in its adoption, I find myself overwhelmed with a sense of Divine munificence.[9]

The Bill of Rights thus succeeded because it came in direct response to contemporary concerns respecting the specific range and degrees of freedom sanctioned by the Constitution. Hence, after the document's final ratification in 1789, the nation's architects took up the task of enumerating explicit rights more specifically – among them, seeking to place all sects and churches on equal footing before the nation's law, completing their work in December, 1791.

Making religious freedom the very first phase of the First Amendment, in a noteworthy economy of words, therefore, the amended Constitution provided a double guarantee: first, that Congress would do nothing extraordinary to favor, promote, or endow religion in general or any one of its denominations in particular; second, Congress would take no action that would impede, obstruct, or penalize religion's free exercise. In sum, by neither hindering nor helping, government was to leave religion and its freedoms to its citizens alone.[10]

The Founders' thus perceived and created clear distinctions between the issue of church and state and that of faith and politics. Their language was basic and their intent could not be more clear. The federal government would not enfranchise any denomination or sect as the "national religion" and adherence to any particular religious creed would not be a bar or benefit to federal office. The intent was that the twin tenets operate in tandem to safeguard the free expression of faith for all.

Notwithstanding a long legacy of religious commitment imbued by her Founders, however, these precepts now stand in jeopardy — as a new wave of liberal social engineers seeks to forge a "god-free" vision for America's future. In their quest to dismantle what the nation's forebears knew as "old-time religion," and in direct contravention of the U.S. Constitution, they seek to inculcate a new theology – the doctrine of secular humanism legally imposed top-down through the powerful force of an extremist counter-cultural judicial agenda. In the prescient words of the 18th century British philosopher Lord Chesterfield: "The modern world is full of old Christian virtues gone bad."[11]

Unfortunately, in this instance, the prime problem is not one of misunderstanding, as the Constitution is written in simple English terms. The difficulty is not one of interpretation either, as there is a multiplicity of documents, most noteworthily the *Federalist Papers*, that expound upon the Founding Fathers' explicit constitutional intent. Nonetheless, depending upon individual agendas and political views, there is today an ever-evolving spate of improbably divergent and often contradictory interpretations of the simple document that was intended to be America's "operating manual."[12]

The implementation problem is further compounded, and confounded, by the fact that radical "judicial activism" – using the judge's bench as a "political soapbox" – has become the norm rather than the exception amongst leftist jurists who subscribe to arbitrary interpretations of law in rewriting legal precedent within the country's courts. In the process, in the place of those God-given rights eloquently articulated and defended in the Constitution, *civil rights* have become the omnibus term for any liberal cause designed to challenge the general will and historic workings of America's democracy and the wishes of her people.[13]

As within the past half century, the Supreme Court has inflicted a nearly unbroken series of assaults upon God and the faith of the Founders with a radically new secular catechism that supplants the Constitution. Indeed, those very values upon which the American nation was founded are now deemed dangerous, destructive, and divisive.[14]

All this, despite the fact that the notion of "the constitutional separation of church and state" is no more than a jurisprudential myth. To the contrary, the explicit intent of the Founding Fathers was to preclude a federal favoring of one Christian denomination over another, as explained by Justice Joseph Story, appointed to the Supreme Court by President Madison in 1811:

> The real object (of the First Amendment) was not to countenance, much less to advance, Mahometanism or Judaism, or infidelity by prostrating Christianity; but to exclude all rivalry among Christian sects, and to prevent any national ecclesiastical establishment which would give to an hierarchy the exclusive patronage of the national government. It thus cut off the means of religious persecution and of subversion of the rights of conscience in matters of religion almost from the days of the Apostles to the present age. . . .
> Probably at the time of the adoption of the Constitution, and of the First Amendment to it . . .the general, if not universal, sentiment in America was that Christianity ought to receive encouragement from the State, in so far as that was not incompatible with previous legal rights and the freedom of religious worship. Any attempt to level all religions and to make it a matter of state policy to hold all utter indifference would have created universal disapprobation, if not universal indignation.[15]

Concerning religion, in fact, the First Amendment only states that "Congress shall make no law respecting an establishment of religion nor prohibiting the free exercise thereof." Not only are the words "separation" "church" or "state" not found within the First Amendment, that phrase is not to be found in *any* official founding document, nor is there official document whatsoever that mandates that government be overtly hostile to religion.[16]

Such documents suggest, in fact, just the opposite. According to the daily *Congressional Records* for June 8 to September 25, 1789 – the period wherein the ninety Founders in the First Congress framed the First Amendment that was formally ratified in 1791 – the Congressmen repeatedly emphasized that what they were trying to expressly prevent was that which they had experienced in Europe – the establishment by the federal government of a single national church – as was the Anglican hegemony in England – to the exclusion of all others. In proclaiming America's independence from England in 1776, the Founders had concurrently severed ties with the Anglican Church, the established Church of England, and they vividly wanted to keep it that way in their new nation.[17]

Their original intent thus could not have been more clear. Accordingly, the initial version of the First Amendment – as crafted by James Madison with its original wording being: "*nor shall any national religion be established*" – was introduced into the House on June 8, 1789 and later into the Senate on September 3, 1789, stating: "Congress shall not make any law establishing any religious *denomination*." It was subsequently amended to read: "Congress shall make no law establishing any *particular denomination*." It was then amended to read: "Congress shall make no law establishing any religious *denomination* in preference to another." The final version passed on that day ultimately read: "Congress shall make no law establishing religion *nor prohibiting the free exercise thereof.*"[18]

Accordingly, there was not going to be, by Congressional fiat, an officially enfranchised denomination in America, as the objective was two-fold: (1) to provide an *establishment clause* to preclude establishment of a single national religion; yet, in so doing, (2) to concurrently provide a *free exercise* clause to prohibit government from interfering with the public's religious expression; alternately put, to preclude a federal separation of biblical principles from the public marketplace.[19] In this manner, both clauses restricted the action of the federal government; yet neither restricted the actions of citizens – provisos enacted in the belief that liberty for all would ensure liberty for each.[20]

Indeed, Fisher Ames – the Founding Father who wrote the final version of the First Amendment – subsequently crafted a missive wherein he expressed concern that the *Bible* might become deluged by a proliferation of other books and thereby become under-employed as a textbook in the nation's public school system. He therefore warned that the Scriptures should never be pushed to the back of the American classroom:

> What, then, if these (new) books for children are retained — should not the *Bible* regain the place it once held as a schoolbook?[21]

Ames concluded his treatise by stressing that the reality that the *Bible* was the prime source of sound morals in America was a further reason why it should never be separated from the classroom. This, then, was the view of a foremost Founder, indeed the one who authored the First Amendment's precise wording – who makes clear that it was intended only to limit the power of government, not that of the people or of organized religion. It is not surprising, then, that in the *Congressional Record's* discussion of the Founders' intense debate leading to the passage of the First Amendment, nowhere is the term "separation of church and state" ever mentioned.[22]

Accordingly, Dr. Benjamin Rush, one of early America's leading educators — a signer of the Declaration of Independence who later served in the administrations of Presidents Adams, Jefferson, and Madison, and the first of the nation's architects to call for free public schools, thereby earning him the title of the "Father of the Public Schools under the Constitution" — in arguing why the *Bible* should never be taken out of the American classroom, explained:

> In contemplating the political institutions of the United States, (if we remove the *Bible* from schools), I lament that we waste much time and money in punishing crimes and take so little pains to prevent them.[23]

Noah Webster, yet another Founder, further explained this dimension to their original intent:

> All the miseries and evils which men suffer from vice, crime, ambition, injustice, oppression, slavery, and war proceed from neglecting the precepts contained in the *Bible*.[24]

That the Founders did not conspire to see biblical precepts excluded from American society was underscored in President John Adams' address to the U.S. military on October 11, 1798:"We have no government armed with the power capable of contending with human passions unbridled by morality and religion. Our Constitution was made for a moral and religious people. It is wholly inadequate to the government of any other."[25]

Did the nation's architects contemplate that the First Amendment would be used as an instrument to separate religious principles from public affairs? To the contrary, they believed that it would preserve those values in public life.[26] George Washington, in his Farewell Address, in fact, explicitly affirmed that it was the intent of American policy that religion should never be removed from the public arena – openly commending religion and morality as foremost cornerstones for reinforcing *political* prosperity as well:

> Of all of the dispositions and habits that lead to political prosperity, religion and morality are indispensable supports. . . . Let us with caution indulge the supposition that morality can be maintained without religion. Whatever may be conceded to the influence of refined education on minds . . . reason and experience both forbid us to expect that national morality can prevail in the exclusion of religious principle. . . .Where is the security for property, for reputation, for life, if the sense

of religious obligation deserts the oaths which are the instruments of investigation in courts of justice?[27]

Such writings by the foremost amongst the nation's Founders thus make eminently evident that they did not embrace the specious notion that the "separation of church and state" that is today imposed upon the conduct of public life in the United States was a mandate of the Constitution that they wrote. Yet the very wording that the Founders created to *encourage* the free exercise of religion is now instead being interpreted by the courts to *prohibit* it. [28]

## II. UNDERPINNINGS OF THE MYTH OF SEPARATION: THE LOCUS OF THE DEBATE

If the phrase "separation of church and state" itself does not appear in any official founding document, what then, is its source – and how did it become associated with the First Amendment as a constitutional doctrine? These are critical questions. For the "separation of church and state" issue did not evolve in a vacuum – making the course of its evolution, and thus, by implication, the questions' answers, though circuitous, germane.

The incipient catalyst is clear. On October 7, 1801, the Danbury Baptist Association, a consortium of churches located in the Connecticut Valley, drafted a letter to President Thomas Jefferson congratulating him on his election to the presidency while concurrently arguing that freedom of religion was an inalienable God-given right – not a governmentally-granted one. Though they recognized that the nation's founding was firmly predicated upon freedom *of* religion, not freedom *from* religion, they concurrently feared that for a guarantee of religious freedom to even appear in the Bill of Rights was to cede to the government powers to regulate the free exercise of religion – powers that they strongly felt it should not have.[29]

On January 1, 1802, a full eleven years after the First Amendment was adopted, therefore, in somewhat of a sidebar *apologia* embedded in a courtesy response to a political congratulatory missive, Jefferson responded in a private letter to the Danbury Baptist Association concurring in the belief that mankind were accountable only to God for their faith and worship, not to the government. He assured them that there was no reason to fear that the government would regulate religious expression, for the First Amendment had built "a wall of separation between church and state." In his exact words:

> Believing with you that religion is a matter which lies solely between man and God . . . I contemplate with sovereign reverence that act of the whole American people which declared that their legislature "shall make no law respecting an establishment of religion or prohibiting the free exercise thereof," thus building a wall of separation between Church and State.[30]

The intent? In Jefferson's own terms, in multiple iterations:

> I consider the United States government as interdicted by the Constitution from in-

ter-meddling with religious institutions, their doctrines, discipline, or exercises. This results not only from the provision that no law shall be made respecting the establishment or free exercise of religion, but also from that which reserves for the States the powers not delegated to the United States. *No power to prescribe any religious exercise or assume authority in any religious discipline has been delegated to the General Government. It must then rest with the States . . . .*[31]
In matters of religion, I have considered that its free exercise is placed by the Constitution independent of the powers of the General Government. I have therefore undertaken, on no occasion, to prescribe the religious exercise suited to them, but have left them, as the Constitution found them, under the direction and discipline of the church or state authorities as acknowledged by the several religious societies.[32]

Indeed, throughout his entire political career and beyond, Jefferson had feared just such federal judicial encroachment upon states' rights. In 1825, just one year before his death, he wrote: "I see . . . with the deepest affliction, the rapid strides with which the federal bench of our government is advancing toward the usurpation of all of the rights reserved to the States, and the consolidation in itself of all powers, foreign and domestic. . . ."[33]

This assertion thus firmly built upon his earlier determination in 1820 – in proposing that judges be limited to six year terms, with term renewals subject to approval by both Houses of Congress – that: "The judiciary of the United States is a subtle corps of sappers and miners constantly working underground to undermine the foundations of our confederated fabric. They are construing our Constitution away from a coordination of a general and special government to a general and supreme one alone."[34]

With the combination of these words, then, Jefferson's intent could not made more evident: that the "wall of separation" was erected not to limit public religious expression but rather to expressly provide security against government interference with those expressions, whether public or private.

It may be more irony than coincidence, therefore, that on the very day that the First Amendment was passed, September 24, 1789, the Congress passed a resolution calling for a "National Day of Prayer" which President Washington then agreed to proclaim — and that two days after issuing his seemingly landmark "separation of church and state" letter to the Danbury Baptists, President Jefferson attended Sunday church services in the House of Representatives chambers — thereby strongly suggesting that while he officially opposed a federal religious establishment, he nonetheless personally encouraged, and symbolically supported, the free expression of religion even in a public place.[35]

It is not sheer coincidence either that the "Northwest Ordinance of 1787," which proclaimed: "Religion, morality, and knowledge being necessary to good government" – was reenacted by the First Congress immediately after it had agreed to the final wording of the First Amendment in 1789. Certainly, it did not deem the two documents to be incompatible.[36]

In conjunction with another question related to the role of religion and governance posed while en route to a religious service at Christ Church on Capital Hill, Jefferson – who had opened the Treasury, War Office, and Supreme Court chambers for religious purposes – reportedly responded: "Sir, no nation has ever existed or been governed without religion; nor can it be." Such an affirmation, of course, would build upon Jefferson's aforesaid rescript on the assurance of religious liberty in Virginia that it "was meant to comprehend, within the mantle of its protection, the Jew and the Gentile, the Christian and the Mahometan, the Hindu, and infidels of every denomination."[37]

In affirmation of that commitment, he also supported congressional resolutions that appropriated federal funds to provide Christian chaplain services to sundry Indian tribes — and the nation's "Articles of War," which he signed on April 10, 1806: "Earnestly recommended that all officers and soldiers diligently attend divine services."[38]

Notwithstanding, it must be said that matters of "church and state" within a polity aspiring to be a "Christian nation," from the onset, was a problematic issue. Jesus himself, in John 18:36, had declared that "my kingdom is not of this world" — and in Matthew 22:21: "Render onto Caesar the things that are Caesar's; and unto God the things that are God's" — and upon such foundations, many of the Church Fathers sought to distinguish the church from civil government.[39]

Martin Luther had also sought to depict the church as set apart from the taint of worldly things — differentiating between the "two kingdoms; one, the kingdom of God, the other, the kingdom of the world," and argued that "these two kingdoms must be sharply distinguished" and even that they "must be kept apart." This was a position subscribed to by many of America's early Calvinists and Baptists as well.[40]

But the concept of "separation" gained genuine intensity within American conception of religious liberty only in the nineteenth and twentieth century as part of a growing fear of churches in general and of the papal concept of theocracy in particular. This was a somewhat schizoid evolution, as Protestants often invoked it in seeking to limit Catholic influence in government as they concurrently sought greater public support for their own institutions.[41]

The debate has been complicated by a notion that an absolute separation is the only alternative to a collaboration of church and state – notwithstanding that it is not the issue of separation, but instead the judicial application and interpretation of the Fourteenth Amendment to states, that has opened the door of federal intrusion into traditional expressions of religious liberties.

As in enforcing the first "establishment" clause of the First Amendment to the detriment of its second "religious freedom" clause, the federal court system has gravely confounded its original intent. It was within the vortex of this confluence of conflicting interests that the era of court meddling into America's historic religious freedoms emerged six decades ago.[42]

## III. IF GOD IS ALIVE AND WELL, THEN, IT IS AS A WARD OF THE COURT IN WASHINGTON

### A. God's Standing Before the Court

It was within this complex context, then, that the concept of church/state separation was, at its origin, explicitly designed as a safeguard against governmental interference, public or private, into free religious expression. Later courts expounded upon Jefferson's letter. In *Reynolds v. United States* (1878), for example, the U.S. Supreme Court, incorporating numerous excerpts from it, ruled that "coming as it does from an acknowledged leader of the advocates of the measure (the First Amendment), it (Jefferson's letter) may be accepted almost as an authoritative declaration of the scope and effect of the Amendment thus secured. Congress was deprived of all legislative power over mere (religious) opinion..."[43]

"The rightful purposes of civil government are for its officers to interfere (with religion only) when (religious) principles break out into overt acts against peace and good order. In th(is)... is found the distinction between what properly belongs to the church and what to the state."[44]

The Court, in this manner, thus affirmed its understanding of the Jefferson letter to be that government could involve itself in the exercise of religion only when and if its actions were "subversive of good order" or broke out into "overt acts against peace and good order."[45] This understanding was effectively reaffirmed, moreover, by the late Court Chief Justice William Rehnquist in writing the dissenting opinion in *Wallace v. Jaffrey* (1985):

> Based on proceedings in the House of Representatives, James Madison was undoubtedly the most important architect of the members of the House who deliberated the Amendments which became the Bill of Rights....
> His original language, "nor shall any national religion be established," obviously does not conform to the "wall of separation" between Church and State idea which latter-day commentators have ascribed to him. His explanation on the floor of the meaning of language "that Congress should not establish a religion, nor enforce the legal observance of it by law," is of the same ilk...
> It seems indisputable from these glimpses of Madison's thinking, as reflected on the floor of the House in 1789, that he saw the Amendment as designed to prohibit the establishment of a national religion and perhaps to discriminating among sects. He did not see it as requiring neutrality on the part of the government between religion and irreligion.[46]

Justice Rehnquist was therefore moved to add that the "wall of separation between church and state is a metaphor based on bad history, a metaphor which has proved useless as a guide to judging. It should be frankly and explicitly abandoned."[47] He concluded that: "History must judge whether it was the Father of His

Country (referring to George Washington who signed into law the final version of the Northwest Ordinance on August 7,1789, which proclaimed" religion, morality, and knowledge being necessary to good government"), or a majority of the Court today, who have strayed from its meaning."[48]

As James Madison himself, who prior to becoming president was Jefferson's Secretary of State, in his *Memorial and Remonstrance*, explicitly explained:

> We hold it for a fundamental and undeniable truth that religion or the duty that we owe to our Creator, and the manner of discharging it, can be directed only by reason and conviction, and not by violence or force. The religion, then, of every man must be left to the conviction and conscience of every man; and it is the right of every man to exercise it as these may dictate. This right is, in its nature, an inalienable right.[49]

These explicit disavowals notwithstanding – though Jefferson's Danbury letter was essentially no more than a political campaign document issued in the aftermath of a presidential campaign – and though the precept of a "constitutional separation of church and state" was cited in but two cases in the Supreme Court's first 150 years – it has recurred repeatedly in a wide variety of rulings within the past half century.[50] As today, the very language that the Founders drafted in the First Amendment to ensure freedom of religious expression is now being interpreted by an extremist leftist court system as intended to expressly deny it.[51] The examples, to be discussed presently, are particularly egregious regarding free religious expression in the nation's schools.[52]

Indeed, courts across the nation have even ruled that it is unconstitutional for a kindergarten class to raise the question of whose birthday is celebrated at Christmas[53] — and for a Board of Education to use or refer to the word "God" in any of its writings[54] — and for artwork depicting religious activities to be displayed in school even if that work is deemed to be a cultural classic.[55]

---

\*\*\*

RECENT FEDERAL COURT DECISIONS RESPECTING CLASSROOM FREEDOM OF RELIGIOUS EXPRESSION

\*\*\*"Freedom of speech is guaranteed to students and teachers — unless the topic is religious, at which point it becomes unconstitutional." (*Stein v. Oshinsky*, 348 F.2d 999 (2nd Cir. 1965), *cert denied*, 382 U.S. 957); *Collins v. Chandler Unified School District*, 644 F2d 759 (9th Cir. 1981) *cert. denied*, 454 U.S. 863)

*** "If a student prays over lunch, it is unconstitutional to pray aloud." (*Reed v. Hoven*, 237 F. Supp. 48 (W.D. Mich 1965))
*** "It is unconstitutional for students to see the Ten Commandments lest they read, meditate upon, respect, and obey them." (*Stone v.Graham*, 449 U.S. 39 (1980))
*** "It is unconstitutional for a classroom library to contain books which deal with Christianity, or for a teacher to be seen with a personal copy of a *Bible* at school." (*Roberts v. Madigan*, 705 F. Supp. 1505 (D.C. Colo 1989), 921 F2d 1047 (10th Cir. 1990), *cert. denied*, 112 S. Ct. 3025))
*** "It is unconstitutional for a student to read his *Bible* on his free time or even open his *Bible* at school." (*Gierke v. Blotzer*, CV88-0-883 (U.S.D.C. Neb. 1989))

***

In some of the more preposterous *non-school-related* federal court decisions regarding freedom of religion:[56]

***

## RECENT FEDERAL COURT DETERMINATIONS RESPECTING NON-SCHOOL RELATED RELIGIOUS FREEDOMS

*** "It is unconstitutional for a war memorial to be erected in the shape of a cross." (*Lowe v. City of Eugene,* 451 P.2d 117 (Sup. Ct. Or. 1969), *cert. denied,* 34 U.S. 876)
*** "It is also unconstitutional for a public cemetery to display a planter in the shape of a cross, lest the viewing cause someone 'emotional distress.'" (*Warsaw v. Tehachapi*, CV F-90-404 EDP (U.S.D.C., E.D. Ca 1990))
*** "Even though its wording may be constitutional, an act becomes unconstitutional if the legislator who introduced it had a religious activity in mind when it was authored."(*Wallace v. Jaffrey,* 472 U.S. 38, 86 (1985))
*** "It is unconstitutional for a nativity scene to be displayed on public property unless it is accompanied by sufficient secular displays to preclude it from appearing religious." (*County of Allegheny v. ACLU*, 106 L. Ed.2d 472 (1989))
*** "It is unconstitutional for school officials to be publicly praised or recognized in an open community meeting if that meeting is sponsored by a religious group." (*Jane Doe v. Santa Fe Independent School District,* Civil Action No. G-95-176 (U.S.D.C., S.D. Tx. 1995))

***

It is thus also not surprising to learn that it has been ruled judicially improper for a copy of the Ten Commandments to be displayed in a courtroom during a murder trial lest jurors be influenced by the command: "Thou shalt not kill."[57] Or that in Pennsylvania, the state Supreme Court overturned the conviction of a criminal convicted in the axe-murdering of a seventy-one-year-old woman while stealing her Social Security check because the prosecutor in the case cited a *Bible* verse in his closing argument.[58]

As today, in a stunning display of "judicial exegesis creep" combined with "Orwellian mind-speak," the courts have interpreted the First Amendment to forbid even a mere mention of God, the *Bible*, the Ten Commandments, or prayer in public places – to the extent that a "God Bless America" banner" erected on a California public school campus to honor those killed on "9/11" was attacked by the ACLU as an unconstitutional establishment of religion – and that as a consequence of *Everson v. Board of Education* (1947*)*, the separation doctrine is now a dictum applied not only at the federal level but to state and local governments as well.[59]

Such a determination thus represents a significant legal departure— as historically, American jurisprudence had distinguished between rights held under the U.S. Constitution and those held under the various state constitutions. Not the least, it took for granted that the Bill of Rights did not constrain the states — that each state imposed its own limitations pursuant to its own bill of rights. When James Madison in 1789 tried to persuade his fellow congressmen to apply the Bill of Rights to the states, in fact, his motion was decisively rejected, as were five other subsequent attempts – clearly indicative of longstanding congressional intent respecting the exclusively *federal* applicability of the Bill of Rights.[60]

Hence, invoking the Fourteenth Amendment – a measure ratified in 1868 only to guarantee the civil rights of emancipated slaves and not to prohibit the exercise of public affairs by the states – to now assert the claim that the federal ban on religious practice also applies to state governments is specious. Even the Supreme Court, in *Waltz v. Tax Commission* (1970), conceded that the precedent that it invoked was based upon an interpretation of recent origin which:

> involved the imposition of new, far-reaching constitutional restraints upon the States. Nationalization of many civil liberties has been the consequence of the Fourteenth Amendment, reversing the historic position that the foundations of those liberties rested largely in state law . . . And so the revolution occasioned by the Fourteenth Amendment has progressed as Article after Article in the Bill of Rights has been incorporated in it and made applicable to the States. . .
> The Establishment Clause (of the First Amendment) was not incorporated in the Fourteenth Amendment until *Everson v. Board of Education* was decided in 1947. . . . The meaning of the Establishment Clause and the Free Exercise Clause has been made applicable to the States for only a few decades at best. . . . It was, for example, not until 1962 that . . . prayers were held to violate the Establishment Clause.[61]

Certainly, this inversion of the Founders' legal documentation in forging the First Amendment runs contrary to their intent. As James Madison, the amendment's architect, said: "The powers delegated by the Constitution to the federal government are few and well defined. Those which are to remain in the State governments are numerous and indefinite."[62] To which Thomas Jefferson added. "The (only) way to have good and safe government is not to trust it all to one but to divide it among many."[63]

A New York court, in *Baer v. Kolmorgen* (1958) likewise conceded that a notion of separation of church and state could not be traced to Founders' provenance; to wit: "Much has been written in recent years concerning Thomas Jefferson's reference in 1802 to a 'wall of separation between church and State. . . Jefferson's figure of speech has received so much attention that one would almost think it is to be found somewhere in our Constitution."[64]

There are powerful indications, in fact, that Jefferson himself subscribed to the same sentiments. In his Second Inaugural Address delivered on March 4, 1805, he asserted: "In matters of religion, I have considered that its free exercise is placed by the Constitution independent of the powers of the General Government."[65]

This position was likewise adopted by the Supreme Court in the aforesaid *Reynolds v. United States* in 1878, when it used Jefferson's letter not to separate church and state but to the contrary — to uphold the precept of free expression of religion.[66] Accordingly, those seeking to divine original intent in the matter of separation of church and state based on Jefferson might due well to listen to the Founder himself – as the fact that the Constitution is silent on the issue does not mean that either the Founders or the First Amendment intended to be hostile to religious practice.[67]

There can be no doubt, therefore, that the federal courts' recent half-century-long sequence of "impenetrable wall" decisions constitutes a direct perversion of the Founding Fathers' ideological construct, whose treatment of religion was intended to safeguard religious liberty – to protect religion from the state, not the state from religion.[68]

Indeed, the First Congress, which had passed the Bill of Rights that incorporated the First Amendment, concurrently elected chaplains whose principal duties included daily delivering opening prayers within its public chambers.[69] Yet rather than understanding the First Amendment's opening lines as a single clause designed to preserve religious freedom, the Court has persisted in finding two clauses embedded within it – an "establishment clause" and a "free exercise clause" – reading each independently, yet with a focus on the former to the detriment of the latter.[70]

Regrettably, to paraphrase eighteenth century American philosopher William James, if one repeats an absurdity often enough, eventually people will believe it. Small wonder, then, that Chief Justice Rehnquist asserted: "The metaphor of a 'wall of separation' is bad history and worse law. . . . It should be frankly and explicitly abandoned." For the progress of civilization enters a bizarre and dangerous stage if the First Amendment is interpreted to mean that citizens may deduce their "politics of meaning" from Karl Marx or Herbert Marcuse or Max Lerner or Ralph Nader but not from the *Bible*.[71]

Indeed, to selectively extract bits and pieces from the First Amendment to construe that it forbids public-private collaboration in things religious, as America's courts have done, is tantamount to further truncating its text to read – "Congress shall make no law" – a redaction that, from a standpoint of the public good, might-likely be a more provident exercise of power.

Notwithstanding, commencing on February 10,1947, in *Everson v. Board of Education*, the Supreme Court, relying upon the imputed words "separation of church and state," ruled that the First Amendment not only prohibited the federal government from showing preference amongst religious sects, but also interpreted the "separation" clause as requiring the federal government to remove religious expression entirely from the public arena; in so doing: (1) banning nondiscriminatory aid in support of any religion; and (2) determining that the prohibition applied not only federally but to the governments of the various states as well.[72]

As articulated by Justice Hugo Black in setting dramatic legal precedent: "In the words of Jefferson, the clause against establishment of religion by law was intended to erect a 'wall of separation' between church and State. . . .The First Amendment has erected a wall between Church and State. That wall must be kept high and impregnable. We cannot approve the slightest breach."[73] In dissent, Justice Wiley Rutledge, quoting Jefferson's "Bill for Establishing Religious Freedom" in Virginia, countered: "I cannot believe that the great author of those words, or the men who made them law, could have joined in this decision."[74]

This ruling was subsequently reaffirmed and reinforced by *Engel v. Vitale* in 1962, which ominously concurrently broadened the definition of the word "church" in the separation clause" to mean "any religious activity."  In so doing, as will be presently described, the Court effectively prohibited many of the conventional public religious activities that the Founders had explicitly encouraged, and participated in, at the very time they were writing the nation's Constitution — in effect, staking out a claim that it knows more than the Founders about their "original intent."[75]

Indeed, in remarkable candor in writing his concurring opinion on the 1947 *Everson* decision school busing decision affirming the so-called "wall of separation" between church and state, Justice Robert Jackson wrote: "It is idle to pretend that this task is one to which we can find in the Constitution one word to help us as judges to decide where the secular ends and the sectarian begins in education. It is a matter on which we can find no law but our own prepossessions." [76]

It is noteworthy nonetheless that even after *Everson*, the Supreme Court in *Zorach v. Clauson* in 1952 continued to uphold the constitutionality of student religious instruction during the school day, albeit that it had to take place off-campus, declaring:

> We are a religious people whose institutions presuppose a Supreme Being. When the State encourages religious instruction or cooperates with religious authorities by adjusting the schedule of public events to sectarian needs, it follows the best of our traditions. For it then respects the religious nature of our people and accommodates public service to their spiritual needs.
> To hold that it may not would be to find in the Constitution a requirement that the government show callous indifference to religious groups. That would be prefer-

ring those who believe in no religion over those who do believe.... We find no constitutional requirement that makes it necessary for the government to be hostile to religion ....[77]

Based on this rationale and analogous case law, then, legal historian E.R. Norman concludes: "the separation of church and state in the federal constitution of the United States was not originally intended to disconnect Christianity and public life; it was a device to prevent the supremacy of one sect over another"[78] — in other words, it was aimed at denying denominational monopoly while preserving religious freedoms.

## B. Expelling God from School

This ruling, however, would prove to be amongst God's last dying gasps within the U.S. federal court system – as within the past half century, judicial interpretation would dramatically deteriorate from judicious tolerance to a distinct intolerant one in matters of religion. As commencing in 1947 -1948, in *Everson v. Board of Education* and *McCollum v. Board of Education* respectively, taking Jefferson's nine word phrase — "building a wall of separation between church and state" — the Court effectively outlawed all voluntary religious instruction conducted in the nation's public schools, thereby deciding, in the words of Justice Black that "we cannot approve the slightest breach."[79]

The litany of litigated intolerance, therefore, is long but mixed. In *McCollum*, in ruling against elective courses in religion in public schools when protested by a local atheist, the Court granted legal standing to the plaintiff's grievances in asserting that: "she has every right to be, and is, an avowed atheist."[80] Thus, the sensitivities of a single individual ostensibly personally offended by a practice to which she was not a direct party were granted higher legal standing than the wishes of an entire community school district – Jews, Catholics, and Protestants alike – operating as a volunteer task force who instituted and supported non-denominational religious instruction classes for fourth to ninth graders which were provided at no expense to the school.[81]

Fifteen years later, in *Abington Township v. Schempp* (1963), on the other hand, the Court held that: "The state may not establish a 'religion of secularism' in the sense of affirmatively opposing or showing hostility to religion – lending preference "to those who believe in no religion over those who do believe."[82] Two decades later, the U.S. West Virginia District, in *Crocker v. Sorenson* (1983) similarly ruled that: "The First Amendment was never intended to insulate our public institutions from any mention of God, the *Bible*, or religion. When such insulation occurs, another religion, such as secular humanism, is effectively established."[83]

Both decisions thus affirmed the "common sense doctrine" articulated by Justice William O. Douglas writing the majority opinion in *Zorach v. Clauson*. in 1952:

The First Amendment does not say that in every and all respects there should be a separation of Church and State. Rather, it studiously defines the manner, the specific ways in which there should be no concert or union or dependency one on the other. That is the *common sense* of the matter. Otherwise, the State and religion would be aliens to each other – hostile, suspicious, and even unfriendly. Churches could not be required to pay even property taxes. Municipalities would not be permitted to render police or fire protection to religious groups. Policemen who helped parishioners into their places of worship would violate the Constitution. Prayers in our legislative halls; the appeals to the Almighty in the messages of the Chief Executive; the proclamations making Thanksgiving Day a holiday; "so help me God" in our courtroom oaths — these and all other references to the Almighty that run through our laws, our public rituals, and our ceremonies would be flouting the First Amendment. A fastidious atheist or agnostic could even object to the supplication with which this Court opens each session: "God save the United States and this Honorable Court."[84]

Regrettably, however, this "common sense doctrine" has subsequently been utterly juridically abandoned. In 1962, pursuant to *Engel v. Vitale*, school prayer was banned, effectively holding that a verbal prayer offered in a school is unconstitutional even if it is voluntary and denominationally neutral. The simple 22-word prayer in question, in which no pupil was compelled to join, was seemingly innocuous: "Almighty God: we acknowledge our dependence upon Thee, and we beg Thy blessings upon us, our parents, and our Country."[85]

Notwithstanding, the Supreme Court, the Honorable Justice Hugo Black again presiding, citing no legal precedents for its decision, in determining that "the public domain is out of bounds for God,"[86] held that:

Neither the fact that the prayer may be denominationally neutral nor the fact that its observance on the part of students is voluntary can serve to free it from the limitations of the (First Amendment). . . . Prayer in its public school system breaches the constitutional wall of separation between Church and State.[87]

Writing in dissent, Justice Potter Stewart countered that he could not see how an "official religion" is established by letting those who want to say a prayer say it."[88] Notwithstanding, a year later, in a follow-on case announced in June, 1963, the Court ruled that the Lord's Prayer and daily Bible readings in public schools were unconstitutional as well.[89]

Thus, despite the clear intent of the Founders, and the biblical admonitions of the Scriptures contained in Ezra 61:10 to "pray for those in authority,"[90] those in authority ruled that such prayers for them, if they take place at all, will not take place in a classroom. Seeking to justify its bizarre decision, even the Court conceded:

A union of government and religion tends to destroy government and to degrade religion. . . .[91] It is true that New York's . . . prayer . . . does not amount to the total establishment of one religious sect to the exclusion of all others. . . . *The prayer seems relatively insignificant when compared to the governmental encroachments upon religion which were common 200 years ago.*[92]

## Portents of the Precipitous Death of God 83

Astoundingly, then, the Court was alleging that the Founder-authors of the Constitution habitually violated the very governing document that they had so carefully crafted – and that it, the Court, two centuries later, understood their original intent far more than they! But did it really?[93] The first four U.S. presidents didn't think so: —

* George Washington said that "true government affords to government its greatest support;"[94]
* John Adams asserted that "religion and virtue are the only foundations . . . of republicanism and of all free government;"[95]
* Thomas Jefferson contributed that: "I have always said, and will always say, that studious perusal of the Sacred Volume will make us better citizens;[96] whereas
* James Madison affirmed that "religion . . . is the basis and foundation of government."[97]

As John Adams succinctly summed it: "Our Constitution was made for a moral and religious people" [98] — sentiments echoed in George Washington's assertion: "It is impossible to rightly govern . . . without God and the *Bible*."[99]

Indeed, in its ruling, in redefining its definition of "church" to include any public religious activity whatsoever, the Court effectively equated school prayer to an "obnoxious act" — to wit: "Attempts to enforce acts to so great a proportion of citizens tend to enervate the laws in general and to slacken the bonds of society" — and explained that: "state-sponsored school prayer violates the First Amendment" because "it interferes with an individual's freedom to believe, to worship, and to express himself according to the dictates of his own conscience."[100]

In 1963, in *School District of Abington Township v. Schempp*, moreover, voluntary daily reading from the *Bible* within public schools was declared unconstitutional as well. In this decision, the Court sweepingly ruled that: "The (First) Amendment's purpose was not to strike merely at the official establishment of a single sect. . . . It was to create a complete and permanent separation of the spheres of religious activity and civil authority."[101]

Alternately put, henceforth, "separation of church and state" no longer meant only that the federal government could not establish a national denomination, but that public religious expressions must be kept separate from the public square as well. Once again, then, though paying nominal lip service to the original intent of the Founders, it blatantly contravened it. [102] Explaining its rationale, it ruled:

> This Court has decisively settled that the First Amendment mandate the "Congress shall make no law respecting an establishment of religion or prohibiting the free exercise thereof'" has been made wholly applicable to States by the Fourteenth Amendment. . . .
> The First Amendment, in turn, declares that Congress shall make no law respecting an establishment of religion or prohibiting the free exercise thereof. The Fourteenth Amendment has rendered the legislatures of the states as incompetent as Congress to enact such laws.[103]

It dd not matter to the Court that this conclusion directly contravened the 1833 majority opinion in *Barron v. Baltimore* written by Chief Justice John Marshall that the Bill of Rights restricted only federal governance – a decision firmly founded upon an accurate reading of legislative intent – as the very Congress that enacted the Fourteenth Amendment, on six separate and distinct occasions, subsequently explicitly rejected initiatives to link it to the First Amendment.

In *Abington*, however, the Court summarily dismissed these deliberations. Instead, three quarters of a century after the fact, it stipulated that 'we alone" are qualified to determine what Congress and seventy years of subsequent court decisions *should have said* respecting the Fourteenth Amendment.[104]

In a court decision more egregious still, in a 1970 New Jersey Supreme Court decree allowed to stand by the U.S. Supreme Court, the act of students voluntarily arriving early to read remarks made by chaplains to the U.S. Congress *verbatim* from the *Congressional Record* was deemed to be an unconstitutional practice – in so doing, asserting a claim of the State to the very lives of the children; to wit:

"It is hereby declared to be a principle governing the law of this state that children under the jurisdiction of said court are wards of the state . . . which may intervene to safeguard them from neglect or injury. . . ."[105]

"It is a religious exercise to read from the *Congressional Record* "remarks" of the chaplain. . . . Reading from the *Congressional Record* may be an unconstitutional infringement upon the First Amendment."[106]

"A school program for religious exercise is not saved from being unconstitutional establishment by providing for permissive attendance . . . A period for the free exercise of religion . . . is unconstitutional establishment of religion and not essential to the free exercise of religion."[107]

If one is to literally interpret this ruling, then, acting in a presumptive "*in loco parentis*" role, the court did not want *its* children to be exposed to the free exercise of religion by voluntarily, on their own time, reading prayers delivered by federally-funded chaplains of an equal branch of government, the U.S. Congress. Politburo, be proud![108]

In November, 1980, in *Stone v. Graham*, moreover, a Kentucky law mandating posting of the Ten Commandments in classrooms was overturned because of the mythically-constitutionally-prescribed doctrine of the "separation of church and state" – on the pretext that "they serve no secular purpose," and that "if portions of the New Testament were read without explanation . . . they could be psychologically harmful to the child." To wit:

> If the posted copies of the Ten Commandments are to have any effect at all, it will be to induce schoolchildren to read, mediate upon, perhaps to venerate and obey, the Commandments. . . . This is not a permissive state objective under the Establishment Clause[109]

— thereby declaring as unconstitutional the embodiment of what the Founders had embraced as the very cornerstone of civilized moral law, while concurrently establishing the notion that exposure to biblical teachings could cause lasting damage to the values of "the court's children."[110]

In this watershed decision, the U.S. Supreme Court thus forbade school children from even seeing the Ten Commandments – as such fundamental concepts as "thou shalt not steal" and "thou shalt not kill" were now judicially interpreted to be corrupting precepts amongst the nation's youth.[111]

For a posting of three-millennia-old religious principles, the nation's foremost jurists ruled, was tantamount to establishing a state-sponsored religion – that the mere presence of such ideas as honesty, marital fidelity, and respect for parents might influence impressionable young minds – that it runs counter to the countercultural *zeitgest* – and this, modern justice cannot not tolerate – with the faith of the Founders thus being ever more relegated to nothing more than a mere curious relic of a more enlightened past.[112]

Yet the jurists were not yet done. In 1980, in *Brandon v. Board of Education*, the federal court system held that students arriving at school early before the start of classes to engage in voluntary prayer was unconstitutional. In 1992, in *Lee v. Weisman*, all prayers at high school football games and graduation ceremonies were prohibited. In 2000, students were forbidden from praying over loudspeakers at high school football games as well.[113]

In 1982, in considering the constitutionality of Alabama's "voluntary moment of meditation" law in *Wallace v. Jaffrey*, the Supreme Court held that: "It is not the activity itself that concerns us; it is the purpose of the activity."[114] In seeking to ascertain the intent of the legislator who had authored the bill, it found that: "The 'prime sponsor' of the bill . . . explained that it was an effort to return voluntary prayer to our public schools.'"[115] Therefore, the statute was:

> invalid because the sole purpose . . . was an effort by the State of Alabama to encourage a religious activity.. . .(It) is a law respecting the establishment of religion within the meaning of the First Amendment.[116]

In other words, the Court ruled that while meditation itself contravened no law, the statute itself became unconstitutional because its sponsor's motives were incipiently religious and thus impure – making more evident than ever that *Comintern* thought-control today reigns supreme in the nation's federal court system.[117]

Yet the beat goes on. In New Jersey, school officials prevented a grade school student from reading his favorite story because it came from the *Bible* — and in another case, barred an elementary school student from handing out gifts pencils bearing the inscription "Jesus loves the little children" and candy canes bearing attached cards referring to the birth of Jesus — and in Pennsylvania, a teacher's assistant was suspended from school because she wore a necklace with a cross.[118]

In Alaska, public school students were told that they could not use the word "Christmas" in school because it had the word "Christ" in it – that the word could not appear in their conversations or even in their notebooks and that they could not exchange Christmas cards or gifts. In Virginia, a federal court ruled that a homosexual newspaper may be distributed on a high school campus but a religious newspaper could not.[119] In Colorado, an elementary school teacher was compelled to stop teaching Christmas carols because of alleged violations of church and state.

And in Nebraska, a ten-year-old child was prohibited from reading his *Bible* during free time at school.[120]

In a Colorado case, a federal judge ruled that a teacher could not been seen in school carrying his personal *Bible* and also stipulated that a classroom library containing 237 books must remove two bearing Christian titles. In another ironic case, at the very time the "American Civil Liberties Union" (ACLU) – the legalistic societal battering ram of the liberal left – was in Louisiana challenging the right of teachers to conduct voluntary private prayer during school recess, its counterpart in Tennessee was suing the city of Nashville for prohibiting the practice of fortune-telling on its public premises.[121]

*Ad infinitum* – as pursuant to the radical judicial agenda of the ACLU, religious values are today being systematically expunged from the nation's schools. The germane questions, in these instances, thus become: where is the national church that is being "established" by the individual acts of faith being purged, and where is the coercion to believe in it?

The net effect of such modern disparate "judicial legislating," however, is that the American corpus of civil law, as interpreted by the U.S. Supreme Court, has today become a tangled polyglot of conflicting provisions as it pertains to the nation's schools which have been juridically scrubbed of every vestige of those firm religious precepts upon which America was founded. As in a litigious litany of judicial double standards:[122]

* Though the Supreme Court opens its sessions every day with prayer, the nation's institutions of public learning are forbidden from doing so.
* Though it is constitutional for U.S. governmental chaplains to pray, it is unconstitutional for students to hear or read those prayers.
* Though it is constitutional to display the Ten Commandments on public property, including in the U.S. Supreme Court, it is unconstitutional for students to see them.
* Though it is constitutional to commence public meetings with invocations, it is unconstitutional to allow students to hear those invocations.
* Though witches are allowed in the classroom at Halloween in October, Christ isn't allowed in at Christmas in December.

Indeed, the nation's courts, at the instigation, in no small part, of the ACLU – who have become to free religious thought in the Christian West what the Taliban are to free religious thought in the Islamic East – have today so intimidated the public schools that they now go to absurd lengths to excise any reference whatsoever to a Supreme Being — to the extent that a California school recently prohibited a teacher from providing his students with "excerpts from the Declaration of Independence, the diaries of George Washington and John Adams, the writings of William Penn, and various state constitutions because of the documents' references to God."[123]

Again, to what end? Saying prayers at public sporting events, reciting "under God" in the Pledge of Allegiance, and experiencing a moment of silent meditation do not constitute mandated, top-down enforcement of religious practice or belief.

To the contrary, such expressions of faith are no more than basic conventions dedicated to the precepts of morality and patriotism as employed by a civil society that is not openly hostile to religion.[124]

## C. Expunging God From Public Life

But the ongoing judicial assault on God in America today extends well beyond the schools. On June 27, 2002, the Ninth Circuit Court of Appeals in San Francisco decided that the words "under God" in the Pledge of Allegiance also were a violation of the separation of church and state. Notwithstanding that the use of the phrase was fully consonant with the tenets of the Constitution's framers, that Lincoln had used it in the Gettysburg address, and that the Supreme Court had long ruled that no one could involuntarily be compelled to cite the Pledge, the "anti-God" component of the judiciary could not abide even this free will exercise of America's most profound expression of patriotism.[125]

In August, 2003, moreover, in gestapo-like fashion, pursuant to an order of U.S. District Court Judge Myron Thompson, a 350 pound monument bearing an inscription of the Ten Commandments – the spiritual basis of American law, and as such, carved into the U.S. Supreme Court Building in Washington, D.C. – was forcibly dragged, over strong local public objection, under the supervision of counter-cultural "morals police," from the Alabama Judicial Building.[126]

Thus culminated yet another successful judicial attempt to remove every vestige of God from the public square –with Alabama Chief Supreme Court Justice Roy Moore also subsequently removed from office three months later for "obstruction of justice" for resisting this federal intrusion into his courtroom. What's worse, Alabama's citizens were forced to reimburse the ACLU $540,000 in tax dollars to cover its attorneys fees and expenses for its role in effecting this abomination.[127]

The legal pretext for removing monuments such as the Ten Commandments issues, of course, stems from judicial reference to the First Amendment's "establishment of religion" clause. But the rationale is utterly specious. Monuments are not laws; a public square is not the Congress; and the Ten Commandments are not a religion. Indeed, every major world religion subscribes to their fundamental precepts.[128]

In California, in 1990, in *Warsaw v. Tehachapi*, the U.S. District Court likewise determined that a public cemetery couldn't maintain a planter in the shape of a cross since the mere sight of it could cause "emotional distress" to passers-by and thereby constitute "injury in fact." In Oregon, a war memorial in the shape of a cross was similarly ruled unconstitutional. In Nevada, a fire station was forced to remove from its premises a cross placed in remembrance of a colleague who had lost his life in the line of duty.[129]

Similarly, backed by the courts, the California ACLU – the same ACLU that, by federal court order, got the Boy Scouts of America kicked out of a San Diego park which they had leased for camping purposes for decades on the grounds that it was a "religious organization" – forced Los Angeles County to remove a tiny cross from its official municipal seal on the grounds that it violated the "separation-of-church-and-state-doctrine" – despite the fact the cross represented the *historical* founding of Los Angeles by Catholic missionaries and wasn't advocating *religion* in any way.[130]

Constitutionally, of course, such modern exegetical judicial rational is founded upon questionable logic if there is any logic to be found at all. It is, in fact, doubtless what Thomas Jefferson had in mind when he wrote that: "The germ of dissolution of our federal government is in . . . the federal judiciary, working like gravity by night and day . . . advancing its noiseless step like a thief, over the field of jurisdiction, until all shall be usurped by from the States" — thus "to consider judges as ultimate arbiters of all constitutional questions (is) a dangerous doctrine that would place us under the despotism of an oligarchy. . . . The Constitution has erected no such single tribunal."[131]

James Madison, in like manner, warned: "As the courts are generally last in making decisions (on laws), it results to them, by refusing or not refusing to execute a law, to stamp its final character. This makes the Judiciary paramount in fact to the Legislature, which was never intended and can never be proper."[132]

Alexander Hamilton, in turn, in *Federalist No. 81*, argued that it was never the Founders' intent to give to the federal courts the power to strike down laws: "In the first place, there is not a single syllable in the plan under consideration which directly empowers the national courts to construe the laws according to the spirit of the Constitution."[133]

All of which led Jefferson to pessimistically conclude of the courts already in his day: "The Constitution . . . is a mere thing of wax . . . in the hands of the judiciary, which they may twist and shape into any form they please. . . .They have retreated into the judiciary as a stronghold . . . and from that battery, all works of republicanism are to be beaten down and erased."[134]

Thus spake the Founding Fathers. Indeed, if sheer volume is any relevant indication of their intent, it may be noteworthy that in its enumeration of powers, the Constitution devotes 255 lines of expressed powers to the Congress — and 114 lines to the President – but only 44 lines to the Courts. The simple reason: the Founders did not contemplate a powerful judicial system and thus did not feel the need to place powerful constraints upon it.[135]

What is happening in America's courts today, therefore, is not about an abstract legal theory respecting the "separation of church and State," it is about the courts, as one of the three principal arms of state, meddling in the people's First-Amendment-guaranteed right to freedom of worship and religious expression. For if "original intent" now means nothing, what is left to judicially interpret? [136]

Were Congress to promulgate a law prohibiting under-aged youth from praying and reading the *Bible*, as the Court by fiat has done, the Court would rightly rule the act to be patently illegal. But regrettably Lady Justice is no longer blind in America! Her blindfold has been snatched away by leftist-leaning courts who have betrayed the very Constitution that they have sworn to uphold – in so doing, routinely making law, that if enacted by Congress, would ruled unconstitutional. By so doing, a simple majority of five members of a nine member Court – unelected officials not directly answerable to the people – has thus usurped the power of the land.[137]

Indeed, this is a power triumphantly proclaimed by the Court itself in *Wallace v. Jeffrey* (1984) when it ruled: "Federal district courts and circuit courts are bound to adhere to the controlling decisions of this Supreme Court. . . . A precedent of this Court must be followed by the lower federal courts no matter how misguided the judges of those courts may think it to be. . . . Only this Court may overrule one of its precedents."[138]

This ruling comes in affirmation of a determination originally established in *State Board of Education v. Board of Education of Netcong*, (1970); that: "Trial courts cannot claim right to independent determination of the United States Constitution and is obligated to apply the law as pronounced by superior judicial authority."[139] Given these realities, then, there can be but two possible outcomes to this Promethean jurisprudential struggle: either the Constitution must constrain the judges, or the judges will destroy the Constitution.[140]

The true absurdity, however, is that this entire corpus of errant "separation " law is founded upon nine words in a private political campaign letter from Thomas Jefferson to a religious group taken entirely out of context by the federal courts. Accordingly, given that:

> (1) Jefferson wrote his letter in 1802, thirteen years after Congress passed the First Amendment;
> (2) Jefferson was not a delegate to the 1787 Constitutional Convention nor was he member of the Congress in 1789 when the First Amendment was drafted;
> (3) Nor was he a member of any state legislature or ratifying convention involved with the First Amendment at this time — as he was serving as U.S. Minister to France throughout this entire period — it is patently obvious that:
> (4) Jefferson was not physically positioned to speak competently to the intent of the Founders respecting the original intent of the First Amendment;
> (5) His actual words issued in private have been twisted to construe a meaning exactly opposite of what he said; to wit: "that the state must be protected from the church;" and that there is therefore
> (6) no "wall of separation" embedded within the Constitution, unless it is a wall intended by the Founders to keep government out of the affairs of the church.[141]

This was, in fact, the early conclusion of the Court as well, in ruling in *Church of the Holy Trinity v. U.S.* in 1892 that:

> No purpose of action against religion can be imputed to any legislation, state or national, because this is a religious people. . . . This is a Christian nation.[142]

In sum, the cancer of radical secularism has now metastasized throughout the nation's entire judicial system — as the infamous "wall of separation" has, in just six decades, turned the soul of America from being a "Christian nation" to that of an agnostic state hostile to its own religious heritage – one wherein the concerns of a whole community may be subordinated to the perceived sensitivities of a single

90    *Chapter Three*

self-serving atheist.

As commencing with *McCollum v. Board of Education* in 1948, and continuing to the present day, America's jurisprudence respecting the role of religion in pubic life has set upon a dangerous and patently misguided course – for in interpreting "church" to mean any religious activity, the federal courts now hold as unconstitutional even many of the regular daily religious practices of the Founders who produced both Constitution and its landmark First Amendment.[143]

## IV. Judicial Activism Run Amok

Accordingly, notwithstanding the flawed legal precedents involved, what is incontrovertible is that America's ever-evolving judicially-mandated church-state bifurcation has not stemmed from happenstance. Instead, it has issued from the carefully constructed designs of the extremist left and its liberal Court surrogates. For despite the fact that Christian values were explicitly built into the structure of the nation by the Founders, today's political elites have decided that they, and the founding documents that they forged, no longer have a place in the nation's public life.[144]

How else can one explain Justice Ruth Bader Ginsberg's declaration that she and her fellow justices now look to international law as the basis for their decisions, as she did in a speech to the American Constitution Society in 2003? — or Justice Stephen Breyer's questioning of the Constitution as appropriate for governing America in the future, as he did on ABC's *This Week* in 2004? The answers are as obvious as they are unsettling: America's judiciary is gradually, and increasingly, drifting away from the high legal principles upon which the nation was founded and descending into the cess pit of a godless proletarian society.[145]

For there is no question that within recent decades, the courts have discovered "rights" within the Constitution that are neither part of the enumerated nor unenumerated entitlements designed to be protected by that document, notwithstanding that it is not their defined role to find or establish rights that are not constitutionally permitted. For that precious document's framers clearly intended to create a limited constitutional republic – a polity with islands of democratic power in a sea of liberty, not a sea of statist powers surrounding isolated islands of liberty.[146]

The core question thus arises, given that a tiny handful of non-believers cannot be compelled to recite the "under God" pledge, do they concurrently have the right to impose their atheism on the vast majority of those Americans whose beliefs both now and historically have defined America as a religious nation? The California-based Ninth Circuit Court of Appeals believes they do.[147]

Irrespective of the grim reality that if judges can interpret the Constitution or its derivative laws in a manner not intended by their original makers, and that the nation's founding precepts thus become meaningless, regrettably, the fact is that, as Justice Charles Evans Hughes said, " the Constitution is what the judges say it is."[148] The new difference now, however, is that while in the past, the question was *how* to read the Constitution, under the new approach the question has become *whether* to read the Constitution at all.[149]

It is not surprising, then, that the *Bible* – the sacred document upon which all executive, legislative, and judicial public oaths historically have been taken – is now already banned in some legislatures, schools, and graduation ceremonies – and is becoming increasingly unwelcome in the nation's courtrooms as well. And thus it is that unlike pornography and free speech – which are cherished First Amendment rights in the view of the present courts – the free expression of religion has been banned from the public square by judicial fiat.[150]

Already concerned about these dangers in his time, Abraham Lincoln in his First Inaugural Address, delivered on March 4, 1861, warned that: "The candid citizen must confess that if the policy of the government upon vital questions affecting the whole people is to be irrevocably fixed by the decisions of the Supreme Court, the instant they are made . . . the people will have ceased to be their own rulers, having . . . resigned their government into the hands of that eminent tribunal."[151]

Small wonder that after three decades on the Supreme court bench, the late Chief Justice William Rehnquist would accuse the nation's judiciary of: "bristling with hostility to all things religious in public life." Small wonder also that Whittaker Chambers in *Witness* would write: "History is cluttered with the wreckage of nations that became indifferent to their God and died." For in the past half century, the courts have moved from recognizing the vital role that religion plays in a republic to erratically allowing mere symbolic vestiges of it at their sublime tolerance.[152]

Indeed, at a time when fourth-fifths of America confess to faith-based moorings, a small liberal leftist fringe is being permitted to dictate the nation's religious values. In this bizarre but sinister process, people who aspire to a religious faith have permitted themselves to be psychologically intimidated by secular humanists who disparage their willingness to fight for their beliefs.

They have instead too often sacrificed those beliefs in a quest to reassure their accusers that they too are well intentioned and full of compassion and really aren't "bigots" – a leftist pejorative term perhaps best defined as describing "those who are winning arguments vis-à-vis liberals." In the war for those social and moral issues that once defined America's greatness, therefore, many have largely fled the battlefield, in effect becoming conscientious objectors in the politically correct nonsense that is the ongoing cultural war.[153]

As a consequence of this ideological devolution, the nation has permitted leftist, activist courts to redefine the First Amendment as sanctioning public policy as advocated by Karl Marx, Betty Friedan, and Al Sharpton, but not on tenets prescribed by the *Bible*. To quote Ronald Reagan in December, 1984: "We even had to pass a law – pass a special law in Congress a few weeks ago – to allow student prayer groups the same access to school rooms after classes that a 'Young Marxist Society' would already enjoy with no opposition." [154]

In all of these determinations, then, the Court has overturned the constitutionality of policy choices reflecting historic values made in the ordinary political process, only to substitute radical new policies to further the social agenda of political radicals. Decisions of any comparable importance reversing that course, on the other hand, are conspicuous by their absence – as in the guise of enforcing the Constitution, the Court has instead enacted the agenda of the counter-cultural revolution.[155]

Indeed, the effect of the judicial interventions since the 1950s onset of the so-called "Warren Court" has been overwhelmingly to undermine or overthrow traditional American beliefs and practices on basic issues of domestic social policy. Yet in its sanctimonious arbitrariness, there is no oversight respecting its decisions; it is not only above the law, its decisions, as it insists, are the law – a reality that led Justice Robert Marshall to assert: "We are not final because we are infallible, but we are infallible because we are final."[156]

The consummate irony, however, is that today – hewing to Alexis de Tocqueville's observation that religion is foremost amongst America's political institutions because it is "indispensable to the maintenance of republican institutions," the United States remains an overwhelming practicing Christian nation – with the vast majority of her populace describing themselves as "Christian" – with 54.7 percent self-identifying as Protestant, 22 percent as Catholic, and another 2.7 percent as "other Christian," according to a 2004 survey by the "Pew Forum on Religion and Public Life." That is, as calculated, nearly 80 percent of the nation's populace.[157]

Notwithstanding, America appears to be legally entering a "post-Christian age" – witnessing a dramatic shift away from longstanding civic practices inculcated by religion – societal well being, communal attachment, altruism, and the sanctity of commitment that have been her historic sources of strength, and instead toward a militant secularism focused predominantly upon self.[158]

In the process, traditional cultural values are under challenge. School systems founded on the classics are being transformed into propaganda centers for secular humanistic counter-cultural diversity. The news media and other major national institutions are becoming *un*-Christian, even *anti*-Christian. America appears to be entering its post-Christian age, in fact, through a seemingly fervent quest to validate the assertions of German philosopher Nietzsche that: "God is dead . . . and we have killed Him."[159]

There is thus no question, then, that America has lost her moral bearing, as the triage of her traditional values makes manifest. No less a jurist than Sandra Day O'Connor, who delivered the Supreme Court's decision in *Hudson vs. Macmillan*, wrote, in fact, of "those evolving standards of decency that mark the progress of a maturing society."[160]

With such sentiments, she epitomizes the symptoms of the modern activist court – that justices are today mandated to interpret the law beyond the scope of the Constitution – thereby allowing them to venture freely into uncharted moral and ethical waters to unilaterally determine how Americans should act and think. As Lino Graglia, professor of law at the University of Texas, has asserted:

> The thing to know to comprehend about contemporary constitutional law is that,

almost without exception, the effect of rulings of unconstitutionality over the past four decades has been to enact the policy preferences of the cultural elite on the far left of the American political spectrum.[161]

To which his university colleague Stanford Levinson appends: "The death of constitutionalism may be the central event of our time, just as the death of God was that of the past century."[162]

In sum, today's judges no longer seemingly feel constrained by the defining dicta of the nation's foremost governing documents, as they fervently work to alter the nation's laws to conform them to their own political ideologies.

They have, in the process, instead moved from their constitutionally-defined function of interpreting the law – "judicial constructionism," strictly interpreting the law, yet not making it – to a manifestly unconstitutional one of legislatively rewriting it, a function that is not their job. For constitutions are not expository writings. They are instead the repository of the values, ideas, and symbols that constitute a society's well being.[163]

The U.S. Constitution, of course, can legally be changed through the amendment process – as it has been seventeen times since the passage of its first ten amendments now known as the "Bill of Rights." Undoubtedly also, there remain some fine legal constructionist federal judges committed to the upholding of due process. Yet today, too many jurists see themselves not as humble guardians of a two-centuries-old sacred governing contract between America and her people, but rather as high priests of an emerging new social order destined to chart the course of civilization in a new and more enlightened globalist world.[164]

Again, it bears repeating that those are not the conditions of their appointments. For if the Constitution can indeed be changed on the whimsy of jurists, then the nation has no real constitution at all. Whatever happened to that strict constructionist interpretation is the cornerstone of both just jurisprudence and natural law — now having been replaced by revolutionary value judgement made by non-elected judicial partisans?[165]

What happened to that system of "checks and balances" amongst the three branches of government contemplated by the Founders when they carefully debated and wrote the Constitution in Philadelphia in 1787? The reality is that, by absolute law, the Supreme Court is "supreme" only over the other federal courts – and Congress explicitly retains the constitutional power by legislative act to restrict the jurisdiction of the federal courts.[166]

Notwithstanding, the unconstrained judicial rampaging of the courts continues, as at the bottom line, liberals despise religion because it is a religious substitute for secular liberalism, and they can't stand the competition, with the ongoing judicial trashing of the Ten Commandments particularly egregious – giving rise to a multitude of jurisprudential questions, among them:

"Which of the Ten Commandments violate deeply-held cherished liberal judicial beliefs? Is it:"

— Remember the Sabbath Day to keep it holy . . .?

— Honor thy father and thy mother. . . .?
— Thou shall not kill. . . .?
— Thou shall not commit adultery. . . .?
— Thou shall not steal. . . .?
— Thou shall not bear false witness against thy neighbor. . . .

These are precepts that have enjoyed wide subscription throughout the course of human history. "The Ten Commandments and the Sermon on the Mount contain my religion," John Adams proclaimed. The Reverend John Witherspoon, signer of the Declaration of Independence and mentor to James Madison, called them "the sum of moral law." Daniel Webster said of them: "If we and our posterity shall be true to the Christian religion, if we and they shall live in the fear of God and respect His Commandments. . . . then we shall have the highest hopes for the future fortunes of our country."[167]

Harry Truman concurred: "The fundamental basis of this nation's laws were given to Moses on the Mount."[168] Whereas Ronald Reagan apprised: "We must start with the Ten Commandments. If we lived by the Golden Rule, then there would be no need for other laws."[169] In a May 6, 1983 speech, Reagan added:"If we could just keep remembering that Moses brought down from the mountain the Ten Commandment, not ten suggestions — and if those of us who live for the Lord could remember that He wants us to love our Lord and our neighbor, then there is no limit to the problems that we could solve or the mountains that we could move as a mighty force for good."[170]

The possibility cannot be discounted, of course, that the conceptual recognition problem here at work may simply be one of remembrance as President Reagan also suggested — that the commandments have now have been out-of-sight for so long that few know precisely what they really are or what they say.[171] So again, precisely what is it to which the counter-culturalists and their judicial cohorts, using the Constitution as a pretext, object in such dicta so as to justify their unconditional and absolute removal from schools, courtrooms, and other public places? What noble ideals do they violate?

On their face, the Ten Commandments appear neither draconian nor esoteric in their prescription. Indeed, they are not just legal constructs within the Western values system, nor are they mere Judeo-Christian idiosyncrasies. They are instead part of a continuum of "Natural Law" that has existed since the dawn of time. Indeed, subscribing to anything less would be barbarous to the cause of civilization as mankind has known it in the course of written history.

Hence, Thucydides, in his *History of the Peloponnesian War*, was moved to write: "For of the Gods, we believe, and of the men we know, that by a necessity of their nature wherever they have the power, they always rule. And in our case, since we neither enacted this law, nor when it was enacted were the first to use it, but found it in existence, and expect to leave it in existence for all time." Sophocles, the 5$^{th}$ century B.C. Greek poet, in his tragedy *Antigone*, likewise demonstrated that ancient Greece employed such immortal concepts of Natural Law.[172]

The Roman Republic, successor to democratic Greece, also fully accepted such universal laws of morality and human interaction. Thus, the Roman Senator-Philosopher Cicero would proclaim:

> There is, in fact, a true law, namely right reason, which is in accordance with nature, which applies to all men and is interchangeable and eternal.... It will not lay down one rule at Rome and another at Athens, nor will it be one rule today and another tomorrow. But there will be one rule, eternal, binding at all times and upon all peoples.[173]

In the first century A.D., St. Paul similarly equated the *Bible's* "Ten Commandments" with Natural Law – observing that the Gentiles, for whom the mandates were not incorporated within their scriptures, nonetheless observed them, because, as he expresses in Romans 2:14-15, they had them "written in their hearts."[174] Why, then," Martin Luther asks in his 15th century catechism, "does one teach the Ten Commandments? Because Natural Law was never so well-written as by Moses!"[175]

Thus, the compatibility of the Ten Commandments with the workings of Natural Law is nearly fully universally subscribed. Yet in a modern context, using the ACLU and the U.S. Supreme Court as their legal battering rams, counterculturalists, in *Stone v. Graham (*1980), have succeeded in banning the posting of the Ten Commandments in American public schools.[176]

The practical ramifications? – American students are precluded from reading them, and teachers are prevented from teaching them, with the net result that the next generation of national leaders may never know that many of the nation's civil and criminal laws – "Thou shalt not kill;" "Thou shalt not steal;" "Thou shalt not commit adultery" – all are derived from the biblical Ten Commandments or even the underlying moral precepts for why such mandates should be fastidiously obeyed.[177]

Several years ago, *Nightline's* Ted Koppel, echoing President Reagan, in a university commencement address, asserted that the Ten Commandments are far more than merely "ten tentative suggestions" to be considered when addressing the nation's moral and cultural challenges.

It is unfortunate, therefore, that today, this sage counsel appears to have been, for all intents, forgotten. For to quote contemporary social commentator Kenneth Woodward: "Good hymns are works of art, not ideology. Their integrity deserves respect and so do the traditions from whence they came."[178]

Great civilizations *do* die from core value cultural rot. One needs only to recall what happened to the golden age of ancient Greece, to the once mighty Roman Empire, and to Adolph Hitler's vaunted "Third Reich" that he proclaimed would last a thousand years. All three died when they came to condone civil conduct that contravened the workings of Natural Law. Indeed, the pages of history are strewn with the remains of ruined societies that thought they could reject Natural Law with impunity. Is it sheer accident, then, that the twentieth century's most demonic mass murderers – Hitler, Stalin, Mao Zedong, and Pol Pot – were all militant atheists?[179]

Nevertheless, ongoing attempts to politically and judicially deconstruct religious conviction within America egregiously continues in contravention of the cogent lessons of the past. John Adams believed that her Constitution requires "a religious and moral people." Thomas Jefferson's First Inaugural Address invoked "that infinite power which rules the destiny of the universe . . . to lead our counsels to what is best." James Madison asserted that "we have staked our future . . . upon the capacity of each of us to govern ourselves in accordance with the Ten Commandments of God" – a commitment to Divine Law affirmed in John Kennedy's Inaugural Address that "the rights of man come not from the state but from the hand of God."[180]

It is no coincidence, therefore, that the nascent nation's Declaration of Independence made clear that the rights that it was proclaiming were God-inspired and God-given and could never be taken away by kings or governments:

> We hold these truths to be self-evident, that all men are created equal, and that *they are endowed by their Creator with certain unalienable Rights*, that among these are Life, Liberty, and the Pursuit of Happiness.[181]

Powerful words that the Founders employed to construct the foundations of "God's nation:"

— "Self evident," that universal truths divined through reason are its raison d'être;
— "Creator," that a Supreme Being guides the destiny of nations and their citizens;
— "Unalienable rights" that are defined by God's Law which no government can take away; and
— "Liberty and the pursuit of happiness" as unimpeachable parts of the human birthright.[182]

Now, however, those precious precepts have been abandoned. The nation's court system has banned public display of the Ten Commandments on federal property, claiming that it violates the very Constitution that Madison led in authoring. They reject, and likely would be appalled at, Madison's belief that "before any man can be considered a member of civil society, he must first be considered as a subject of the Governor of the Universe."[183]

As today, American governance is powerfully shaped by secular elites who maintain that religion and patriotism are mere opiates for the masses – self-delusions of the uneducated that can be cured through radical reindoctrination if detected and corrected early on. They feel that (i) a belief in God, if He or She exists at all, is irrational, dangerous to democracy, and has no place in public life; (ii) that any mention of God in national life or as the basis for law or governmental action is both unconstitutional and reprehensible; (iii) that "right and wrong" can be subjectively defined without recourse to God's law, and (iv) that it is logically impossible to deem otherwise.

This is a federal court system, it must be recalled, that has taken the positions:

\* That the specific, literal language of the First Amendment must be abandoned;
\* That in its place should be substituted the nebulous concept of a "wall of separa-

tion between church and state" that has no literal basis in any founding document;
* That the term "establishment of religion" means every "religion, religious organization, or institution," regardless of its form or religious function;
* That "an establishment of religion" also means financial support of religion in any form;
* That it likewise forbids the commingling of religious and secular instruction in any way; and
* That to even think otherwise, as in the case of legislative intent, is equally unconstitutional.[184]

What kind of precedent does this set – when the nation's court system presumes two centuries after the fact to be able to respectively divine what Jefferson and Madison meant even as their open declarations proclaim otherwise — directly contradicting what those two great Founders wrote in order to be able to deliver a decision of what the modern court thinks "it ought to be?

Every president in the nation's history has approved the use of public funds for religious purposes, including monies for military and congressional chaplains, and in the era of Jefferson and Madison, both sons of Episcopalians, for missionaries to the American Indians. Their actions, in fact, clearly convey their intent:[185]

### Actions of Jefferson and Madison Regarding Freedom of Religion[186]

| Thomas Jefferson: | James Madison: |
| --- | --- |
| * Supported the use of tax funds to pay the chaplains of the Congress and the U.S. Armed Services.<br>* Recommended a "School of Theology" for training clergymen in the public education system of the State of Virginia.<br>*Designated a special room at the University of Virginia for religious worship.<br>*Supported the use of tax money to promote religion and religious education amongst the Indians. | * Supported the use of tax funds to pay the chaplains of the Congress and the U.S. Armed Services.<br>* Served on the Congressional Committee that planned and operated the chaplain system for the Congress.<br>* Argued that the word "establish" in the First Amendment applied only federally.<br>*Supported the use of tax money to promote religion and religious education amongst the Indians. |

Thus, it is clear that both Jefferson and Madison supported equally the "no establishment of religion" and "freedom of religious liberties" clauses of the First Amendment. Jefferson's "Bill for Establishing Religious Freedom" designed to disestablish the Anglican Church in Virginia, enacted in 1786, and Madison's "Memorial and Remonstrance Against Religious Assessments," penned in 1785 in protest of the use of Virginia public funds to pay teachers of the Christian religion, clearly affirm their support of the "establishment clause."[187]

Yet Jefferson concurrently advocated that tax-supported College of William and Mary maintain a "perpetual mission among the Indian tribes" to provide instruction in " the principles of Christianity;" and wanted a professorial chair at the University of Virginia that would develop "the Proofs of the being of God, the Creator, Preserver, and Supreme Ruler of the universe."[188]

He also commended to the Congress a treaty with the Kaskaskia Indians that provided federal funds for a Catholic priest to minister to their spiritual needs, and gave federal land grants to charitable societies dedicated to propagating the Gospel amongst the Indians.[189]

Jefferson likewise introduced into the Virginia Assembly legislation (1) "annulling marriages prohibited by Levitical law;" (2)" punishing disturbers of religious worship and Sabbath breakers;" and (3) "appointing days of fasting and thanksgiving." A new Constitution that he proposed for the state contained a reference to the "Sovereign Disposer of all human events." As the state's highest elected official, he thus found no particular difficulty advocating religious issues and religion, and the Christian religion in particular.[190]

James Madison, in turn, was a member of the committee that recommended the Congressional chaplain system.[191] In 1785, he introduced into the Virginia Assembly "A Bill for Punishing Disturbers of Religious Worship and Sabbath Breakers" which sought to impose a ten shilling fine for every offense of working on Sunday.[192] In that same year, he introduced "A Bill for Appointing Days of Public Fasting and Thanksgiving."[193] Thus, the Founding Fathers leave no doubt that while they wanted to prevent the establishment of a national religion, preservation of free exercise religious practice was an equal policy concern.[194]

Accordingly, if what America's Founders, in their wisdom, deliberately put into the Constitution is to be disregarded by the Court, and its exact opposite – a legal position that, in the form of a proposed constitutional amendment, has been rejected eleven times by the Congress in the nation's history – is now to be adopted and enforced merely because the doctrine fits the political predispositions and zeal of those jurists who happen to be serving at any given time – then the Constitution disintegrates from its status as supreme law into mere historic curiosity.[195] In the famous admonition of Chief Justice John Marshall: "We must never forget that it is a *Constitution* that we are expounding."[196]

Yet that is precisely what is happening in America today. For if the First Amendment can be construed as to constrain rather than promote religious freedom, and the Fourteenth Amendment can be tortured into prohibiting the states from having laws or constitutional provisions addressing religion, then those two amendments and the Founders' intent will have been decimated *in toto*, and atheism – having been transformed into the national religion – will have won.[197]

Indeed, anticipating this problem already in his time in speaking to the Founders' original intent, Jefferson himself perhaps explained it best: "On every question of construction, we must carry ourselves back to the time when the Constitution was adopted, recollect the spirit manifest in the debates, and instead of trying to determine what meaning can be squeezed out of the text, or invented against it, conform to the probable one in which it was passed."[198]

To which James Wilson, one of only six Founders to have signed both the Declaration of Independence and the Constitution, appended: "The first and governing maxim in the interpretation of a statute is to discover the meaning of those who made it." As Justice Oliver Wendell Holmes alternately put it: "A page of history is worth a volume of logic."[199]

Hence, to ignore the Founders' intent in favor of judicial predilection is a precipitous policy course whose outcome can only end in cultural disaster. For in the last analysis, whenever any society has abandoned its respect for its venerated values – its civic, social, and economic institutions and its respect for the rule of law — that nation, at that point, has experienced the onset of its ultimate demise.[200]

Fully cognizant that America has given the world prosperity, liberty, and democracy – the best that has been thought and taught – that she remains a country well worth fighting for and the last best hope of earth – the question therefore must be asked: "Will this be America's fate as well?"

In the quest for remedy, legal recourse thus must focus not on the establishment clause *per se*, but instead upon the universally constitutionally guaranteed right to free speech – reflecting the reality that faith is foremost among the requisite survival values for a free society. For in the words of both John Kennedy and Ronald Reagan, liberty is a gift of God, not an indulgence of the federal government. As Samuel Huntington has similarly assessed: "Those countries that are the most religious tend to be the most nationalistic."[201]

One reality is certain: If the Republic and the values for which it stood for two centuries are to now persevere — if its people are to continue to enjoy "the blessings of Liberty to ourselves and our Posterity" that its Constitution prescribes — then America must once again restore her erstwhile framework of moral order based upon the foundation principles of her forefathers – leaders of the stature of George Washington, John Adams, Thomas Jefferson, and James Madison – all of whom were aware of the portent of the scriptural admonitions:[202]

> When the righteous are in authority, the people rejoice;
> (Proverbs 29:2)
> and
> Blessed is the nation whose God is the Lord!
> (Psalm 33:12)

# Chapter Four
# The Ideology of the Counter-Culture

*Is there any alternative other than the dictatorship of an 'elite' over the people?*

—1960s pop counter-cultural philosopher Herbert Marcuse

### I. Portents of the Death of God

Is God dead? — asked *Time Magazine* on an April 8, 1966 cover featuring foreboding trends that portended His obituary. Similar proclamations have subsequently issued from a multitude of sources. Indeed, the posited death of God had been a recurring theme in modern history. As expressed by Friedrich Nietzsche's madman: "Whither is God? I shall tell you. We have killed Him – you and I."[1] To which Dostoevsky notoriously appended: "If God is dead, then everything is permitted!"[2]

Commencing in the 1960s, this notion of the death of God has permuted into a post-theocratic"feel good" secular ideology devoid of inner meaning – turning the very term *"god"* into a concept bearing little more in meaning than its palindrome *"dog."* In this ongoing process of "religious secularization," both the church and the traditional family have been subordinated as historic socializing forces. Once the twin bedrocks of American existence, they have become mere alternate lifestyle options amongst many – the "open church," the "singles culture," homosexuality, cohabitation, communal living, and the like.[3]

The 1960s were an historic American watershed, as new centers of power, in the name of what was euphemistically called by some "rich kids' radicalism — interests vested with too much to live with, and too little to live for — triumphed over older values – urban over rural, secular liberalism over orthodox religion, flag-burning over patriotism, and hedonistic lifestyles over a traditional family ethic. Ephemeral "ecstasy" seemingly had prevailed.[4]

Accordingly, atavistic "counter-culturalism," as it is today preached and practiced within America, has become a multi-headed hydra. As defined in one acclaimed analysis, it is:

> a leftist political ideology that sees all cultures, their mores and their institutions, as essentially equal. No culture is considered superior or inferior to any other; it is merely different. Criticism of other cultures, especially non-Western/minority cultures, is labeled "insensitive" or bigoted.
> There is one major exception, however. Euro-American culture, with its Judeo-Christian underpinnings, is not only criticized, but often condemned, accused of racism, sexism, and classism.[5]

Succinctly put, counter-culturalism views Euro-American culture as not having been of abiding value to non-Western and minority cultures; hence, its values and truths must be discarded as specious and irrelevant. As aptly encapsulated by social commentator Dinesh D'Souza, the phenomenon "represents a denial of all Western claims to truth."[6]

How did this deconstruction happen? How did America lose her historic roots? The nation's inception was founded upon an inspiring vision. John Winthrop, the Pilgrim preacher on the Arabella, likened her to a "city on a hill." Drawing upon the Scriptures, he proclaimed;

> Ye are the light of the world. A city that is set on a hill cannot be hid. . . . [7]
> Let your lights so shine before men that they shall see your good works and glorify your Father which is in heaven.[8]

For two centuries, drawing upon the wisdom and aspirations of the Founders, America prospered in that vision. But today, she has lost that lofty status and harbors much that should concern her – the collapse of morality enforced by law – multiculturalism and political correctness– intellectual elites experimenting with new ideas that are not only revolutionary but alien to her founding fundamental beliefs – and finally, the rise of irreligiousity and a growing disrespect for human life. Consequently, she has come to a moment of crisis like none other in her history.[9]

For in the process of deconstructing the old order in which church and state shared a concern for the common good, the nation's core values are instead now being revolutionarily reinterpreted and dumbed down daily by its leftist political and educational establishments. In the classroom, the grand accomplishments of Western civilization–along with its entire canon of great literature –are being radically redefined and attendant social sciences are being reformed to conform to a secular social code of "moral relativism."[10]

What does this latter phrase mean? Simply this: as historic religion and expressions of faith are being officially being banished from the public square, in the absence of commonly held absolutes that have traditionally derived from faith, all values have become "relative." Longstanding ethics standards are being portrayed as arbitrary, authoritarian, and fascist – and concepts such as "right" and "wrong" are being condemned as totalitarian absolutism in the ongoing end game to overthrow the nation's legacy of Christian virtue and replace it with a self-serving form of cultist paganism.[11]

Concurrently, students are being told that Western culture is imperialist and exploitive by its very nature – characterized by racism, misogyny, and greed – and that the notion of its noble purpose is a fraud perpetuated by a self-serving patriarchy. At best, Western values are vacuous. At worst, they contravene the rich diversity of other regions of the world. In the process, the traditional "three Rs" – reading, writing, and arithmetic – have been replace by the three "Ss" — "self esteem," "sensitivity," and "safe sex."[12]

Accordingly, the nation today stands afflicted by three attriting forces:

— "cultural relativism," which holds that the traditional values of Western civilization are one-sided, bigoted, and destructive;
— "historical revisionism" that seeks to rewrite history in a way that better comports with the humanist "moral relativist" code; and
— a pernicious, suffocating form of "political correctness' that seeks to censor and destroy the free expression of ideas contrary to these goals – notwithstanding that censorship in the name of political correctness is tantamount to putting a band-aid over a metastasizing melanoma.[13]

As across the nation, the *cognescenti* – the *philosophes* and the *illluminati* — are working actively to undermine the legacy of the Founders. New societally remedial "expert systems" are being devised by the elites in government, the judicial system, academia, and the media – the extremist vanguard of a brave new leftist world waiting to be born.[14] But what they have actually done has been no more than to diminish America's standing before the planet wherein she was long admired for her traditional values of benevolence and the pursuit of self-determination – a vision that once was euphemistically called "pursuit of the American dream."

As a consequence, America has lost her erstwhile status as moral exemplar. While she is still regarded as the planet's premier economic and political power, she has lost the respect for decency that she once enjoyed. When the world views America now, she is no longer seen as a "shining city on a hill" but instead as a nation in peril – a civilization in decline. The faith and commitment of the Founders has become a relic of a long gone past. Like ancient Ozymandius glaring arrogantly to the heavens, as counter-culturalism proceeds, the nation's epitaph is being written upon the sarcophagi of the most damning cultural and moral failure of the age.[15]

Yet it need not be thus. For despite the *detritus* of recent political polemic, America has thrived socioeconomically because she has historically tacked religiously. She has endured far-out Surgeon Generals advocating the free distribution of condoms in elementary schools and legalizing narcotics nationwide — even as drugs destroy inner cities supplied by drug dealers who recognize no legal limits, leaving the nation's urban areas, the sources of her erstwhile industrial strength, in lingering mordant decline.[16]

At the same time, "welfare politics" – policies sustained by handout addiction – have created a vast "constituency of dependency" empowered by four generations of recipients, as the promise of cradle-to-grave support has gravely undermined the nation's erstwhile values of "work ethic," self-reliance, and integrity. Individual initiative thus today is no longer considered the most promising path to prosperity —as governmental largesse and public sector handouts have become foremost means to immediate self-gratification.[17]

But by thus looting the treasury, by constantly increasing the tax burden upon a declining number of taxpayers, and by incurring disastrous levels of debt through deficit spending, leftist-leaning politicians have undermined the nation's long term economic future by securing their own careers through buying off the votes of the nation's economic underclass.[18]

Tragically, in the process, the historic role of family as the social glue of society is being systematically destroyed. As graphically assessed by sociologist Amitai Etzioni in invoking the need to restore the traditional role of home and community, if modern Americans ran their businesses they way they now run their homes, the entire nation would grind to an immediate halt.[19]

More tragically still, such programs have done no more than to destroy hopes for a better future held by the would-be beneficiaries. As assessed by *Newsweek* columnist Joe Klein:

> It is impossible, of course, to pinpoint the precise moment when moral relativism became acceptable public policy — but in the Sixties, the structures of moral authority were systematically removed from the poorest neighborhoods.
> A series of legal judgments made it harder for teachers to discipline their students and for housing projects to screen their tenants; the cops on the street were seen as an occupying force and removed. Moral consequences of programs such as welfare were never considered.
> Instead of nurturing virtue, popular culture celebrated intemperance — and while intemperance, as Adam Smith pointed out 200 years ago, may addle the rich, it devastates the poor.[20]

America is thus succumbing to a process of gradual societal regression – as the progression of cultural decline continues to unfold as an incremental process. Best described as the 'Durkheim constant," as defined by French sociologist Emile Durkheim, it posits that there is a finite limit to the amount of deviant behavior that any society can "afford to recognize." As behavior worsens, the postulate holds, society gradually accommodates it by readjusting its pre-existing standards downward so that conduct once considered to be reprehensible eventually becomes the norm.[21]

Absent its clinical nomenclature, sociologist and former New York Senator

Daniel Moynihan simply called the process: "defining deviancy down." As he articulately put it:

> The amount of deviant behavior in American society has increased beyond the levels that the community can afford to recognize, and that accordingly, we have been redefining deviancy so as to accept much conduct previously stigmatized, and also raising the normal level in categories wherein behavior is now abnormal by any earlier standard.[22]

Yet this finding again comes as no surprise. Reflect upon the gravity of the Supreme Courts November, 1980 ruling that the Ten Commandments could not be posted upon a Kentucky classroom wall because viewing the mandate of Mosaic law could "induce children to read, meditate upon, perhaps to venerate and obey, the commandments" For they might then be dissuaded from killing, stealing, and committing adultery – while marital fidelity, honesty, respect for parents, and religious faith might concurrently be irrevocably restored. As historian Will Durant cogently assessed: "There is no significant example in history before our time of a society successfully maintaining moral life without religion."[23]

## II. DEFINING DEVIANCY DOWN

### A. The Cancer of Counter-Culturalism

By what other means could these sub-cultural values have become multicultural postulates – created in a counter-cultural revolution forged by leftist secularists opposed to historic Judeo-Christian values for self-serving political reasons – radical ideologues who, though they deplore its precepts, would rather be forced to recite the Lord's Prayer in a public school than to concede the laudatory role of traditional American society as a moral beacon to the world?

Hence, America's current clash of religious and secular cultures – indeed "clash of civilizations" – has become a civilization war. But unlike the Civil War of the 1860s, which pitted North versus South, commerce against agriculture, and urban vis-à-vis rural interests and tradition, America's "Second Civil War," commencing in the 1960s, has been launched on multiple vectors moving outward everywhere into society.

Unlike its more physically-engaged predecessor, moreover, refuge from its psychological impacts cannot be sought in the country's primary institutions – its rich religious, cultural, and political organizations and its families – for that is precisely where, and against which, this war is being waged — on school, history, language, religion, anti-military, and family fronts.[24]

Such counter-cultural conflict, and its strategic social battering ram – the tactics of "political correctness" run amok – thus share deep and tangled roots, tracing their origins to breakaway Marxist movements evolving in the 1930s that sought to defeat the Western system of democratic capitalism not by challenging the economic system that nurtured it but rather by undermining the traditional moral culture that supported it and lent it its enduring strength.[25]

Amongst its earliest champions were neo-Marxists: Herbert Marcuse, Theodor Adorno, Antonio Gramsci, Max Horkheimer, Walter Benjamin, and Jurgen Habermas – all radical scholars who commenced their proselytizing at the Frankfurt School of Social Research and then went on to comprise the dogmatic vanguard that laid the ideological foundations for America's 1960s "hippy" ivory tower socialist intellectual revolution. In a remarkable confluence of cresting radical leftist ideological currents, their arrivals coincided with the rise of the anti-Vietnam-war movement on U.S. campuses.[26]

Foremost among the newly arrived Neo-Marxist reformers was the apostle of libidinal utopia, Marcuse, often credited – if "credit" is the proper word – as being the "father of the New Left," who would lead anti-Establishment rallies on politically-active campuses throughout the United States commencing in the mid-1960s.[27] Indeed, it was he who taught the cult children of Woodstock and Haight-Ashbury the very language of revolution.[28]

Advancing an incendiary counter-cultural ideological didactic championed by Marcuse – a doctrinaire academic first affiliated in the 1930s and 1940s with Columbia University, then at mid-career in the 1950s and 1960s at Brandeis University, and later with the University of California-La Jolla – the so-called "New Left" dogma thus took root, as articulated in his master work, *Counter-Revolution and Revolt,* which proclaims:

> If the New Left emphasizes the struggle for a restoration of nature, if it demands a new sexual morality . . . then it fights against those material conditions imposed by the capitalist system and their reproduction.[29]

Indeed, in the "Political Preface" to a 1966 screed titled *Eros and Civilization*, Marcuse openly called for all-out revolution against the "political machine, the corporate machine, and the cultural and educational machine . . . of affluent Western society;" in so doing, invoking a revolt against the very civic, social, and intellectual foundations that have historically defined American values.[30]

In this quest — in a jewel of opacity bizarrely blending the pretentious with the patently profane labeled "liberating tolerance," a precursor to the "politics of meaning" that would later become the mantra of the Clinton Administration — he demanded not just equal, but "extra-equal" primacy for the "New Left," and sinisterly called for the use of "extra-legal means if legal ones have proved to be inadequate."[31]

The movement's targeted recruits were radical youth, black militants, feminists, Third World revolutionaries, homosexuals, and the anti-social and alienated — all self-determined, self-proclaimed angry victimized voices deemed persecuted by "the West." Central to its campaign – in a manner not unlike Adolf Hitler in the 1930s seeking to revive the spirit of a fallen people by finding suitable scapegoats upon which to blame their fall – it launched its effort to make innate patriotism and traditional values its first victims, and to demonize those who support them as "politically incorrect" and ideologically beyond the pale.[32]

Adopting: "Make love, not war!" – "It is forbidden to forbid!" – and "Sex, Drugs, and Rock and Roll!" its working slogans, the New Left thus became a prime motivating force for late 1960s college students, imbued by Marcusian zeal, for shouting down defenders of the U.S. war effort in Vietnam — in the process, concurrently welcoming anti-war activists denigrating those who did fight as "baby killers," "genocidal," and "racist"– while shouting "Hey, Hey, LBJ! How many kids did you kill today" – and burning American flags while waving their North Vietnamese counterparts.[33]

What Marcus offered, in fact – under the guise of an imposed Sovietization of intellectual life wherein values are determined not by their intrinsic qualities, but by the degree to which they hue to the official party line – was "intellectual cover for cowardice," a way for war protestors to dodge the draft while arrogating to themselves an aura of moral superiority over those who nobly served.

Theirs was a watershed in America's cultural evolution – as "Vietnam" became a conveniently powerful metaphor for their conviction that "Amerika's" polity, economy, society, and culture were inherently corrupt. Oblivious to, or perhaps wedded to, the nihilistic political realities that their objectives would invoke, their protests largely involved their self-perceived moral superiority vis-à-vis the corresponding shortcomings of their home country.[34]

Ultimately, in fact, these new secular liberal leftists were able to penetrate to the very highest levels of U.S. government – with Clinton social policy advisor and architect of its signature byline, "the politics of meaning," Michael Lerner – later to become editor of *Tikkun* – explaining the Clintons' and other members of the "New Left's" affinity for the inspiration of the Marcusian didactic thusly:

> Marcuse remained an inspiration to many of us because he unashamed embraced the need for utopian vision and a revolutionary metaphysic that could recognize human needs that transcend economic security, individual rights, or the struggle for inclusion or non-discrimination within an oppressive social reality.[35]

Continuing his thesis, Learner explained that: "Reacting against the selfishness and materialism that are sanctified by the free market — and that undermine the ability to sustain loving relationships — people hunger for communities of meaning that provide ethical and spiritual purpose. . . . (as) the freedom obtained through free market economies increasingly feels empty, and people in fact become trapped and dominated by a subtler but equally coercive power now operating by shaping their consent rather than opposing it."[36]

## B. Metastasizing of the "Marcusian Didactic"

Building upon the works of Rousseau and Marx to create a torqued concept of liberty distinctly at odds with historic First Amendment doctrines, therefore, the alternative analytic framework of Herbert Marcuse and his disciples, though employing traditional terms of reference, frequently assigned to them radically different meanings.[37]

In a 1965 essay titled "Repressive Tolerance," for instance, Marcuse concluded that the "neutral tolerance" for ideas supposedly prevailing in America in the 1960s was, in reality, a highly selective tolerance that benefited only the rich and powerful. Such an approach, he said, served to the express social advantage of the well-positioned to the detriment of those lacking such facilities, thereby serving the "cause of oppression" and "established machinery of discrimination."[38]

For Marcuse, then, so long as society was held captive by perceived pervasive institutionalized economic and social inequality – so long as the holders of power maintained their control through manipulation and indoctrination of the masses — which he characterized as "regressive practices" – "indiscriminate tolerance" would perforce serve what he deemed to be parochial and highly discriminatory interests of regression.[39]

In contravention, he contended, reopening channels of tolerance and liberation presently blocked by "organized repression and indoctrination" must, at times, be forcibly accomplished by "apparently undemocratic means." In a cosmic spasm of sophistry, he thus suggested that such means could include "withdrawal of toleration of speech and assembly from groups and movements which promote aggressive policies, armament, chauvinism, or discrimination on the grounds of race or religion" – all "reactionary" ideas.[40]

For "liberating tolerance," Marcuse wrote, in contrast to "indiscriminate tolerance," would be a new double standard of "intolerance against movements from the Right and tolerance of movements from the Left." This duality, moreover, would "extend to the stage of action as well as of the discussion of propaganda, of deed as well as of word" — because, for him, words had consequences, and if their consequences were to be avoided, then the words themselves must perforce be silenced.[41]

Thus, the assault on organized religion in America was launched, as the Marcusian premise – one which separated his political philosophy from the until then accrued body of First Amendment jurisprudence – was that liberty, as it had evolved, was, in effect, a "zero-sum game;" to wit: an "exercise of civil rights by those who don't have them presupposed their withdrawal by those who prevent their exercise."[42]

For Marcuse, therefore, the application of such "undemocratic," albeit necessary, actions, would foster a bold new society distinguished by universal tolerance and freedom – as to forge a society of *universal tolerance*, one could not tolerate reactionary ideas.

In this dogmatic "reversal" process, Marcuse conceded, the censorship of ideas was essential because ubiquitous regressive notions were dangerously susceptible to being rapidly translated into practice. Indeed, for Marcuse, censorship, though temporal, must nonetheless be deeply pervasive. But once its incipient objective had been achieved, there would be no further need for such "anti-democratic" expedients, which were, in the last analysis, designed to redress present imbalances between the "oppressor" and the "oppressed."[43]

The ultimate result, he promised, would be to recreate genuine freedom so that the words "freedom" and "liberty" could again reassert their true meanings. These Marcusian prescriptions, then, form the doctrinal underpinnings of modern counter-culturalism as well as the model for the assault on free speech, operating from its academic bridgehead, now ongoing throughout America. That they have, in fact, now succeeded is captured in Thomas Sowell's somber assessment that "Marxism now continues to flourish on American college campuses as perhaps nowhere else in the world."

Cuncurrently, the intellectual output – the graduates – of America's radicalized higher education system has percolated out into society at large, creating the similarly-biased leftists liberal judiciary and media that the nation now endures — and whose societal contributions this inquiry seeks to document.

## III. THE COUNTER-CULTURAL AGENDA

### A. Counter-Culturalism and Its Secular Apostles

What America confronts today, then, with the gradual, but steady, evolution of the counter-cultural movement, is no less than the destruction of those fundamental precepts that underlie the nation's historic founding, equally of a religious heritage and a liberal democratic being. Yet there can be no escaping that freedom of patriotic religious expression is quintessential to a free society. The First Amendment has served the American republic well. Compromising its safeguards puts her liberties at risk. For as Alexis de Tocqueville wrote of her: "It is by the enjoyment of a dangerous freedom that Americans learn the art of rendering the dangers to freedom less formidable."[44]

Indeed, in a commentary on what political correctness impositions respecting free speech portend for patriotism in America, even the liberal social philosopher Richard Rorty writes of fellow ivory tower elitists:

> Many of the exceptions to this rule are found in colleges and universities, in academic departments that have become sanctuaries for left wing political views.... (They have done a great deal for) women, African Americans, gay men, and lesbians.... But there is a problem with this left: it is unpatriotic.[45]

The insights of Rorty are echoed in those of Alan Bloom. Writing *The Closing of the American Mind* in 1987, he postulates that the tendency of academics to discard two millennia of learning codified in the great works of Western civilization constitutes "an intellectual suicide" tantamount to that which precipitated the Dark Ages. If the American empire is to survive, he argues, it will be because her people choose to recognize their heritage and traditions and reject those who would denigrate and deconstruct them. Bloom asserts:[46]

> This is the great moment in American history, the one for which we shall forever be judged. For just as in politics, the responsibility for the fate of freedom in the world has devolved upon our regime, so the fate of philosophy in the world has

devolved upon our universities, and the two are related as they have never been before.... The gravity of our given task is great, and it is very much in doubt how the future will judge our stewardship.[47]

The words of Rorty and Bloom are paralleled in the writings of modern philosopher Susan Haack's *Manifesto of a Passionate Moderate*, wherein she argues that though the goals of the counter-culturalists may well be laudable, they "seem to have encouraged the idea that truth, evidence, and reason are tools of oppression, an idea as tragic as it is bizarre."[48]

Her assessment is profound. For a principal argument articulated by those who advocate their counter-cultural cause is that, albeit secular, it is philosophically "democratic" in its essence. Ever-emphatic in their assertions, they are convinced that Americans are sufficiently sanguine about the sanctity of the concept of democracy that they will accept anything so labeled unequivocally.[49]

Yet nothing could be further from the truth. For in rejecting the Founders' classic prescriptions for faith-based patriotism to champion the virtues of humanistic secularism, as "New Wave Leftism" does, is itself contrary to the foundations of traditional democratic freedoms which have their roots in individual rights.[50]

There can be no doubt that the suppression of individual rights to free expression throughout history – as in the case of Nazi Germany and the erstwhile Soviet Union – brought with it the death of democracy and freedom in its wake. Hence, the inherent error of extremist counter-culturalist rhetoric – as once individual rights are subordinated to those of an ideologically determined few, democracy becomes an empty shell.[51]

## B. Counter-Culturalism and the Rule of Law

The outcome of this ideological confrontation thus is not inconsequential. For pursuant to the counter-cultural agenda, its proponents would, and, in fact, now work to:[52]

— Ban the Ten Commandments from all institutions of higher learning, courts, and other public places;
— Censor First-Amendment-guaranteed "free speech" as a violation of political correctness doctrine;
— Rewrite history texts to discredit traditional American heroes and replace them with counter-cultural ones;
— Legally compel Boy Scouts to accept atheists and homosexuals within their ranks;
— Promote same sex marriages;
— Forbid voluntary prayer in schools;
— Condemn Christopher Columbus as an Indian murderer and exploiter;
— Portray traditional Judeo-Christian values as obstacles to "diversity;" ironically often indicting them for the very practices that they seek in the Boy Scouts; and
— Encourage American flag-burning in support of their parochial causes.

For traditionalists and patriots, this is a prolonged bad dream. But for the new radicals, it is "God damn America!" "God is dead, and we did it for the kids," as Abbie Hoffman, paraphrasing Nietzsche, proclaimed – paraphrasing ideas that the Reverend Jesse Wright has recently reincarnated. To which Malcolm X appended: "I don't see an American dream. I see an American nightmare!"[53]

The net result is an amalgam of a secular elite scorning historic fundamental values – of counter-cultural nihilists demeaning traditional ideals – a society wherein adherence to classic religious values has been described by contemporary politicians as a manifestation of "bitterness" – a vulgar practice that serves only as an opiate for the masses — as "Let them have religion" has become the leftist *cognescenti's* analogue to Marie Antoinette's: "Let them eat cake!"[54]

Today, that phenomenon thrives as an elitist, occultist counter-cultural doctrine imposed top-down upon humanity at large. As 1960s hippie philosopher Herbert Marcuse, progenitor of the notion of "discriminating intolerance," rhetorically asserted: "Is there any alternative other than the dictatorship of an 'elite' over the people?"[55]

It is the illogic of this specie, of course, that has given way to wanton societal libido – accompanied by such literary travesties as dismissed 1960 Harvard professor Timothy Leary's *Politics of Ecstasy* as well as the rock opera: *Jesus Christ Superstar* and the cult film: *Rosemary's Baby*.[56] Epitomizing its prevailing spirit, Adrian Mitchell's near blasphemic poem: "The Liberal Christ Gives an Interview" proclaims:

> I would have preached a golden sermon,
> But I didn't like the Mount.
> And I would have fed the fifty thousand,
> But the press wasn't there to count. . . .
> I would have turned water into wine,
> But I couldn't get a license.
> And I would have been crucified and died,
> But like – you know how it is.[57]

Theirs is, then, not a moral beacon. As noted social philosopher Os Guinness aptly phrased it: "No liberal theology is ever a new theology. It is merely base secular premises shifted to a religious dimension."[58]

As a consequence, today America has become a civilization whose intellectual subculture is at war with its core founding ideals – a phenomenon almost unprecedented in history – a cultural cancer perhaps only best clinically described as a manifestation of the aforesaid "Durkheim constant."[59]

In the process, America's "special calling" – her "manifest destiny" – her noble sense of mission, stewardship, and service – has been lightly shed. Thus, a debilitating form of societal entropy has replaced a faith-based cultural legacy– for as one looks back to history, what once appeared to be revolutionary in its time becomes familiar in the rearview mirror of hindsight.

Such developments, of course, run counter to the course of history. America, as demonstrated throughout this inquiry, was founded explicitly upon the bedrock of her conservative religious values. "It has been the will of Heaven," John Adams asserted in 1776, "that we should be thrown into existence in a period when the great philosophers and lawgivers of antiquity would have wished to live. . . . How few of the human race have ever had the opportunity of choosing a system of government for themselves and for their children?"[60]

The source of Adams' wonderment would find vivid expression Founder George Mason's *Virginia Declaration*:

> No free government nor the blessings of liberty can be preserved to any people but by a firm adherence to justice, moderation, temperance, frugality, and virtue, and by frequent recurrence to fundamental principles.[61]

There are defining moments in history – for Rome, Caesar crossing the Rubicon; for England, Sir Francis Drake's defeat of Spanish Armada; for the United States, the Declaration of Independence; for France, the 1789 revolution; and for Russia, the fall of the Berlin wall exactly two centuries later – in so doing, capping the apogee of the "American century."[62]

Today, at the close of that vaunted century, America herself again faces just such a moment – an epistemological crisis of her own making. She has strayed far from her historic religious roots. She has responded with band-aid remedies to the metastasizing demise of her historic values – the moral equivalent of taking aspirin for appendicitis.

She must decide what type of nation she wishes to be. Like the *Pax Romana* and *Pax Britannica* before it, the *pax Americana* has a shelf-life. "A house divided against itself cannot stand," the Scriptures assert. The clock is ticking on the "American hour" — with the current generation of Americans answerable for the choices that they make.[63]

## IV. Is Counter-Culturalist "Political Correctness" Itself Politically Correct?

Accordingly, it must be clearly recognized that so-called "political correctness" is merely the flagship of a massive counter-culturalist anti-American armada – a force whose outright assault on citizenship denigrates the value of the national birthright. Indeed, all of their disparate subversive initiatives, ongoing historiographic reconstruction foremost among them, are no less than battles deliberately waged in an all-out war on the U.S. national identity — an assault on homeland values possibly unprecedented in human history — precepts in conflict with every aspect of American culture and values as they have been understood and revered for the past two centuries.[64]

"Political correctness" – neutralization through intimidation – thus is, as openly proclaimed by its proponents, one of the foremost Marcusian inventions expressly designed to effect the destruction of the American socioeconomic system – instilling fear in the responsible, inhibiting enlightening discussion, bashing those who believe otherwise, and destroying the classic values that the nation engenders. As in its modern understanding, doctrinaire insistence on its use is no more than the imposition of censorship on any and all traditional ideas to which one is opposed.[65]

Indeed, the very notion of "political correctness" is itself a direct frontal assault upon the First Amendment doctrine of unfettered free speech. For what began as a polite means to counter communicational incivility has instead mutated into a tool for controlling civilization itself – a didactic that betrays cherished historic legacy, replacing that longstanding tradition of assimilation that is the nation's social glue with cultural, ethnic and racial fragmentation.[66]

During the past couple of decades, Americans have, in fact, gained fairly good insight into what political correctness really means – to wit: no more than compelling people to conform to dogmas advanced by advocates of a secular counter-culturalist agenda. For when individuals, higher education students, for instance, do not comply, they are usually disciplined and sometimes even expelled in a classic example of reverse bigotry practiced in the guise of eliminating bigotry.[67]

Their goal is thereby to manufacture seeming virtue out of deliberately-fostered guilt – reflecting a curious symmetry that exists at both ends of the political spectrum – the fact that the fanatics on the Left are mirror images of the zealots on the Right – but with one defining difference. While the "Right" seeks to zealously preserve traditional American values, the Left seeks to decimate them with its tortured vision of a utopian socialistic totalitarian state.[68] Thus, it endlessly endeavors to transform a failed past into a redemptive future. Turning Santayana's famous warning inside out, it proponents refuse to learn from their past precisely because they want to repeat it.[69]

The approach enjoys powerful historic precedent. The communists of the former Soviet Union and the fascists of Hitler's Germany viscerally employed just such political correctness long before the current crop of counter-culturalists stumbled onto it, thereby propelling themselves prominently onto the political scene – with speech or action not in line with prescribed doctrine subject to stern and severe punishment.[70]

The modern counter-culturalist tactics for enforcing conformity with political correctness doctrine thus are powerfully reminiscent of, and analogous to, the communistic-fascist approach. For while they may not actually send the politically incorrect to Siberia or Buchenwald, they nonetheless impose draconian punishments upon those who do not march goose-step in conformity to their dogmas and rigidly enforced norms. Indeed, their handiwork has spread beyond that, now infesting the nation's academia, media, and courts alike.[71]

## A. Academia

As amongst their successes, higher education's politically correct enforcers have, in many instances, gained the power to suspend or expel students who do not conform to their arcane speech codes. On many campuses, they can, in fact, concurrently coerce students into joining specially-designed politically correct "sensitivity sessions" that are tantamount to brainwashing. While they are telling the general public that they support "diversity," therefore, it is not diversity of opinion that they are supporting, but rather a mandated strict conformity to the dogmas of their own diverse personal proclivities.[72]

In the process, many institutions of higher education have created special policing units to enforce their politically correct manifestos. It is becoming increasingly apparent, in fact, that there is little that a 20th century KGB agent could do that a 21st century counter-culturalist cop today cannot do better by employing identical totalitarian "tools of trade" explicitly designed to fight one form of perceived bigotry by creating another. Indeed, they have created their own vocabularies and nomenclatures to carry out their brainwashing missions.[73]

Much-publicized debate over attempts to enforce "politically correctness" on college campuses in the name of "diversity" has, in fact, underscored the extent to which higher education has been transformed into a propagandistic institution – indeed, a netherworld focused intently upon radical ideological indoctrination – a perpetuation of partisan politics by other means. The evocative issues that they invoke: the "politics of oppression, dependency, and victimization."[74]

For increasingly, academic study is no longer organized around core intellectual disciplines – history, linguistics, science, mathematics, and engineering – but is instead explicitly designed to cater to the ambitions, demands, and whims of politically-approved marginalized groups. So consummately successful has the quest been, in fact, that the highest achievements of Western civilization have somehow become technologically off-limits or inaccessible to certain groups because they are portrayed as not of an appropriate ethnic background, race, sex, or intellect to comprehend them.[75]

It is as if the teachings of Jesus or Socrates, because they were white Mediterranean males, are somehow unapproachable by, or unintelligible to, contemporary non-WASP college students. The racial and sexual implications of such assumptions, especially when advanced by counter-cultural proponents, are thus as patently ironic as they are ludicrous, as what they are advocating is nothing less than a concession of intellectual inferiority– and with it, intellectual entropy inseminated through institutional means.[76]

The sheer folly of such an outcome is readily self-evident. Would not a classics major gain more self-esteem, and indeed a better future, through a mastery of classics literature than in picking up political clichés and slogans from 1960s radicals now being recycled into today's "post-colonial" history classes?[77] Perhaps the challenge is not new. As early as 1776, an age that anticipated the University of California-Berkeley by two centuries, Adam Smith complained that contemporary institutions of higher learning were teaching "a mere useless and pedantic heap of sophistry."[78]

Notwithstanding, it goes without saying that, as with most dictatorial movements, in the quest for absolute conformity, the tyranny of "political correctness" has abjectly abused the rhetoric of decency and interpersonal consideration to silence its dissenters. How gratifying it must be to know that one is perforce on the side of the angels simply by endorsing and adhering to the official party line![79] To again quote social theorist Alan Bloom:

> Our universities today have become the battleground of a struggle between liberal democracy and radical, or one might say, even totalitarian egalitarianism.[80]

Indeed, today, censorship imposed in the name of political correctness has so traumatized academic debate that it is often impossible to even clinically define a social problem as a precursor to its resolution. Yet the operations of such didactic disciplinary agendas are particularly destructive when they are applied in respected learning institutions ostensibly dedicated to free and objective intellectual inquiry. Not only do they foster intimidation while enforcing slavish conformity, they concurrently assault the very foundations requisite for a free and open exchange of ideas.[81]

For while it is impossible for free academic inquiry to flourish where thought police prevail, the intellectual apparatus of the 1960s counter-culturalists now dominating academia is built explicitly for such ideological repression, not intellectual exploration. In their quest to reinterpret history, in fact, they ignore those factors that *do* shape history – faith, patriotism, the struggle for freedom, and the quest for self-determination,[82]

Yet their ideological taxonomies are not genuine frameworks for sociological analysis, they are instead political expressions of resentment predicated upon perceived socioeconomic repression – little more than facile media for expressing grievances more appropriate for attacking objective analysis than for sustaining it. They are anti-intellectualism carried to its ultimate limit, as there is a clear distinction between an individualistic society and a counter-cultural one that America's higher education system fails recognize.[83]

Indeed, collectively, the competing dogmas expressed in common cause are often not even mutually compatible, but are instead market baskets of disparate ideologies, many even in conflict with one another. What empowers them to coexist congenially in spite of gross logical inconsistencies is a shared sense of injury and resentment against that traditional culture, and its inherent values, shared by the vast majority of patriotic Americans.[84]

For the bottom line on political correctness is that it is predicated on the specious notion that only the self-anointed "socially and politically informed" – the intellectual elite, and particularly those who prevail in academia – have the wisdom and the right to decide the "greater good" for the nation and its people.

## B. The Media

But the principal problems posed by ongoing attempted counter-cultural suppression of free thought under the pretext of "political correctness" are not just those presented by academicians, they pervade the world of journalism as well — and they are not just confined to the realm of lower-rung street reporters but extend from top-to-bottom.

At a mid-1990s "American Society of Newspaper Editors" annual convention, Bob Haiman, director of the Florida-based "Poynter Institute for Media Studies," polled attendees as to whether they perceived political correctness to be a problem, defining it as: "a rigid orthodoxy, usually of a doctrinaire liberal tilt, which precludes acceptability of a contrary viewpoint and allows those who insist on a contrary view to be ridiculed, shunned, denounced, or silenced."[85]

Of the 41 editors polled, 38 answered that, "yes," the doctrine of political correctness did indeed lead to a tilt and tint to their news coverage and inhibited vigorous and candid debate – but only two would permit themselves to be identified or quoted.[86]

Hence, as with the indoctrination programs in academia described, many news organizations have degenerated into diverse polyglots of the same kinds of dysfunctional sub-cultures as now obtain on America's college campuses, wherein transgressions against the prevailing party line can result in ideological ostracization, if not outright excommunication. Small wonder, then, that columnist Sam Fulwood of the *Los Angeles Times* has reduced media objectivity, and the notion of a quest for even-handedness, to "among the many lies we like to tell about journalism."[87]

Thus it also is that today, within the nation's classrooms and newsrooms alike, an extremist "counter-cultural symbiosis" has become a sacred intellectual mantra – with an academic cliché that has penetrated journalism to its detriment holding that reality is no more than an abstract set of power relationships wherein those in control – the so-called "power elite" so reviled by the Marcusian-neo-Marxists – are empowered to impose their wanton social vision and self-serving wills upon less-systemically-well-endowed opinions.[88]

## C. The Courts

More egregious still, the counter-cultural revolution, as demonstrated in Chapter 3, has perniciously infected America's judicial system as well. As in their quest for political correctness absolute, the courts have subordinated the rule of law to social biases in favor of "lifestyle" determinants that celebrate group identity and radical personal autonomy in basic moral matters.

Consequently, there is today a fundamental disconnect between America's erstwhile jurisprudential cornerstone, its system of constitutional law, and the traditional values by which Americans have lived and continue to wish to live– those foundational institutions that have undergirded American moral life for four centuries and that of the West for two millennia.[89]

Societal values are not immutable. They inevitably change – sometimes for the better – to adjust to evolving circumstance. Those mores that guided a parochial, essentially agrarian 19th century society may not be entirely appropriate for a more global 21st century one. But the pace of that change, and the role of law in effecting it, are questions of primary importance to the type of society that Americans aspires to be — and should develop as a function of popular volition, and not as a litany of whimsical edicts of an extremist liberal court system.[90]

Such questions, evolving within the framework for change contemplated by a democratic form of government, thus are intended to be resolved by the nation's private institutions – families, communities, schools, and churches – and seldom, if ever, by court decisions that seek to impose top-down legal and moral consensus – and certainly not within a crucible wherein natural moral evolution is preempted by minority moral preference arbitrarily enforced by judicial fiat.[91]

Notwithstanding, in an age wherein judicial activism has replaced constitutional constructionism as the cornerstone of law, the Constitution, intended by the Founders as the guarantor of basic rights, is instead now steadily being reshaped into a tool for depriving mainstream citizens of their most fundamental right, the right to freedom of self-expression. In the process, under the torqued interpretations of the court, flag desecration and nude dancing have been proclaimed protected free speech; whereas prayer in school is not; and racial discrimination, in the form of arbitrary quotas, has been sanctioned as a preferred basis for public sector decision-making.[92]

Concurrently, as shown, "separation of church and state"– a political campaign phrase appearing nowhere in the Constitution, Declaration of Independence, or Federalist papers — has become the "constitutional" basis for framing the role of religion in American society. As what the cultural left calls the "mainstream" has instead become a polluted cesspool that has grossly overflowed its banks and continues to wreak devastation upon the landscape of the nation's traditional morality and cherished core values.[93]

Indeed, some of the judicial efforts at legislating morality would be outright risible were they not so socially devastating. There has a time in the nation's recent history, for instance, when the assignment of children by race to public schools was constitutionally permissible, another when it was constitutionally prohibited, and yet another, as now, when it is sometimes constitutionally required — the overarching legal mandate seemingly fluctuating with the circumstance, with the court, and with the whimsy of the judge.[94]

In each of these determinations, then, the Court has overturned the constitutionality of policy choices reflecting historic values made in the ordinary political process, only to substitute radical policies to further the social agenda of the political left. Decisions of any comparable importance reversing that course, on the other hand, are conspicuous by their absence – as in the guise of enforcing the Constitution, the Court has instead enacted the agenda of the counter-cultural revolution.[95]

Indeed, the effect of such judicial interventions since the 1950s onset of the so-called "Warren Court" has been overwhelmingly to undermine or overthrow traditional American beliefs and practices on basic issues of domestic social policy. Yet in its sanctimonious arbitrariness, there is no oversight respecting its decisions; it is not only above the law, its decisions, as it insists, are the law. In the aforesaid words of Justice Charles Evans Hughes: "The Constitution is what judges say it is."[96] To which Justice Robert Marshall famously appended: "We are not final because we are infallible, but we are infallible because we are final."[97]

Notwithstanding, there are perforce beliefs that bind together any great society – values that lend it its character and that its people deem precious and hold dear – and must be held inviolate. As absent them, as the great 19th century champion of the philosophy of liberty, John Stuart Mill, explicitly warned, the potential for societal devolution is accentuated:

> In all political societies which have a durable existence, there has been some fixed point; something upon which men agreed in holding sacred; which might or might not be lawful to contest in theory, but which no one could either fear or hope to be shaken in practice. . . .
> But when the questioning of these fundamental principles is the habitual condition of the body politic . . . the state is virtually in a position of civil war against itself and can no longer remain free from it in act or fact.[98]

The latter is, in fact, the state of that judicially-inflicted "society-building" that actively afflicts America today. Yet the framing of constitutional law – absent the Constitution – policy-making for the nation as a whole by a mere majority of nine unelected lawyers – is the antithesis of a system whose principles of federalism, the separation of powers, and representative self-governance were the basis for its founding.[99] As Texas law professor Lino Graglia has asserted:

> Judicial usurpation of legislative power has now become so common and complete, in fact that the Supreme Court has become our most powerful and important instrument of government in terms of determining the nature and quality of American life.[100]

To which Supreme Court Justice Antonin Scalia appends:

> What secret knowledge, one must wonder, is breathed into lawyers when they become Justices of this Court that enables them to discern that a practice which the text of the Constitution does not clearly prescribe, and which our people have regarded as constitutional for 200 years, is unconstitutional? . . . Day by day, case by case, (the Supreme Court) is busily designing a Constitution for a country that I do not recognize.[101]

Alexis de Tocqueville clearly understood these consummate dangers when, in noting that "scarcely any political question arises in the United States that is not resolved, sooner or later, into a judicial question," wrote in his treatise, *Democracy in America*:

> The President, who exercises a limited power, may err without causing great mischief in the state. Congress may decide amiss without utterly destroying the Union, because the electoral body in which the Congress originated may cause it to be retracted by changing its members. But if the Supreme Court is ever composed of imprudent or bad men, the Union may be plunged into anarchy or civil war.[102]

The judicial bottom line, then, remains that the essence of democratic governance is the right of the people to engage in public deliberation over what is right and what is wrong and to then decide how those rights and wrongs are translated into what is legal or illegal. Conversely, the elevation of juridically-created notions of "right and wrong" to trump collective moral judgements made by the people as citizens undermines constitutionalism as conceived by the Founding Fathers and was practiced by America for most of its first two centuries.[103]

As such, the current pervasiveness of rampant, unbridled "political correctness" – be it academic, journalistic, or judicially-mandated – to achieve bureaucratically-conceived standards of morality and "social justice" remains an all-too-prevalent corrosive nonsense perpetuated by the nation's far-out left that is wholly incompatible with any previous vision ever held for a moral, egalitarian society.

For in favoring "group rights" over "individual rights" and the "rule of the enlightened" over "the will of the people," its logic makes no concessions to historic standards of decency and traditional concepts of right and wrong. It has instead produced a bizarre twilight of reality unprecedented in human history – a civilization whose intellectual culture is at odds with its ideals of civilization itself. It is a new wave démarche inimical to the rule of law, contrary to the nation's proclaimed political *raison d'être* — and directly defies America's longstanding legacy of normative traditions respecting inter-personal civility and common courtesy.[104]

Such is the state of traditional religious values in America today – a war being waged against a nation's civilization and its culture virtually unprecedented in human history. However egregious their campaign in its multifaceted dimensions, however, no initiative is more illustrative of their pernicious intent than the current sweeping and unending efforts to turn the concept of "Christmas" into its antithesis.

## V. THE CRUCIFIXION OF CHRISTMAS

Ongoing effort to dismantle religion as the centerpiece of U.S. national existence, as demonstrated. has been a foremost feature of the counter-cultural crusade – as the First Amendment guarantee that — "Congress shall make no law respecting an establishment of religion, or prohibiting the free exercise thereof" — has invariably of late been interpreted as meaning the exact opposite of what it says.

The Founders' original intent is clear – government was not to establish a state religion. It was instead to ensure freedom *of* religion, not freedom *from* religion– neutrality amongst religions, and not a choice between "religion" and "irreligion" – as the amendment is now interpreted by the nation's courts and political elites.[105]

The counter-culturalist assault on Christmas, aimed at "de-Christifying" its religious celebration, has been ubiquitously and egregiously abetted by ACLU, the legal arm of the liberal left – an institution committed to achieving through the courts what it cannot win through democratic process – and an affiliated cabal of radical, cultist secularist groups – including so-called "humanists," moral relativists, trial lawyers, and guilt-wracked liberal Christians – who view pornography as First-Amendment-protected free speech, but *Bible*-reading and school prayer as constitutional violations.[106] It is thus not surprising that a popular bumper sticker around notoriously liberal Eugene, Oregon reads: "So Many Christians, So Few Lions"(!)[107]

Initiated by the Supreme Court's efforts to expunge Christian (and at times, Jewish Hanukkah) symbols from America's social fabric, in *Lynch v. Donnelly* (1984), it ruled that a Christmas crèche on public property in Pawtucket, Rhode Island could be displayed only if its sole purpose was not religious and that it be accompanied by such secular displays as a Santa Claus, Christmas trees, snowmen, and other such secular *accoutrement*.[108]

In a subsequent ruling, *Allegheny v. ACLU* (1989), the Court declared a Christmas crèche in a public area in Pittsburgh to be unconstitutional even though it was accompanied by such non-religious displays because its symbolism was nonetheless predominantly religious. Alternately put, the symbolism of the Divine birth must not only be intermixed with secular objects, it must have a preponderant non-religious purpose as well.[109]

The bottom line being that Christian symbols may not communicate what they were designed to communicate; for if they do, they are unconstitutional in the eyes of the nation's highest court as molded by ACLU activism. Indeed, the latter has now even taken as its mandate a course of visiting municipal seasonal displays to judge whether religious displays have been sufficiently degraded by secular objects as to pass their interpretation of constitutional muster.

From the northeast coast, therefore, the secular "taking Christ out of Christmas" movement spread to Covington, Georgia; to Mustang, Oklahoma, to Baldwin City, Kansas; to Plano, Texas; to Eugene, Oregon; to Indianapolis, Indiana; to Maplewood, New Jersey; to San Jose, California, onward through the heartland of America, and whenever and wherever else the counter-culturalists have been judicially active — banning Christmas trees, classic religious hymns, nativity crèches, Christmas calendars, Christmas sweaters, gifts bearing the name of Jesus, and even red and green wrapping paper (!)[110]

In conjunction, red poinsettias also were banned from the Ramsey County Courthouse in Minnesota because someone deemed them to be a "Christian symbol;" the city of Pittsburgh renamed the Christmas season "Sparkle Days" lest anyone be offended; and the Plano, Texas Independent School District banned wearing of red and green clothing at school "winter break" parties. It also forbade students from writing "Merry Christmas" in seasonal cards that they sent to members of the U.S. military stationed in Iraq.[111]

In Rochester, Minnesota, two thirteen-year-old girls were suspended from school for actually having the audacity to wear red and green clothing; and in a Queens, New York school district, while the display of a Jewish *menora* and an Islamic star and crescent were allowed, a Christian nativity scene was not.[112]

At the Coral Street Elementary School in State College, Pennsylvania, children were led in a chant of "Kwanzaa." while Christmas carols were concurrent stripped of all religious content. At Pattison Elementary School in Katy, Texas, not only were Christmas carols banned, but students were threatened with grade reductions for refusing to sing songs celebrating other religious faiths. Thus, American children today are compelled to chant tribal dirges in school holiday concerts, but not "Hark the Herald Angels Sing" and "Rudolph the Red Nosed Reindeer."[113]

A New Jersey teacher was forced by an ACLU lawsuit to abandon plans to take children to see the Broadway version of *A Christmas Carol*. A school district in California has prohibited teachers from mentioning Christmas or wearing Christmas jewelry. More broadly in the campaign for ubiquitous godlessness, in Panama City, Florida, a principal banned a biblical study group from calling themselves the "Fellowship of Christian Students" and forbade them from advertising notice of their meetings. A Dallas, Texas secondary school administrator was reprimanded for forwarding a copy of President Bush's "Proclamation of a National Day of Prayer" via the school's E-Mail system.[114]

In the 1994 San Jose incident, the city was forced to remove its traditional *seasonal* crèche from its park display because it was deemed "insensitive" to non-Christian peoples. But as columnist and social commentator Linda Chavez noted at the time: "The city officials showed no similar sensitivities two weeks earlier when a group of Christians protested the unveiling of a *permanent* exhibit in its public park of an eight-foot statue honoring the Aztec god Quetzalcoatl." The defining difference? The crèche was paid for with private funds. The Indian statue, on the other hand, was financed with $500,000 in taxpayer dollars (!)[115]

Rapidly following suit, the United States Post Service, in 1995 ceased allowing signs on its premises that proclaim: "Merry Christmas!" Nor does it any longer print and issue stamps containing replicas of the Virgin Mary and the Christ Child, as it had in 1994. But in true counter-culturalist fashion, Kwanzaa displays are allowed, and in September, 2007, the Post Office once again reissued its annual "Eid" festive stamp commemorating the Muslim celebration of the close of their month of fasting: Ramadan.[116]

The net result? In many areas of the country, TV stations that have no problem wishing viewers "Happy Kwanzaa" "Mazel Tov," or "Blessed Ramadan" have been traumatized into forbidding "Merry Christmas." In Dubai, Bahrain, Jordan and elsewhere throughout the Muslim world, Christmas is out there for all to see. But in the United States – a polity once called by the Founders and the U.S. Supreme Court a "Christian nation" – the institution is under siege by those whose atavistic faith is "political correctness," and who, in its worship, constantly, and successfully, raise complaints, protests, threats, and litigation against competing creeds.[117]

In the process, "Christmas trees" — in fact, not a "Christian tradition" at all, but rather a pagan practice dating back to the ancient Druids in England – have been judicially banned and children's choirs have been banished — as the classic Christmas hymn "*Silent Night*" – together with *Away in a Manger* and *O Holy Night* – has been reduced to a self-fulfilling prophecy. Indeed, the Scarsdale, New York school district even banned the singing of "Frosty the Snowman," presumably because of the threat that Frosty posed to the separation of church and state – as in the spirit of counter-cultural "tolerance," no vestige of even celebratory *Christmas-like* carols can be tolerated.[118]

Not content to stop there, the counter-culturalist crusade is, in several places, succeeding in getting "Christmas" renamed as the "Winter Festival" or "Winterval." Hence, while many people of faith are working to "Preserve Christ in Christmas," the counter-culturalists are feverishly trying to eliminate its dwindling remnants – to, in effect, '"de-Christianize" the holiday by calling it "X-Mas" or even worse. Merry Sparkle Days, everyone![119]

Yet to what end? Why does free speech protect the rights of child pornographers but not Christians? Because the First Amendment makes hostility to religion equally as unconstitutional as the establishment of a state religion, the overarching question perforce becomes: Why is it a matter of federal juridical concern that someone might want to rejoice in the reality that: "Christ the Savior is born?"

Christmas – a seasonal event observed by 96 percent of all Americans according to recent polling – is just that, "Christmas.' It is universally known for what it is – commemoration of the birth of Christ, not the Druids' winter solstice or the ancient Romans' *saturnalia,* both of which antedated it and whose parallels, if perpetuated, would render its celebration hollow. Happy Solstice! Hail to Winter![120]

The crucial question thus becomes: don't counter-culturalists, the ACLU, and the courts have better to things do than to make would-be constitutional criminals out of tiny children whose only crime is that they want to sing Christmas carols? As one wag has perhaps most aptly described it: "The reason the ACLU is jealous of manger scenes is that it has neither wise men nor virgins amongst its membership!"[121]

For at the bottom line, the radically secularist ACLU notwithstanding, religious faith is not base pornography, a societal corrosive needing to be excised by an all-knowing court. For as this inquiry has demonstrated, there is, in fact, no "separation of church and state" doctrine addressed in the Constitution – only language prohibiting the government from lending preference to one religious sect over another – as it does when it allows the public posting of Kwanzaa posters and Ramadan stamps but not their Christmas counterparts.

Thus, while a Christian may, in precept, be personally offended by a Jewish Star of David or an Islamic star and crescent, there is in America today no legal mandate that denies, nor legal mechanism that can deny, nor should there be, Jews or Muslims their lawful right to display them. A free and decent society instead relies on peer pressure armed with moral suasion to socialize intolerant individuals out of dim-witted bigotry and into a spirit of accommodation.[122]

Religion – be it Christian, Jewish, Islamic, Hindu, or Buddhist – is a socializing influence, the social glue that binds a nation's fabric. The cultural war therefore is on, as Christmas today has become the litmus test of the nation's willingness to abide by its Constitution respecting free speech, as asserted by Richard Thompson, founder of the "Thomas Moore Law Center" in Ann Arbor:

> The "establishment clause" (embedded within the First Amendment to the Constitution) was never meant to prohibit religious displays or the influence of religion on government. It was really meant to prevent government's intrusion into religion.[123]

Onward Christian lawyers! The battle for Christmas is joined![124]

It is, nonetheless, the incessant spate of such pernicious counter-cultural claptrap engaged by the residual radical roots of the 1960s "Free Love," anti-capitalism, anti-war movement that moved French social commentator Jean-François Revel to describe them thusly:

> To say that a system that has done more than any other to spread well-being and social justice deserved to die, as did the young rebels commencing in the Sixties, was to reveal a profound and thorough gap between reality and the concepts needed to comprehend reality. . . .
> Yet they chose as their political role models men like Fidel Castro, Mao Zedong, and Ché Guevera whose deeds were not in the area of good government but mass terrorism, not social justice but economic incompetence, not expansion of liberty but criminality.[125]

This, then, is the fractious and invidious state of the intellectual reign of terror being waged by the *cognoscenti* under the rubric of "political correctness" throughout much of America today. This is how the political party of Adlai Stevenson, John Kennedy, and Daniel Patrick Moynihan has now morphed into that of Michael Moore, Al Franken, and Al Sharpton. In the words of historian Victor David Hanson: "The Radical Left is courting disaster and threatens to destroy the credibility of true liberals who are apparently fearful of condemning the rampant madness in their midst."[126]

Does this, then, make the counter-culturalists intrinsically evil perforce? Here again, the great English philosopher-politician Edmund Burke may offer insight, who, in contending that; "I revere men in functions that belong to them, but not beyond" — in conceding that they "may do the worst of things without being the worst of men" — nonetheless concluded that: "It is no excuse for presumptuous ignorance that it is driven by insolent passion."[127]

## VI. THE SOCIETAL IMPACT OF THE COUNTER-CULTURAL REVOLUTION

Yet unabashedly, the counter-culturalists proceed. This despite the fact that amongst the cultures that they aggrandize and adore, there is no nobility to the values to which the profess to aspire. The Aztecs made their prisoners-of-war human sacrifices, then turned their flesh into a ceremonial stew, and were likewise not adverse to ripping out the hearts of virgins and children in supplication to their gods; the Kukuku culture of New Guinea likewise cannibalized its prisoners of war; the Toltecs of Mexico engaged in human sacrifice; the Inca Indians of Peru also engaged in cannibalism and child sacrifice; and the Auca Indians of East Equador put chronically-crying babies into purpose-built holes wherein they were trampled to death.[128]

Even today, sanctioned wife-beatings throughout much of southwest Asia are not uncommon. Indian subcontinent widows, through the practice of *sati*, are often burned alive on the funeral pyres of their deceased husbands' cremations — and many young African women, particularly in East Africa, are subjected to female clitoridectomies.[129]

Can anyone objectively argue that these practices were Western formulations? Can anyone seriously doubt that the forced genital mutilation of women is a traditional African practice and not some arcane custom introduced by colonialism? Some role models to feel good about, exult, and emulate!

This also despite the fact that it was native Africans who sold fellow Africans, at times, even their own people, to predatory European slave merchants; that slavery lasted far longer in Africa and Asia than it did in Europe and America, being abolished in Ethiopia in 1942, in Saudi Arabia in 1962, in India in 1976, in Mauritania in the 1980s, and may still continue in many parts of the Sudan.[130]

This too, despite the reality that closer to home in North and Central America, slavery was practiced by Indian tribes long before the white man arrived; that the Pima Indians of Arizona enslaved members of the Apache and Yuma tribes; that the Illinois Indians at times bartered their slaves with the Ottawa and Iroquois Indians; that the Mohawk tribe derived its name from its practice of eating human flesh; that the Mayans engaged in human sacrifice; and that myriad other cannibalisms, human sacrifices, and scalping perpetrated by peoples admired by the counterculturalists concurrently took place. Of this, of course, their chronicles say nothing.[131]

Never mind either that countervailing Western values are neither whimsical nor happenstance – that they are – indeed pioneered – the world's unique source of the noble precepts of individual liberty: human rights, democratic self-determination, equality before the law, and religious and cultural freedom. These are European and American ideas – not Asian, not African, nor Middle Eastern, except infrequently by emulation – precepts that remain the planet's most precious cultural legacy and to which the entire globe today aspires.[132]

It was America, in fact, not non-Western cultures, that in 1865 first abolished slavery – and that over the stiff resistance of Middle East and African slave-traffickers who were selling their own brothers into involuntary servitude. It is Anglo-Saxon democracy that today attracts the peoples of all creeds and continents – and inspires them with dreams of self-determination.

When Chinese students died vainly seeking democracy in Tiananmen Square in 1989, as Arthur Schlesinger has noted, they were not bearing representations of Confucius or Lenin or Chairman Mao but rather replicas of the Statue of Liberty – doubtless aware that though America didn't murder 100 million of her innocent citizens, Joseph Stalin did; and that Chairman Mao had murdered 30 million of his own as well.[133]

Critics of the U.S. system also must explain the religious freedom safeguard of the First Amendment, the 19th century policies that established free public schools for all, the post-Civil War reaffirmations of liberty and full equality before the law embedded in the Thirteenth, Fourteenth, and Fifteenth Amendments, and the universal political suffrage established by the Nineteenth Amendment.[134]

It was likewise the "old-guard Washington establishment" that initiated the

Civil Rights Act of 1964 — strongly supported by 80 percent of all Republicans and 61 percent of Democrats in the House; and 82 percent of all Republicans and 69 percent of Democrats in the Senate — led by Senate Minority Leader Everett McKinley Dirksen (R-Illinois) – while concurrently vigorously opposed by such ranking southern Democratic senators as Albert Gore of Tennessee, Richard Russell of Georgia, and Robert Byrd of West Virginia — initiatives enacted well before the counter-cultural movement began to gain its momentum in the mid-to-late 1960s – all inconvenient realities that America's liberal media does not deem worthy to recollect.[135]

Indeed, though today whole libraries of books are being rewritten in the quest to prove that a free market system characterized by its openness and tolerance is actually a regimen of oppression, they are being written by the same crowd that four decades ago was assuring society that one communistic government after another was a "workers' paradise" – at the very time that the workers themselves were doing their utmost to escape their so-called utopias, often losing their lives in their attempts.[136]

There is, in fact, something morbidly ironic in the New Left's use of "ethnocentrism" to flog the West for chauvinism, since both the idea and the modern application of the concept of egalitarianism have been distinctly Western. Indeed, as her immigration record shows, never has there been a society more open to other cultures than that of America – nor has there ever been a place on the planet wherein minorities, be they racial or ethnic, or women or homosexuals, for that matter – have enjoyed greater freedoms than in the United States.[137]

The system's naysayers likewise are at a loss to explain why people from all over the world, legally or illegally, seek to emigrate here. They do so not because they believe that America is perfect, but because they are convinced that this system of governance offers greater individual freedoms, personal dignity, and economic opportunity than anywhere else on the planet.

They do so because they understand that their choice is not between a counter-culturalist nirvana and societal repression but instead between the rich rewards of a proven benevolent culture and the degeneracy of a communal barbarism that is reduced to promoting equality at the bottom because it is doctrinally-deficient in offering economic opportunities to ascend to the top.[138]

In short, only through blatant historical revisionism and raucous politicking has a small liberal lunatic fringe been able arrogate to itself the right to redefine and dictate, indeed "dumb down," the values of America in seeking victory in a cultural war that cannot be won through other, more noble, means – precisely the types of ideologically corrupted secular elitists that British statesman-historian Lord Thomas Macaulay doubtless had in mind when he presciently predicted in a letter to an American friend in 1857:

> Your Republic will be fearfully plundered and laid waste by barbarians in the twentieth century just as the Roman Empire was in the fifth; with this difference: that the Huns and Vandals will have been engendered within your own country, by your own institutions.[139]

The cogency of Lord Macaulay's warning lies in just how accurate it was. For a nation does not collapse always and only by being overrun by "barbarian" hoards. Sometimes the most dreaded of aliens threats are already in its midst. This was the case of ancient Rome. Yet the irony for the Goths who would claim the throne of Caesar, for all their efforts, what they found was already an empty chair. There was no glory left.[140]

Thus civilizations rise and die — a stark reminder of which is encapsulated in the poignant observation of early 20$^{th}$ century American journalist and social commentator Walter Lippman that: "We should remember that when Shakespeare was alive, there were no Americans, when Virgil was alive, there were no Englishmen, and when Homer was alive, there were no Romans." *Sic transit gloria!*[141]

In the 1930s, European philosopher José Ortega y Gassett wrote: "Civilization is, above all, the will to live in common. . . . Barbarism is the tendency to disassociation. Accordingly, all barbarous epics have been times of human scatterings, separate from and hostile to, one another." Counter-culturalism is no less than barbarism so-defined, and as analysis reveals, it has brought America to the threshold of a more barbarous age.[142]

## VII. THE DEMISE OF AMERICA AS A MORAL EXEMPLAR TO THE WORLD

Hence, based both on analogy and historical example, it is clear that the cogency of Lord Macaulay's century-and-a-half-old somber warning imperils America hauntingly still, as her people have come to a moment of crisis like no other in her history. She has entered an age wherein she is being pressured by judges, educators, and other political elites into experimenting with secular ideas that are not merely revolutionary, they are alien to her being. She is being led into a great unknown by admonitions that her history and her traditional values and ideals are no longer valid.[143]

Once she stood as a beacon of integrity and virtue – a nation dedicated to the pursuit of freedom and prosperity – a moral exemplar to the world. Today, when the rest of the planet views America, they no longer see "a City on a Hill." They see instead a civilization in decline, conflicted by the confounding of her once cherished values – phenomena which caused the late Arthur Schlesinger to vainly ask: "Is there still an 'American ideal,' and if so, what is it?"[144]

The follies of such historical revisionism and social revaluation are readily self-evident. For "counter-culturalism" is little more than a politically-orchestrated scam of "ethnic cleansing" designed to transform an otherwise admirable appreciation for diverse cultures into an adversarial aberration that seeks to dilute that of America – a form of ethical polytheism – moral orders of a diverse pantheon of ideological gods that must be critically examined in light of its manifest inconsistencies for rightly what it is.[145]

The manifestations are many. Republican democracy, the nation's founding tenet foremost among them, is predicated upon the precept of "majority rule." Why, then, despite this nation's commitment to majority rule, should the religious views of the vast majority be subordinated to the whims and sensitivities, real or imagined, of a single atheist? Why should the majority's right to cite God in the national Pledge of Allegiance be trampled merely because some self-professing militant claims that it offends his or her sensibilities? How is it that quoting the *Bible* has now come to be defined as "hate speech."[146]

Why is abortion a "personal matter," yet sexual preference is not? Why should the power of the State be invoked to force the general populace, through public education, to accept the social behavior of what homosexuals, a discreet minority, elect to do in the privacy of their bedrooms as an acceptable alternative lifestyle? Where is it taught that believing otherwise is bigotry? These are private matters, many would argue, better left precisely there.[147]

Indeed, why is it that America, almost by definition, is always wrong? Why is it that liberals, when they go abroad, lavish praise social conditions that they deplore and condemn at home? Why was it "noble" domestically when, for more than a century, East Coast liberals politically cohabited with segregationists and dutifully attended black Southern Baptist Sunday services, but suddenly became "ignoble" when Midwest political conservatives developed an aggressive so-called "southern strategy" to reach out to white Southern Baptist congregations?[148]

Such efforts to redefine America for self-gratifying leftist political purposes not only fly in the face of logic, they fly in the face of history – as man's past is strewn with the triage of nations that tried to elevate the primacy of embedded subcultures over their bedrock ethnic and cultural base – as the precipitous path to decline and ultimate dissolution from such a wayward course is inescapable.

For a counter-cultural America will, in short time, ultimately and inexorably concurrently become a multi-creedal one, with groups with differing cultures espousing distinctive values rooted in those creeds and the subcultures that underlie them – and that development, as the examples of empires past vividly demonstrate, will inevitably hasten her demise.[149]

It thus bears repeating that neo-Marxist "political correctness" – the forcible imposition of one's personal views and ideologies upon another – whether issuing from a renegade political left or a radical religious right – is equally wrong. As a nation's values are not whimsy or happenstance. They are instead components of a common cause that works for the people that it serves and for that reason, they live and die for them.

That is the focus of the creed that made America great, yet one that today stands gravely threatened by its counter-cultural counterpart. For high-minded ethereal screeds cobbled together by unrepresentative, and in some cases, even slightly deranged, members of *the intelligentsia* are not scriptural perforce. Rather they are too often, mere neo-Marxist psycho-babble.

It is consummately ironic, therefore, that those socialists still seeking the demise of "traditional America" are fighting on a battlefield wherein their greater war already has been lost. For the fall of the Berlin Wall 1989 ushered in new realities that are both dramatic and profound – as the entire planet watched with utter fascination while the Soviet Union collapsed under its own dead weight, seemingly done in by capitalism and the strategic defense policies pioneered by Ronald Reagan. World communism's long-held dream of godless global domination, it appeared, had been extinguished.[150]

The once serious threat of domestic communism has apparently gone into defilade as well. Indeed, in 1970, perennial Socialist Party presidential candidate Norman Thomas and longstanding American Communist Party presidential candidate Gus Hall both dropped their bids for the nation's highest office conceding that in the existing political climate, they could not succeed.

It is only on university campuses, populated by a generation of social drop-out ideologues schooled in faddish 1960s neo-Marxism, then, that the hopes for a communistic recrudescence of "intellectuals" – notoriously defined by mid-twentieth century Bishop Fulton Sheen as "those educated beyond the limits of their intellects" – continue to prevail.[151] Yet as sociologist Robert Conquest has asserted, while "New Leftist" intellectuals may say they believe in social justice and freedom of thought, they instead rely upon communistic dogmatism, social oppression, and Marxist-style-thought-control to maintain their power base.[152]

This is the paradoxical conundrum that pervades America today. For unfortunately, retrograde radical liberals remain in charge of the ivy-covered halls – fulfilling George Santayana's keen observation that "fanaticism consists of redoubling your efforts when you have lost your aim." In the meantime, unless this course is soon reversed, intellectual freedom in America will have been lost, and Hebert Marcuse, the Frankfurt school, and Karl Marx will have won.[153]

When he spoke at Westminster college in Missouri in March, 1946, addressing the advance of global communism, Winston Churchill proclaimed: "From Stettin in the Baltic to Trieste in the Adriatic, an iron curtain has descended across the continent of Europe."[154] Well known words, but in that same famed "Iron Curtain" speech, Britain's then ex-prime minister uttered other lesser known, but equal cogent, admonitions as well — among them the time-tested truism that:

> freedom of speech and thought should reign; and that courts of justice, independent of the executive, unbiased in any part, should administer laws which have received the broad assent of large majorities or are consecrated by time or custom.[155]

The values that Churchill espoused were not unfamiliar to his audience. Indeed, they were those classic American values championed by her Founders who had dutifully cast them into their Declaration of Independence and Constitution – cherished beliefs that vividly distinguish American and Western civilization from the barbarism of both atavistic communism and totalitarian fascism.[156]

Today, six decades later, with much of the nation's history now unlearned and forgotten, those noble traditions cannot be blithely taken for granted. For a new iron curtain has descended, this time not on Eastern Europe but instead on free thought in America nationwide – as unfettered debate on social issues is no longer fostered, and ideologically, much of the *intelligentsia* is as resolutely leftist as it is anti-

American. As the republic is now passing through a profound cultural revolution – the unleashing of a radicalized social transformation for which it is not prepared.[157]

In one of the most memorable speeches of his long, illustrious career, distinguished conservative philosopher Russell Kirk in 1992, in the immediate wake of the fall of the Berlin Wall, queried:

> America has now overcome the ideological culture of the Union of Soviet Socialist Republics. But in the decade of this victory, are Americans to forswear the beneficent culture that they inherited? For a civilization to arise and flower, many centuries are required; but the indifference or hostility of a single generation may suffice to work that civilization's ruin.[158]

How unfortunate it now is, therefore, that out of thousands of years of suffering and oppression, a beacon that had come to burn so brightly for nearly than two and a half centuries, espousing the revolutionary idea that America could be free – master of her own governance, free to worship her own God, dazzling the entire world not only with her power and progress, but with her innate goodness – should now be threatened with extinction by "new wave" intellectual proponents of those identical socialist ideologies that precipitated the planet's longstanding massive outpouring of suffering and oppression in the first place.[159]

For the great melting pot has today been callously corrupted by self-serving neo-Marxist disciples — a fate now all-too-blithely accepted by Americans oblivious to the reality that every country needs its cause, a distinguishing ideology, a creed that embodies those precepts in which it most profoundly believes, as the monumental remnants of that internal cultural alienation that brought about the demise of ancient Egypt, Greece, Carthage, and Rome leaves little residual doubt.[160]

The United States is today, therefore, a polity at risk – a nation intellectually held hostage by radical ideologues that must be taken back. Democracy is a fragile flower. Its success requires an educated populace respecting the same corpus of law, aspiring to the same freedoms, relying upon the same bedrock ethical and religious foundations for its bearing, and united against common challenges and threats.[161]

In 84 B.C., the Roman general Sulla asked: "Now that the universe offers us no more enemies, what will be the fate of the Republic?" His answer came a few decades later when it collapsed into the autocracy of Caesarism. When godless communism lost its doctrinal appeal in the late 1980s, ending the Cold War, the Soviet Union concurrently lost its collective identity and fragmented into sixteen separate states, each claiming an identity of its own as defined by its unique, rediscovered culture and history. Absent religion, and her historic faith-based motivation, will this be America's fate as well?[162]

# PART III
# The Challenge

Every individual necessarily labors to render the annual revenue of the society as great as he can. He generally, indeed, neither intends to promote the public interest nor knows how much he is promoting it. . . . He intends only his own gain, and he is in this, as in many other cases, *led by an invisible hand* to promote an end which was no part of his intention. Nor is it always the worse for the society that it was no part of it. For by pursuing his own interest, he frequently promotes that of the society more effectively than when he really intends to promote it.

—Scottish Economic Philosopher Adam Smith, *Wealth of Nations*, 1776

# Chapter Five
# God's "Invisible Economic Hand"

> God moves in mysterious ways,
> His wonders to perform.
> He plants his footsteps in the sea,
> And rides upon the storm.
>
> —18th century British poet William Cowper

## I. "Economic Man" and Profit Motive

### A. The Quest for Remedy

Opening chapters have shown that those qualities of faith, patriotism, honor, and work ethic that made the twentieth century "the American century" have since been corroded by an ominous counter-cultural crusade. Critical questions thus become: "Is there ready remedy" — and if so: "Can it be reached by taking the nation back to its historic roots?

The facts of life remain largely economic – survival is economic, social welfare is economic, crime is economic. Thus, that is where the quest for remedy must begin. The next two chapters seek remedy based on lessons learned.

America, and her national ambitions, have historically been imbued with optimism. As articulated by American poet Henry Wadsworth Longfellow in his epic *Ship of State*:

> Sail on, sail on, O Ship of State:
> Sail on, O Union, strong and great!
> Humanity with all its fears;
> With the hopes of future years;
> Is hanging breathless on thy fate![1]

A paean to ever-optimistic U.S. aspiration, this amalgam of faith and determination is the American national creed.

The role of religion in stimulating productive economic activity, not only within America but as the catalyst for Western civilization's renaissance, has long been a topic of scholarly debate. From the teachings of Jesus on the criticality of a Christian to be diligent in all of his activities, to the strictures of the Church on interest-bearing transactions based upon prohibitions of "usury" in the Middle Ages, to the notion of the "Protestant work ethic" introduced by John Calvin to usher in the Renaissance — the lessons of history become quintessentially important. As today, the stewardship of once prudent economic policy enjoyed as late as a half century ago has mutated into sheer political malfeasance.[2]

Yet reckless economic policies that cater to special interests to the detriment of the general interest have brought down great civilizations. In his 1997 work indicting the American version of the called "the Judas economy," William Wolman, chief economist for *Newsweek* – exploring whether ongoing outsourcing is no more than prudent downsizing or instead part of a cultural revolution – states:

> The best historians have noticed in each major phase in the development of capitalism, the leading country of the capitalist world goes through a period of "financialization," wherein the most important economic dynamic is the creation and trading off abstract financial instruments rather than the production of genuine goods and services.[3]

Because this phase of economic devolution heralds the onset of that fiscal deterioration that invariably brings down civilizations through imperial overstretch, the role of financial excess in societal collapse must perforce be carefully contemplated – focusing, in particular, upon the role of faith-based profit motive in driving a nation to produce those cherished goods and services whose successful marketing then becomes the lifeblood of its economy.

The 1990s – which Allan Greenspan called a decade of profligate "irrational exuberance" characterized by unwarranted public and private debt and spending – set the process into motion, invoking a financial downward spiral that reinvokes the wisdom of economic history in the quest for remedy.[4]

The reason reverts to basic economics. Classic theory holds that the main objective of any successful development initiative is to create wealth — and that net wealth is derived primarily through the production of exportable goods and services. Such production, in turn, results from a process of free market innovation — finding new ways to employ resources more effectively to create the things that customers need and want.[5]

Only private enterprise is equal to this challenge — as government doesn't create wealth, it consumes it. Its proper role in public policy, therefore, must be to facilitate, or at least not hinder, the private sector in its vital task of combining financial, human, and natural resources to produce those marketable, aspired cherished goods and services that contribute to wealth creation.

For nations promote building of wealth not by implementing new public programs per se, but rather by stimulating new private sector business investment. Generally, this goal is best approached by reducing, not increasing, the public sector role in the private sector marketplace.

Indeed, in those success scenarios where public intervention has made a significant growth impact, positive results have been produced primarily because policy makers have actively sought to create an operating environment propitious for private sector entrepreneurship to evolve – as that is precisely what sound entrepreneurship does: "putting people to work doing things needing to get done."[6]

Relaxed tax and regulatory *milieux* have almost invariably been the foci of such enlightened policy efforts. For leading-edge economic development remains a free market process, not a legislated act. To the extent that it can be impacted by public policy, therefore, such policy must be aimed at the goals of both changing public attitudes toward private profit and removing public barriers to private sector growth.

This reality remains the foremost challenge to sound, balanced development operating within a free market system wherein such development enjoys a certain self-generating "reciprocity." For it is dynamic economic growth that fuels technological innovation and scientific progress. It is such economic growth that raises living standards for the rich and poor alike and ultimately defeats poverty. It is such growth that provides the vital social overhead capital that underwrites the arts and sciences that lend quality to human life.

As true liberty is achieved through three sets of societal institutions – economic, cultural, and political. The goal of economic institutions is to transform poverty into ambience and open up dynamic vistas of opportunity for the development of human talent. The goal of cultural institutions is to inculcate those habits and ideas that empower the human mind to realize the full panoply of its potentials. And the goal of political institutions operating within a free market economy must be to afford access for humankind to the paths of sound self-government and personal responsibility.[7] The correlation and subsequent challenge of these synergies, as assessed by de Tocqueville, is that:

> Americans are pleased to explain almost all of the actions of their lives with the aid of self-interest; they complacently show how the enlightened love of themselves constantly brings them to aid each other and disposes them willingly to sacrifice a part of their time and their wealth to the good of the state. . . .
> I have already said enough to put Anglo-American civilization in its true context. It is the product of two elements which elsewhere have often been at war with one another, but which in America, it was somehow possible to incorporate into each other forming a marvelous combination. I mean *the spirit of religion* and *the spirit of freedom.*[8]

The compelling social case for such democratic capitalism, however, has been perhaps best made by the twentieth century theologian Reinhold Niebuhr in asserting that: "Because humans are sometimes capable of acting justly, democracy is possible. Because humans do not always act justly democracy is necessary."[9]

Hence, because people within a democracy do not invariably promote those virtues necessary for maintaining authentic human freedom, government exists. It exists to ensure ample production of the requisite economic growth that lends ambience to human existence. While government cannot create such growth — and indeed, can often be its enemy — it can nonetheless aspire to establish settings favorable for it to take place, secure environments that encourage businesses to take those financial risks in quest of equitable returns that enable civilization to progress.

## B. The Historic Models

Historically, two distinctly Calvinistic precepts – "work ethic" imbued by "profit motive" – have been the economic engines powering such *laissez faire* entrepreneurial success – producing models for governance worthy of contemplation within America today.

Preceding analysis makes clear that the Founders did not contemplate statist economic governance. Indeed, history leaves little doubt that they aspired to a free market process functioning within the framework of a republican form of government — a model designed for "economic man," as defined by Sottish economic philosopher Adam Smith in his famed *Wealth of Nations*, which appeared in 1776 — the same year that their Declaration of Independence was proclaimed.

Between them, the twin documents – one just a few pages long, the other more than 800 pages in length – form the architectural *corpus juris* for forging modern socioeconomically successful nation states. Their aggregate message is both seminal and illuminating.

As it is the challenge of economists and historians – and also overarchingly of would-be public policy makers – to ponder why twenty two separate civilizations have risen and fallen in man's brief sojourn on the planet. What caused them to ascend? What precipitated their demise? What are the implications of the messages resonating from those profound socioeconomic evolutions in forging public governance?

This inquiry produces findings demonstrating that in the ascendancies of most free societies, a series of crucial economic interactions eventually coalesce. To wit: as man's *modus operandi* ascends from merely acquiring the necessities of sheer survival to a more sedentary lifestyle, the ambitions of "*economic man*" concomitantly rise.

For *economic man* is "acquisitive man" – as his society matures, so do his ambitions. In his quest for material gain, therefore, he is increasingly driven to convert current earnings into savings in order to accumulate and invest his "surplus capital" in future cherished goods and services. And it is these individual and collective savings, committed on the promise of a fair return, that generate the investment capital that underwrites those productivity-enhancing technological breakthroughs that empower societies to progress.

It is free society's ability and willingness to divert those savings into non-economic intellectual and aesthetic activities, in turn, that produce those scientific, literary, and artistic achievements that are the hallmark of civilization. It is the accumulation of such wealth that enables its owners to both finance the development of "intellectual property" and to fund the activities of educational institutions.

It is the cumulative volume of a society's savings, made up of the contributions of its institutions and individual members, moreover, that ultimately determines its living standard – that liberates "*economic man*" from the need to focus exclusively upon basic necessities and, in the end, distinguishes between his merely eking out a living and attaining the highest levels of culture.

For sustained social progress, almost without exception, is achieved through the effective employment of the creative resources of private individuals. But why is this reality, in fact, the case? What motivates individuals and compels them in their incessant striving to succeed? These are valid questions for any nation seeking to build a sound economic future founded upon individual responsibility by aspiring to learn from the accumulated wisdom of the past.

Without question, within most modern Western cultures, the term that best captures the indomitable human quest to succeed is "profit motive" – the pursuit of which was called by Adam Smith "enlightened self interest." Indeed, the insatiable search for profit drives a person's every economic activity — his or her willingness to work, penchant to invest, and eagerness to save.

Yet profit motivation is encouraged not only by a desire to succeed but equally from a favorable operating milieu and an opportunity to equitably compete. Conversely, though highly durable, its perishability remains a function of economic circumstance. It can be ruined by unfavorable market conditions; undone by inordinate taxation; subjugated by excessive regulation; decimated by unfair competition — and overwhelmed by the coalescing of all of those factors into a repressive business climate.

Hence, the pursuit of profit is quintessential for any civilization to advance. It is the driving force that produces "economic surplus" – the capital needed for investments in those non-economic aesthetic and intellectual developments – in art, architecture, literature, music, philosophy, and science – that lend ambience to human life.

Private economic surplus keys all of those essential economic interactions that are at the essence of sustained human progress. It is private surplus capital that creates the social overhead capital that finances technological innovation and cultural development. Those great societies that have reached civilization's socioeconomic apogee at any time in history, in fact, have all been distinguished by this one outstanding attribute – private economic surplus.

Indeed, a precondition for any civilization to advance is that it possess such capital surplus – in the form of cash, industrial goods, and/or agricultural products –

in excess of that needed for immediate survival. For such surplus can then be channeled into more creative enterprises of a non-economically essential intellectual or aesthetic nature. Exactly for this reason, then, the cultural apogee of any civilization coalesces precisely at that point where its economic decline commences to set in.[10]

Yet economic surplus presupposes private healthy business activity – and the operation of an economic milieu wherein healthy profit-taking can take place. Sound public sector fiscal policies must concurrently create confidence in investors, therefore, that capital commitments to entrepreneurial activity will lead to profitable downstream undertakings.

Such business confidence, in turn, must be sufficient to foster deferred consumption — savings from both corporate profits and personal salaries — so that investments in other economic enterprises can continue to take place. This surplus must not be limited to affluent capitalists, moreover, for laborers too must be rewarded with adequate wage compensation to induce them both to be productive and to be high demand consumers.

Capitalistic operation thus is an holistic process – a means of organizing resources, both natural and human, to produce economic surplus. Its productive activities are propelled by the vaunted workings of the competitive free market – of Adam Smith's "invisible hand" coordinating market exchange amongst individuals and firms – which is at once the secret of its success and the source of its remarkable resilience and self-regulating adaptability.

## II. "Profit Motive" and the Course of Economic History

### A. The Calvinistic Model

That "economic surplus" is quintessential to the advance of civilizations is central to the workings of free market process. Its inverse corollary, however, is that when government taxes away that surplus, it sows the seed corn of its own inevitable demise. For those individuals, empires, and eras most successful throughout history have invariably been those characterized by indomitable entrepreneurial spirit. The deaths of such empires and eras, in turn, have usually occurred when onerous public policies have suffocated that competitive spirit most often nurtured at the roots of its private enterprise foundations.

To understand why this reality is, in fact, the case, one must delve more deeply still into the motivations of economic man – and it is here that recourse to history's cogent lessons becomes insightful. For it is clear that the transformed Roman Empire that would devolve into early medieval Christian Europe sank into the mire that would become its Dark Ages not due to external force but rather to the revenue costs of the internal bureaucratic complexity required to govern its domain.

Most devastating was still was its 9th century decision, by administrative fiat, to impose, under the rubric of "usury," the Church's ban on interest-bearing transactions in a quest to make all profit-making a function of the theocratic state –

thereby monopolizing for itself all commercial resources of the realm, with the dismal feudalism of the Middle Ages the inexorable result. Indeed, it would take the revolutionary free market ideologies of the Protestant Reformation commencing in the 16th century to reverse this dismal economic course. How that process transpired is illuminating.[11]

A century has now passed since noted German socioeconomist Max Weber (d. 1920) produced his renowned, albeit controversial, work: *The Protestant Ethic and the Spirit of Capitalism,* which opened with the evocative paragraphs:

> A first glance at occupational statistics of any country of mixed religious composition readily brings to light with remarkable frequency a situation that has at several times provoked discussion in the Catholic press. . . . namely the fact that business leaders and the owners of capital, as well as the highest grades of skilled labor, and even more so, the technically and commercially trained personnel of modern enterprises, are overwhelmingly Protestant.[12]

Weber's analysis proceeds to search for answers as to why this reality is, in fact, the case. He purports to find them in Calvinistic doctrine, '*l'esprit calviniste,*' "which – unlike medieval Catholicism's banning as "avarice" the quest for capital fructification – turned "profit-motive" into a distinct religious virtue – equally as a sign of redemption and a devout act of faith – the technique of seeing God manifest in the capitalistic success of "rational economic man."[13]

By thus transporting the abstract principle of religious liberty into the pragmatic field of economics – making the marketplace its chapel by reconciling the Christian goal of salvation with the commercial goal of rational consumption, he asserts, Calvinism forever slammed the doors of the staid monasteries shut behind them. For if, in fact, the Church had suffocated medieval "profit motive" and the "quest for filthy lucre"– *"turpe lucrum, auri sacri fames"* – based on the verse in the Old Testament book of Deuteronomy:

> Thou shalt not lend upon usury to thy brother; usury of money; usury of victuals, usury of anything that is lent upon usury[14]

— 16th century Calvinists rescued it with the spiritual sanction of the Book of Proverbs: "See a man diligent in his business; he shall stand before kings"[15]

— as well as Deuteronomy's admonition: "Remember the Lord thy God: for it is He that giveth thee power to make wealth."[16]

Diligent workers, Calvin thus contended, are the Lord's foot soldiers — a conviction taking as its scriptural sustenance *Matthew* 5:16:

> Let your lights so shine before men that they may see your good works, and glorify your Father who is in heaven"

— and culminating in the counsel of *Matthew* 7:12: "By their fruits, you shall know them."[17]

In Calvin's words: "God . . . by ingrafting us into his Son, constitutes us anew to be lords of the world, that we may lawfully use all of our own wealth with which he supplies us."[18] Accordingly, humankind were created not merely to react passively to the world around them but to actively shape their operating environment.

It is not surprising, then, that the biblical "Parable of the Talents" – Luke 19: 11-26 – whose joyous proclamation: "Well done, good and faithful servant; thou has been faithful over a few things, I will make thee ruler over many things" – became favored scripture in the Protestant capitalist's "Gospel."

For simply put, in reformists' eyes, the "business of business" was the Lord's business, and each time one earned honest profit, he was doing the Lord's work (!) Or as Calvin himself aptly phrased it in his commentary upon Genesis 2:"Everyone must remember that he is God's steward in all that he possesses."[19]

Accordingly, the earning of profit now became for the devout not just an obligation nor a mere effort to earn one's "daily bread," but instead a capitalistic obligation that later would find vivid expression in the admonition of Benjamin Franklin: "Remember that time is money.... He who idly loses five shillings worth of time loses five shillings and might just as prudently throw them into the sea."[20]

Diligent labor thus became a religious ritual as well as an essential element of early Western capitalism, as Calvin – in establishing a unique theological *"laissez faire"* that lifted his writings to an impact status like none other of the modern age save the *Bible* – likewise elevated to lofty status the role of *economic virtue* as a prime precondition for salvation.

For under it, man ascertains his calling as one of "God's elect" in his struggles with daily business life. Alternately put, by allowing individualism to replace collective consciousness, thereby igniting personal economic energies, it gave full free play to the workings of Adam Smith's vaunted "invisible hand."[21]

But unlike more classic religions whose adherents earn their salvation through a vast accumulation of good works, the Calvinist proves his redemption through a series of self-serving acts that take place within an overarching economic system wherein industry, utility, diligence, thrift, frugality, and sobriety are amongst faith's foremost pillars. As in the religious *"New Politic,"* to quote Max Weber:

> Today it is no longer necessary to seek the support of an ethical force, but instead *"weltanshauung"* is determined by the position of politico-commercial and politico-social interests; a man who does not soon adapt himself to those conditions indispensable for success under the capitalistic system is either left behind or goes under.[22]

In this profound economic transformation, then, enterprise and mercantile endeavor became at once both Christian virtues and societal contributions to the goal of establishing an economic order worthy of the Kingdom of Christ. For in striving to earn profit within the marketplace of "free will," man demonstrates the unequivocal signs of his election to salvation – and in so doing, promotes the greater glory of God – *in majorem gloriam Dei!* [23]

Within this reformed process, moreover, there is no longer room for the human cycle of sin, repentance, atonement, and release over which the medieval Church had long presided – as in this new doctrine, redemption through temporal punishment cannot restore a state of grace. For man is on his own recognizance. He must earn his own election. Or more succinctly put in modern terms: "God helps those who help themselves!"

By sanctioning, and indeed glorifying, self-serving ends, Calvinism thus overcame the mentality that man would only work because, and as long as, he was poor. For in giving new life to the virtues of heretofore suspect successful business endeavors, it was a religion formed of, and for, bourgeois entrepreneurs who actively functioned within the real time "marketplace of life" — an eminently practical doctrine that would lend inspiration to the capitalistic spirit manifest in the determination of that rugged Dutch sea captain who asserted that he "would go through Hell for capital gain, though it would likely scorch his sails (!)"[24]

Hence, after Calvin, in the words of British economic historian R.H. Tawney: "The good Christian was no longer at all greatly dissimilar from 'economic man.'" For in his global view, the aim of "enterprise" is:

> not personal salvation, but the glorification of God, to be sought not by prayer only, but by action – sanctification of the world through strife and labor. For Calvinism, with all of its repudiation of personal merit, is intensely practical. Good works are not a way of attaining salvation, but are indispensable as proof that salvation has been achieved . . . .
> So now, far from there being an inevitable collision of the requirements of business and the claims of religion, they walk hand-in-hand. Through fortunate dispensation, the virtues enjoined on Christians: diligence, moderation, sobriety, and thrift, are the qualities conducive to success.[25]

Accordingly, when the West emerged from its self-inflicted Dark Ages through the restoration of profit motive in the economic marketplace, a new Renaissance of art and culture concurrently burst into bloom, first in Italy, from whence it spread to France, England, and the rest of Europe. The rediscovery of classical ideas stirred an awakening of imagination that led to a revitalization of civilization. The Renaissance, and the Reformation which followed in 1517, would thus become the cultural vehicles that would transport the Christian faith first into Europe, and from there around the world.[26]

Though Calvin offered an eminently pragmatic economic doctrine that was unique to the Christian West, however, he was no pioneer. For elements of the so-called "Protestant ethic" can be found in the varied doctrines and dogmas of other, equally zealous "theocratic elites" as well. Amongst them, Islam similarly exhorts its followers to the utmost of productive labor; and certainly the tenets of Judaism have played no small role in the industriousness that has characterized its devout.

It is likely no accident, therefore, that the last two major civilizations to dominate the planet – the "Muslim East" and the "Christian West" – have both been driven by the identical impetus — "profit motive" – as the "Protestant Ethic" and the "Islamic Ethic" appeal to, and indeed are mirror images of each other, in capturing the acquisitive instincts of man.

The prerequisites for both, in fact, are basic – man's incessant drive for material gain in an insatiable quest for capital surplus to acquire life's amenities while operating within the boundaries of a competitive free market safeguarded by the workings of the rule of law. It is the more modern role of taxation and regulation in incentivizing or suppressing natural human economic motivation, therefore, that are the ultimate economic determinants in the rise and fall of nation states.[27]

For at the market-driven bottom line, the costs of bureaucratic complexity, when excessive, vitiate an economy – making their moderation perforce a foremost policy priority and concern. Thus, the advocates of limited government must not be seen as "anti-government" per se, as some would charge. Rather, they are merely hostile to concentrations of coercive public power and to its arbitrary use.

Equally attuned to the lessons of economic history and the perils of unconstrained bureaucracy, they stand for constitutionally limited government possessing the delegated authority and means to protect human rights, yet not so powerful as to destroy or negate them.[28]

This was, in fact, what England's *Magna Carta* signed by King John in 1215 A.D. was really all about – that taxation and regulation could not be imposed without the consent of the governed – as likewise was the vital message of America's Declaration of Independence and her Constitution, together with its appended "Bill of Rights."[29]

## B. The Founders and the Calvinistic Model

That the Founders learned well the utility of the "Calvimistic economic model" was evident at the country's inception in Virginia, America's first colony – a region crying out for, but initially lacking – profit-driven economic motivation. For though the first settlers arrived in Jamestown in May, 1607 found uncommonly fertile soil and a cornucopia of wild meats, fish, and fruits, within six months, the vast majority of the original settlers were dead, primarily from famine. Two years later moreover, six months after a second wave of 500 émigrés arrived to settle in Virginia, an astounding 440 of them were dead from starvation and disease as well.[30]

The cause for such triage amidst a land of plenty? As described by one eyewitness, it was "want of providence, industrie, and government, and not the barrenness and defect of the Countrie, as is generally supposed."[31]

Yet how could there be such an utter lack of industry? Direct testimony suggests that the problem was one of incentive – as the arrivals were indentured servants with no financial stake in their productive outputs – as all that they produced went into a common pool to support the colony, with any surplus destined for their sponsor, the "Virginia Company." With no direct link between output and reward, therefore, there was no overarching motive to produce — and the residents responded with predictable indifference.[32]

This situation would lead to the famed edict of Captain Smith, leader of the Jamestown colony, paraphrasing biblical II Thessalonians 3:10: "You must obey this now for a Law, that he that will not work shall not eat, except by sickness he be disabled."[33] Indeed, when in 1611, the British government sent Sir Thomas Dale to marshal the colony, he noted that while most of the initial settlers had starved to death, those who remained of them were nonetheless occupying their time in indolent activity on the streets. He thus immediately identified as the problem the colonial system of communal leadership.[34]

His solution: that each citizen of the colony be given three acres of land and required to work no more than one month per year during the non-harvest season to contribute to the colony's common treasury. In exchange, each sharecropper was required to remit to the colony a lump sum tax of two and one-half barrels of corn each year.[35]

With profit motive bred of property rights thus restored, the Virginia colony prospered. In the words of Matthew Andrews: "As soon as the settlers were thrown upon their own resources and recognizance, and each freeman had acquired the right of owning property, the colonists quickly developed what became the distinguishing characteristic of future Americans — an aptitude for all kinds of craftsmanship coupled with an innate genius for experimentation and invention."[36]

The three-acre land grant system worked so well, in fact, that the colony's private property system was soon greatly expanded. As explained in one studied analysis:

> As private land holdings replaced common ownership, work incentives improved; and full return for individual effort became a reality, superceding output-sharing arrangements. In 1614, private land holdings of three acres were allowed.
> A second and more significant step toward private property came in 1618 with establishment of the "head-right" system. Under this system, any settler who paid his way to Virginia was given fifty acres and another fifty acres for anyone else whose transportation he paid. In 1623 – only sixteen years after the first Jamestown settlers had arrived – all land-holdings were thus converted to private ownership.[37]

Soon, with the introduction of similar systems across the northeast region, including at the Massachusetts Plymouth Colony on Cape Cod, such private sector land reforms produced a remarkable economic transformation ushered in by the introduction of a profit-driven capitalistic system that promoted industriousness in place of indolence.[38]

Accordingly, the colonies' newly-won economic freedoms – secured property rights combined with moderate taxation – soon produced economic abundance, as the colonists set out to harness the nation's fertile soil and other resources in ways unachievable in earlier communal production arrangements.[39]

Throughout New England, a vibrant new shipping industry also developed. Atlantic coast whaling likewise led to a whale oil industry that would serve as a source of home lighting throughout the nation for a century. Concurrently, shipbuilding rapidly evolved to the extent that by nation's birth in 1776, New England possessed the third-largest maritime fleet in the world and was building ships for England.[40]

The nation's Founders — aware of this early legacy of indolence and sloth, as well as its resolution, and cognizant of Calvin's catechisms — were thus determined to devise a lasting remedy in the form of democratic capitalism. For as Founder Samuel Adams cogently observed: "The importance of piety and religion;

of industry and frugality; of prudence, economy, regularity, and an even government, all ... are essential to the well-being of a family."[41]

Initially, the Founders faced great challenges, as articulated in their bill of economic grievances delineated in the Declaration of Independence. Complaining of the king's tax collectors, Thomas Jefferson wrote: "He has erected a multitude of New Offices and sent hither swarms of Officers to harass our People and eat out their substance." The Declaration likewise condemned the king for his protectionist trade policy vis-à-vis the colonies: "For cutting off our Trade with all parts of the world." Concurrently, the king was denounced "for imposing taxes upon us without our Consent."[42]

Indeed, the First Continental Congress was formed in direct response to the "Stamp Act," which required a formal fee-based British governmental notarization of all official documents promulgated in the colonies. This so-called "Stamp Act Congress" was soon to achieve high profile — coining the phrase "no taxation without representation" — and mobilized such public outrage that the British Parliament was pressured to repeal the act in 1776 — as faith-based confidence in the virtue of their cause led the Founders into political revolution. [43]

Auspicious beginnings indeed. Two centuries later, however, that spirit of collegiality intended for financial coexistence of church and state within America contemplated by the Founders has tragically broken down.

For while religious creed has traditionally called for a ten percent *tithe*, the U.S. government's share of GDP now often exceeds 20 percent. Thus, while the *Bible* commands the devout to "render unto Caesar the things that are Caesar's, and render unto God the things that are God's," today, Caesar demands twice as much as God — and while God's deacons may too often pass the plate, they don't threaten, seize homes, fine, or imprison for failure to comply.[44]

Notwithstanding, such an outcome too did not come absent scriptural warning. When the people of Israel asked God for a king so that they could "be like all other nations," the Prophet Samuel explicitly warned that the king would then use his mandate to create bureaucracy, conscript their sons and daughters to serve it, and lay heavy taxes upon them to serve it – findings that suggest why Samuel was properly called a "prophet (!)"[45]

## III. THE BIBLICAL ECONOMIC MODEL

The Founding Fathers, as documented, in forging their economic vision sought counsel from the Scriptures – heeding closely the guidance of English epic poet John Milton that "the *Bible* doth more clearly teach the solid rules of civil government than all the eloquence of Greece and Rome."[46] Of their 3,154 most prominent quotes, as shown in Chapter 2, in fact, 34 percent came from the *Bible* – four times more than Montesquieu or Blackstone, and twelve times more than Locke.[47]

Thus, driven by powerful biblical influence, America's creation is the sum of its parts, transcending any one of them. In the words of religious historian Theodore

Motley: "American democracy was the result of all that was great in bygone times. All led up to it. It embodies all. Mount Sinai is in it; Greece is in it; Egypt is in it; Rome is in it; England is in it; all the arts are in it; as well as all of the reformations and discoveries."[48]

Accordingly deeming the *Bible* to be America's "*Magna Carta*," and cognizant of the counsel of Proverbs 14:34 that: "Righteousness exalteth a nation," George Washington, in his Farewell Address, admonished: "Of all of the dispositions and habitudes which lead to political prosperity, religion and morality are indispensable supports."[49]

The Founders thus drew heavily upon theological analogy in forging the nation's economic governance — making a cursory review of the "biblical economic model" insightful. For in establishing a scriptural "capitalistic contract' amongst the governed and God, Deuteronomy 8: 18 and Genesis 1:28 stipulate:

> \*\* Remember the Lord thy God: for it is he that giveth thee power to get wealth that he may establish his covenant which he sware unto thy fathers, as it is this day;[50] and
> \*\* And God blessed them and God said unto them: Be fruitful and multiply and replenish the earth and subdue it; and have dominion over the fish of the sea, and over the fowl of the air, and over every living thing that moveth on the earth.[51]

The specific terms and conditions of such a "dominion covenant" were to be as follows:

> \*\* I will give thee the treasures of darkness, and the hidden riches of secret places, that thou may know that I, the Lord, which call thee by thy name, am the God of Israel;[52]
> \*\* And all of these blessings shall come unto thee, and overtake thee, if thou shalt harken unto the voice of the Lord thy God.[53]

It was, moreover, to be a covenant denominated in treasure. As in America, on a gold monetary system established by the Founders that prevailed for the first two centuries of her existence up to August 15, 1971, wealth in biblical time was denominated in a precious metals standard, as the *Bible* suggests in referring to the "land of Havilah, where there is gold; and the gold of that land is good.[54]

Gold and silver were, in fact, standard units of account because, as Genesis 24: 22 indicates. their values could be determined by a standard weight, the *shekel*. Thus, the Psalmist David, in Psalms 119: 127, values the commandments of God "above gold, above fine gold."

Thus, King Asa of Judah paid tribute to Ben-Hadad, king of Syria, in gold and silver, as I Kings 15:18-19 indicates; the wealth of Abraham was likewise measured in gold and silver as well as cattle, as Genesis 13:2 asserts; and the land in Ephron where Abraham buried his wife Sarah was purchased with four hundred *shekels* of silver according to Genesis 23:1-20. Indeed, over 350 references to precious metals appear as entries in one prominent biblical concordance.[55]

In conjunction with a precious-metals denominated monetary system, the Scriptures likewise called for a uncorrupted uniform system of weights and measures — a mandate designated by the Founders as amongst the seventeen federal functions delineated in the Constitution as well — as biblical businessman were exhorted to honesty and fairness in their business transactions.

As articulated in Leviticus 19: 35-37: "Ye shall do no unrighteousness in judgment; in meteyard, in weight, or in measure. Just balances, just weights, a just *ephah*, and a just *hin* shall ye have." Accordingly, the Israelis were rebuked in Isaiah 1:22 for debasing their currency with the indictment: "Your silver has become dross."[56]

Just weights and measures were a particularly critical imperative in biblical times as monetary transactions frequently were carried out not in struck coins but in gold bullion – ingots measured in weight by *shekels* – a term derived from the root *sekel*, which in Hebrew conveyed the notion of counting as well as weighing.[57]

In the era of the biblical prophets, people thus settled debts by producing given weights of precious metals. Hence, the stipulation of Proverbs 16: 11 — "A just weight and balance are the Lord's, and the weights of the bag (in the merchant's wallet) are his work" — refers to both honest weights and good money. Indeed, even at the time of Jesus, the practice of weighing money rather than counting it was prevalent — and scales likewise were employed by money-changers to determine that the weights of struck coins then in circulation had not been deliberately diminished by counterfeiters.[58]

A theistic approach to economic administration as contemplated by the Founders is scripturally documented as well:[59]

**The Scriptural Model for Economic Governance**

| Tenet: | Verse(s): | Provision: |
|---|---|---|
| The biblical sanction for civil governance: | I Samuel 8:19-22 | 19. Nevertheless, the people refused to obey the voice of Samuel; and they said: Nay, but we will have a king over us; 20. That we also may be like all the nations; and that our king may judge us, and go out before us, and fight our battles. 21. And Samuel heard all of the words of the people, and he rehearsed them in the ears of the Lord. 22. And the Lord said to Samuel: Hearken unto their voice and make them a king.[60] |
| Civil governance is a covenant of governance with the consent of the governed; | Exodus 19: 5,8 | If you will indeed obey My voice and keep My covenant, then you shall be my own possession among all the peoples. . . . And the people answered together and said: "All that the Lord has spoken, we will do." |
| | Proverbs 11:14 | Where there is no counsel, the people fall, but in a multitude of counselors, there is safety. |

| Tenet: | Verse(s): | Provision: |
|---|---|---|
| *Separation of powers: | Matthew 22:21 and Mark 12: 17 | Render unto Caesar the things that are Caesar's; and unto God the things that are God's.[61] |
| *The rule of law: | Romans 7:16 | I consent unto the rule of law that it is good. |
|  | I Timothy 1: 8 | We know that the law is good if a man use it lawfully." [62] |
| *Created equal by God: | Acts 10: 34 | God is no respecter of persons; |
|  | Galatians 3:28 | There is neither Greek nor Jew, there is neither bond nor free, there is neither male nor female: for ye are all one in Christ Jesus. |
| *That government, to these ends, is mandated "to ensure domestic tranquility:" and | I Timothy 2:2 | Therefore the people are to pray for "kings and all that are in authority; that we may lead a quiet and peaceable life in all godliness and honesty." |
| *Promote the general welfare: and | Romans 13:3-4 | For rulers are not a terror to good works, but to evil. Wilt thou then not be afraid of power? Do that which is good and thou shalt have the praise of the same: For he is the minister of God to thee for good." |
| *Secure the blessings of liberty: | Leviticus 25: 10 | Proclaim liberty unto all the land, unto all the inhabitants thereof. |
| By equality in treatment, including ensuring an equitable rate of rate of taxation for all: | Exodus 30:11-15 | 11. "And the Lord spake unto Moses: 12 When thou takest the sum of the children of Israel after their number . . . !3. This they shall give, every one that passeth among them that are numbered, half a *shekel* after the *shekel* of the sanctuary: an half *shekel* shall be the offering of the Lord 14. Everyone that passeth among them that are numbered, from twenty years and above, shall give an offering unto the Lord. 15. *The rich shall not give more, and the poor shall not give less*, than half a *shekel* when they give an offering unto the Lord . . ." |

In this manner, graduated taxation was thus scripturally forbidden – making its imposition equally contrary to biblical prescription, to the express original intent of the Founding Fathers, and to Article I, Section 8 of the Constitution which stipulates that: "all taxation be uniform throughout the United States" – a proviso only to be undone in 1913 by the Sixteenth Amendment.[63]

Accordingly, while the Apostle Paul admonishes in Romans 13:7 that citizens are to: "render therefore to all that is due unto them: tribute to whom tribute is due; custom to whom custom is due" – the federal government, in supplanting the nuclear family and the community in their historic functions – and by confiscating 20 percent of national income in tax revenue, as it currently does each year – has concurrently doubled its scripturally-prescribed tax take to pay for the responsibility of that usurpation.[64]

This is, then, a policy course in direct contravention of biblical prescription. For the Scriptures clearly provide that families are to take care of their own, as stipulated by I Timothy 5: 3-4: "Honor widows that are widows indeed. But if any widow have children or nephews, let them first sow piety at home and requite their parents; for that is good and acceptable before God."[65]

The economic model that obtains today in America today, therefore, is neither scriptural nor is it the handiwork of a free market economic model. It is instead amongst the foremost machinations of the prototypic welfare state — and analogous to that of the "Seven Years of Famine" in ancient Egypt when the pharaonic minister Joseph levied a 20 percent production tax on all citizens, as described in Genesis 47: 20, 23-24:

> And Joseph bought all of the land of Egypt for the Pharaoh; for the Egyptians sold every man his field because the famine prevailed over them; so the land became Pharaoh's. . . .
> Then Joseph said unto the people: Behold I have bought you this day and your land for the Pharaoh. Lo, here is seed for you and ye shall sow the land. And it shall come to pass in the increase, that ye shall give the fifth part unto Pharaoh; and four parts shall be your own for seed of the field, and for your food and for them of your household . .[66]

As a consequence, while God still only seeks ten percent of income, government has not only confiscated the double portion that He has allocated to heads-of-household to provide for familial care, but employed citizens must now work until April 23 to pay their annual taxes in cost, more than their outlays food, clothing, and housing combined –a circumstance making them, in effect, tax-bonded sharecroppers for a profligate Congress.[67]

As with a greater tax share, government preempts increasingly more areas of society that historically has belonged to individuals, families, and religious institutions that benefit from their tithes. Given that the federal government has already preempted the traditional family's role in education, charity, and caring for the poor, this reality may best explain why it treats religion with hostility — it views it an economic competitor.[68]

The Scriptures likewise promote Calvinistic diligence – being replete with verses extolling diligence crafted in pursuit of the "Calvinistic work ethic." The Fourth Commandment, banning nonessential labor on the Sabbath, the seventh day, concurrently assumed that they were to be productively engaged throughout the first six. They make clear, moreover, that it is demonstrable performance, not labor alone, that is rewarded:[69]

---

***

### On the Biblical Prescription for Diligence:

* "Let your lights so shine before men that they may see your good works, and glorify your Father who is in heaven." (Matthew 5:16)
* "If any man's work abide which he has built thereupon, he shall receive a reward." (I Corinthians 3:14)
* "He becometh poor that dealeth with a slack hand; but the hand of the diligent maketh rich." (Proverbs 10:4)
* "See a man diligent in his business; he shall stand before kings." (Proverbs 22:29)
* "The substance of a diligent man is precious." (Proverbs 12:27)
* "And whatsoever ye do, do it heartily as to the Lord." (Colossians 3:23/ I Corinthians 10:31)
* "But we beseech you, brethren, that ye increase more and more. (I Thessalonians 4:11)
* "If any would not work, neither should he eat." (II Thessalonians 3:10)
* "Arise, work, and may the Lord be with you." (I Chronicles 22:16)

***

---

## IV. Fulfilling the Founders' Mandate for an Amalgamated Economic Model

Analysis to this point has revealed that the Founders' economic vision for America was to be an amalgam of classic Graeco-Roman economic precepts, biblical economic values, and European renaissance "enlightenment" socioeconomic concepts. Close scrutiny of how these values have coalesced to forge American democratic capitalism is illuminating.

### A. The Ideological Underpinnings of the Founders' Economic Model

In any quest for economic remedy, public policy matters. America today faces tectonic economic watersheds. Her existence has spanned twenty three decades. But just because a civilization has been around for two or three centuries is not *prima facie* proof that it will last forever. Indeed, the nation is precariously positioned today where Great Britain was at the turn of the Twentieth Century.

While time remains, therefore, it faces a defining choice between righting its economic policy course or following powers past, ancient, medieval, and more recent, into the trash bin of second-ranked global powers. Cognizant of these sobering precedents, learning the cogent lessons of that past can better position it to prepare for its strategic future.

America was founded on the precept of "democratic capitalism"– a somewhat improbable conjoining of terms inasmuch as the driving force of democracy is equality; of capitalism, inequality. The apparent incongruity is echoed in the concerns of the Founding Fathers. Thomas Jefferson's idyllic world was one wherein democracy prevailed. In arguing for a "national bank," conversely, Alexander Hamilton contemplated one where capital reigned supreme.

Yet the issue was effectively resolved with the establishment of an amalgamated system – one wherein the operations of capitalistic process are modulated and moderated by the corresponding workings of democratic process. The consummate success of this hybrid system of governance is reflected in many realities – among them, that even few of the most devout libertarians would today deny the utility of institutions such as Social Security or the "Federal Deposit Insurance Corporation."

Early on, in fact, the issue was joined in federalist jurisprudence. For the Constitution didn't limit what citizens could do – it merely prescribed what was permissible for the federal government to do – stipulating that any act not expressly permitted for it was specifically forbidden to it — the Tenth Amendment making explicit that those powers not sanctioned for it are denied.

To wit: "Those powers not delegated to the United States by the Constitution nor prohibited by it to the States, are reserved to the States respectively, or to the people." Indeed, on the *precise limits* of federal economic jurisdiction, Article 1, Section 8, states only that: "The Congress shall have the power . . . to regulate Commerce with foreign Nations, and among the several States, and with Indian Tribes."[62]

Hence, the federal government was empowered to regulate the commerce of indigenous tribes, that between foreign governments, and on an interstate basis only – and, in no way, to reign supreme over all things socioeconomic; to wit, to "govern" the private sector.

For all other tasks – education, crime control, business regulation, *ad infinitum* – are specifically reserved for the states or for the people. In this dichotomy, each jurisdiction cannot constitutionally interfere in the affairs of the other – as each sovereign government is held in jurisdictional check by the Constitution, whose higher law is proclaimed supreme in Article 6, paragraph 2.[63]

In the ageless words of James Madison: "The powers delegated by the Constitution to the federal government are few and well defined."[64] To which Thomas Jefferson presciently appended. "The way to have good and safe government is not to trust it all to one but to divide it among the many."[65]

Such, however, is not now the reality– as the federal government, like that of ancient Rome, has, over time, evolved into a hegemonic monolith administered by a massive sea of faceless bureaucrats. As today, it meddles in all aspects of human life – from birth, through education, through employment, through retirement, and ultimately, to death, and, at times, beyond.

In this quest, the federal government employs just less than three million employees to oversee the activities of just over three hundred million citizens. Whereas the ratio of civil service employees stood at 1:8,500 in 1789, it stands at 1:100 today – with each federal employee financed by taxes and paid to regulate some aspect or aspects of citizens' lives – and with state and local governments having concurrently experienced similar payroll growths.[66]

In the process, it taxes citizens not only in their first years of income but throughout their lives – from when they first commit their meager after-tax savings to those investments intended to secure their retirements, to the very estates that they have built as legacies to their children when they die. The result is not only a country that the Founders would not recognize, it is a malfeasance of economic governance, a denial of the lessons offered by the planet's economic past.

As economic history, as revealed, portrays in vivid terms the dramatic elevation of society through time powered by the private pursuit of profit motive in an unfettered free marketplace, a steady evolution that ranks amongst humankind's foremost monuments to progress. Yet today, civilization's prized legacy of "democratic capitalism" — and with it, many of America's hard won economic freedoms – instead stand gravely threatened from within, challenged by the wanton policy extravagances of her public sector and the exorbitant bureaucratic transaction costs that they engender.

Such costs, a product of profligate public spending, matter because they vitiate that private profit motive that throughout history has been the primal force impelling progress — the fuel that powers the economic engine that drives the march of civilization. They matter because "big government" – regulation and other gratuitous public service – clearly has its price.

Its toll comes in the form of taxes and oppressive governmental regulatory processes that sap vigor from the productive private sector – while its financial multiplier effects erode the free economy in a variety of other ways. As described by economist Milton Friedman:

> None of this means that government doesn't have a very real function. Indeed, the tragedy is that because government is doing so many things that it shouldn't be doing, it performs the functions that it ought to be performing badly.
> The basic functions of government are to defend the nation against its foreign enemies, to prevent the coercion of some individuals by others within the country, and to provide means for deciding on our rules, and to adjudicate disputes. . . .
> The net result has been that government has become a self-generating monstrosity. Abraham Lincoln talked at length about a government of the people, by the people, and for the people. What we now have is a government of the people, run by the bureaucrats — including legislators, who have themselves become bureaucrats – and for the bureaucrats.[67]

Yet government cannot build progress because it cannot create. It can only take and reallocate. It cannot produce anything, including jobs that it did not arbitrarily take in the first place. Because "bureaucratic transaction costs" systematically attenuate the earnings of private businesses, thereby undermining their global trade competitiveness, moreover, the afflicted jurisdiction, through down-sizing and industrial out-migration, invariably continues to lose higher paying production jobs which, as the "outsourcing" phenomenon makes clear, are most often replaced with lower-paying service jobs.

In seeking prospective remedy to the resulting deteriorating jobs and incomes situation, it is critical to again bear mind that the facts of life remain largely economic. Healthy macroeconomies produce robust private economic well-being, whereas deteriorating ones precipitate correspondingly adverse consequences. Unemployment is economic. Welfare is economic. Crime is economic. Unaffordable healthcare is economic. America's world, therefore, is one unequivocally economically-driven.

Americans, as good citizens accepting this reality, are willing to pay taxes — but they concurrently seek, and expect, value for their tax investments. In attempting to meet this reasonable expectation, the key policy question thus becomes – how does government within a democracy, faced with the need to win favor with voters by filling insatiable consumer demand, still preserve property earned through the pursuit of private profit, while, at the same time, limiting the growth of government to control the public debt and deficit.

Mindful that the burgeoning public cost of mounting bureaucratic complexity is the internal undoing of most civilizations, defining the proper role of government in the lives of the citizens of the embryonic nation was a clear concern of the nation's Founders. As articulated by her first president George Washington:"Government is not reason; it is not eloquence. It is force. Like a fire, it is a dangerous servant and a fearful master."[68]

John Adams, in 1772, similarly asserted that "the only maxim of a free government should be to trust no man living with the power to endanger liberty."[69] To these ends, James Madison, in *Federalist No. 10,* compellingly warned against: "that old trick of turning every contingency into a new resource for accumulating force within the government."[70] Whereas, the "First American Democrat," Thomas Jefferson similarly wrote:

> The natural progress of things is for liberty to yield and government to gain . . . The greatest calamity that could befall us would be submission to a government of unlimited powers. . . .
> The public debt is the greatest danger to be feared by a republican government. To preserve our independence, we must not let rulers load us with perpetual debt. We must make our choice between economy and liberty, or profusion and servitude.[71]

In his First Inaugural Address, Jefferson similarly proclaimed: "A wise and frugal government, which restricts men from injuring one another, must leave them otherwise free to regulate their own pursuits of industry, and shall not take from the mouths of men bread that they have earned."[72]

Jefferson likewise said: "I place economy among the first and most important virtues, and public debt as greatest of all dangers"[73]— and later in his career, would despairingly add: "Were we to be directed from Washington when to sow and when to reap, we would soon want for our bread!"[74]

Thus, the issues of government's role, and the tax costs required to sustain it, are longstanding. John Locke, the early 18th century British philosopher-statesman whose conservative political ideas inspired the Founders, believed that not debt, but the "preservation of private property" should be the ultimate end of government; whereas his slightly later 18th century French counterpart, Montesquieu, in like manner, maintained that public taxes were no more than that part of any person's property relinquished in order to secure protection for that part which remained.[75]

Operating within this ideological framework of an overarching sense of public need to protect private possessions, then, while the "republican" Hamilton espoused that "a national debt can be unto us a blessing," the "democrat" Jefferson believed that "limiting the purpose and size of government" could best meet the private property needs of "workers, farmers, and small businessmen"– the nation's citizens at large."[76]

Indeed, this was America's "social contract" with her people, as delineated by Jefferson within the "Declaration of Independence," the legally recognized principle that all were "created equal and endowed by their Creator with certain inalienable rights, among them, life, liberty, and the pursuit of happiness" – not happiness itself per se, but nonetheless a level playing field in its pursuit.

This precept meant that they could not be bound by the sovereign will of the British king to pay taxes to sustain His Majesty's empire. For in the *new* United States, the people would reign sovereign, with the government reduced to the role of servant set up with a limited, carefully circumscribed mandate to fulfil with the consent of the governed in the course of safeguarding their private property rights.[77]

Today, however, the demarcation of the respective ideological roles amongst the parties has become less clear. For while Hamilton's Republican political heirs now preach, if not always practice, fiscal responsibility and balanced budgets, they instead preside over record federal deficits. Jefferson's Democrats, on the other hand, despite his aspirations to limited government, have come to believe that larger, more assertive government is necessary to achieve their income redistribution goals.

Yet ironically, the very programs that they espouse are today devastating Jefferson's aspired prime constituency – those "workers, farmers, and small businessmen" who are the nation's productive citizens – as their onerous tax costs undermine and destroy people's abilities to help themselves.

Indeed, in a tragic spiral, as the tax burden occasioned by those costs grow increasingly more onerous, still more citizens are forced into the public sector dependency cycle at the expense of those productive citizens who remain. Thus it is that, to paraphrase Tom Brokaw's epic documentary of the WW-II era, *The Greatest Generation*, the successor offspring to that noble "generation that gave" have now been transformed into "the generation that took."[78]

Benjamin Franklin once averred that: "nothing is certain except death and taxes" – the modern response to which is: "At least death never gets any worse!" But though such tax-consuming "big government" has long historic precedent, today its role is expanding in an unprecedented way– as business management expert

Peter Drucker, in his seminal work: *The Age of Discontinuity,* concludes:

> There is mounting evidence that government is big rather than strong; that it is flabby rather than powerful; that it costs a great deal but doesn't achieve very much.
> There is mounting evidence also that citizens less and less believe in government and are becoming increasingly disenchanted with it. Government is sick – and at a time when we need strong, healthy government.[79]

The effects of such bloated government, which some have called "*demosclerosis,*" can be devastating. As throughout history, the world's great imperial powers – 3rd century Rome, 9th century Baghdad, 16th century Spain, and 19th century Britain – whose ascendancies were all initially founded upon the inherent strengths of durable private economies that enabled them to be net exporters of capital – all eventually lost their global primacies due to the mounting taxes needed to cover burgeoning domestic public debt produced by public sector fiscal excess.[80]

## B. The Founders' Economic Model and the Quest for Remedy

Such a danger clearly was a foremost concern at the time of the founding of the American Republic. Indeed, Jefferson, in many missives, argued: "Loading up the nation with debt and leaving it for the following generation to pay is morally irresponsible. No nation has a right to contract debt for a period longer than the person contracting it can expect to live."[81] Accordingly, upon reflection, he called upon the fledgling American democracy to:

> Declare in the Constitution that they are forming that neither the legislature nor the nation can validly contract more debt than they can pay. . . .
> I wish it were possible to obtain a single amendment to our Constitution. I would be willing to depend upon that alone for reduction of administration of our government to the genuine principles of its Constitution.
> What I mean is an additional article taking from the federal government the power of borrowing.[82]

The Founders were thus well attuned to the lessons of economic history as well as to the sage scriptural admonition that: "A good man leaveth an inheritance to his children's children."[83]

Historically, in fact, America has long honored an implicit social contract to leave a productive legacy for her offspring. But today, a wantonly permissive public sector short-sightedness has set in that has left that contract in shambles. For in blithely passing off the burgeoning federal debt to her lineage, America stands in direct contravention of both historic warning and Divine admonition – as generations yet unborn will bear the burden of the current budgetary process. In so doing, a group is unabashedly being taxed that has no vote – an act that precipitated the Founders' original political revolt — "taxation without representation" — which they equated with tyranny.

Accordingly, the American Revolution of 1776 was, at its roots, a capitalistic revolution – an economic protest against attempts by England's King George III to tyrannically impose his country's interventionist, anti-capitalist system of mercantilism upon the colonies. As a consequence, foremost amongst the Declaration of Independence grievances were numerous economic ones.[84]

The British king, for instance, was denounced for "imposing taxes on us without our consent." These protests came after a series of tax levies – the Navigation Acts, the Townshend Acts, the Stamp Act, and the Tea Act most noteworthy among them – imposed by imperial fiat over the three decades leading up to 1776 – significantly increased tariffs and taxation on the colonies.[86]

Hence, numerous specific safeguards were built into the Constitution of 1789. The Contracts Clause prohibited any laws abridging freedom of contract. The Commerce Clause outlawed protectionist tariffs in interstate commerce, in effect, making the country a free trade zone. This clause, it must be recalled, applied only to *interstate* commerce, not to the regulation of *intrastate* commerce, a function reserved exclusively to states.[87]

The Due Process Clause, in turn, protected private property by stipulating that no person "shall be deprived of life, liberty, or property without due process of law;" whereas the Constitution likewise mandated that all taxation as then conceived be uniform with the unequivocal words: "All Duties, Imposts, and Excises shall be uniform throughout the United States," whose proceeds were then to be dedicated to "promote the general welfare," benefits afforded to all citizens, not to special interest welfare as is the case today.[88]

In enumerating these powers, the Founders made their intent clear. James Madison, in *Federalist #45*, wrote: "The powers delegated by the proposed Constitution to the federal government are few and defined, Those which are to remain in the State governments are numerous and indefinite. The former will be exercised principally on external objects, such as war, peace, negotiation, and foreign commerce."[89]

Indeed, Madison, widely acknowledged as "Father of the Constitution," in *Federalist Paper No. 45*, explicitly warned the Congress that the "general welfare" clause of the Constitution was never intended to become a "Pandora's "Box" for special interest legislation. Building upon his assertion that: "If Congress can do whatever in their discretion by money. . . government is no longer a limited one possessing enumerated powers, but an indefinite one subject to particular exceptions."[90] Thomas Jefferson was similarly moved to append the clarification: "Congress has no unlimited powers to provide for the general welfare, only those specifically enumerated."[91]

Jefferson's contention thus built upon the provision of Article 1, Section 8 of the Constitution which authorizes Congress to tax and spend for "the general welfare of the United States" — a clause intended by the Founders as a limit on federal power — to wit: the federal government can tax and spend only for that which benefits the nation *generally*, not for the *specific* welfare of groups or individuals.

Succinctly put, the federal government was empowered to, and limited from exceeding, providing for the "common defense and general welfare of the United

States;" which as defined by Article 1, Section 8, consists of seventeen discrete functions, cited in their order of appearance within the text of the amendment as follows:[92]

| | |
|---|---|
| (1) contracting debt; | (10) punishing pirates; |
| (2) regulating foreign commerce; | (11) declaring war; |
| (3) establishing rules for naturalization; | (12) raising & supporting armies; |
| (4) collecting taxes and coining money; | (13) providing for a navy; |
| (5) establishing weights and measures; | (14) regulating naval & land forces; |
| (6) punishing counterfeiting; | (15) calling forth the militia; |
| (7) establishing a postal system and roads; | (16) organizing the militia; and |
| (8) promoting science; | (17) administering the nation's capital. |
| (9) establishing a judicial system; | |

Alternately put, the federal government was constrained to making laws through such enumerated powers as the regulation of interstate and foreign commerce, coining currency, operating post offices, providing copyright protection, enforcng laws for citizenship, and maintaining the armed forces. Hence, while the states were prohibited from interfering in these distinct federal functions, all other governmental powers were mandated to them — and the national government was expressly forbidden from meddling in them.[93]

Today, however, such is not the case, for as noted, the federal government has now grown from three original departments with a handful of employees to fifteen cabinet-level departments, hundreds of federal agencies, and nearly three million employees – in the process, usurping practically every power constitutionally consigned to the states.[94]

This was a possibility of grave concern to James Madison – in his vigorous assertion that: "I cannot undertake to lay my finger on that article in the Constitution which granted to Congress of expending, on objects of benevolence, the money of their constituents"[95] – who further explained when he prophetically wrote that:

> If the Congress can apply money indefinitely to the general welfare, and are the sole and supreme judges of the general welfare, they may take care of religion into their own hands; they may take into their own hands the education of children, establishing in like manner, schools throughout the Union; they may undertake the regulation of *all* roads, other than post roads.
> In short, everything from the highest object of State legislation down to the most minute object of policy, would be thrown under the power of the Congress; for every object that I have mentioned would admit the application of money, and might be called, if Congress pleased, provisions for the *general welfare*.[96]

In the supporting argument of Thomas Jefferson in arguing against federal banking legislation proposed by Alexander Hamilton:

> The Constitution allows only the means which are "necessary," not those that are merely convenient for effecting the enumerated powers. Had such a latitude of construction been allowed to this phrase, as to give any non-enumerated power, it will go to every one; for there is no one which ingenuity may not torture into a convenience, in some way or another, to some one of so long a list of enumerated

powers; it would swallow up all of the delegated powers.[97]

Summarily stated, in Madison's and Jefferson's view, the scope of spending appropriated by Congress within its constitutionally enumerated powers must perforce be spent for the *general* welfare, not for specific individuals or regions, groups of persons, or special interests – no pork barrel, no earmarks.[98]

This was, in fact, a position endorsed by the Supreme Court as well as late as 1936, when it ruled in *U.S. v. Butler* that the term "general welfare" implies that government may not tax and spend for the welfare of "specific" socioeconomic groups – in so doing, noting that "the power to confer or withhold unlimited benefits is the power to coerce and to destroy."[99]

The Founders thus, with great deliberation, framed a distinct, yet discrete, vision for America's public administration framed as one of limited governance. Indeed, indicative of its circumscription, the following fiscal model reflects how the FY 2007-2008 Federal Budget would have looked had Congress incorporated just those seventeen functions that it can legally incorporate pursuant to the Article I, Section 8, "Duties and Responsibilities," prescriptions of the Constitution – while stripping out those functions expressly prohibited to it and reserved for the states and the people by the Tenth Amendment. The regression, which employs estimated budgetary outlays, by function, is as follows: "Common defense" functions, cited as numerically delineated, are listed in Paradigm 1:

Paradigm 1

| Mandate Cost (Millions) | Budget Category: | Line: |
|---|---|---|
| A. *Common Defense* | | |
| $571,869 | 050 Total National Defense= | —which includes (10) punishing pirates (11) declaring war (12) raising and supporting armies (13) providing for the navy (14) regulating naval and land forces (15) calling forth the militia (16) organizing the militia |
| $72,401 | 700 Cost of Veterans Benefits= | |
| $7,428 | 920 Homeland Security | —includes: (3) establishing rules for naturalization |
| Total = $651,698 | | |

"General welfare" functions, again cited as numerically delineated, in turn. are listed in Paradigm 2.

158                                     Chapter Five

| Paradigm 2 | | |
|---|---|---|
| Mandate Cost (Millions) | Budget Category: | Line: |
| B. *General Welfare* | | |
| $251,541 | 900 | Treasuries Function include:<br>(1) contracting debt and<br>(4) collecting taxes and coining money<br><br>— Total Net Interest on Debt $239,153<br>—Treasury Functions<br>  —IRS $10,438<br>  —US Mint $1,950 |
| $35,071 | 050 | Includes:<br>(2) regulating foreign commerce=<br>—Total International Affairs |
| | 372/400 | Includes:<br>(7) establishing a postal system & roads=<br>which includes |
| | 372 | —Postal Service ($5,715) |
| | 400 | —Total Transportation $74,607 |
| $558 | 370 | Includes:<br>(5) establishing weights and measures =<br><br>which is the current responsibility of<br>—National Institutes for Science & Technology= |
| $24,862 | 250 | Includes:<br>(8) promoting science which includes:<br>—Total Federal Science & Technology |
| $35,407 | 750 | Includes:<br>(6) punishing counterfeiting; and<br>(9) establishing a judicial system= |
| $34,602 | | which include:<br>—Total Administration of Justice<br>which incorporates<br>  —Federal Judicial Activities: $9,756<br>  —Federal Law Enforcement: $24,846 |
| $3,936 | 800 | Includes:<br>(17) Administering the Nation's capital=<br><br>which includes:<br>  —Legislative Functions: $3,141<br>  —Executive Functions: $517<br>  —Payments to District of Columbia: $278 |
| Total=$420,267 | | |
| AGGREGATE TOTAL FY 2007 FEDERAL BUDGET AS PRESCRIBED BY THE FOUNDING FATHERS<br>$1,071,965 | | |
| Source: *Budget of the United States, FY 2008* | | |

The results produced by a constitutionally-prescribed and proscribed federal budget are thus shown to be quite extraordinary – revealing that by strictly adhering to the Founding Fathers' fiscal mandate, the country could have eliminated all federal income taxation, and still have produced a $431 billion annual budget surplus in FY 2007-2008 – as follows:

| Paradigm 3 | |
|---|---|
| Category | $US (Millions) |
| *Total Estimated FY 2007 Federal Budgetary Outlays | $2,784,267 |
| *Total Estimated Actual Individual and Corporate Income Tax Collections FY 2007 | $1,510,900 |
| *Total FY 2007 Federal Budget If Constructed IAW the Founding Fathers' Constitutional Mandate: | $1,071,965 |
| *Amount Available to Reduce the Federal Deficit After Achieving a Balanced Federal Budget While Also Eliminating All Federal U.S. Income Taxation | $438,935 |

Thus it may be shown that inordinate income taxation is the costly price that America pays for the "New Deal" and the "Great Society." The data further reveal that a succession of such annual budgetary surpluses using static revenue projections would enable the country to eliminate its present $12 trillion-dollar-plus federal debt – now standing at over at $40,000 for each and every citizen – and that, in less than two decades. Alternately, assuming dynamic revenue scoring of the economic stimulus projected to be produced by elimination of U.S. income taxation in its entirety would show the entire national debt being repaid within a decade.

Indeed, the results would be more remarkable still had just *those discrete portions* of the DOD, Homeland Security, State, Justice, and Transportation budgets that were the Founders' original intent been employed – but which were nonetheless incorporated intact within the model both because they are now integrated national functions that the individual states cannot be reasonably expected to unilaterally perform on behalf of their residents – as well as to preclude equivocation over just what part of a given budget, say the Defense budget, is actually "defense," etc.

Amazing what America could accomplish were she to just elect Congresses committed to the Founders' rule of law. For cutting the federal budget in the manner contemplated by them would not only produce a budget in full fiscal balance, it would likewise meet the mandate that Jesus clearly had in mind when he admonished that good citizens share equally between state and church – government and God – when he instructed in Matthew 22:21 and Mark 12:17 to: "Render unto Caesar the things that are Caesar's; and unto God the things that are God's."[100]

# Chapter Six
# Education in the Founders' Vision for America

*Train up a child in the way he should go; and when he is old, he will not depart from it.*

—Proverbs 22:6

Education is the critical complement of economics in society-building. Indeed, it is far more than that. It is the primary power engine of economic growth. So integral is it to the development process that it may unequivocally be asserted that it *is* the very essence of economic advance.

Education matters because it is the impetus propelling the technological progress that drives the course of civilizations. It matters because it epitomizes the fruits of those cultural blessings that issue from a free society. Education is the future of a nation – as well as a prime beneficiary of that "capital surplus" that derives from prudent tax and regulatory policies.

For civilization flows from freedoms – freedom from political oppression, freedom from the subjugation of economic regulation, freedom from the need to devote the total of one's energies to the exigencies of sheer survival so that they may be redirected to the arts and sciences.

Education is, in fact, the anvil upon which society is forged. It is, in the words of historians Will and Ariel Durant, "the transmission of civilization."[1] H.G. Wells, in his *Outline of History*, declared that "history is a race between education and catastrophe."[2] Franklin Roosevelt, echoing Plato, called learning the "foundation of democracy."[3]

As Henry David Thoreau put it: "I know of no fact more encouraging than that of man's ability to elevate his life through conscious endeavor."[4] To which Victor Hugo contributed: "He who opens the door of the schoolhouse closes the doors of the jail."[5] Indeed, the Bible itself, in Matthew 28-19, counsels: "Go ye, therefore, and teach all nations . . ."

Creating sound educational infrastructures thus is quintessentially important to the process of building a civilization. For if the courts have indeed adopted the neo-Marxist position that school children are "wards of the state,"[6] – a lower court determination described in Chapter 3 that the Supreme Court has allowed to stand– then society must clearly come to grips with the reality of the determination of Abraham Lincoln that: "The philosophy of the schoolroom in one generation will be the philosophy of government in the next."[7]

Alternately put, whoever controls the schools sets the goals for the nation, establishes its religious values, and ultimately controls its future. From the academies of ancient Sparta and Athens to medieval Notre Dame of Paris and Al-Azhar of Cairo, on to Harvard and Yale, education has been the principal means of cultural advance.[8]

Accordingly, "the government must be capable of offering greater education and better instruction to people than they would demand from it," opined 19th century British economic philosopher John Stuart Mill. "Education, therefore, is one of those things that a government should provide for its people." This was a position adopted by America's Founders as well, and was a clear aspiration in their attempts to forge public education policy – building upon a history of longstanding tradition.

Given academia's foremost role of preserving and transmitting knowledge – of being a civilization's conservator of tradition and cultural values – then, it is distressing to contemplate the base, self-serving propagandistic role to which it has been reduced in the humanities departments of many of even the finest colleges and universities throughout America today.

For liberal dogma not withstanding, it is not the state that is the wellhead fount of societal advance. To the contrary, name a single statist society that enjoys a rich cultural heritage? There are none. Milton Friedman speaks precisely to this point:

> Great advances of civilization, whether in architecture or painting, in science or literature, industry or agriculture, have never come from centralized governments. Columbus did not set out to seek a new route to China in response to a majority directive of parliament. . . .
> No government can duplicate the variety and diversity of individual action. At any moment in time ..... by imposing uniform standards in schooling, road construction, or sanitation, central government can undoubtedly improve the level of performance in many localities and perhaps even the average of all communities. But in the process, government would replace progress with stagnation, it would substitute uniform mediocrity for that variety essential for experimentation that can bring tomorrow's laggards above today's mean.[9]

Education is also a mandate of government — a vital, indeed, quintessential, public sector function if progressive civilization is to advance. For that reason, the U.S. Constitution, Article I, Section 8, makes "progress in the arts and useful science" an explicit governmental function – thus again making manifest the Founders' abiding foresight and intent.

Education likewise is an intangible societal building block whose long term repayment horizons put it beyond the grasp of most private sector investment models. The reason is its fungibility. For while physical capital can always be repossessed and resold, such is not the case for human capital. Yet it is indispensable for long term success in the economic development process.[10]

Such knowledge-based imperatives thus become critical as America moves still further into the 21st century – as within the "new economy," successful technological development strategy will be founded squarely upon state-of-the-art education and "top-to-bottom" workforce training – as in the 21st century development process, education's potentials are limited only by the horizons of humankind's creativity.[11]

For in its most pragmatic context, education sets into motion a cyclic progression — fostering applied research, which leads to new products and processes, which result in new businesses, which provide jobs, which create economic surpluses produced by wages and profits, which contribute public revenues for further funding education — all of which impel civil progress.

Knowledge is, moreover, a prime source of global strength. It has always conferred power upon those who have it and know how to properly use it. For education fuels an economy by shaping society at the hands of its productive people. Unlike tools or machines, which can only be used by one person at any given time, moreover, the same body of knowledge can be employed by many different users simultaneously – and when employed to its optimal productivity, can generate still more new knowledge and information.

Knowledge is no longer just a resource, then, it is *the prime resource* that powers modern civilization – shaping America's society while driving her economy. Indeed, the proliferation and dissemination of knowledge to increasingly greater numbers concurrently holds the crucial key to both political sovereignty and future economic progress. For just as the last century's "Industrial Age" required horsepower, so the "new economy" requires brainpower. But in planning its development, its roadmap must be carefully crafted to national strengths and values.

As knowledge in any society is no less than the corpus of those individual ideas and philosophies that forge its distinct character – and in the ongoing quest for economic and societal success, ideas matter. Recall the words of John Maynard Keynes who, cognizant of this reality, in the closing sentence of his famed General Theory of Employment, concludes: "Sooner or later, it is ideas, not vested interests, that are dangerous for good or evil."[12]

At the economic bottom line, then, the inherent strength of any nation lies in the capacity of its productive populace to produce – employing skills that are at once upgradable and renewable. The talents of a nation's workforce are what make it unique — and can thus make it uniquely successful in the evolving world economy — as it is sound, in-depth education that is the prime catalyst that makes productivity enhanced through technology possible. Education thereby serves the industrial economy by making it more efficient, linking future ability to prosper with present ability to educate and empower a workforce.

Human resource development thus becomes of paramount importance in any comprehensive 21$^{st}$ century economic strategy. Its imperative arises both because returns on human capital are now constantly rising relative to those on financial capital, and because such investments aid the efforts of a jurisdiction's citizens to add value to the global economy.

For in the international marketplace, workers can command higher wages and better jobs only by adding more value to their products and services than do their counterparts abroad – thereby offsetting higher earnings with greater productivities to produce those necessarily balanced unit labor costs that preclude inflation from engulfing the economy.

While in the "Industrial Revolution," the economic balance of power dramatically shifted from labor to financial capital, moreover, within the "Knowledge-Based Revolution," the value of human capital is rapidly reascending – replacing monetary assets as the prime vehicle for prosperity and growth. Because it reduces the need for raw materials, labor, space, time, and dollar capital, acquired knowledge is, in fact, the force singularly driving economic advance as the nation moves ever further into the 21$^{st}$ century.

## II. Education and the Founders' Vision

Education was a paramount priority for the nation's Founders as well – and characteristically, it commenced with their desire to preserve religious freedoms. The colonists' commitment to ruling America in accordance with God's will and Christian values extended to, and indeed was embodied by, education, at the founding of the republic, patriot, politician, and publisher Samuel Adams, in 1771, affirmed:

> Let divines and philosophers, statesmen and patriots, unite their endeavors to renovate the age by impressing the mind of men of the importance of educating boys and girls, of inculcating in the minds of youths the fear and love of the Deity and universal philosophy, and in subordination to these great principles, the love of their country; of instructing them in the art of self-government, without which they can never act a wise part in the government of societies, great or small; in short, of leading them in the study and practice of the exalted virtues of the Christian system.[13]

To these ends, Adams, called by many the "Father of the American Revolution," proposed that "Committees of Correspondence" be established throughout the colonies so that people could be educated to the extent that they could deductively reason their rights and political convictions based on biblical principles – desiring that the colonies be united "not by external bonds but by the vital force of distinctive ideals and principles."[14]

Indeed, America's early educational infrastructure was expressly built upon the nation's irrevocable commitment to imparting knowledge and preserving a panoply of freedoms – political, personal, and religious freedoms foremost among them – in its quest to build a "biblical commonwealth" – and to then pass the torch of that knowledge on to forthcoming generations.[15]

As its initial settlers, many of whom had suffered persecution for their religious beliefs in Europe, believed that it was biblical illiteracy – and the attendant inability to distinguish right from wrong – that was the incipient cause of civic abuse. In education, therefore, they were fervent believers in the counsel of biblical Deuteronomy 6:5-7:

> And thou shalt love the Lord thy God with all thine heart, and with all thy soul, and with all thy might. And these words, which I commend to thee this day, shall be in thine heart; and thou shall teach them diligently to thy children, and shall talk of them when thou sittest in thine house; and when thou walkest by the way; and when thou liest down, and when thou riseth up;[16] — as well as: Hosea 4:6: My people are destroyed for lack of knowledge;"[17] — Proverbs 1:5,7: "A wise man will hear and increase learning . . . but fools despise wisdom and instruction;"[18] — and Proverbs 22:6: "Train up a child in the way he should go; and when he is old, he will not depart from it."
>
> Such convictions were, in fact, explicitly articulated by many of the Founding Fathers, among them:[19]

---

***

## THE LINKAGE BETWEEN EDUCATION AND RELIGION AS PERCEIVED BY THE FOUNDING FATHERS [20]

Reason and experience forbid us to expect that national morality can prevail to the exclusion of religious principle. . . . Promote, then, as an object of primary importance, institutions for the general diffusion of knowledge

– GEORGE WASHINGTON, First President of the United States.[21]

Religion is the only basis of good morals; therefore education should teach the precepts of religion and the duties of man toward God

– GOUVERNEUR MORRIS, Signer of the Constitution.[22]

> You have received a public education the purpose whereof hath been to qualify you the better to serve your Creator and your country. . . .Your first great duties, if you are sensible, then, are those you owe to Heaven, your Creator and Redeemer. Let these be ever present to your minds and exemplified in your lives and conduct
>
> – WILLIAM SAMUEL JOHNSON, *Signer of the Constitution.*[23]
>
> Education leads the youth beyond mere outside show and will impress their minds with a profound reverence of the Deity. . . . It will excite in them a just regard for Divine revelation
>
> – SAMUEL ADAMS, Signer of the Declaration of Independence.[24]
>
> The only foundation for a useful education in a republic is to be laid in religion. Without this, there can be no virtue, and without virtue, there can be no liberty; as liberty is the object and lifeblood of all republican governments. . . . Let the children, therefore, be instructed in the principles and obligations of the Christian religion
>
> – BENJAMIN RUSH, Signer of the Declaration of Independence.[25]
>
> \*\*\*

In short, the Founders believed that not to teach a student "the Ten Commandments, the Lord's Prayer, and the Sermon on the Mount would be the same as to not teach him the multiplication tables and the rules of syntax."[26]

Consistent with the counsel of Matthew 28:18: "Go ye, therefore, and teach all nations," then, the nation's earliest efforts at public education were attempts to preempt those perceived abuses of power that can be inflicted upon a biblically-illiterate people. As Thomas Jefferson — defining a liberal education as "reading, writing and common arithmatick" . . . followed by the reading of Graecian, Roman, English and American history. . . (to make the beneficiaries) worthy to receive and guard the sacred deposit of the rights and liberties of their fellow citizens" — said:

> It cannot be doubted that in the United States the instruction of people powerfully contributes to the support of the democratic republic; and that will always be the case, I think, where the instruction that enlightens the mind is not separated from the education responsible for moral manners.[27]

Like Jefferson, James Madison too not only expected schools to provide instruction in Greek, Latin, geography, and the higher branches of numerical arithmetic, together with Grecian, Roman, and American history, he also expected them to instill "the first elements of morality" into the students' minds.[28] John Quincy Adams concurred: "To a man of liberal education, the study of history is not only useful and important, but altogether indispensable, and with regard to the history contained in the *Bible*."[29]

This imperative, as articulated by another founder, Noah Webster, "America's Schoolmaster," was predicated upon his conviction that "the Christian religion is the most important and one of the first things in which all children, under a free government, ought to be instructed. . . . No truth is more evident to my mind than that the Christian religion must be the basis of any government intended to secure the rights and privileges of a free people."[30] Accordingly, Webster aspired to an educational system that would "discipline our youth in early life in the sound maxims of moral, political, and religious duties," contending that:

> All miseries and evils which men suffer from vice, crime, ambition, injustice, oppression, slavery and war proceed from their despising or neglecting the precepts contained in the *Bible*. . . .
> In my view, the Christian religion is the most important and one of the first things that all children, under a free government, ought to be instructed. . . . No truth is more evident to my mind than that the Christian religion must be the basis of any government intended to secure the rights and privileges of a free people.[31]

This was a position earlier advanced by Benjamin Franklin as well. To wit: "A nation of well informed men who have been taught to know and prize the rights which God has given them cannot be enslaved. It is in the region of ignorance that tyranny begins."[32]

Echoing Rush and Franklin, Fisher Ames, another Founder, in arguing for the primacy of the *Bible* as a classroom tool, argued: "Should not the *Bible* regain the place that it once held as a school book?"[33] — and Benjamin Rush, a contemporary, concurred that: "In contemplating the political institutions of the United States, if we remove the *Bible* from the schools, I lament that we waste too much time and money punishing crimes and take so little pains to prevent them."[34]

In like manner, educator William McGuffey, a Presbyterian clergyman and author of a famed set of childhood readers, of their content, asserted: "For copious extracts from the Sacred Scriptures, (I make) no apology."[35] Thus, taking heed from the biblical admonition: "My people are destroyed for lack of knowledge"[36] – the nation's first public school laws – affectionately then known as the "that old deluder Satan" laws explicitly designed to ensure that students would know how to read the *Bible* – were enacted in Massachusetts in 1642 and in Connecticut in 1647, mandating:

> It being a chief project of that old deluder, Satan, to keep men from the knowledge of the Scriptures . . , It is therefore ordered that . . . after the Lord hath increased (a settlement) to the number of fifty households, they shall then forthwith appoint one within their town to teach all children as shall resort to him, to write and read . . . And it is further ordered that when any town shall increase to the number of one hundred families or householders, they shall set up a grammar school . . . to instruct youths so that they may be fitted for the university.[37]

Early on, taxation likewise was established within the colonies to fund public education, Maryland, the Carolinas, and Georgia being amongst the earliest — and such laws were often accompanied by supportive literacy laws such as that of Connecticut enacted in 1690:

> The (legislature) observing that . . . there are many persons unable to read the English tongue and thereby incapable to read the Holy Word of God or the good laws of this colony . . . it is ordered that all parents and masters shall cause their respective children and servants, as they are capable, to read distinctly the English tongue.[38]

Indeed, to ensure that biblical literacy was achieved, the Dorchester, Massachusetts school system in 1645 mandated that its schoolmaster "each second day in the weeke shall call his schollers together betweene 12 and one of the Clock to examine them what they have learned on the Saboath day proceeding (and) . . . Every sixth day of the weeke shall catechise his schollers in the principles of the Christian religion."[39]

To further such early attempts at education, books would be brought in from England, often by incoming immigrants a few volumes at a time, throughout the 18th century. Various manuals to provide guidance for education within the colonies – such as John Brinsley's *A Consolation for Our Grammar Schooles*, produced in 1622, was designed to preserve the purity of the English language of a people dwelling in such a faraway land, explicitly referring to Virginia – and took as its express goal to improve the "country grammar schooles" and to "expand the Kingdom of Christ, especially among the heathen Indians" – and a few books likewise were printed in America herself, such as the *Bay Psalm Book* of 1640.[40]

The Protestants who settled the English colonies greatly valued the school, therefore, because it taught their children to read the *Bible*, which was deemed the seminal document guiding early colonial life and education. Beside it in the classroom was the so-called "horn-book," which was a small, wooden paddle-shaped instrument upon which was inscribed the Lord's Prayer, the alphabet, basic numerals, and sundry other reading materials, which were covered by transparent horn that lent the instrument its name.[41]

Complementing the "horn-book" as a teaching tool was a small, multipurpose reader titled the *New England Primer* – a widely-circulated text conveying a distinctly Calvinistic standpoint respecting sin and salvation, law and gospel, which is estimated to have been produced in over three million copies – as well as Noah Webster's spelling book, Lindley Murray's grammar, and Warren Colburn's arithmetic. A concurrent spelling and grammar text, *A New Guide to the English Tongue* (1740), employed extensively throughout early New England schools, began its first lesson with all of its words no longer than three letters, as follows:

> No man may put off the Law of God.
> The way of God is no ill way.
> My joy is in God all the Day.
> A bad man is a foe to God.[42]

Slightly later, the famed *McGuffey's Readers* – primers *cum* religious indoctrination instruments – commenced with a lyric recital of the alphabet, beginning:

> With Adam's fall;
> We sinned all.[43]

Indicative of its genre and teaching mode, in *McGuffey's Fifth Eclectic Reader* – part of a series that would ultimately sell over 120 million copies between 1836 and 1920 – in a typically preachy essay by one William Ellery Channing titled "Religion: the Only Basis of Society," one finds:

> Pure and undefiled religion is to do good; and it follows very plainly that if God is to be the Author and Friend of Society, then recognition of Him must enforce all social duty, and enlightened piety must give its whole strength to public order.[44]

Similarly, in early America, as a self-professing Christian nation, New England colonial colleges were established with the express mission to "further the gospel of Christ in all disciplines." Already within a century of the arrival of the first settlers at Jamestown, three colleges had been established in the colonies. Amongst them, the College of William and Mary was founded in Williamsburg, Virginia in 1692 with the objective that: "The youth may be piously enacted in good letters and manners and that the Christian faith may be propagated . . . to the glory of Almighty God."[45]

Nine of America's first ten earliest major colleges were, in fact, created by ecclesiastical denominations:

| Religious Provenance of America's Earliest Major Colleges[46] | | |
|---|---|---|
| Harvard | 1638 | Congregationalists |
| William and Mary | 1693 | Episcopalians |
| Yale | 1700 | Congregationalists |
| Princeton | 1746 | Presbyterians |
| University of Pennsylvania | 1747 | Individuals and the State, although it relied upon the Churches for financial support and has been under Christian control |
| Columbia | 1759 | Episcopalians |
| Brown | 1764 | Baptists |
| Rutgers | 1770 | Dutch Reformed |
| Dartmouth | 1770 | Congregationalists |
| Hampton Sydney | 1775 | Presbyterians |

Indeed, an 1884 census of education found that of the 370 colleges then in America, 309 were religious denominational colleges.[47]

Thus it was that Harvard College (later to become Harvard University in 1693) – founded by Calvinistic Puritans of Massachusetts in 1636, sixteen years after their arrival in the New World – adopted as its motto: *Veritas Christo et Ecclesiae* (Truth

170                                    Chapter Six

for Christ and Church). In this *modus operandi*, the school's 1636 rules for students stipulated:

> Let all students be plainly instructed and earnestly pressed to consider well that the main end of his life and studies is to know God and Jesus Christ which is eternal life (John 17:3), and therefore to lay Christ at the bottom as the only foundation of sound knowledge and learning.
> And seeing that the Lord only giveth wisdom, let every one set himself by prayer in secret to seek it of him. (Proverbs 2:3). Everyone shall so exercise himself in reading of the Scriptures twice a day that he shall be ready to give such an account of his proficiency therein.[48]

Harvard's admission standards therefore were stringent: "When any scholar is able to understand Tully or any such classical author, extemporize and make and speak in true Latin in verse and prose; . . . and decline perfectly the paradigms of nouns and verbs in the Greek tongue, let him then, and not before, be capable of admission into the college."[49]

A typical school day at Harvard, as experienced by student and future president John Adams, consisted of regular daily prayers and Scriptures reading at 6:00 AM; followed by breakfast; classes at 8:00 AM; more classes and studies throughout the day; and evening prayers at 5:00 PM. Saturdays were set aside for theological studies, memorizing works of dogmatic theology, and taking turns reading aloud passages from the Scriptures and expounding upon their meanings before fellow students.[50]

The express objective of Yale's founders, a university established in 1699 by ten clergymen, in like manner, was that the "Westminster Confessional be diligently read in the Latin and well studied by all Schollars . . . for the upholding of the Christian protestant Religion by a succession of Learned and Orthodox men." To this end, its mission was to "propagate in this Wilderness the Blessed Reformed Protestant religion."[51] Indeed, when its classes began in 1701, Yale required that:

> The Scriptures . . . morning and evening, are to be read by the students at prayer times in the school . . . studiously endeavoring in the education of said students to promote the power and purity of religion. . . . so that every student shall consider the main end to his study is the wit to know God in Jesus Christ and answerably to lead a Godly, sober life.[52]

Princeton University, founded by the Presbyterians in 1746, whose official motto was "Under God's Power, She Flourishes," similarly took as its mission that:

> Every student shall attend worship in the college hall morning and evening at the hours appointed, and shall behave with gravity and reverence during the service. Every student shall attend public worship on the Sabbath. . . . Beside the public exercises of religious worship on the Sabbath, there shall be assigned to each class certain exercises for their religious instruction suited to the age and standing of the pupils . . . and no student belonging to any class shall neglect them.[53]

Indicative of the educational preeminence of Princeton, during the twenty-six years that Founder John Witherspoon served as its president, from 1768 to 1794, the school produced 478 male graduates, an average of about eighteen per year. Of them, 114 became ministers; one, James Madison, became President; another Aaron Burr, became Vice President; 30 were United States senators; 3 were U.S. Supreme Court justices;13 were state governors; and 9 constituted one-sixth of the 55 delegates to the 1787 Constitutional Convention.[54]

The express goal of King's College, created in 1754 as the precursor to Columbia University, likewise was to: "teach and engage children to know God in Jesus Christ and to love and serve Him . . . and to train them up in all virtual habits and all such useful knowledge as may render them . . . useful to the public weal in their generations." Its admissions requirements thus specified that "no candidate shall be admitted into the college . . . unless:

> he shall be able to render into English . . . the Gospels from the Greek. . . . It is also expected that all students attend public worship on Sunday.[55]

When John Jay enrolled in at the college at the age of fourteen in 1759, the entrance prerequisite was to "give a rational account of the Latin and Greek grammars,'" read the first three of Tully's *Select Orations* and the first three books of *Aeneid*, and translate the first ten chapters of St. Johns's Gospel from Greek into Latin.[56] By 1785, they had evolved as follows:

> No candidate shall be admitted into the College . . . unless he shall be able to render into English Caesar's *Commentaries of the Gallic War* . . . the four Orations of Cicero against Catiline . . . and the Gospels from the Greek . . . and turn English into grammatical Latin, and shall understand the first rules of Arithmetic . . . with the rule of three.[57]

The College of William and Mary, chartered in 1692, similarly took as its express mission that "the youth may be piously enacted in good letters and manners, and that the Christian faith may be propagated to the glory of the Almighty God" – and to this end, a working knowledge of Greek was a prerequisite to admission.[58]

Rutgers, established in 1766, in turn, was the creation and doctrinal bridgehead of the Dutch Reformed Church. Its official motto: "Sun of Righteousness: Shine Upon the West Also" – a slogan that it borrowed from the Netherlands' University of Utrecht logo: "Sun of Righteousness: Shine Upon Us" – derived from the biblical verses: Malachi 4:2 and Matthew 13:43.[59]

Indeed, 106 of the first 108 colleges in America – many of which took as a prime mission producing clergymen and educated laities for their denominations – were founded on the Christian faith – almost invariably with a clergyman as college president — and by 1860, of the nation's 246 colleges, 229 were religious institutions.[60] In the words of social historian Henry May:

> From the very beginnings, the express purpose of colonial education had been to preserve society against barbarism, and so far as possible, against sin. Inculcation of a saving truth was a primary responsibility of churches, but schools were necessary to promote written means of revelation.[61]

At the onset of the Republic, therefore, public education dedicated to service of God was amongst its foremost distinguishing features – with its purview and administration largely a requirement and function of the individual states. For though the federal Constitution did not explicitly address education, its subsequent influence upon the discipline has been both manifold and profound. Instead, relying upon the doctrine of reserved powers delineated in the Tenth Amendment, the prime responsibility for education was not only delegated to the states but concurrently served to preclude the federal government from interference in its execution.[62]

Nonetheless, the Founders retained an abiding interest in fostering learning. The foremost goal of public education in the early United States, as they perceived it, was succinctly articulated by George Washington on May 12, 1779 to chiefs of the Delaware Indian tribe: "You do well to wish to learn our arts and way of life, and above all, the religion of Jesus Christ. This will make you a happier people than you are. Congress will do its utmost to assist you in this wise intention."[63] In his famed Farewell Address, in turn, he reiterated the familiar words:

> Promote, therefore, as an object of primary importance, institutions for the general diffusion of knowledge. For in proportion as the structure of government gives force to public opinion, it is essential that the public option should be so enlightened.[64]

Echoing this assertion, John Adams, in a letter to his son on the importance of education in 1777, asserted that it is necessary to teach the next generation about America's founding principles in order to preserve the freedom and independence that so many of his fellow countrymen had sacrificed to achieve.[65]

Writing from his official ambassadorial posting to Paris in 1786, Thomas Jefferson similarly asserted that only through education could peoples preserve their freedoms and ensure their individual happiness. Education, therefore, he proclaimed, "is the business of the state to provide, and that through a general plan." In like manner, the nation's very first Chief Justice, John Jay, considered "knowledge to be the soul of the republic" — and the nation's fourth President, James Madison, declared that "knowledge will forever govern ignorance; and a people who mean to be their own governors must arm themselves with the power that knowledge gives."[66]

As a result, in the words of Jefferson, America's schools became what he called the "keepers of the vestal flame" – the principal institutions entrusted with passing on the nation's identity and mission in the interests of civility and unity. They were to be the nexus whereat differences, bred of creed and class, could be reconciled.[67]

The Founding Fathers themselves, it deserves restating, were, by no means, illiterate men. To the contrary, they were extraordinarily erudite. Thus, John Adams in 1776, as noted, would rejoice: "It has been the will of Heaven that we should be thrown into existence at a period when the greatest philosophers and law givers of antiquity would have wished to live. . . . How few of the human race have ever had the opportunity of choosing a system of government for themselves and for their children!"[68]

Endowed with this rich intellectual legacy, then, it is no surprise that Article III of the "Northwest Ordinance," enacted in 1787 and reenacted in 1789, stipulated that: "Religion, morality, and knowledge, being necessary to good government and the happiness of mankind, schools and the means of education shall be forever encouraged." This clause makes vividly clear, in fact, that it was the intent of the First Congress that a prime responsibility of the nation's public school system was to instill religious and cultural values within the citizens of the realm.[69]

While this proviso at its inception applied only to the original territories of the United States as of 1789 – Indiana, Illinois, Michigan, Minnesota, Ohio, and Wisconsin – moreover, it was gradually also extended to other territories as they were incorporated into the United States, including Mississippi, Alabama, Missouri, Arkansas, Kansas, and Nebraska – all of which replicated the language of the "Northwest Ordinance" respecting the establishment of public education.[70]

In this spirit, the Continental Congress in March, 1775, recommended that the central section of every township be reserved for the support of education; and that the one-mile-square area adjoining it to the north be reserved for the support of religion.[71] Thus it was that America's public schools indeed became the nation's "keepers of the vestal flame" – and grew to be the principal institution entrusted not only with imparting knowledge but with preserving and then passing on the nation's identity and mission from generation-to-generation, inculcating a reverence for faith, unity, civility, and American ideals which were their *raison d'être*.[72]

Indeed, until the mid-20th century, the nation's public school system was its central institution charged with building patriotism and adherence to civic values through its cultural assimilation processes. Its formal creation was, in fact, in large part, dictated and shaped by a perceived need for the "Americanization" of citizens, particularly immigrants – as the nation looked to education as the optimal way to transmit Anglo-American values and preserve civic institutions.[73]

To these ends, the local schools offered civics classes that stressed American principles, history, and ideals. In the words of social analyst Stephen Steinberg: "More than any other factor, the public school system undermined the capacity of immigrant groups to transmit their native cultures to American-born children."

These were critical undertakings all – for as aptly articulated in the eloquence of Ronald Reagan: "If we ever forget what we did, then we won't know who we are."[74]

## II. THE STATUS OF K-12 EDUCATION WITHIN CONTEMPORARY AMERICA

It is a national tragedy, therefore, that public education is in serious trouble throughout America today. Statistics suggest that as many as three million people graduate from her K-12 (elementary and secondary) schools as functional illiterates each year. Many cannot read above a third grade level. They cannot perform simple mathematics. They cannot keep a checkbook. And in many cases, they cannot earn a subsistence income. Indeed, many cannot even fill out an employment application without someone reading it to them. Yet this outcome comes as no surprise.[75]

For the problems afflicting the nation's K-12 system directly correlate to, and indeed, feed into, those that pervade its higher education system today – representing a tragic deterioration of a precious national asset. For very much like America's village churches of the 17th and 18th centuries, her local public schools, were, as described, originally designed as places wherein useful knowledge, as well as character and personal integrity, were instilled in her children from their earliest years. Just as the country's first universities were founded as colleges embracing religion, so her common K-12 schools were founded as places where reading, writing, history, science, and math were taught within a moral setting structured to mold the nation's youth into adults of character.[76]

Rather than stripping students of their earliest-instilled knowledge and values, then — as is now happening throughout the local school system in its frenetic dash to supplant traditional beliefs with a leftist humanistic creed — teachers sought to build character upon the foundations of the traits that their pupils had learned in their homes and in their churches.[77]

Foremost amongst America's K-12 educational challenges today, therefore, go to the core issue of the propriety of its general curriculum. For whereas American schools used to teach reading, writing, arithmetic, history, and geography, today they have deteriorated into mere cells for counter-cultural indoctrination.

How dramatically things have changed – and for so little cogent reason. As for education to work at any level, there must be standards. At the K-12 level, students must develop skills in the fundamentals that allow them to acquire the reservoirs of knowledge that they will need not merely to compete at the universities but to enjoy successful careers and serve as good citizens.

Unfortunately, the generation that produced "Woodstock" also has developed an educational system that has stranded millions of young people in a limbo of academic mediocrity and unmet academic aspirations. As a consequence, the public schools – erstwhile equalizers of American society – have degenerated into little more that Petrie dishes for liberal social engineering.[78]

As today, after more than two centuries of presumptive "progress," U.S. high school graduates about to enter college have almost no practical knowledge of their

*Education in the Founders' Vision for America* 175

nation's history and only a rudimentary command of the nation's official language, English, let alone any knowledge of Latin or Greek. Some see this educational downsizing, in fact, as part of an intentional, carefully constructed liberal "dumbing-down" of education that has led, in turn, to a general collapse of social, cultural, and moral standards throughout both the nation's K-12 and higher education systems; from there percolating out into society as a whole.[79]

For by the close of the 1960s, noted sociologist Catherine Iserbyt writes, the so-called "educational progressives" had ensconced themselves within the academic system at all levels, and operating from this power base, have advanced a radical new philosophy that: "American education would henceforth concern itself with the importance of the 'group' rather than the individual" – and in this process, public education would no longer focus upon the teaching of history, language, mathematics, and the sciences, but instead upon the student's emotional health and socialization.[80]

Indicative of this "new wave" educational approach, the "National Education Association" (NEA), America's largest teacher's union, promptly proclaimed that the traditional teaching of "reading, writing, and arithmetic" had now been overtaken by the need for public schools to become "agents of social change." Theodore Sizer, former dean of the Harvard School of Education, has synopsized the goals of such "outcome-based-education" processes as that of a desire to "move away from nationalism toward the concept of 'world family.'"[81]

Indicative of the *"spirit of the age,"* John Dewey, referred to by many as the father of modern education," and then honorary president of the NEA, wrote:

> I believe that the true center of correlation on the school subjects is not science, not literature, not geography, but the child's social activities. . . . I believe that the school is primarily a social institution. . . . The teacher's business is simply to determine, on the basis of larger experience and riper wisdom, how the discipline of life shall come to the child. . . . All the questions of grading the child and his promotions should be determined by reference to the same standard. Examinations are of use only to the extent that they test the child's fitness for social life.[82]

To which, former NEA president Catherine Barrett, in openly endorsing continuing political indoctrination aimed at social transformation in the nation's K-12 system, in an address to its membership in 1975, appended:

> First, we must help all of our people to understand that education is a concept, not a place. We will not confuse "schooling" with education. The school will be the community, the community the school. . . .We must recognize that the so-called basic skills, which currently represent nearly the total effort in elementary schools, will be taught in one-quarter of the present school day.
> The remaining time will be devoted to what is truly fundamental and basic — time for academic inquiry, time for students to develop their own interests, for a dialogue between students and teachers; more than a dispenser of information; the teacher will be a conveyor of values, a philosopher.[83]

More egregious still, reminiscent of the "mind-speak" of the novel *1984*, the counsel of education professor Charles Pierce at Harvard – called by some the "People's Republic of Cambridge" – instantaneously becomes germane:

> Every child in America entering school at the age of five is mentally ill because he comes to school with certain allegiances toward the founding fathers, toward elected officials, toward his parents, toward a belief in a super-natural Being, toward the sovereignty of this nation as a separate entity, It is up to teachers to make sick children well by creating the international children of the future.[84]

It is not surprising, therefore, that today, the primary and secondary schools' priority focus has shifted from the hard core academic disciplines to diverse and superfluous counter-cultural agendas addressed to such ephemeral matters as how to build "self-esteem" absent criticism or honest grading, being "citizens of the world," understanding how western culture destroys indigenous societies, and learning how to practice safe sex.[85]

Such a curricular course, as shown, contravenes American educational tradition. Historically, the nation's schools were designed to be agents of cultural unification. They taught patriotism and cultural values. Immigrants speaking not a word of English were placed in English-only class-rooms, and soon they were proficient in the language.[86]

But today, under the guise of preserving notions of "self-worth," the nation's education system has become the forward battle staging area in the attempts of modern liberals to dismantle American culture.[87] Yet to the degree that such forays into counter-cultural fantasy come at the expense of classroom time more usefully spent on more economically productive academic disciplines, to what productive end? [88]

Nowhere are the results of this arcane education process more clear than in the initially proposed "National Standards" testing which asked 7th-8th graders to address how "Columbus's description of the peaceful and pleasant nature of the Carib Indians contrasts with his treatment of them." Never mind that the cheerful, pleasant Carib Indians were cannibals who tortured and ate their male captives. Students were concurrently instructed to consider the achievements of Aztec civilization but not their practice of human sacrifice.[89]

There was no mention in the testing of Daniel Webster, Robert E. Lee, Alexander Graham Bell, Albert Einstein, Jonas Salk, or the Wright Brothers. But Joseph McCarthy and McCarthyism is cited nineteen times, the Ku Klux Klan seventeen. The reasons for the founding of the "National Organization for Women" (NOW) were deemed exceptionally newsworthy; the forming of the First Congress was not.[90]

In a subsequent edition of the testing that did prevail, students are asked to analyze modern feminism, described as "compelling in its analysis of women's problems and the solutions offered." Students are simultaneously given a thorough founding in Watergate as well as the keen insight that Ronald Reagan was known as "Herbert Hoover with a smile."[91]

Since none of these "vital topics" appear on Scholastic Aptitude Tests, it is not surprising that SAT scores are in decline – as those student who come out of high school may do so with higher self-esteem, together with more powerful testosterone and estrogen, but relatively little, if any, ability to perform intellectually.

And it is equally not surprising that employers throughout America are finding America's secondary school graduates entering the workplace wholly unprepared to compete for 21$^{st}$ century jobs – as decreasing competence is inevitable in an educational system wherein intellect has lost its virtue, abandoning its quest for truth in favor of the pursuit of extremist political ends.[92]

The bottom line, however, is that because humankind is educable, the overarching goal of public education must be to produce successful people, not merely "politically correct "ones. Neither society nor the individual is made better if the principal output of a nation's education system is sensitive, albeit affable, dolts.

Damage done to national well-being by the leftists' quest for radical educational reengineering thus is incalculable. Recognizing this reality themselves, in fact, the educators have tried to cover it up – removing entire traditional sections of the SAT that examine student abilities to reason and reach logical comparisons and conclusions.

Indeed, after more than two decades of declining SAT scores, test developers decided to give all participants a gratuitous "100 point bonus," thereby effectively deliberately disguising the fact that American secondary students preparing for college are now far less knowledgeable than were their predecessors just two generations ago.[93]

But such subterfuge can only go so far – as the ongoing deliberate "dumbing down" of American education has become a crisis that threatens the very future of the Republic. For while K-12 school officials and college administrators continue to deny these facts, the truth is undeniable – as reflected in graduates unable to hold modern high tech jobs, employers whose earnings are diluted by the need to retrain and educate high school graduates – and by universities themselves that must constantly lower their admissions standards to accommodate new categories of underperforming students who must then undergo months of remedial training to empower them to compete at a college academic level.[94]

Such realities as deliberate "dumbing-down" and subsequent ideological reprogramming of K-12 students thus should be matters of the grave concern for all Americans, as economist Thomas Sowell makes clear:

> Creating mindless followers is one of the most dangerous things that our public schools are doing. Young people who know only how to vent their emotions, and not how to weigh opposing arguments through logic and evidence, are sitting ducks for the next talented demagogue who comes along in some cult or movement, including some like those that put the Nazis in power in Germany. . . .

At one time, the educator's creed was: "We are here to teach you how to think, not what to think. Today, our schools across the country, at the expense of how to think, are teaching students what to think — whether about the environment, the war, social policy, or whatever."[95]

In essence, then, in recent decades, America's youth have been taught that learning is a mere minor annoyance on the path to unlimited self-indulgence – being allowed to coast through elementary and secondary school learning with only superficial intellectual exertion, all the while being assured that they were the "best and the brightest," the finest that the nation could produce.

But such a policy has its price — as there has been massively mounting evidence that this approach has instead merely made them more susceptible to ideological indoctrination in the liberal counter-cultural and social cant now being inculcated throughout the nation's schools.[96]

Yet at the academic bottom line, turning K-12 students into reprogrammable automatons is probably not good public policy — notwithstanding that as a result of the shifting emphasis away from core curricula into the ethereal and the aesthetic, the evolution of American educational malaise has endured a long gestation,

Already as early as a half a century ago, Professor James Coleman, in his massive 1966 study, *Equality of Educational Opportunity*, concluded that the nation's ineffective public school system was making no discernable impact in either eliminating or even moderating disparities of achievement amongst students – concluding that problem was programmatic and systemic, and could not be solved by simply spending more money on it.[97]

In 1983, moreover, the "National Commission on Excellence in Education's" famed *Nation at Risk* report in 1983 proceeded to identify further alarming signs of intellectual decay, moving it to call the graduating products of the nation's K-12 schools a "rising tide of mediocrity:" To wit:

> Our recent unchallenged preeminence in commerce, industry, sciences, and technological innovation is being overtaken by competitors throughout the world...... What was unimaginable a generation ago has begun to occur – others are matching and even surpassing our educational attainments. . . .[98]
>
> Had a foreign power attempted to impose upon America the mediocre educational performance that exists today, we might well have viewed it as an act of war. As it stands, we have allowed it to happen to ourselves. . . . we have, in effect, been committing an act of unthinking, unilateral educational disarmament.[99]

Seven years later, in 1990, the U.S. Department of Education further conceded:

> Large proportions, perhaps more than half, of our elementary, middle, and high school students are unable to demonstrate competency in challenging subject matter in English, mathematics, science, history, and geography. Furthermore, even fewer of them appear to be able to use their minds well.[100]

Regrettably today, as the nation moves ever further into the 21st century, all evidence is that neither its warning has been heeded nor has the downturn been reversed — that far too little progress has been made in the quest to restore educational excellence. As today, far too many U.S. school systems remain foundering islands of incompetence in a sea of public policy indifference. In the warning of economist Milton Friedman: "The amount spent per pupil in the past thirty years has tripled in real terms after allowing for inflation. Although input has tripled, output has been going down. Schools have been deteriorating."[101]

Accordingly, now even America's "best and brightest" — the approximately two million K-12 students whose testing actually *does* rank them in the top five percent in national achievement — as shown, often seriously trail their counterparts in other countries, and the best students in the critical areas of science and math, in particular, rank merely "at the bottom of the best" of other industrialized nations. U.S. 12th grade students, for example, recently performed well below the international average of 21 countries on a test of general knowledge of science and mathematic; whereas 11 nations outperformed them in a 15 nation assessment of advanced mathematics skills.

More recently, the Organization for Economic Cooperation and Development (OECD) "Program for International Student Assessment"(PISA) in 2006 determined that "American students ranked 33rd among world industrialized countries in science literacy and 27th in math competence.[102]

Studies of twenty countries done by the National Center for Educational Statistics similarly revealed that thirteen-year-old Americans ranked thirteenth amongst their global counterparts in science and fifteenth in mathematics. Amongst the countries that ranked higher in both subjects were Korea, Taiwan, Switzerland, Russia, Israel, Slovenia, Canada, France, and Hungary.[103]

In the latest example, in Michigan, in the spring of 2007, in pre-college qualification testing, just 51 percent of the junior-level students tested passed the English portion of the test; an even lower 47 percent passed the math portion; and an abysmal 40 percent passed the writing portion of the statewide so-called "Merit Exam." What is needed in the American K-12 system, then, is not more pedagogical claptrap of union-driven teachers telling students how worthy yet oppressed they are but instead more focus upon teaching the hard core disciplines.[104]

In civic affairs, random testing similarly found that today's K-12 students lack an understanding of even the most rudimentary principles of modern governance – revealing that just 42 percent of thirteen-year-olds and 74 percent of seventeen-year-olds could give an acceptable answer to the question: "what is democracy?" — and only 37 percent of seventeen-year-olds could describe how presidential candidates are nominated.[105]

Regrettably, such civically-illiterate K-12 students grow up to be American voters. As a consequence, a survey of 1,004 U.S. adults found that 46 percent of the respondents did not know that the original purpose of the Constitution was to create a federal government and define its purpose; 26 percent believed that it was framed to declare independence from Great Britain; only 41 percent correctly identified the Bill of Rights as the first ten amendments to the Constitution; whereas 27 percent thought that it is the preamble to the Constitution.[106]

What's worse, the national *high school dropout rate* has increased since 1983. Of those pupils who reach the ninth grade level, a full one-third disappear before high school grade graduation. Another one-third finish high school but aren't, in any way, ready for college or the workplace. Only the upper one-third of students, then, leave high school actually prepared for productive citizenship.

America's business competitors meanwhile are advancing and surpassing her. Of the twenty foremost developed nations, she ranks 16th in high school graduation rates and 14th in college graduation rates. Yet that list doesn't include China and India, still classified as "developing countries," but who are nonetheless are becoming her rapidly emerging premier trade competitors.

As a consequence, the nation now ranks 49th in the world in overall literacy; 28th out of forty countries in mathematical literacy; behind the European Union in producing science and engineering graduates as well as scientific literature — and its front line production workers lack basic skills to the degree that American businesses must spend over $30 billion annually on remedial education and training.

Small wonder that in 2001, the bipartisan Hart-Rudman "Commission on National Security" found that after terrorism, the second greatest threat to national security is the failure of math and science education. Indeed, in a unanimous consensus, it found that this educational failure is a greater threat to America's present well-being than any conceivable conventional war within the next quarter century.

The problem is not primarily one of money – as the United States already outspends most other major industrial nations per capita on K-12 education, while their students consistently outperform those here. A Cato Institute study has found that whereas federal educational spending, in real terms, stood at about $25 billion in 1960, it now approaches $110 billion and continues to grow, Indeed, since 1980 alone, funding for American public schools from all sources has more than doubled.[107]

Yet the needless diversion of finite education resources to non-educationally productive causes plays out in the results – and the results are devastating. In the 2006-2007 academic year, spending in Washington D.C. schools stood at $10,103 per student, the highest in the nation after Alaska. But only twelve percent of the district's eighth grade public school students could read at eighth grade levels in 2005 and only seven percent could do eighth grade mathematics. By contrast, in Iowa and South Dakota, both of which spend far less per pupil than Washington D.C., more than a third of the eighth grade pupils could read and perform mathematics at or above eighth grade levels.[108] In the words of economist Walter Williams:

> If money were the answer, Washington public schools would be the best in the nation – if not the world. . . . With a 'student-teacher ratio' of 15.8, they also have smaller-than-average class size.
> What is the ultimate result? In only one of the city's 19 high schools do as many as 50 percent of its students test as proficient in reading, and at no school are 50 percent of the students proficient in math.[109]

Hence, while federal solutions have typically consistently proposed more brick and mortar, American children still can't read and calculate their math. Fiscal realities suggest, therefore, that the remedy for the nation's educational deficiencies lies not in increased expenditures of tax dollars, but rather in the more productive use of the training resources that actually have been made available.

For succinctly put, and as a definitive Hudson Institute study makes clear, it is disastrously poor classroom productivity, not too little spending, that is the central cause of the expanding crisis now enveloping America's K-12 education system. To again quote Thomas Sowell:[110]

> Our education system is turning out increasing numbers of people who have no skills that anyone would pay for out of his own pocket. They thus have little choice but to become busybodies in government or in programs paid for with taxpayers' money or foundation grants designed to get taxpayer money later. This is called "public service."

Indeed, at a time when current economic, demographic, and competitive forces have combined to create a workplace wherein one's basic learning tools are of paramount importance, the present elementary and secondary school systems operating within many regions of America are actually regressing in their abilities to impart the job skills needed by high school graduates entering the work force. Small wonder also, then, that a multitude of major high tech industry executive told the 2007 "National Governors Association Convention" that America's public K-12 schools "no longer make the grade."[111]

The key public policy question thus becomes: can such regression be reversed? While there may be no single solution, it is clear that better teachers must be supported by sounder education policies, lending promise to some combination of a significant number of prospective remedies — among them, restoring the primacy of the hard core disciplines — mathematics, science, history, civics, and communications — in the K-12 curriculum, annual teacher competency testing, better productivity controls, and development of superior vocational training.

Such reform cannot come soon enough — as over 90 percent of all future jobs will require at least a high school education. Thus, to prosper, America cannot continue to allow her educational focus to lag behind the pace of technological change. For already, as noted, declining literacy and numeracy is denying many young people access to even entry level jobs. Yet no small part of the problem stems from the underutilization of *existing* educational resources which, if used more productively, would enable the nation's K-12 educational infrastructure to do more with less.

As today, America remains committed to the 180 day school year — a relic of the economic dictates of an agrarian age wherein children were required to spend their summer months working on their family farms — an industrial phenomenon that is no longer a prime societal concern. By contrast, the more urban offspring of her principal trade competitors in Europe and Japan now spend 220 to 240 days in the K-l2 classroom. Germany, for example, requires her high school students to study core "hard discipline" academic subjects 3,528 hours per year, compared with just 1,460 hours for America's youth.[112]

In like manner, typical Japanese K-l2 students receive an average of 5 hours per day of homework, compared with one hour for their U.S. counterparts. This is doubtless a significant factor why Japanese students consistently score at median 70 percent achievement levels on standardized mathematics scores, compared with 40 percent for American students; and 67 percent on science scores, contrasted with 55 percent for U.S. teenagers.[113]

The notion that America can somehow achieve educational parity with her principal trade competitors with dramatically lower levels of intellectual commitment thus constitutes an academic arrogance that cannot continue if the nation to remain an economic superpower.

But systemic overhaul of the attendance dimension to the K-12 training process is not the total solution. For in tandem with consideration given for extending the school year quantitatively, a concerted focus also must be lent to improving it *qualitatively* — to make better use of the time that *is* available

As presently, much of a typical American school day is spent — indeed often wasted — on non-academic activities. No more than 40 percent of U.S. high school students' productive classroom time, for instance, is now spent on the combination of math, science, history, civics, geography, and foreign languages — less than one half that of their German, French, and Japanese counterparts.

If America's schools are going to effectively compete intellectually, then, they must begin *by getting back to basics* – commencing with immediate reinstatement of a primary focus on communications skills, mathematics, and the scientific disciplines. Greater opportunity for the acquisition of "fast track skills" as well as increased incentives for *individual* students to excel likewise are required if the nation's graduates are gain a secure foothold on the path to successfully competing in the highly sophisticated 21$^{st}$ century job market.

Though such trends must be reversed, they are not irreversible. In her founding years, as shown, America's citizens were amongst the most literate on earth. The education of her youth has always been her path to progress. She now stands at a crucial crossroad confronting a critical public policy choice: will she rescue the education of her coming generations or forever consign them to menial labor and their nation to the ranks of second rate economic progress?

### III. THE CONTINUING CAUSES OF THE DISINTEGRATION OF AMERICAN EDUCATION AT THE K-12 LEVEL

The diffusion of counter-cultural influence thus has now percolated devastatingly down into America's basic educational foundations – portending a socioeconomic catastrophe of epic proportions if permitted to proceed. For all of civilization, as demonstrated, has been built upon a strong educational infrastructure – a reality that applies to the economic as well as social dimensions that are the focus of this inquiry. The quest to preserve America's economic might as well as preserve her historic values, therefore, must perforce commence in her K-12 classrooms.

For economic growth in the Information Age depends less upon a nation's ability to work harder than smarter. Such growth derives from two principal sources: commitment — growth in total hours worked and — productivity — growth in output per hour. Historically, about one-quarter of all productivity growth has relied upon increased educational attainment. That ratio will expand significantly in coming decades, moreover, as retiring baby boomers reduce the total number of hours worked, and economic growth tends to rely increasingly on productivity-enhancing investments.[114]

The nation's economic security likewise relies upon education and training to enhance the work-related skills that people need to ensure their employability in a world wherein multiple job and even occupational changes over a lifetime is becoming the norm. The requisite increase in human capital stock, however, can only be bought by equal measures of education, training, and practice, and can best be measured by, among other things, formal schooling and on-the-job training.

In this quest, as noted, America spends prodigious sums of money. In 2006, the nation paid $8,287 annually for each child in public schools – twice what it was spending three decades ago. The rising cost of education, in fact, has outpaced practically every other public sector spending benchmark for nearly a generation.[115]

But money alone does not buy quality education. In the mid-1990s, the *National Assessment of Educational Progress* (NAEP) found that while New York typically spends over 150 percent more on K-12 education than does Utah, 72 percent of Utah students were ranked academically "proficient" contrasted with 62 percent in New York. The Czech Republic spends about one-third as much per pupil as does the United States and enjoys a world ranking of 6$^{th}$ in math and 2$^{nd}$ in science, contrasted with an American ranking of 28$^{th}$ in math and 17$^{th}$ in science.[116]

The key determinant, therefore is not the quantitative one of how much money is being spent, but rather a qualitative one of how well it is spent. While New York City spends $11,172 per child in its school system, for instance only 40 percent of its $16 billion education budget winds up in the classroom. The remaining 60 percent goes to bureaucracy and infrastructure.[117]

Accordingly, America today is no longer the most educated nation in the world. She is instead ranked seventh after Canada, Finland, Japan, South Korea, Norway, and Switzerland. A recent Academy of Science study has found her students well below the international average in a ranking of 12$^{th}$ graders within twenty-one countries on general knowledge in math and science.[118] Overall, the studies show, the United States ranks twenty-fifth among forty-one industrialized countries in math and science – as she is developing the scholastic profile of a third world nation.[119]

The bottom line: U.S. schools are now failing drastically in their abilities to impart the hard core job skills that students elsewhere in the world are mastering. Only about 40 percent of U.S. high school seniors come to college prepared in algebra. Only a quarter are ready for college science. Only 56 percent meet the recommended core curriculum for college-bound students. Technological innovation has historically empowered the United States to be the global leader. Her crisis in math and science education now not only threatens her position as a global innovator, therefore, but as high tech jobs increasingly leave the country, her national security is jeopardized as well.[120]

For the reality is that today, one-third of all American jobs demand high tech skills. There is another six million job requirements for scientists and engineers. The Labor Department estimates that 260,000 new math and science teachers are needed in the present 2008-2009 school year – and they have their work cut out for them.[121]

But the qualitative dimension to the K-12 education challenge extends deeper still. Most local school districts today must contend with sizable numbers of poorly trained and educated teachers, teacher union arrogance and intransigence, administrative incompetence, community apathy, and too many parents who neither nurture nor discipline their children, nor encourage learning, nor meet with teachers to ensure quality instruction in reading, mathematics, and other basic skills.[122]

Teachers unions are a particularly critical component of the problem, invariably insisting that their membership be paid based on seniority rather than on-the-job performance that a merit-based system provides. In this process, better teachers are not rewarded with higher pay nor are substandard ones docked and demoted.

Instead, the sole criterion for upward salary mobility is that the longer that one works, level of classroom achievement notwithstanding, the better one is paid. Indeed, after a half decade of their handiwork, even Albert Shanker, head of the nation's second largest teachers' union, was moved to concede:

> Ninety-five percent of the kids who go to college in the United States would not be admitted to college anywhere else in the world.[123]

To again recall Jefferson: "If a nation expects to be both ignorant and free in a state of civilization, it expects to be what never was and never will be."[124] Recommendations explicitly designed to remedy such shortcomings are presented in the Appendix to this inquiry.

# EPILOGUE
# God, Governance, and "Deicide"

> "Something there is that does not love a wall,
> that wants it down."
>
> —American Poet Laureate Robert Frost,
> The Mending Wall

## I. "Separation of Church and State:" Mending or Dividing Wall?

"For what avail the plough or sail, or land or life, if freedom fail," the 19th century American poet Ralph Waldo Emerson asked in paean to his hometown Boston on Independence Day, 1873.[1] If freedom fail! That is a critical reflection a century and a half later, as America stands poised at the onset of her second decade of the Twenty First Century contemplating that very prospect.

At the very least, the religious dimension to freedom in America is now threatened – as the ongoing assault on it reflected in the specious juridic exegesis of the now famed 1802 letter of Thomas Jefferson to the Danbury Baptist Association addressing "the separation of church and state" makes clear. Calling the phrase "a misleading metaphor," former Chief Justice William Rehnquist, writing the dissenting opinion in *Wallace v. Jeffrey* (1985), excoriated its modern interpretations as "based on bad history."[2]

Aristotle said that: "the greatest thing to be by far is a masterpiece of metaphor."[3] Yet the converse is true as well. Subsequent judicial action has unequivocally demonstrated that Justice Rehnquist was indeed correct – that metaphors can create their own realities; and that, in this case, an expression of speech designed to facilitate the interaction of church and state with clarifying constitutional language that, in retrospect, to some appears enigmatic, today has been inverted by modern radical courts to subvert its original intent.[4]

American poet laureate Robert Front's determination — "something there is that does not love a wall; that wants it down" — manifest in his classic *Mending Wall* becomes cogent here.[5] For when Justice Hugo Black, in *Everson v. Board of Education* (1947), proclaimed that the First Amendment: "in the words of Jefferson . . . erected a 'wall of separation between church and State that must be kept high and impregnable," he dramatically transformed the national dialogue, indeed the very nature, of the critical interface of God and governance in America.[6]

Black's ruling was, in fact, a juristic watershed, as today, the so-called "wall of separation" has become the jurisprudential motif – the *locus classicus* – in defining the constitutional role of role of religion in American public life.

Yet America had ample warning, Four years before, in an unrelated case, *Tiller v. Atlantic Coast Railroad Co.* (1943), Justice Felix Frankfurter – arguing that courts too often use metaphors in attempts to mask what they are unwilling to admit: that they lack precedential paradigms, thereby substituting metaphors to create new realities – warned that: "A phrase begins life as a literary expression; its felicity leads to lazy repetition; and repetition soon establishes it as a legal formula indiscriminately used to express different and sometimes contradictory ideas."[7]

In like manner, a year after Black's initial ruling, Justice Stanley Reed protested in a follow-on case that "a rule of law should not be drawn from a figure of speech."[8] As a consequence, as Justice Oliver Wendell Holmes observed nearly a century and a half before: "It is one of the misfortunes of the law that ideas become encrusted in phrases and thereafter for a long time cease to provoke further analysis."[9]

Regrettably, notwithstanding that it is impossible to build sound constitutional doctrine upon the foundations of simplistic, often mistaken, interpretations of political history — and never mind that Jefferson was in France throughout the time that the First Amendment was debated and then promulgated into law — his somewhat cavalier 1802 political courtesy letter to the Danbury Baptists typecasting the "establishment clause" has served to undermine the workings of constructive judicial interpretation of religion within the nation for over the past half century; in so doing, beckoning the vanguard of the secular barbarians to the gate.[10]

## II. THE BARBARIANS AT THE GATE

As analysis has shown, America enjoys deep religious roots. She has a profound history that has shaped her mind, her law, and her institutions. Her roots are grounded in Eurocentric Judeo-Christian tradition. Today, these values are threatened at the hands of extremist social engineers abetted by an equally radically leftist court. Yet history shows that from a cultural cohesiveness standpoint, such trends are terminally toxic and must be irrevocably reversed.[11]

Two millennia ago, Roman citizens recoiled at the prospect of Carthaginian military leader Hannibal attacking their city-state. He did, in fact, ultimately reach the city's gates by moving his army on elephants across the Alps, but there he was fortuitously stopped – and Rome wouldn't fall for another seven centuries. It was instead a different enemy that felled the empire – the cancer of a polity weakened from within by disintegrating social values and crumbling institutions.[12]

Recall that in 1857, Lord Macaulay predicted a similar fate for the United States: that the American republic would be undone in the 20$^{th}$ century by its own Huns and Vandals "engendered within your own country by your own institutions."[13]

Though the 20th century has now come and gone, Lord Macaulay may have well been right. As today, there is indeed an enemy at the gates of the American republic set into motion in the second half of the 20$^{th}$ century– a counter-cultural revolution that has shaken it to its social roots. As a consequence, the nation is forgetting those values that once made it great — abandoning the principles set forth by the Founders that, in their time, were revolutionary — while losing respect for that supremacy of the Constitution that unites the national cause.[14]

In the immortal words of Daniel Webster: "Hold on, my friends, to the Constitution and to the Republic for which it stands. Miracles do not cluster, and what has happened once in 6,000 years may not happen again. Hold on to the Constitution, for if the American Constitution should fail, there will be anarchy throughout the world."[15]

Not heeding that noble warning, today, the Constitution has been twisted and subverted – shaped by extremist ultra-left judges to mean not what it says but what they want it to mean – overturning the law of the land and the rule of the people while justifying their distortions by rationalizing that it was a document written for another time – with the consequence that a judicial notion now prevails that faith in a transcendent God is superfluous to the way the nation governs its affairs.[16]

Yet recall the prescient warning of George Washington:

> Of all the dispositions and habits which lead to political prosperity, religion, and morality are the indispensable supports. In vain would that man claim the tribute of patriotism who should labor to subvert these great pillars of human happiness, these firmest props of the duties of men and citizens. The mere politician, equally with the pious man, ought to respect and cherish them. . . .
> Let it simply be asked where is the security for property, for reputation, for life, if the senses of religious obligation desert the oaths which are the instruments of investigation in Courts of Justice?
> And let us with caution indulge the supposition that morality can be maintained without religion. Whatever may be conceded to the influence of refined education on minds of peculiar structure, reason and experience both forbid us to expect that national morality can prevail in exclusion of religious principle.[17]

Today, the foundation of America's traditional values infrastructure is imperiled, the Founders' handiwork ignored – sacrificed on the altar of a rabid "new wave" counter-cultural ideology that renders the nation more vulnerable to subversion from within than to actual forceful domination or asymmetric terrorist forces applied from without.

### III. Lessons for America Today

Franklin Roosevelt – who believed that "man born in the image of God will not forever suffer the oppressor's sword" – in his famed "Four Freedoms" speech, framed the challenges elegantly:

> We can accept only a world consecrated to freedom of speeches and expressions – freedom of every person to worship God in his own way – freedom from want – and freedom from terrorism. Is such a world impossible of attainment? The Magna Carta, the Declaration of Independence, the Constitution of the United States, the Emancipation Proclamation, and every other milestone of human progress – all were ideals which seemed impossible of attainment – yet they were attained.[18]

The challenge, in many ways, speaks to the fundamental operating milieu of modern politics wherein in recent decades, the Republican Party has been cast as the party of "morality;" whereas the Democratic Party is perceived as the party of "compassion.' The dichotomy has been simply, but well, articulated by Democratic Party Chairman Howard Dean: "My faith does not inform my public policy."[19] A century ago, the three-time Democratic Party nominee for president William Jennings Bryan, on the other hand, called his support for liberally progressive causes "applied Christianity." Today, such no longer is the moral test of governance. The case for consolidated "moral compassion" has been lost.[20]

Six hundred years before the birth of Christ, when the people of Israel fell from their faith, the word of God, through the Prophet Jeremiah, admonished: "Let not the wise man glory in his wisdom, nor the mighty man in his might, nor the rich man in his riches. Let them boast in this alone: that they truly know me and understand that I am the Lord of judgment and of righteousness whose love is steadfast."[21] Later, through the Prophet Ezekiel, God declared. "I will set my glory among the nations; all the nations shall see my judgement which I have executed and my hand which I have laid on them."[22]

Facts of history show, in equal measure, that religion must thus be judged both by the quality of rulers that it produces and the anarchic political atheism that it rejects. A nation deprived of its history will be despised in its posterity. Whatever use or misuse America now may make of her priceless faith-driven inheritance, therefore, she would nonetheless do well to be reminded from whence it came.[23]

Given the fact that prophets are, in fact, no less than historians facing backward; that prophecies are not so much the outline of history as history is the outline of prophecy, and that history is the record of the working of God's plan, America thus stands duly warned. In 1993, Hungarian historical philosopher John Lukacs, in *The End of the Twentieth Century*, wrote that America's prestige and presence in the world are finished — that though her influence may continue for a time, the "American Century" has prematurely come to an end. What lies ahead, he predicted, is a time of trouble that will threaten the nation's very foundations.[24]

Journalist David Halberstam, in his 1992 work *The Next Century*, similarly laid the foundations for this argument, contending that America has been a nation needlessly burdened by the "myth of empire" for some time, with the incivility of the post-Watergate political era a manifestation of the dishonesty and flawed assumptions of her recent litany of leaders.[25]

Maybe these seers are simply wrong. Perhaps America has not yet reached her point of no return. Ancient Egypt experienced three major incarnations before ultimately succumbing to the yoke of Rome. Greece, in turn, enjoyed two major revivals, while Rome itself had three. But the corrosive manifestations of the disease of cultural dissolution clearly now are present.[26]

A society is a composite of its ideals and its mores. Its legacies matter. If there are no religious values firing the soul of a people, there is no civic comity wherewith to build a nation. As asserted in the "Introduction," social historian Samuel Huntington has found that: "those countries that are more religious tend to be more nationalist;"[27] whereas Rousseau stated: "Never was a state founded that did not have religion as its basis."[28]

It bears repeating: today, as her social values become ever more corrupted by the rise of counter-culturalism; as her civic values are concurrently diminished, as manifest in a sharp decline in patriotism and work ethic; and as she squanders her religious legacy, America confronts survival issues replete with peril that she has not faced before.[29]

As analysis has shown, the ongoing national decline of religio-social values has been attended by a demise of economic values – as the nation's social character has been transformed from an entrepreneurial ethic into an entitlements one — its erstwhile innate dynamism lying victim to the excesses of the New Deal and the Great Society.

FDR's grand strategy, as articulated by his political advisor Harry Hopkins was: "tax and spend, spend and spend, and elect and elect."[30] As for the Great Society, it can be equally cynically dismissed. As Ronald Reagan famously lamented: "Lyndon Johnson declared a "war on poverty" and lost!"[31] Today, the chickens have indeed come home to roost – and as a consequence, government endures "bureaucratic elephantiasis" with its onerous transaction costs producing debilitating public debt – with the national debt approaching twelve trillion dollars, some $40,000 per citizen – and with the Environmental Protection Agency now probably the world's largest government bureaucracy since the Soviet Union is no more.

To pay for such political largesse, the cost of government at all levels – federal, state, local, and payroll taxes – now takes 47 percent of the average citizens' paychecks – up from 7 percent in 1916 and 28 percent in 1950. Federal state, and local taxes alone, as noted, caused them to work until April 23 in 2008 just to pay the costs of public governance – longer than they worked to pay for their housing, food, and clothing costs combined.[32]

Add in the more than 10 percent of wasted national income hidden in regulatory costs, and it becomes evident that government consumes some 57 percent of all the earnings that the nation's workers had intended as commitments to sustain their daily lives – in effect, cutting potential private living standards by significantly more than half.[33]

Such realities mean that average taxpayers must now work until the beginning of August each year to bear the sundry burdens of government before they start working for themselves. And while some may be willing to pass a portion of that cost along to their children in the form of deficits, some things cannot be postponed — as the interest on that debt must be paid annually and increases exponentially.

As a consequence, for many, the "American Dream" has become an ever more distant mirage – with John Kennedy's "boats lifted by the rising tide" now foundering in their moorings on an seemingly insurmountable, but entirely avoidable, bureaucratic reef — as the purpose of prudent public policy should aim to make the poor richer, not the rich poorer.

For when public sector overburden breaks the backs of productive people through onerous taxation or excessive regulation – or both – the need for still more government is irrevocably invoked. But as British social commentator John Grigg has aptly put it: "It is not the duty of the State to facilitate the heavenly redemption of the rich by impoverishing them on earth."[34]

It need not have come to this. At the country's founding, James Madison explicitly warned that: "if Congress can do whatever in their discretion by money . . . . government is no longer a limited one possessing enumerated powers, but an indefinite one subject to particular exceptions" – a phenomenon the he also clearly anticipated when he said that: "enlightened statesmen will not always be at the helm."[35]

Thomas Jefferson, in turn, wrote: "The public debt is the greatest danger to be feared by a republican government. To preserve our independence, we must not let rulers load us with perpetual debt. We must make our choice between economy and liberty, or profusion and servitude."[36] Thomas Paine similarly graphically observed at the onset of the U.S. Revolution in 1776 that:

> When we survey the wretched condition of man under systems of government, dragged from his home by one power or driven out by another, and impoverished by taxes more than by enemies, it becomes evident that those systems are bad, and that a revolution in the principle and construction of governments is necessary.[37]

Yet history simultaneously makes clear that this was, by no means, a danger limited to the American experience. For Thomas Paine's political contemporary, the Baron de Montesquieu, at the time of the French Revolution in 1789, likewise warned his own country of: "the dangers to freedom-seeking peoples when their countries come to be ruined by the oppression of fiscal extortion by government – causing otherwise good men who fail to comply with its demands to be condemned as villains."[38] These, then, are admonitions that any nation ignores at its peril. For throughout the course of history, tax laws have more deprived peoples of their liberties than have invading armies.

Voltaire famously observed that: "the state is a device for taking money from one set of pockets and putting it into another;"[39] — to James Madison concurred in admonishing the consummate dangers of "over taxation of the more productive few at the hands of the less productive many"[40] — whereas George Bernard Shaw wryly appended the corollary that "a government that robs Peter to pay Paul can usually depend on the support of Paul."[41]

It must be readily recalled, however, that it was onerous financial burden caused by "imperial overstretch" – by a decline in social values encompassing a decline in patriotism and work ethic that occasioned the ultimately intolerable tax and fiscal regime — that brought down ancient Rome.

Civilizations die through atrophy and attrition. Rome was not vanquished by barbarians – she had wasted away long before the already entrenched barbarians who, acting as duly enfranchised citizens, effected their *coup d'état*. She died when she forgot what being Roman meant. As a consequence, when the Goths came to claim the power of Caesar, they found the throne no longer there.[42]

As this inquiry has shown, America was born with a special mission. As elegantly captured in verse by famed theologian and Yale President Timothy Dwight in 1771:

> Round thy broad fields more glorious Romes arise;
> With pomp and splendor brightening all the skies;
> Europe and Asia with surprise behold;
> Thy temples starred with gems and roofed with gold. . . .[43]

This was indeed the spirit that captured America's first two centuries. A century after Dwight's poignant paean, theologian Josiah Strong orated: "Surely to be Christian and Anglo Saxon, and an American in this generation is to stand on the very mountaintop of privilege."[44] Whereas novelist Herman Melville wrote: "We Americans are the peculiar chosen people – the Israel of our time; we bear the ark of the liberties of the world."[45]

God is not yet finished with America. But to succeed, she must work to ensure that her noble past remains mere prologue to her vital future. In the past two federal elections, 2006 and 2008, her electorate have voted for "change," with the jury still out on the result. Whether the outcome be positive or merely proof positive of the abiding axiom — "every disaster is change" — only time will tell.

As America has entered an age of unknown and unprecedented change – producing times that are at once complex, challenging, and compelling. To quote Ralph Waldo Emerson:

> If there is any period in which one would desire to be born, is it not the "age of revolution:" when the old and new stand side-by-side and admit of being compared; when the energies of all are searched by fear and fueled by hope; exploring whether the historic glories of the old can be compensated by the rich possibilities

of the new?[46]

America is no longer a colossus standing astride the planet. Ronald Reagan in 1990 turned over a nation unsurpassed in history in its global supremacy. Today, her unipolar world is gone, replaced by a competing array of rising, aspiring powers. Yet she retains her destiny in her hands. She is heir to the legacies of faith and fiscal prudence bequeathed by the nation's Founding Fathers. In the 1920s, and again in the 1980s, she arose phoenix-like from the economic ashes to restore her erstwhile financial diligence. She continues to preside at the mantle of history, but for how long?

In her ongoing vacillation, in her quest for remedy, she would again do well to return to the remarkable architectural vision of the Founders as they derived them from the Scriptures:[47]

> Unless the Lord builds the house, those who build it labor in vain;
> (Psalm 127:1)

and

> Blessed is the nation whose God is the Lord.
> (Psalm 33:12)

As President Kennedy said in closing his immortal Inaugural Address on January 20, 1961: "Here on earth, God's work must truly be our own!"

# PART IV
# The Cure

*Who knows what Master laid thy keel;
What workman wrought thy ribs of steel;
Who made each mast and sail and rope;
What anvils rang, what hammers beat;
In what a forge and what a heat;
Were shaped the anchors of thy hope.*

—From American poet Henry Wadsworth Longfellow's epic: "*Ship of State*"

# Appendix A
# Civic Governance: "Covenantial Change"

> I will give thee the treasures of darkness, and the hidden riches of secret places, that thou may know that I, the Lord, which call thee by thy name, am the God of Israel.
>
> *Bible*, Isaiah 45: 35

## I. THE ECONOMIC CONTRACT WITH AMERICA

### A. Dispelling Economic Myths

The Founders' socioeconomic vision for America, as shown, drew heavily upon the biblical model, the classic wisdom of the ancients, and the philosophies of the Enlightenment, which coalesced to produce the design architecture for a quite remarkable and unique societal blueprint. Such models, as also shown, tended to be "covenantial" — founded upon an explicit social contract between governance and governed. As explained by the 19th century champion of the philosophy of liberty, John Stuart Mill:

> In all political societies which have a durable existence, there has been some fixed point; something upon which men agreed in holding sacred; which might or might

196                                        *Appendix A*

not be lawful to contest in theory, but which no one could either fear or hope to be shaken in practice. . . .
But when questioning of these fundamental principles is the habitual condition of the body politic . . . the state is virtually in a position of civil war against itself and cannot remain free from it in act or fact.[1]

Indeed, such a covenant was crafted at the nation's inception, as articulated by John Winthrop, leader of the Massachusetts Bay Colony, while still aboard the ship Arabella in 1630. Invoking themes common to St. Augustine's *City of God* a millennium before, he proclaimed:

Thus stands the cause between God and us. We are entered into Covenant with Him for this work. We have taken a Commission; the Lord has given us leave to draw our own Articles. . . If we shall neglect the observation of these Articles, which are the ends we have propounded . . . the Lord will surely break out in wrath against us, be revenged of such a perjured people, and make us know the price of a breach of such a Covenant.[2]

In drafting the preamble to the Massachusetts Constitution, as noted John Adams similarly wrote:

The body politic is formed by a voluntary association of individuals. It is a social compact by which the whole people covenants with each citizen, and each citizen with the whole people, that all should be governed by certain laws for the common good.[3]

Concurrently, in language clearly anticipating the Declaration of Independence, he declared: "All human beings have rights, rights that cannot be repealed or restrained by human laws, rights derived from the great Legislator of the universe." Thus, he saw the settlement of America as "the opening of a grand scene and design in Providence."[4]

Consistent with the biblical covenant of Exodus 19:4 — "Ye have seen what I have done unto the Egyptians and how I now bare you on eagles' wings " — this was, in fact, America's explicit "social contract" with her people, as delineated by Thomas Jefferson within the "Declaration of Independence," the legally recognized principle that all men were "created equal and endowed by their Creator with . . . unalienable rights, among them, life, liberty, and the pursuit of happiness" – not happiness itself per se, as shown, but nonetheless a level playing field in its pursuit.

Once liberated, this would become the Founders's mantra – a diverse people bound together by national ideals as articulated in the Declaration of Independence, the Constitution, and Lincoln's Gettysburg Address – in short, they became "Americans," patriots devoted to a common cause– a phenomenon ably captured by Arthur Schlesinger:

The American Creed envisaged a nation composed of individuals making their own choices and accountable to themselves, not a nation based upon inviolable ethnic communities. For our values are not matters of whim or happenstance. History has given them to us. They are anchored in our national experience, in our great national documents, in our national heroes, in our folkways, our traditions, and our standards. Our values work for us, and for that reason, we live and die by them.[5]

This, then, was the nascent nation's "deal with God." As described by FDR, America is "the lasting concord between men and nations, founded on the principles of Christianity."[6]

This inquiry has concurrently underscored critical fiscal, economic, and educational challenges that now imperil the nation's future because governance has strayed far from the Founders' sweeping vision. Seeking remedy, this appendix outlines the conceptual framework for a "new economic covenant" between U.S. government and its people – a new economic "Contract with America" underpinned by the educational infrastructure needed to support it.

Regrettably this imperative is crucial if America is to transcend her current socioeconomic drift. As too often today, public fiscal and commercial policy has been forged by those who thrive in a "politics of victimization" bred of a consummate liberal faith in voter economic ignorance. This is no sheer happenstance. John Kennedy's 1960s Commerce Secretary Luther Hodges perhaps articulated the philosophy best: "If ignorance paid dividends, most Americans could make a fortune on what they don't know about the American economic system."[7]

Yet most Americans are not economically ignorant – instead they often become confused by slick politicians offering ultra-leftist notions designed to confuse them. Foremost among them is the "corporate tax myth" – the idea that corporations actually pay taxes and hence can bear the bulk of the nation's fiscal burden. Indeed, in the history of civilization, no successful one ever has – only paying customers do.

Notwithstanding, for years, "tax and spend" politicians have been able to financially underwrite economic wants of their special interest constituencies by perpetuating the illusion that they are committed friends of the voting middle class by seeking to shift taxes onto "rich corporations." This recurring spate of "campaign stump sophistry" not only insults voters' intelligence, it is no more than a patent fraud to semantically disguise what is — in essence, a highly regressive sales tax upon consumers that ironically apportions its greatest impact upon the lowest income groups.

Indeed, commercial and industrial firms, by definition, cannot pay taxes because they are mere "legal constructs." In this capacity, they act only as governmentally-enfranchised "tax collection pass-through agents" for downstream consumers who must bear the ultimate tax burden as capitalized into the prices of goods and services that they buy. In other words, while businesses do, in fact, write "tax checks," they are no more than governmental financial intermediaries – collecting money from their shareholders, employees, and customers and transferring it to public treasuries.

Levying "corporate taxation," therefore, is, in reality, no more than a dissembling political shell game – that of determining who should bear the brunt of tax burden incidence in the first round of collection – the vendor, or its customer to whom it is invariably passed on perforce. Were it any other way, in fact, the firm would soon be out of business. Thus it is that, in the last analysis, tax impact *always* falls only upon households and the people who comprise them.

It is not surprising, then, that traditional liberal politicians are so enamored of the *electoral utility* of the "corporate income tax myth." For in the Robin Hood guise of taxing the rich while giving to the poor, it is an extremely useful revenue tool for surreptitiously confiscating the earnings of the middle class.

What's worse, in levying upon the productivities of vital industrial job-generators in escalating relationship to their demonstrable degrees of success, it kills the geese that lay the jurisdiction's most prized "golden eggs" – meaningful, productive jobs. For job-export, in the form of foreign "*outsourcing,*" can be, and indeed, to a great extent, already is, the inexorable result.

What the liberals effectively have done, therefore, is to merely "privatize" individual income tax collection – a strategy that, from an efficiency standpoint, probably does make certain economic sense to the extent that the private sector likely can collect taxes more effectively than the present array of federal bureaucracies. The problem, however, lies in the reality that by that using private corporations as tax collectors, the proceeds become capitalized into the cost of exports, which then undermine the nation's quest for global trade competitiveness – and the great domestic job-creation that such exports bring.

The same phenomenon holds true for individual tax collection – the quest to shift a greater share of the tax burden onto the affluent. Yet these are precisely those individuals whose productive investments will create America's future jobs – and who will prudently tax-shelter their incomes if taxes on them become too onerous. This is sheer neo-Marxist folly - a "Potemkinesque House of Cards" built of class warfare political pandering.

Today, due to imprudent public tax policies that not only make production costs but also workers's salaries inordinately expensive, outsourcing continues to consume American jobs at an alarming rate. Reflecting these economic and fiscal realities, the question thus posed is this. If as a consequence, because of the nation's imprudent tax and fiscal policies, China is going to be the world's major manufacturer, and India is going to be the world's prime service provider, where do those realities leave the United States?

## B. Restoring Fiscal Responsibility at the Federal Level.

The economic and fiscal trends cited are alarming and ones that must be expeditiously reversed if America is to preserve her global economic primacy. To these ends, the quest for effective financial and economic remedy must commence with federal policies directly aimed at fiscal restoration; to wit:, a ten plank "New Economic Contract with America" — as follows:

## TENET 1: Make Sure That What the Federal Government Spends Is Constitutional

This goal can best be reached by implementing no federally-funded program without first consulting the Constitution to ascertain if it is a constitutionally-permitted function. The requisite analytic vehicle for determination of legality can be realized by enacting Congressman John Shadegg's proposed "Enumerated Powers Act," which would provide:

> "Each Act of Congress shall contain a concise and definite statement of the constitutional authority relied upon for the enactment of each portion of that Act."

This measure, if enacted, would thus require Congress to specify the statutory basis of authority in the U.S. Constitution as a basis for passage of each law that it enacts.

## TENET 2: Restrict Federal Spending to a Constant 20 Percent Share of GDP

### (1) The Policy Approach

Given the magnitude of fiscal policy shortfalls documented in Chapter 5, spending limitation must become the remedial cornerstone to effective budget balancing, providing safeguards that ensure the goal of federal financial responsibility. It is a critical imperative. For in addressing the question: which is preferable - a two trillion dollar budget with a $500 million dollar deficit or a two and one half trillion dollar balanced budget with 25 percent higher taxes? – the answer is "neither" if true economic prosperity predicated upon fiscal sanity is to prevail.

The concept's critics will invariably counter that both spending limitation and a balanced budget requirement frustrate the process of "representative government" – and raise the cogent question: "Isn't this what we elect our legislators to do?" But the reality lies in the corresponding question: "Are they doing it today?" That answer is clearly "no."

Conversely, when it is argued that mandatory limits to the ability to spend are required, such a démarche is not a denial of the workings of democratic process but merely a call for a judicious separation of the power to tax from the power to spend for which there is strong historic precedent. Indeed, Britain's thirteenth century "Magna Carta," generally hailed as the foundation stone of democratic enlightenment – did precisely that. The executive branch, the King, could spend but could not tax. The legislative branch, the Parliament, could tax but could not spend.

This separation of official functions protocol thereafter became the cornerstone for successful economic governance and remains a valid prototype to the present day. For within this delimited process, legislators retain their basic right to conceptualize and legislate. But they are now compelled to do so more judiciously ever-mindful of resource constraints. To this extent, then, mandated fiscal restraint is no less than a reaffirmation of the time-tested precept of responsible representative government: "There is your budget. Now manage it in the most effective way."

This approach thus becomes a monumentally progressive step to the extent that if government is ultimately to learn to live within its means, its ability to grow must be constrained to its capability to grow its underlying sustaining economy. Indeed, historically, precise *de facto* ratios have evolved to divide resources between those in public service and those whom they purport to serve.

The "*tithe,*" for instance, came as an explicit declaration by the Church that it was entitled to a lawful tenth of private earnings. Indeed, this 10 percent levy, the "*decuma,*" prevailed throughout much of the ancient world – Rome, Greece, India, and China – for millennia. In the United States however, federal spending predicated upon government's "capital take" from the economy for most of the past half century has hovered around double this amount at twenty percent of "gross domestic product" (GDP) level, as shown in *Paradigm 1*.

Paradigm 1

Total Federal Annual Outlays as Percentage of GDP

| Year | Total Outlays as % of GDP |
| --- | --- |
| 1970 | 19.3% |
| 1975 | 21.3% |
| 1980 | 21.7% |
| 1985 | 22.8% |
| 1990 | 21.8% |
| 1995 | 20.7% |
| 2000 | 18.4% |
| 2001 | 18.6% |
| 2002 | 19.4% |
| 2003 | 19.9% |
| 2004 | 19.8% |
| 2005 | 20.2% |
| 2009 (est) | 20.9% |

Source: Table 1.2—Historical Tables, *U.S. Budget, FY 2006*

Indeed, in recent decades, as the tabular data make clear, it has, at times crept well above the twenty percent "Plimsoll Mark." Yet history's lessons make clear that such upward drift must end if prosperity is to issue from the private sector. Firm spending ceilings must be established to explicitly fix the relationship of public consumption to private production before the rapacious appetite of government ingests still more intolerable levels of productive private enterprise.

One prime way that such outlay ceilings could effectively be built, as noted, is by constitutionally limiting future governmental spending growth, except in serious cases of defense or domestic emergency – insurrection, war, or other carefully delineated incidence of *force majeure* – to a strict 20 percent of GDP uppermost limit – with the preceding year's GDP the basis for circumscribing this year's appropriations.

Any excess of public revenue intake above this threshold could then be consigned, as a first priority, to eliminating the current federal debt — and thereafter to a "rainy day fund" to provide government with resources to enable it to engage in compensatory counter-cyclical budgeting in times of severe economic downturn.

This fund could be further augmented, and future economic growth strengthened, in turn, by levying a "penalty clause" on increased expenditures in inflationary periods. For every 2 percent increase in inflation, for example, government could be required to reduce its nominal spending by 1 percent – thereby rebating to taxpayers fifty percent of all revenue benefits produced by "bracket creep." The fiscal responsibility mandate could be strengthened further still by requiring that no less than 10 percent of the federal government's thereby limited revenue intake each year be consigned to debt reduction.

The case for such a revolutionary policy course thus is, at once, both compelling and simple. Relative shares of GDP are firmly fixed so that both the public and private sectors are guaranteed proportional allocations of national productive output. By linking spending to production, moreover, the close connection between economic growth and government's capacity to distribute benefits is concurrently underscored.

Directly tying public spending to GDP growth makes psychological sense as well – producing a powerful public incentive to promote private profits that does not now exist for bureaucrats. For with fixed budgetary constraints linked to economic growth, by contributing to private industrial and commercial productivity, bureaucrats get a ever-rising tranche of tax revenues – and hence, get to spend more money.

In the natural selection process, moreover, those wasteful expenditures and needless regulations that impose financial obligations upon private enterprises would no longer be regarded as "free," or even desirable – but would perforce be weighed against their opportunity costs of aggrandized bureaucracy foregone. Thus, however inadvertently perhaps, public servants would come to be actively working to achieve cost savings that concurrently serve the private economic interest.

For when every addition on the public sector spending side mandates an equivalent subtraction, it dramatically changes both the calculus and the equilibrium of the bureaucratic fiscal equation. As rather than ratcheting up spending through the unrestrained power to tax – rather than rejoicing in each other's spoils – for the first time, federal agencies would be put into direct competition with each other for fixed value budgetary assets; as henceforth, in a "zero-sum budget," more revenue for one would be less revenue for the other.

Indeed, in an era of finite fiscal resources, such an intense intramural quest for improved internal efficiency might even eventually come to be deemed as a highly salutary in-house bureaucratic byproduct. The true winner in such a scenario, however, would be America's taxpaying citizens. For not only would government be given an overt incentive to reduce both its spiraling spending and inflation, but its direct take from their wallets would be reduced in relative terms as well.

## (1) Policy Implementation

The policy goals of TENET 2, can, in turn, perhaps best achieved by a two-pronged approach of redirecting the commitment of public revenues to optimal economic use and by subjecting recurring federal programs and regulations to continuous performance review – objectives realizable through a six-step bureaucratic reform process, as follows:

### Step 1: Create a Federal "Rainy Day" Trust

A budget-balancing constitutional amendment fixing federal outlays as a percentage share of GDP could concurrently stipulate that revenues received in excess of the threshold ceiling be consigned to a "Federal Economic Stabilization Trust." The fund could initially be structured to served as a "fiscal restoration fund" – with its full proceeds dedicated to reducing the federal debt – and once eliminated, retooled as a "rainy day" fund forcing government to save in economic upturns for less buoyant economic times. If such an approach sounds not radical but rather rational, that is because it is really no more than what those heads of household who aspire to be financially prudent now already do in their private lives.

Preceding analysis has made clear that economic growth through fiscal responsibility and stability is a national challenge invoking federal solutions. Thus, there is no better place to start than within the U.S. government itself. To this end, creation of a "rainy day fund" would allow for counter-cyclical budgeting in periods of economic downturn without raising taxes – using financial surpluses built up in good times to offset deficits incurred in bad times.

At the same time, the approach decisively rejects the conventional wisdom oft held by those in government that the solution to recession is to remove capital from the productive private sector in the form of tax increases to underwrite costs of pasting of legislative band-aids over critical economic wounds. To the contrary, it moderates the rate of taxation while preserving essential services – thereby restoring revenue-producing income growth to private industry.

### STEP 2: Provide "Sunset Clauses" for All New Programs Promulgated

Ronald Reagan, paraphrasing General Hugh Johnson, once observed, that "the nearest thing to immortality in this world is a governmental bureau."[8] Yet were the promulgation of new bureaucratic programs to be accompanied by the devolution of old ones – if that vital "creative destruction," breaking down the old to make way for the new that takes place in free market process also worked within the halls of government, its present problems of inefficiency and obsolescence would not now be so self-compounding. Today, however, such is not the case – as bureaucratic dinosaurs remain very much alive and well openly roaming streets and alleys within Washington's beltway foraging upon economically-sustaining private profits.

Incorporating "sunset provisions" into every newly created program that requires substantial recurring commitments of federal funds – thereby mandatorily subjecting its performance to periodic review – would effectively attack this Jurassic anomaly. For under this approach, public programs that do not produce demonstrably cost-effective positive performance reviews would be scrutinized on an ongoing basis to ascertain their continuing merit. Recognizing the inherent efficacy of this approach, fiscal analyst Chris Edwards of the Cato Institute has recommended that:

> Congress needs to get serious about the need to 'sunset' all federal programs on a rotating basis of every eight years. Programs would then be automatically terminated unless specifically reauthorized.[9]

There is a compelling argument to be made, in fact, that only through incorporating such "sunset clauses" in the enabling legislation of all future major revenue-consuming programs can the nation be assured of the comprehensive public oversight required to ensure they remain cost-effective.

Today, the nation's leadership unfortunately only "sunsets" productive federal tax cuts. Why not more providently "sunset" federal spending instead? Considerations for renewal at the time of sunset should include the program or policy's constitutional compliance as would be required by TENET 1, as well as its amenity to privatization as determined by "Steps 3- 6," which follow.

## STEP 3: Ascertain the True Costs of Governmental Functions

Accurately determining the public sector costs of services delivery is critical to any decision to proceed with privatization. This goal can best be accomplished, in turn, by a shift in federal accounting procedure from "fund accounting" to "financial accounting" practices. The distinction is not semantic but instead is operationally critical. For fund accounting identifies only the *direct* costs of governmental services delivery. It does not quantify such indirect inputs as capital costs, administrative overhead, and public employee fringe benefits — factors that can make actual operational costs as much as 30 percent greater than budgeted costs.[10]

"Financial accounting" differs from fund accounting in quantifying these "hidden liabilities" in that, in addition to line item budgetary expenditures, it also calculates a program's indirect costs, opportunity costs, and privatization conversion cost. A national shift to this more comprehensive "total cost" accounting system — using standardized accounting practices — would thus provide the requisite data to enable federal privatization to proceed more intelligently and effectively. For in employing it, public policy makers and private sector vendors alike would be able to optimally gauge the cost trade-offs of privatization initiatives as they are proposed, deliberated, and bid.

## STEP 4: Establish Public Competition as a Market-Driven Process

In establishing market-driven federal privatization, the "Governmental Restructuring Implementation Committee" approach introduced by the provincial government of British Columbia also merits careful contemplation. Pursuant to it, the committee formally entertains private sector bids to perform select public sector functions in a six-step process of bid submission and evaluation.

Should a similar system be contemplated in America, once the full costs of public programs have been established through the reformed governmental accounting practices suggested in Step 3, a "Joint Congressional Committee on Governmental Restructuring" could be created parallel and equal to, and operating in tandem with, the respective Congressional Budget Committees. This new committee would exist not to create more federal bureaucracy, but rather to reduce it by engaging in extensive, ongoing budgetary review to identify appropriate program candidates for privatization.

Its overarching fiscal mission, however, would be to solicit, receive, and evaluate proposals from private firms to directly "bid out" specific functions of the federal budget now being performed by public agencies. Were a private firm convinced that it could better administer the country's parks than the National Park Service, for instance, it would be permitted, indeed, encouraged, to submit a bid.

If, in turn, the bid were to be favorably evaluated, the function's parent agency would be given a prescribed limited period to justify why it should continue as a public sector function. Should it fail to do so to the Committee's satisfaction, the latter could then recommend to its parallel Budget Committees that the activity be privatized and cease to be funded publicly.

Implementation of this approach would thus constitute a revolutionary budgetary advance. For in effect, government would be "reinvented" by retooling Congress — allowing for the workings of competitive market process in the provision of public services. In this course, the same market-driven efficiencies that now provide America with the highest living standards in the world would be made universally available to her citizens in the provision of their public services – all predicated upon the Tenth Amendment premise that those functions not specified constitutionally for the federal government must be turned over to the people or the states to perform.

## STEP 5: Require Privatization Impact Statements for Major New Federal Programs

In tandem with oversight reforms for existing bureaucratic programs, prudent public policy oversight simultaneously effectively mandates that major recurring executive program or policy initiatives under legislative consideration for implementation or renewal be accompanied by privatization impact statements. Such statements should require that their proponent public agencies justify why they can perform what they propose in more cost effective ways than can the private sector — while employing the identical types of stringent cost-benefit analyses that all private firms must undertake to compete and survive.

These statements could be mandatorily generated by the proponent agency advocating the new program or policy and made publicly available on a widespread basis prior to consideration by the primary committee evaluating the measure in the legislative house of origin — thereby enabling business firms and private citizens alike to readily ascertain their capabilities to "bid out" the proposed initiative from the public into the private sector.

## STEP 6: Use "ESOPS" to Promote Public Competition

To further expand venues and opportunities for privatization, special financial and tax incentives to promote the formation of privatized "employee stock ownership programs" ("ESOPS") would likewise play a constructive role in encouraging public employees to "bid out" their current missions as private sector activities.

For often, those actually currently doing the job are the best judges of whether their functions can, or should, be privatized. They are those whose accrued expertise is needed to ensure that essential services are delivered for the best price in tax dollars. They thus should be afforded every opportunity to compete for their own jobs as private functions – while concurrently transforming current tax-consumers into future taxpayers.

For the nation's economic interests are not best served if the cost savings from privatization are merely consumed by corresponding increased public assistance payments required to sustain erstwhile public employees displaced by the privatization transfer – as there is no positive public policy goal achieved in a "zero-sum" exchange whereby unemployment is merely displaced from the private to the erstwhile public sector.

ESOP incentives targeted to rational privatization initiatives can readily resolve this problem. For by altering the nature of the incentives offered to the public employees, bureaucratic impediments to greater productivity are broken through profit motivation induced by free market means.

At the same time, public employee unions should be afforded full opportunity as well to "bid in" quantitative and qualitative improvements to their members' on-the-job performances if they wish to maintain them as public sector functions and thereby forestall their privatization. Through such competitive means, therefore, privatization can be institutionalized as a more vibrant, across-the-board, no-holds-barred competitive bidding process.

TENET 3. Eliminate "Middle Class Taxation" Altogether.

Such a proposal would deny radical liberals the opportunity to indulge yet another economic myth – that of the overtaxed financial underclass. For were there to be no middle class taxation whatsoever, there would no case for a "middle class tax cut" — which summarizes the compelling case why this tenet should also be made a centerpiece of the "Economic Convenant."

How can this reform best be approached? In individual income taxation, the officially-defined single taxpayer "poverty index" could be established as the foundational basis for individual deductions each year – with additional $7,000 deductions for each dependent thereafter. This is no budget-buster – but rather an amalgam of the best features of the existing John Lindner "fair tax" and Dick Armey "flat tax" proposals.

Economic analyses of the Congress themselves tell the story. Unfortunately, due to data collation lag, it presently is limited to fully compatible FY 2005-2006 data. But this is the illuminating message that they convey.

| Quintile: | Millions of Households | Average Pre-Tax Income in 2005 Current Dollars | Effective Individual Income Tax Rate Before Deductions | Share of Individual Income Tax Liabilities |
|---|---|---|---|---|
| Lowest | 24.1 | $15,900 | -6.5% | -2.9% |
| 2nd | 22.0 | $37,400 | -1.0% | -0.9% |
| Middle | 22.2 | $58,500 | 3.0% | 4.4% |
| 4th | 22.6 | $85,200 | 6.0% | 13.1% |
| Highest | 23.1 | $231,300+ | 14.1% | 86.3% |
| Total | 114.5 | $84,800 | 9.0% | 100.0% |
| Top 10% | 11.7 | $339,100 | 16.0% | 72.7% |
| Top 5% | 5.8 | $520,200 | 17.6% | 60.7% |
| Top 1% | 1.1 | $1,558,500 | 19.4% | 38.8% |

Who Paid America's Federal Individual Income Taxes in 2005

Source: Congressional Budget Office. *Historical Effective Tax Rates: 1975 to 2005 (Washington: December 2007)*

The data thus show that the bottom 40 percent of federal tax filers now pay no individual income taxes at all– whereas the middle 20 percent pay just 4.4 percent. Based again upon 2008 Congressional Budget Office (CBO) data releases, $927.2 billion in federal individual income taxes were collected in FY 2005-2006. That reality means that just $40.8 billion (4.4% of $927.2) must be found to make an elimination of middle class taxation proposal revenue neutral – while concurrently resulting in the reality that the lowest earning 59.7 percent of America's tax filing households would pay no federal income taxes whatsoever.[11]

How can this tax cut be paid in a revenue neutral solution? One possibility would be by simply by cutting overall government spending across-the-board. With the CBO data showing $2,472.2 billion in outlays in FY 2005-2006, for instance, overall federal spending would have had to be cut by a mere 1.65 percent — or alternately, by eliminating a few special interest programs with no significant human impact constituencies — or through six months of the "peace dividend" that will result from bringing home the American brigades made possible by the consummate success of the "surge" in Iraq. Reflecting that the Constitution mandates the federal government to do no more than about 40 percent of what it is now doing, and explicitly forbids it from doing the other 60 percent, the cuts should not be difficult to either make or justify.

Alternately, and more radically, a 17 percent national sales tax on consumption to replace current taxes on production income would meet present federal revenue requirements – while allowing consumers to more prudently gauge the personal costs of their consumption – and simultaneously totally eliminating tax forms, the IRS, and ongoing excessive collection and compliance costs.

## TENET 4. ELIMINATE THE CAPITAL GAINS TAX ALTOGETHER.

Tax cuts on capital work. The cause goes to the essence of macroeconomic performance. A prime reason for the documentable dramatic "tax yield/tax rate" inverse reciprocity, of course, is that while moderate tax rates inspire greater personal and corporate investment in productive activity, rapidly progressive tax rates seldom, if ever, actually redistribute income; they merely redistribute taxpayers from highly taxable to less taxable economic activities.

Indeed, it is estimated that high-tax-driven recourse to tax shelters now costs the economy about 18 percent in growth each year – a massive $2 trillion loss in GDP! For precisely this reason, former Federal Reserve Chairman Alan Greenspan has asserted of the capital gains tax: "Its major impact, as far as I can judge, is to impede entrepreneurial activity and capital formation. . . . I have argued that the appropriate capital gains tax rate is zero."[12]

This phenomenon is equally dramatically demonstrated in the fiscal reality documented in annual U.S. budgetary statistics revealing that immediately after the 1990 Bush/Democratic Congress tax increase, aggregate tax receipts from America's uppermost tier of taxpayers actually declined by $6.5 billion, or 6.1 percent in 1991, even as their tax rates rose. Conversely, when tax levels are decreased, the proceeds from their levies multiply. When the top capital gains tax rate was decreased from 39.9 to 28.0 percent in 1978, the federal revenue it produced rose from $9.1 billion to $11.9 billion. When President Reagan further cut the capital gains tax rate from 28 to 20 percent, revenue from its proceeds grew from $12.8 billion to $18.7 billion.

After the top capital gains tax rate was restored to 28 percent by the "Tax Reform Act of 1986," but was then again cut back to 20 percent in 1996, moreover, not only did the tax yields again surge dramatically, but the national economy grew by a dynamic 4.5 percent in 1997, 4.2 percent in 1998, 4.5 percent in 1999, and 3.7 percent in 2000.

In like manner, in the first three years after President George W. Bush further reduced the capital gains tax rate from 20 percent to 15 percent, instead of declining by $5.4 billion as had been projected by the congressional Joint Committee on Taxation, the tax yield more than doubled from a projected $57 billion to $133 billion!

Tax cuts work. Indeed, as the entire course of modern fiscal history proves, tax cuts on capital are invariably revenue enhancers, not attriters. The concurrent financial reality, however, is that the capital gains tax drains the lifeblood of the retirement savings of ordinary people – their pension funds and 401Ks. Eliminating it in its entirety, therefore, is a "win/win" economic situation for all.

## TENET 5: REFORM THE FEDERAL REGULATIONS PROMULGATIONS PROCESS

With federal regulation now costing American consumers an estimated 10 percent of national income in compliance costs, this policy reform could best be accomplished through a four-step administrative oversight process as follows:

### STEP 1: Institutionalize Regulatory Budgeting in the Policy Formulation Process

To lend focus to the costs of public regulation, mandatory promulgation of a annual "Federal Regulatory Budget" should be made a paramount policy priority. Pursuant to it, to empower effective Congressional oversight, the Executive Branch should each year be required to develop in significant detail accurate estimates of the regulatory costs imposed by the full operational spectrum of agencies and programs over which it presides.

Each year, in turn, the Congress would be statutorily required to formally approve the "Federal Regulatory Budget," making such policy adjustments as it prudently deems necessary. By making explicit the costs of the federal regulatory burden, then, this process would enable direct cross-checks between the administrative costs officially sanctioned by government and those actually run up by executive agencies in pursuit of their statutory mandates.

It would concurrently mandate legislative – as well as proponent agency – approval of imposed compliance costs; in so doing, making possible a "regulatory report card" by specific agency and program that would constitute a critical first step toward fiscal remedy by forcing bureaucratic and political officials alike to directly confront the market costs of the regulations that they impose.

## STEP 2: Provide for Detailed Cost Benefit Analyses for Each New Rule Proposed

In 1995, Congress directed the "Office of Management and Budget" to assess the economic impact of all federal regulation. A concurrent measure, "Executive Order 12866," required federal agencies to analyze the market effects of proposed rules economically significant to the degree that they impose private sector costs exceeding $100 million.

Today, such initiatives, however laudatory, have proven to be subjective in their focus and do not go far enough. To quote economist Richard Rahn: "Too few governmental regulations are today subjected to rigorous cost-benefit tests. Many governmental agencies do not take the requirement seriously, act in good faith, or even present accurate data. For regulators have a strong incentive to underestimate the true costs of their regulations."[13]

The reality that each year's new tranche of federal regulations costs the economy another fifty billion dollars or more in opportunity costs, therefore, mandates a new oversight assessment approach — one requiring that regulations subject to Congressional oversight be accompanied by objective, cost-benefit analyses standardized across federal agencies in formats that provide both direct and "contextual" information – and in so doing, monetize the values of *effects*, as well as accurately assess the *costs*, of each promulgation proposed, thereby forecasting the net benefits to society over time.

Such statements — which would require a clear demonstration that the incremental benefits of a regulatory initiative proposed actually exceed its incremental costs — should also incorporate not only economic assessments but technological risk and small business impact assessments and be developed by each proponent agency concurrent with its preparation of each administrative proposal submitted for review.

Such analyses should, in turn, become the basis for Congressional determination of whether any given federal rule or regulation has produced sufficient benefit as to justify its continuance over time. For by making the agency cost-benefit review more discerning, the nation's "regulatory report card" can ensure that unwarranted growth of the "regulatory state" is taken seriously by enabling better federal policy decision-making based on superior economic information.

## STEP 3: Make the Regulatory Approvals Process "Elective" Rather Than Rejective

Submitting administrative rules approval to direct Congressional jurisdiction would likewise make a material contribution to restoring proper oversight in rules promulgation. Pursuant to such a "hands-on" oversight approach, each Congressional committee could be made explicitly responsible for those rules promulgated by those federal agencies subject to its jurisdiction – and required to endorse each rule by record roll call vote ninety days prior to its proposed effective date.

In effect, then, this approach would compel the Congress to approve those follow-on policy mechanisms implemented to enforce the laws that they pass, in addition to the laws themselves. By mandating that all new regulations be mandatorily endorsed, rather than merely tacitly accepted, by Congressional committee, this promulgation reform would thus effectively "regulate the regulators" by requiring greater managerial oversight on the part of elected officials.

STEP 4: Provide "Sunset Clauses" for All New Regulations Promulgated

Just as for recurring federal *programs* described in TENET 2 above, beyond promulgations reform, "sunset clauses," prescribing fixed date terminations for each new federal *rule* enacted can also ensure focused periodic, circumspect reconsideration of regulatory policies. For only through systematic regulatory review can proper stewardship provide that rules continue to serve the public good for which they were originally intended.

Recourse to this sunset law approach thus introduces two highly salutary effects into the public-policy making system. First, it requires elected officials to periodically validate whether past regulations remain valid. Second, it creates a deliberate natural policy inertia — for by requiring bureaucracies to rectify past follies, it reduces their time available to create new ones.

## TENET 6: ELIMINATE "SPECIAL INTEREST APPROPRIATIONS EARMARKS" ALTOGETHER.

Special interest appropriation earmarks are the bane of America's budgetary existence. Office of Management and Budget data reveal that in FY 2005-2006, there were 13,492 congressionally-imposed earmarks totaling $18,938,657,000 enacted. Had they been prohibited, reduction of only 0.89% of general federal spending would have been needed to eliminate middle class taxation altogether as recommended in TENET 3. Among the more ludicrous fiscal excesses, in FY 2005-2006, U.S. taxpayers spent $3 billion on subsidies to 25,000 cotton farmers possessing average net worths exceeding one million dollars.

For economic liberals, this is a particularly pernicious violation of a good faith covenant, as they explicitly campaigned for Congress in 2006 on a pledge of ending special interest appropriations earmarks. Yet once in the majority, they did not. Not only did they preserve them, but Congressional Research Service data show that there were again 11,737 special interest earmarks totaling $16,872 billion embedded within the FY 2008 appropriations bills.

## TENET 7. REFORM CORPORATE TAXATION THROUGH FIRST-YEAR EXPENSING OF INVESTMENTS

To preserve their economic primacies, nations must produce things that people need and want. Yet U.S. manufacturing's share of national GDP has been cut in half within the past quarter century. Concurrently, U.S. Bureau of Economic Analysis (BEA) data show that the U.S. global trade deficit in goods in 2007 stood at $819.4 billion, more than 5.9 percent of GDP. No small part of the problem is that America now endures the second highest corporate tax rate amongst the major industrialized countries of the "Organization for Economic Cooperation and Development " (OECD).[14]

A significant remedy would be to streamline U.S. production lines through productivity-enhancing investments to render them more competitive within the global marketplace. An obvious first step to this end, in turn, is to r*eplace investment amortization with "expensing."*

This tax reform is overarchingly critical for preserving the vitality of American manufacturing. As under present tax rules, business investments in capital equipment may be depreciated for specified periods of up to a maximum number of years. This approach means that a machine purchased for a million dollars assembly production line might be eligible for a "tax write off" at the rate of $100,000 per year for perhaps a decade.

"Expensing," on the other hand, permits deduction of the full $1 million in the year of purchase rather then apportioning it over a prolonged depreciation period. Revenue neutral, therefore – because the actual amount of write-off remains the same, with only the immediate deduction replacing a prolonged time-phased one – this approach can serve as a monumental incentive for promoting job-creating investments in major manufacturing industries – auto, steel, other durable goods, and the like – that now endure high capital production expansion costs.

Concurrently, the nation should strive to reduce the present corporate top marginal income tax rate to bring it more in line with those of America's principal global trade competitors. Today, as noted, the United States levies the second highest corporate tax rate amongst the OECD countries, trailing only economically moribund Japan. Hence, just as her competitors are cutting their corporate tax levies to compete at optimum within the global marketplace, America's government must now do so also if she is to remain a major economic player.

## TENET 8. SHIFT FROM CITIZENSHIP-DRIVEN TO TERRITORIAL OVERSEAS TAXATION

In the quest for U.S. economic restoration, a foremost policy priority – on a par with winning the war on terror – should be to ensure long term U.S. global trade competitiveness. To that end, a "Federal Public-Private Blue Ribbon Task Force on Competitiveness," headed by the Chairman of the Federal Reserve, should be commissioned to examine in detail the entire spectrum of its contributing inputs: structural competitiveness, savings rates, taxing and spending, education and work force training, energy, and pension, health care, and wage insurance in the quest for cost reductions that now lead to job outsourcing.

In fairness, it must be said that the abstract concept of "outsourcing" is not inherently evil. Instead, it is no more than economic common sense. Such comparative advantage is why people outsource their haircuts rather than having their wives cut their hair at home. The nation must take similar recourse to economic common sense in repatriating now-outsourced manufacturing and its quality job-creation potentials. Corporate tax reform is the crucial first step to that end.

The policy possibilities are promising. Among them, America today stands with North Korea and Eritrea as the only nation states in imposing extraterritorial taxation based citizenship rather than levying strict domestic jurisdiction-based taxation. Such trading partners, however, are probably not the optimal development models to be emulated. Not only does this approach preclude U.S. corporations and individuals from competitiveness abroad, it likewise, through prudent business practice, incentivizes American multinationals to seek out overseas reinvestment tax shelters.

Not only would shifting to territorial taxation simplify tax process adherence with established principles of compliance and enforceability, moreover, a major cause of outsourcing would go away. For since repatriated dividends would no longer be taxed, the incentive to keep funds overseas for tax-planning purposes would effectively be removed, thereby promoting the long term in-flow of investment dollars generated by U.S. firms back to the United States – a repatriated total estimated by some to be potentially as high as $13 trillion.

This tax course thus is crucial for America's employment future. For contrary to liberal political polemic, America's corporations do not wallow in excessive profits. To the contrary, studies show that industry-wide, they averaged 5.5 percent in the first half of this decade. Subjecting that 5.5 percent to 34 percent taxation reduces the profit margin to about 3.6 percent; and when state and local taxes are applied, it further declines to around 3 percent – levels whereat even alternate investments in municipal bonds become competitive.

About ten percent of America's present job base derives from exports. This total, if moved from the status of employed to unemployed in 2007, would have raised the unemployment rate of the nation's 146,047,000,000 person civilian employment base from 4.8 percent to 14.4 percent – *making exports the defining difference between U.S. economic prosperity and Hoover-Roosevelt depression-level unemployment.* Building the nation's job base through export promotion tax incentives thus serves America's strategic economic interest.

## TENET 9. PERMANENTLY ESTABLISH 50 PERCENT OF COST JOB TRAINING AND R&D TAX CREDITS

In the current global economy, America's economic preeminence can only be preserved through building leading edge research and development and a state-of-the-art, constantly retrained work force to extract its productivity dividends. Ronald Reagan, in 1981, convincing demonstrated the power of R&D tax credits – in so doing, creating a decade of domestic prosperity.

Indeed, since the "Tax Reform of 1981," American firms have been able to expense R&D costs and claim credits for R&D expenses that exceed average R&D expenditures for the preceding three years. Specifically, the federal tax system allows firms to:

(1) deduct qualified research expenses in the year incurred; and simultaneously
(2) receive a 25 percent credit in increases in qualifying research expenses above the previous three-year running average.

Early Bush-II-era tax reforms *temporarily* prudently doubled this productive tax credit to 50 percent of qualified research expenses– thereby putting the nation and industry into a "fifty-fifty partnership" in the quest to create 21$^{st}$ century-quality jobs. Today, these provisions have expired and must be renewed – as the statutory rate of the current credit is now 25 percent, but the maximum effective rate is actually usually no more than 10 percent because the credit is calculated on the amount of the increase in R&D spending above a base amount.

As underscored in Chapter 6, keenly honed workforce skills are operationally critical as the 21$^{st}$ century "Information Age" continues to unfold – with the types of jobs now being created invariably coming in the high-skilled, knowledge-driven sectors – as within the emerging high tech global market-place, what you learn is what you earn!

When human investments become the prime engines of economic growth, moreover, *everyone gets to play the economic game.* For human-resource-based development policies are those most likely to narrow income gaps by bringing the lower strata up, not dragging the upper strata down. For these compelling reasons, therefore, 50 percent of corporate expenditures for both R&D and work force training should be made fully deductible into federal corporate income taxation.

## TENET 10. ESTABLISH "PORTABLE HEALTH CARE" THROUGH FEDERAL TAX DEDUCTIONS

Providing affordable health care is amongst America's most serious domestic policy challenges. From a public policy standpoint, two ready remedies suggest themselves:

** Solve the health care portability problem by making all medical expenses fully deductible from federal taxable income. Thus, employees would come to "own" their own policies, choosing the ones that best serve their needs, while taking them wherever they wish seeking medical service.

** At the same time, with egregious malpractice suits and attendant legal fees constituting more than 40 percent of all medical costs in America today, these expenditures could be dramatically reduced by statutorily limiting the cost of any judicial award to the level of prevailing workers' compensation rates in the state of jurisdiction, plus an additional one-third of that initial award as legal fees incurred in obtaining the court judgment.

C. Paying for the Economic Contract

How does the America Treasury pay for this panoply of tax reductions? The answer is simple. By balancing the budget on the spending side as suggested in TENET 2, and by eliminating special interest "earmarked" appropriations as recommended by TENET 4 — as revenue neutrality can readily be reached by eliminating from the federal government's jurisdiction some of its most pernicious functions that Article 1, Sections 8 and 9, and the tenth amendment of the Constitution expressly forbid it to do, thereby constraining governmental spending to its present share of GDP.

Again, the economic numbers tell the story. Due to the economic stimulus produced by the Bush II tax cuts, federal outlays in 2007 stood at 19.7 percent of GDP. But in less buoyant economic times, it has risen in recent decades to exceed 24 percent of GDP on an annualized basis. To counter this upwardly spiraling spending drift, there have been recurring calls to focus upon tax limitation, which certainly is a noble goal.

The policy's vulnerable Achilles heel, however is that it can be readily circumvented through deficit spending. That is why while federal revenues stood at $2,568.2 billion in FY 2007-2008, outlays came in at $2,730.2 billion, producing a $162 billion federal deficit. To this extent, then, spending limitation is concurrently tax limitation plus debt limitation.

## II. THE EDUCATIONAL CONTRACT WITH AMERICA

The challenges to the America's educational system posed by the countercultural movement have been amply described in analysis. The conclusions to be drawn are readily evident – no serious academic program can be built upon a foundation of double standards and preferential treatment.[15]

Not only is such a course educationally unsound, it is patently unconstitutional. For democracy is not predicated upon the premise of equal endowment but of equal rights. It does not guarantee success, but it does aspire to equal opportunity – and it is an opportunity extended to individuals, not groups. As true liberal education resolves issues based on idealism, not on special interests – in terms of the weight of moral right – not of political force or civil disobedience in its absence.[16]

Education thus must be structured to serve the national economic interest. Regrettably, education is indeed fungible. Recently, the proportion of U.S. university doctorates awarded to foreign students has risen from 35 percent in 1987 to now approach 50 percent. And whereas 80 percent of foreign born graduates used to remain to pursue careers in the United States in 1985, now the majority now return to their homelands after receiving their university degrees. The obvious key to economic survival, then, is to reengage native Americans in the higher educational process.[17]

Finally, the imparting of knowledge must take place absent cultural, political, or other parochial bias. For as analysis has made clear, an uncritical examination of non-Western cultures in order to favorably contrast them with those of the West is no more than reverse cultural imperialism whereby self-proclaimed intellectuals project personal prejudices onto other cultures to achieve self-serving political ends. Such intellectual distortion has no place in an academia committed to objective scholarly inquiry. Given these manifest realities and complex challenges, then, the following proposals become paramount policy imperatives:[18]

## A. Ensuring Educational Opportunity

Access to equal educational opportunity is a goal that should be a right of all Americans demonstrating worthy performance while concurrently serving the national socioeconomic interest. These objectives can perhaps best be reconciled by establishing "hard discipline" college scholarships for qualifying high school graduates while concurrently reforming education through a national "excellence through education" academic initiative comprised of four components:

** Ensure equal access to higher education to any graduating high school senior meeting stringent national testing levels and demonstrating a need for financial assistance. A civilian equivalent of the GI Bill, providing national college scholarships for the study of mathematics, engineering, and the sciences to bright but needy students, should thus be created as a permanent federal function; and,

** Grant automatic admission to the top 10 percent of every high school class, based on grades, to public colleges and universities regardless of financial circumstance. The federal government should thereby require that public universities grant admission to highly qualified, high school graduates as a condition receipt of federal funding.

Simultaneously:

** Enact as federal law the "All Persons Are Created Equal Civil Rights Act" modeled after the "California Civil Rights Initiative of 1996"– thereby allowing "merit " to be the sole determinant in public sector college admissions, employment, and contracting decisions.

** Require by law that as a condition of institutional funding, all higher education administrators operating within publicly-funded institutions mandatorily receive eight hours of "sensitivity training" taught by a certified constitutional lawyer in the application and enforcement of the First Amendment respecting free speech.

## B. Implementing Pragmatic Education

\*\* *Set explicit federal standards for class size and length of school year* – together with optimal student-to-teacher ratios that ensure that America's children receive the quality in education that they both need and deserve. The school year also should be lengthened to ensure parity with the classroom exposures in schools of principal industrial competitors.

\*\* *Establish a mandatory federal curriculum of hard core subjects and standards of discipline within the classroom.* National standards for math, science, and English should be implemented and continually raised. For if America is determined to preserve her global leadership, she must restore her educational standards to levels consistent with the highest in the world.

\*\* *Make full English language competency a nationwide mandatory requirement for graduation in the nation's K-12 system.* This laudatory goal already was the clear intent of America's earliest settlers, as evidenced in the literacy laws of the State of Connecticut enacted in 1690:

> The (legislature) observing that . . . there are many persons unable to read the English tongue and thereby incapable to read the Holy Word of God or the good laws of this colony . . . it is ordered that all parents and masters shall cause their respective children and servants, as they are capable, to read distinctly the English tongue.[19]

\*\* *Make civics a nationwide mandatory course for graduation in the nation's K-12 system as a condition of public funding.* No individuals can be good citizens unless they are fully cognizant of the laws, rules, and institutions of the political jurisdictions wherein they participate. Civics classes can, in large part, solve this shortcoming – with such education focused upon immigrant students in particular.

\*\* *Restore objectivity to the teachings of history and the indulgence in historiography.* America's universities, colleges, and public schools share a profound responsibility to teach history for its own sake as integral to a requisite intellectual armament of civilized persons – and not to degrade it by permitting its contents to be dictated by political pressure groups, be they ideological, ethnic, racial, religious, or economic. The preservation of the country's legacy and history is far too precious for parochial bias to be allowed to intervene. For national values are imbued by a sense of history and not by whim or happenstance.[20]

\*\* *Implement nationwide proficiency testing teachers.* Each teacher should be tested for proficiency in the subjects taught. Those who excel should receive bonuses; those who fail should be dismissed. Schools that excel should be financially rewarded; schools that don't should go unfunded until they implement the reforms that ensure that they do; and school administrators who can't achieve excellence within their schools should be summarily dismissed.

\*\* *Promote merit-based pay in local school districts to reward teachers who excel while shedding those who are incompetent* – just as every successful private enterprise imbued by profit motive now must to survive. Today, because of tenure and union rules, bad teachers cannot effectively be removed from the education system for years – notwithstanding that those hurt the most by this wholly self-serving unionized approach are the national interest and the children themselves. This gravely flawed approach must be summarily reversed if America is to remain an economic superpower.[21]

# Appendix B
# Financial Meltdown: Crisis of Capitalism or Failure of Federalism?

### I. INTRODUCTION: The Crisis of Capitalism

With a financial *tsunami* of unparalleled magnitude crescendoing across America in the fall of 2008, politicians of all persuasions are now indiscriminately blaming the phenomenon on "capitalistic greed." They point with considerable justification to mounting disparities between historic white collar/blue collar income levels, and posit that a democratic capitalistic system that has served so many so well for so long has somehow now become fatally flawed. The critical question is: "Are they right?"

The raw income numbers seem to support the indictment. Recent analyses of Professor Edward Wolfe of New York University reveal that today:

> * The richest one percent of Americans posses 33 percent of the nation's privately-held wealth.
> * They own 40 percent of its liquid assets – 44 percent of all stocks and mutual funds, 58 percent of all financial securities, 57 percent of all business equity, and 35 percent of all non-residential real estate. [1]

In aggregate, they own more wealth than the bottom 90 percent of America combined — receiving 20 percent of all annual income, a level unprecedented since the 1930s. Indeed, the Chairman of the failed Washington Mutual received $19 million for his meager three week contributions before his institution collapsed in mid-September, 2008. The average CEO, in fact, now earns 531 times more than the average factory worker, up from 42 times that level in 1960.[2]

Disproportionate executive salaries are undeniably a serious problem *sui generis*. But they are a minuscule portion of the current financial meltdown crisis. For a far greater shortcoming has been public sector bureaucratic frustration of the necessary workings of free market process – those acts of "creative destruction" that economist Joseph Schumpeter taught a century ago are "the essential fact of capitalism."[3]

Within this process, it is axiomatic that free markets quintessentially require periodic recession to wring out transactional excess before it becomes excessive – before it coalesces into a giant snowball creating an avalanche that can bring down an economy. It is that giant bureaucratic snowball that has come crashing down on the American financial sector today – and when that occurs, markets overreact, as is happening now.

For because federal bureaucrats have become far too clever in forestalling requisite recession, while concurrently seeking to solve problems that do not lend themselves to public sector cure – in effect, doing little more than postponing the ultimate day of reckoning by kicking the can of responsibility further down the road – the challenge that America faces is not a "crisis of capitalism," as is now superficially alleged. The crisis is not one of inadequate regulation either, but instead a consummate "failure of federalism."

Such disparate data and facts obviously form fabulous fodder for feasting frenzies by pandering politicians seeking to showboat solutions to problems that they do not really understand. The question is: "How relevant are they to the current financial crisis precipitated by the ongoing collapse of the two-decades-long U.S. real estate bubble and the quest for remedy?" This inquiry explores the answers to these questions as well how America got from there to here.

## II. THE FAILURE OF FEDERALISM

The current financial catastrophe should come as no real surprise, since its imminence, together with its underlying causes, have been repeatedly accurately predicted by various noted business analysts, most noteworthy among them Wall Street prognosticator Peter Schiff, in recent years.[4]

Whether they should be seriously considered must now be definitely answered in the affirmative. For when accomplished analysts hypothesize a model, and subsequent events trace a course exactly in accordance with its postulates, one has to intuitively believe that it is right. What is the message from these convergences? How did the nation get from there to here? The answer must be probed in three distinct dimensions:

## (1) The "Community Covenant"

In America, home ownership has historically been forged on a "communal covenant." A citizen wants to own a home. A hometown banker – who has a vested interest in the creditworthiness of his prospective borrower – wants to contract a profitable term mortgage as an asset on his books.

Traditionally, the bank has looked to several factors to collateralize its loan. A 20 percent down payment not only gave the would-be owner a vested interest not to randomly walk away from his commitment, but has, at the same time, demonstrated that he possesses a financial track record of responsible savings that enabled him to aggregate the requisite 20 percent.[5] The requirement to save for a down payment also enhanced the national savings rate and thereby contributed to long term economic security.

Other formulaic factors have concurrently impacted upon the decision to finance. Among them, the would-be borrower should receive a mortgage no greater than twice his annual income. If his annual income was $50,000, then his mortgage ceiling would be $100,000. Were it to be $100,000, then his maximum mortgage size would be $200,000. Other factors impacting upon the financing decision include that his housing costs – mortgage and taxes – should not exceed one-third of his pre-tax annual income.

The economic effect of prudent lending, then, was that it imposed a natural market ceiling on the extent to which aggregate home prices could rise – being limited by the extent that household incomes constrained the size of permissible mortgage payments and the carefully determined down payments that they made possible.[6]

In the process, moreover, while in the past, homeowners took out second mortgages, they usually did so to make home improvements which materially added to the value of their principal asset, their homes. Today, such is not the case. Why? Because within the past half century – as American society has gradually morphed from a productive, high-paying, manufacturing-driven economy into a more consumptive, lower-paying, service-driven one — the public sector has come to be remarkably adept at merely postponing requisite recessions, all predicated on the belief that the good times would last forever. "Irrational exuberance," Alan Greenspan called it.

As a consequence, instead of seeking secondary mortgages for remodeled kitchens, extra insulation, and other home improvements that not only add ambience to life at present but lend value to their principal retirement asset in the future, secondary and tertiary mortgages have been contracted for snowmobiles, prolonged vacations, a sweeping market-basket of job-exporting imported consumer goods, and similar purchases of a more immediate temporal value – most often purchased on credit cards charged, and repeatedly recharged – all secured by the residual equities in their homes and predicated upon the notion that the "housing bubble" would never end.

And with bankers increasingly indemnified by governmental parastatals

222                               Appendix B

backed by federal tax dollar guarantees against mortgage loss, optimizing profitability based on *transactional volume* rather than *loan quality* now became a prudent business decision. Lenders thus made money with each loan origination and would then sell such loans to larger institutions to keep them afloat. Hence, with public sector "securitization," it has become possible for a borrower to obtain a half million dollar mortgage without either a down payment or an exemplary credit record.

The "degeneration of creditworthiness" problem has been attended by a spate of seductive new mortgage products as well– including "adjustable rate mortgages" which transfer traditional interest rate risk from the mortgage lender to the home buyer – and "interest-only" loans which require interest payments only for the first few years of the mortgage — both of which serve as loan enticements by providing low-buy-in costs at the front end of the mortgage, but which then become increasingly back-loaded as it progresses — ultimately creating onerous payment burdens on the borrowers, many often impossible to bear.[7]

The problem was exacerbated by the "Community Reinvestment Act of 1977" which required local bankers to make business loans to sub-prime borrowers within their defined lending areas – as well as the consolidation of individual home town local banks into newly-formed multi-state conglomerates, and the 1999 repeal of the 1933 Glass-Steagall Act which severely circumscribed the activities of conventional banks in investment banking.

The net result has been a shift of the nation's welfare burden from tax dollars to private credit cards – as rather than borrowers banking the savings resulting from low up-front mortgage costs, they have instead been committed to profligate, relatively frivolous, low value, often imported, consumer goods that may contribute materially to employment levels in East Asia, but do little to underpin enduring economic stability within the United Stares. In an economy wherein 70 percent of GDP is generated by consumer spending, and in a society characterized by negative savings rates, this deadly cocktail of improvident lending and borrowing practices is now proving to be financially disastrous, as ongoing events reveal.

Normal, mild periodic purgative business cycle recessions, it bears repeating, in this instance would have arguably served as the proverbial "canaries in the coal mines" – firing warning shots across the bow against the folly of such practices that substitute long term economic security for self-gratification now. How did it come down to this?

## (2) The "Beneficence of Bureaucracy"

Genetically, there can be no doubt that the nexus of America's current economic crisis lies in the "New Deal socioeconomic philosophy" that resulted in the proliferation of multiple "do-gooder" public sector parastatals such as "Freddie Mac" in 1938, and has permeated through the "Great Society" and their legacy offspring ever since. As generically, the approach has metastasized across the public sector board, creating what has been euphemistically called the "nanny state."

More specifically, at the core of the current crisis is a set of triplets — two named "Mae," the other "Mac" — "Fannie May" (Federal National Mortgage Association), "Freddie Mac" (Federal Home Loan Mortgage Corporation), and "Ginnie Mae" (Government National Mortgage Association). Collectively, they are part and parcel of a public sector approach of seeking to extend the American Dream to all through home ownership, even for those who, based on financial track records, creditworthiness, and earnings capabilities, qualify to be renters only.

Indeed, the fingerprints of these financial triplets may be found all over the current meltdown crisis. As the system of "securitization," the practice of purchasing prime residential mortgage assets from original lenders by governmental parastatals who then repackage them into tranches of high yield mortgage-backed securities today lies at the heart of the current capital collapse. In the absence of such federal collateralization, in fact, it is unlikely that a prudent private lender would extend a mortgage to a person with a poor credit or work history making no down payment.

For it is the resultant artificially-appreciated home values that derive from such public sector legerdemain that profit-driven multistate banking chains have been particularly anxious to capture in the form of home equity loans. Superficially, this approach may appear to be a marriage made in heaven for all – unless someone considers the underwriting American taxpayers, of course, but of course, no one ever does.

But while private bankers have been offered "idiot-proof" loans secured by the federal government, the concurrent co-beneficiaries have been a economic class targeted for "Santa Claus politics" – an approach which is, in essence, no more than "tooth fairy economics." For if one's government is going to create a failsafe housing market wherein one can get a half million dollar mortgage with no down payment required – wherein he or she can live free while riding the upswing of an artificially-inflating value structure until his home doubles in worth – and then calculatingly cashes it out, the bounty from the differential is a no-brainer "Monopoly Money" type of windfall with zero risk involved.

Exploiting this opportunity, then, is, again, from a self-serving *individual* standpoint, no more that a sound business decision. But it concurrently is a radical departure from a more conservative era characterized by a commercial practice wherein local bankers judiciously made loans based on established creditworthiness.[8]

## (3) The "Avenging Aftermarket"

Had it been left there, public sector benevolence would have done more than enough to torque the workings of the American economic system. But the activities of the "Mae triplets" concurrently made possible the creation of an expansive subprime mortgage aftermarket as well.

For while their activities were ostensibly to be limited to the prime mortgage market, their abilities to package homogenized hybrids of higher and lesser performing loans – many of which were initiated in the former category, which then degenerated into the latter because of the aforesaid deterioration in due diligence that once went into their contracting – to create a national secondary market for mortgage securities has proven to be the *coup de grace* to the American banking system.

For this practice then cleared the way for Wall Street – with already too much cash chasing too few quality investment products – to design disingenuous way to accommodate the varying qualities of mortgages by splitting the various mortgage pools into different risk, maturity, and rate classes – marketing each separately. By relegating the least creditworthy mortgages to high risk, high yield tranches to be sold primarily to high yield, risk-immaterial institutional investors, it was thus able to qualify the majority of the rest for AAA credit ratings.[9]

Accordingly, Wall Street created what it deemed to be a "win/win" situation for itself – a premier upscale market for the vast majority of its mortgage products – and an enticing sub-prime market for mutual funds and hedge funds whose missions were to seek out high returns in an otherwise low yield investment environment.

But by thus placing the real estate market in conflict with the mortgage market, it has destabilized both – creating an inverted-pyramid mortgage "Ponzi scheme" consisting of multiple-layered tranches of mortgage portfolios all secured at the base by the same set of finite questionable real estate assets–a chimeric house of cards that collapses further still with the removal of each subsequent card. This asset over-leveraging is what lies at the heart of current banking crisis. Thus it is that the American economy finds itself where it finds itself today.

## III. THE PANDERING OF POLITICIANS

That the real estate bubble debacle is the inevitable outcome, however, should come as no surprise – for it is a classic case of what happens when the public sector "cure" itself creates the "crisis" – paving the way for the spread of socialistic recourse further still, as is now happening with the tax-dollar-funded financial bailouts. This reality has been, in fact, a recurring fact of America's past half century. Indeed, it is pandemic to the political process.

As many of the policy problems today evident on both sides of the political divide are intrinsic to the workings of democracy itself – as the system too frequently fosters and regenerates its own socioeconomic problems – reflecting the stark reality that economic progress remains a process, not a act. It cannot be solved with a single bill or within a single congressional session.

Yet legislators, presidents, and governors alike must be reelected every two, four, or six years. In America's "crisis-driven" political process, therefore, they can't afford protracted policy results. They lack both the time and the incentive to wait as patient investment capital wends its way to a successful return. Such on-the-ground political realities thus mandate for them an endless frenetic quest for short term solutions to long term problems and simple solutions to complex problems.

Regrettably, in this policy promulgation process, however, placebos are too often passed off as panaceas — pasting legislative band-aids over critically wounded economic base – while often producing full blown "policy circuses" that stand in steadfast affirmation of the time-proven political axiom that there are two things that one should never see being made – one is sausage, the other law. The problem is compounded by the TV-era "PR" strategic operative rule known as the "Dan Rather syndrome:" To wit: "Don't attempt to accomplish anything that Dan Rather can't explain in 30 seconds!"

Yet if sound governance is to prevail – and effective economic policy is to issue from it – a defining difference between philosophy and platitudes – policy and politics – accomplishment and mere 'bumper sticker slogans' – must be reestablished. For the end result of such superficial thinking, as in the case of the current housing crisis, is that complex structural economic problems too often remain beyond the grasp of the political process.

Hence, they are almost invariably ignored – as lawmakers lavish still more tax dollars not upon building the economy, but upon the inevitable effects of what happens when the economy breaks down: *providing gratuitous tax-funded financial bailouts, increasing welfare payments, expanding unemployment benefits*, and the like. For there, at least, the illusion of perceptible short term political progress can be projected.

The net result, in retrospect, has, therefore, been quite predictable – with the government now clumsily meddling in all aspects of human life. For while as late as 1960, the federal government had little to do with welfare, education, and crime control, by 1975, it dominated them all, setting their rules while subsidizing their existence – with the nation paying a heavy price in the form of an economy grievously attenuated by bureaucratic overburden. As sequentially, in a tragic downward spiral of eroding free market values over the past century:[10]

> (1) The pre-WW-I so-called "Progressive Era" established the precept that the federal government is responsible for all aspects of the economy;
> (2) The New Deal established the notion that no area of life is off limits to government; and
> (3) The Great Society destroyed that sense of self-responsibility that initially had made possible America's great prosperity and freedoms.

In aggregate, then, such inept political handiwork has left America's historic "democratic capitalistic social contract" with her people in shambles — and in a manner wholly oblivious to the cogent lessons of economic history – creating a socioeconomic litany permeated with the triage that occurs when overreaching bureaucrats can't keep their hands off a free market economy.

As within the past century, the nation's social character has been radically transformed from an entrepreneurial ethic into an entitlements one — with a public sector "cure" for every socioeconomic "crisis" and with its erstwhile innate economic dynamism lying victim to the excesses of the New Deal and the Great Society – yet no wonder.

For FDR's grand strategy, as articulated by his political advisor Harry Hopkins was: " tax and spend, spend and spend, and elect and elect."[11] As for the Great Society, it can be equally cynically dismissed. As Ronald Reagan famously lamented: "Lyndon Johnson declared a war on poverty and poverty won!"[12]

## IV. CONCLUSION: Can the Crisis Create a Cure?

"Executive salaries," as noted, have become the featured poster child for pandering politicians pretending to be policy-wise atop the financial meltdown crisis. This is a typically politically reflexive reaction, as undeniably, income disparities now prevalent throughout the marketplace are a high profile financial problem, but they aren't *the housing crisis problem*. Yet misdiagnosing the malady merely complicates the quest for effective cure. For the incontestable reality is that the incipient source of America's ongoing economic faltering is an inane "public sector cure for all" approach that frames the current "failure of federalism" debate.

Today, however, in its insatiable quest to be "all things to all people," government is running out of remedial resources. As in the case of the burst of the housing bubble which underlies the present real estate mortgage collapse, as shown, much of the incipient housing demand has been precipitated by relaxed bank lending standards made possible by federal indemnification against bank loss — combined with "no up-front" borrower financial requirements and relatively low interest rates.

Alternately put, housing speculation bred of irrational exuberance has precipitated an unwarranted housing boom that federal guarantees made possible. But as the exorbitant back-end costs of those developments having finally caught up with the under-financially-endowed borrower pool, the collapse of the real estate financial sector has been the inexorable result.

The reason for the operation of this market dynamic is basic. As borrowers have perceived their property values to be rising in what appeared to be an age of endless, boundless prosperity, their propensities to save have concomitantly diminished. Why bother to save when downsizing one's home and moving in retirement to the Sunbelt Belt can provide a cash windfall through routine cash-outs that will underwrite one's "golden years" costs of living?

Accordingly, monies that might otherwise have gone into provident savings have instead been committed to short term consumption – relatively low value, disposable consumer good credit card purchases funded by multiple sequential series of secondary and tertiary mortgage borrowings – a phenomenon that sustained an artificial boost to the U.S. economy for a time, but has now proven to be economically calamitous.

In an abstract sense, the outcome was unavoidable – as the "housing bubble," like the 1990s "tech bubble" that preceded it, were artificial economic creations that could not be sustained in the long term. Who is to blame? As analysis as shown, those who would condemn "the economic policies of the past *eight* years" are no more than mere political charlatans. For there has been no substantial banking deregulation within the past three decades readily to blame, save that which allowed erstwhile hometown banks to aggregate into multi-state conglomerates. These tragic outcomes are instead structural public sector policy problems that have been coalescing over the past *eighty* years – indeed, ever since Franklin Roosevelt invented "Freddie Mac" in 1938.

More specifically, however, perhaps the more significant share of the blame was accurately assessed by President Bill Clinton himself in mid- September, 2008 when he surprisingly accused congressional Democrats of: "resisting any efforts by Republicans in the Congress or me . . . to set some standards and tighten up a little on Fannie Mae and Freddie Mac."[13] The reason? — as articulated by Fannie Mae CEO Franklin Raines, himself a former Clinton official and Obama campaign policy advisor: "We manage our political risks with the same intensity that we measure our credit and interest risks."[14]

Indeed, to that end, the radical "Mae" and "Mac" parastatals have donated millions of dollars to key congressmen to ensure that no meaningful reform ever will take place to restore equity to the financial markets – a process that works to the advantage of their special interest constituencies that they have carefully first curried, and now corralled, through the" politics of victimization."[15]

In sum, the alleged current "crisis of capitalism" that is manifest in America's ongoing financial meltdown is, in actuality, instead, as charged, a calamitous "failure of federalism." What is the solution? Correctly identifying the problem for what it clearly is an optimal place to start – as paths to remedy then intuitively suggest themselves.

Certainly, blanket financial bailouts predicated upon the proposition of "heads, the government wins, tails the taxpayers lose" – as is presently the case – are no equitable solution. As it is manifestly unjust to ask the financially prudent to continually underwrite the wantonly malfeasant excesses of the financially incompetent. New solutions are required. For when the proposed public sector solution is, in reality, the problem's original cause, the challenge becomes self-compounding.

These are indeed ominous economic harbingers, for as noted in Chapter 5, William Wolman, chief economist for *Newsweek* – as early as 1997, prophetically asserted:

> The best historians have noticed that in each major phase in the development of capitalism, the leading country of the capitalist world goes through a period of "financialization," wherein the most important economic dynamic is creation and trading of abstract financial instruments rather than the production of genuine goods and services. The work of these historians raises a powerful caution about the kinds of trends that we are seeing vis-à-vis the position of the United States in the world economy: the growth of sophisticated high finance is not necessarily a sign of nirvana, but rather an ill omen that the country has entered the last stages of greatness and is headed into trouble.[16]

Wolman continues:

> The United States has now been thrown into a phase of history where finance rules all. Mutual funds and the stock exchange, rather than the research lab and the factory floor, have become central to the culture. The graduating classes of the nation's great business schools, from Harvard to Stanford, flock in droves to investment banking rather than to jobs in the real economy.
> 
> Historically, the financialization of society has been a symbol that the nation's economic position has entered into a phase of deterioration. By the mid-eighteenth century, the Dutch elite, already on the road to decline, had become little more than speculators and rentiers who lived on unearned income, lending their money to any foreign prince or company able to pay the interest.
>
> Britain was at a similar stage by the first decade of the twentieth century. Although its manufacturing industry was losing ground, its financial services had never been stronger – and its elite of investors, bankers, and rentiers, who controlled half of the world's moveable investment capital, were fully confident that finance and investment would make up for any ebb in steel, textiles, and ship-building. They were proved wrong, and those who now proclaim the wonderful wisdom of Wall Street will likewise be shown to be in error.[17]

A decade later, as shown, the wisdom of this prognostication is self-evident. Today, though the outstanding characteristic of the past decade may have been the rise of high tech industry, and its attendant buoyant service economy, within the new global economy, this trend has nonetheless been overwhelmed by the resurgence of the financial sector and its ever-encroaching dominance over the production of goods and services – creating both a new world of weak federal governments and strong central banks, and within it, a powerful new political class of those who trade in global currencies and bond markets.[18]

In this process, America's creative energies have now become focused upon financial engineers specialized in creating complex financial instruments designed to make money out of money – rather than industrial engineers engaged in designing high-powered computers, software, cars, telecommunications, and medical and energy-producing equipment that could improve the lives and productivities of millions.

Concurrently, central bankers have presided over a massive transfer of income from households and private businesses to banks and other financial institutions, transforming the erstwhile world of industrial capitalism into a heretofore unprecedented world of "financial capitalism" – a global "Ponzi scheme" whose portents must be reversed if the economic miracles made possible by the free market are to be preserved – a course that invokes the need not for more "financial bailouts" but for a top-to-bottom industrial "build-out."[19]

To this end, as a point of imminent departure, a modest proposal founded upon a "new economic covenant" between the U.S. government and the American people clearly is invoked. To wit: given that, as manifest in Social Security, a noteworthy goal of public policy should be to contribute to the economic security of citizens, America today calls out for a solution that benefits its citizen-taxpayers, rather than one that, as is presently the case, callously rips them off with no return – a market-based solution rather than a federal one.

To this end, Freddie, Fannie, and Ginnie should be consolidated into a giant "Enterprise America Authority" managed by the Department of Treasury with a revenue bonding structure designed to issue "recovery bonds," backed by the full faith and credit of the federal government, dedicated to backing redeemable bank assets currently within the financial markets – with the hopelessly irredeemably ones bred of financial incompetence allowed to die the deaths that they deserve.

In other words, instead of asking people to sacrifice with no chance of profitable returns, the government should be encouraging them to invest with guaranteed rates of return — thereby allowing them commit their savings to their futures rather than forcibly needlessly requiring then to throw away their tax dollars on financial bailouts without reward in an approach that, in any case, ultimately will not work. In this manner, the financial community can be resurrected through free market means that simultaneously enhance the economic security of citizens.

Concurrently, private financial institutions would benefit as well. No society can survive without financial institutions, and capital surplus bred of private savings is their economic lifeblood. No financial system can survive within a society indulging in negative savings rates. By encouraging private savings rather than profligate consumptive spending, the economic well-being of credit institutions is thereby correspondingly restored.

Americans are a good people who rise to challenges in time of crisis. In the WW-II "Seventh War Bond Issue" – which ran from 9 May to July 4, 1945 — targeted to raising $14 billion from a populace then totaling 160 million citizens, many of them earning only a few thousand dollars a year — nearly double that amount, $26.3 billion, was raised instead – and that in a year when the total federal budget was a mere $56 billion![20]

Patriotism works — and at a time when all the countries of the world are abandoning socialism in droves – including Russia, the erstwhile East Bloc countries, and China – America must not let this generation of perniciously pandering politicians take them there.

# Notes

## Introduction

1. For detailed analysis, please see Appendix B.
2. Jean Jacques Rousseau quoted by C. Galloway 2005, p. 10.
3. Samuel Huntington quoted in A. Lieven 2004, p. 124.
4. Ronald Reagan quoted in W. Federer 2004, pp. 56, 61, 77.
5. Ronald Reagan, Ecumenical Prayer Breakfast, Reunion Arena, Dallas, quoted in W. Federer 2004, p. 56.
6. R. Reagan. "Remarks at the Annual Convention of the National Association of Evangelicals in Orlando, Florida," The Public Papers of Ronald Reagan, Ronald Reagan Presidential Library, at http//www.reagan.utexas.edu/search/speeches/speech_srch.html.
7. Oliver Cromwell quoted in I. Root 1989, pp. 89-81.
8. N. Ferguson 2003, p. 317.
9. The Roman poet Virgil, *Aeneid*, quoted at novaromarespublica.org.
10. J. Addison 1932, p. 280.
11. Kaiser Wilhelm quoted in W. Mead 2007, p. 33.
12. G.K. Chesterton quoted in S. Huntington 2004, p. 48.
13. Alexis de Tocqueville quoted in S. Huntington 2004b, pp.103-105.
14. J.Q. Adams 1821, p. 28.
15. J.Q. Adams 1837, p. 18
16. J. Locke 1986, 49:1.
17. *Bible*. Genesis 12:1-3; W. Hudson 1970, pp. 109 ff.; S. Kennedy 2007, p. 53.
18. Josiah Strong quoted in W. Hudson 1970, pp. 116-117.
19. Thomas Paine quoted in P. Foner 1945, vol. 1, p. 72; O. Guinness 1993, pp. 51-52; K. Armstrong 2000, p. 84.

20. John Adams quoted in J. Moltmann 1995, p.171.; G. Müller-Fahrenholz 2007, p. 14.
21. W. Mead 2007, pp. 312-313.
22. Alexis de Tocqueville 1945, vol. 1, p. 305; G. DeMar 1995, p. 8.
23. Alexis de Tocqueville quoted in W. Berns 2001, p. 43.
24. C. Richard 1994, p. 232; G. Weigel 2005, pp. 69, 83, 102, 108, 112, 143; G. DeMar 1995, p. 84.
25. C. Richard 1994, loc. cit.
26. J. Eidsmoe 2005, p. 71.
27. Henry Commager quoted in C. Richard 1994, pp. 1, 12-14, 19, 35, 232-233.
28. George Washington and John Adams quoted in E. Burns 2006, p. 7; C. Johnson 2006, p. 59; W. McDougall 2004, p. 285; O. Guinness 2001, p. 149; C. Richard 2008, pp. 18, 77; J. Eidsmoe 2005, p. 22; E. Gaustad 1993, p. 85.
29. Thomas Jefferson quoted in E. Burns 2006, loc. cit.; C. Richard 2008, pp. 18-19; S. Kennedy 2007, pp. 45-46; J. Meacham 2006, p. 9.
30. Sources cited, loc. cit.
31. Benjamin Franklin quoted in C. Richard 2008, p. 20.
32. E. Gaustad 1993, p. 103; G. DeMar 1995, pp. 84, 163-165; C. Richard 1994, pp. 39, 50-51, 53 ff.
33. C. Richard 2008, pp.17-19, 79-82, 85, 91-97; idem. 1994, p. 104.
34. James Madison quoted in C. Richard 2008, pp. 82-83.
35. James Madison quoted in C. Richard 1994, p. 140; G. DeMar 1995, p. 84; R. Bellah 1975, p. 23.
36. John Adams quoted in O. Guinness 2001, p. 88; C. Campbell 1994, p. C-6.
37. J. Adams 1971, vol.1, pp. i-iii, xii-xiii; C. Richard 1994, p. 134.
38. J. Adams 1971, pp. xii, 104.
39. John Adams 1850, vol. 4, p. 484; D. Barton 2002, p. 335.
40. Alexander Hamilton quoted in S. Padover 1958, p. 423; J. Eidsmoe 2005, p. 148.
41. Alexander Hamilton and James Madison quoted in C. Richard 2008, pp. 91-95; idem. 1994, p. 104.
42. C. Richard 2008, p. 97.
43. Cicero quoted in C. Richard 2008, p. 100.
44. Livy cited in C. Richard 2008, p. 100.
45. Patrick Henry quoted in C. Richard 2008, pp. 156-158; idem. 1994, pp. 90-91, 100.
46. John Adams quoted in C. Richard 1994, p. 100.
47. John Adams quoted in C. Richard 1994, pp. 88, 100.
48. John Dickinson quoted in C. Richard 1994, p. 88.
49. Thomas Jefferson. "Rights of British America," 1774. ME 1:190, Papers 1:124, quoted at etext.virginia.edu/jefferson/quotations/jeff1210.htm.
50. Thomas Jefferson quoted in C. Richard 1994, p. 119.
51. James Madison quoted in H. Dawson 1890, pp. 334, 360; J. Davis 1984, p. 9.
52. John Adams quoted in C. Richard 2008, loc. cit.; idem. 1994, pp. 19, 85-87; Alexander Hamilton quoted in C. Richard 1994, p. 92.
53. R. Taylor 1977, vol. 1, p. 7; C. Richard 1994, p. 25.
54. John Adams quoted in C. Richard 2008, pp. 18-19; idem. 1994, p. 64; J. Eidsmoe 2005, p. 251; J. Miller 1960, p. 19.
55. R. Taylor 1977, vol. 2, p. 230; C. Richard 1994, pp. 232-233.
56. C. Richard 1994, pp. 85-86.

57. S. Kennedy 2007, pp. 50-51.
58. C. Richard 2008, pp. 124-128; idem. 1994, pp. 70-72.
59. John Adams quoted in C. Richard 2008, pp. 20-21.
60. John Adams quoted in C. Richard 2008, p. 21.
61. C. Campbell 1994, p. C-6; G. DeMar 1995, p. 84.
62. T. Jefferson 1994, vol. 2, pp. 260, 264; John Adams quoted in O. Guinness 2001, p. 88; J. Eidsmoe 2005, p. 11.
63. Source cited, loc. cit.
64. John Adams quoted in E. Sandoz 1984, p. 67.
65. Benjamin Franklin quoted in J. Madison 1840, vol. 2, p. 984; idem. 1911, vol. 1, p. 451; D. Barton 2002, p. 213.
66. Charles Lee quoted in C. Richard 2008, p. 128.
67. John Kennedy quoted at www.quotationspage.com/quotes/John_F._Kennedy.
68. James Russell Lowell quoted in D. Marsh 1970, p. 51; W. Federer 2005, p. 271.
69. O. Guinness 1993, p. 51; R. Bellah 1975, p. 2.
70. William Penn quoted in J. Butler 1990, p. 37.
71. John Adams quoted in E. Tuveson 1968, p. 25; O. Guinness 1993, p. 52.
72. John Adams quoted in J. Miller 1960, p. 311; J. Eidsmoe 2005, p. 253.
73. John Jay quoted in Modern Library 1937, p. 3.
74. A. de Tocqueville 1945, vol. 1, pp. 301, 319; quoted in I. Cornelison 1895, p. 257; W. Skousen 1985, pp. 678-679; O. Guinness 1993, pp. 51, 141.
75. Benjamin Franklin quoted in E. von Kuehnelt-Leddihn 1990, p. 67; A. Schmidt 1997, p. 179.
76. T. Jefferson 1859, vol. 2, p. 232.
77. Thomas Paine quoted in W. McDougall 1997, pp. 20, 23; K. Armstrong 2000, p. 84.
78. Reverend John Winthrop quoted in W. McDougall 1997, pp. 37-38.
79. Reverend George Duffield quoted in W. Hudson 1970, p. 55.
80. Oliver Cromwell quoted in W. Hudson, p. xxviii. President George W. Bush, "Address to a Joint Session of Congress and the American People, September 20, 2001 at http:/www.whitehouse.gov/news/releases/2001/09/print/20010920-8.html.
81. S.F. Smith 1940, no. 141.
82. Abraham Lincoln quoted in N. Gingrich 2008, p. 74.
83. Alexis de Tocqueville quoted in W. Berns 2001, p. 72.
84. P. Buchanan, March 12, 2008, p. 30.
85. W. Cook. July 11, 1994, p. 54.
86. D. Boorstin. July 11, 1994, p. 61.
87. See M. Lerner 1957, passim.
88. John Quincy Adams quoted in W. Mead 2001, p. 185; W. McDougall 1997, p. 36.
89. Colin Powell quoted in L. Ingraham 2003, pp. 319-320.
90. L. Ingraham 2003, p. 320.
91. *Bible*, John 1:5.
92. On this, see S. Huntington 2004b, passim; L. Ingraham 2003, p. 257; W. McDougall 1997, p. 16.
93. In this quest, analysis demonstrates that, like Rome herself when others came to dominate her culture, the nation is losing its sense of what "being Roman means," thereby undermining its traditional core value underpinnings. The resulting cultural chaos is manifest in a loss of patriotism and work ethic, precipitating a mounting welfare burden, resulting in

an onerous fiscal burden that can ultimately bring her down. The phenomenon is not without precedent. It evolved to destroy the Roman and Islamic empires – and it is happening in America today. As one wag put it recently: "Want to know the impacts of illegal immigration? Ask the American Indians?"

94. Herbert Marcuse quoted in R. Fopp 2007, "Introduction."
95. As defined in D. Barton 2002, p. 8; C. Richard 1994, p. vii.
96. Ibid.
97. M. Bradford 1982, p. x; D. Barton 1992, pp. 21-22.

## CHAPTER ONE

1. Jean Jacques Rousseau quoted by C. Galloway 2005, pp. 10 ff.
2. W. Berns 2001, p. 92; C.L. Thompson n.d., p. 68; J. Black 1994, p. 245; C. Galloway 2005, p. 11.
3. Plutarch quoted in C. Galloway 2005, pp.10-12.
4. J. Black 1994, pp. 7-8, 38-39.
5. J. Black 1994, p. 245.
6. W. Berns 2001, p. 92; C. Galloway 2005, p. 11.
7. Will Durant quoted in J. Black 1994, p. 8.
8. M. Singer and P. Bracken 1976, p. 34; J. Davis 1984, p. 34.
9. J. Black 1994, p. 8.
10. Christopher Columbus quoted in D. Barton 2002, p. 76; J. Black 1994, p. 237; G. DeMar 1997, vol. 1, p. 136.
11. Noah Webster quoted in W. Federer 2003, p. 194; O. Guinness 2001, p. 114; M. Berman 2006, p. 249; G. Jackson 2006, pp. 363 ff.; N. Gingrich 2006a, p. 30; J. Eidsmoe 2005, p. 360; M. Beliles and S. McDowell 1992, p. 115.
12. Source cited, loc. cit.
13. A. de Tocqueville 1945, p. 318; O. Guinness 2001, p. 13; H. Kramer and R. Kimball 1999, p.146.
14. J.F. Kennedy 1964, p. 30; C. Galloway 2005, pp. 80, 88.
15. B. Weiss 1966, p. 47.
16. J. Marshall 2006, vol. 12, p. 278; E. Gaustad 1993, pp. 116-117; C. Galloway 2005, pp. 56-58; I. Cornelison 1895, pp. 4 ff.
17. H. Commager 1958, p. 8; H. Hazard 1792, vol. 1 p. 72; D. Barton 2002, p. 76; J. Black 1994, loc. cit.; 24; G. DeMar 1997, vol. 1, p. 137; idem. 1995, p. 52; idem. 2003, pp. 14-15; O. Guinness 1993, p. 149; D. Brewer 1996, p. 14; J. Meacham 2006, pp. 41 ff.; C. Galloway 2005, pp. 48-50. Indeed, as George Mason wrote in the "*Virginia Declaration*": No free government, nor the blessings of liberty, can be preserved by any people, but by a firm adherence to justice, moderation, temperance, frugality, frugality, and virtue, and by frequent recurrence to fundamental principles." ("Virginia Declaration of Rights," June, 1776).
18. C. Galloway 2005, p. 49; M. Beliles and S. McDowell 1992, pp. 80-81.
19. Sources cited, loc. cit.
20. G. Brydon 1947, vol. 1, pp. 26-27; B.F. Morris 2007, pp. 119 ff.
21. E. Hazard 1792, vol. 1, p. 252; D. Barton 2002, p. 77; G. DeMar 1997, vol. 1, pp. 121-122.

22. M. Adler 1968, vol. 1, p. 64; J. Black 1994, p. 240: J.F. Kennedy 1964, p. 30; B. Weiss 1966, p. 26; D. Barton 2002, p. 77; G. DeMar 1997, vol. 1, pp. 135-137; idem. 1995, p. 56; idem. 2003, pp. 15-20; O. Guinness 1993, p. 250; G. Jackson 2006, pp. 45, 369; M. Beliles and D. Anderson 2005, p. 94; D. Brewer 1996, loc. cit,; C. Galloway 2005, pp. 50-53; M. Beliles and S. McDowell 1992, pp. 61 ff.; I. Cornelison 1895, pp. 23 ff.; T. Hall 1930, p. 86.

23. John Winthrop quoted in M. Noll 1983, p. 38; D. Barton 2002, p. 77; D. Brewer 1996, p. 15; C.L. Thompson n.d. pp.105, 125-126, 140, 145; S. Kennedy 2007, pp. 26-27, 37 ff.; G. DeMar 1995, p. 6; idem. 2003, p. 9;J. Eidsmoe 2005, pp. 29-30; J. Meacham 2006, pp. 37, 46 ff.; C. Galloway 2005, pp. 54, 90; W. Miller 1986, p. 212; M. Beliles and S. McDowell 1992, pp. 83 ff.; I. Cornelison 1895, pp. 27 ff.; B.F. Morris 2007, pp. 71 ff., 85 ff. The Puritans, called Pilgrims now, were absolute separatists, making no comprise in their quest for absolute divorce from the established church. Their presence grew rapidly in Massachusetts. Indeed, twelve years from establishing the settlement, their numbers had grown to more that twenty thousand people; they had built fifty towns and villages and set up forty churches, and had founded Harvard College.

24. *Bible*, Matthew 5:14; O. Guinness 1993, p. 13; T. Hall 1930, pp. 85 ff.

25. C. Galloway 2005, pp. 54-55.

26. M. Foster and M. Swanson 1992, p. 93; M. Beliles and D. Anderson 2005, p. 95; D. Brewer 1996, p. 15.

27. H. Commager 1958, p. 23; B. F. Morris 2007, pp. 87 ff.; G. Bancroft 1837, vol. 1, p. 403; L. Hurst 1991, p. D-1; P. Buchanan 2002, pp. 181-182; S. Huntington 2004, p. 43; B. Weiss 1966, p. 30; D. Barton 2002, p.79; G. DeMar 1997, vol. 1, pp. 123-124; idem. 1995, p. 58; idem. 2003, p. 20; C. Galloway 2005, p. 54; M. Beliles and S. McDowell 1992, pp. 86-87; I. Cornelison 1895, pp. 44 ff.; B.F. Morris 2007, pp. 125 ff.

28. H. Commager 1958, p. 26; B. F. Morris 2007, pp. 93-94; E. Hazard 1792, vol. 2, p. 1; J. Butler 1990, p. 214; S. Huntington 2004, p. 84; G. DeMar 1995, pp. 51 ff., 55-56, 70; idem. 1997, vol. 1, pp.121-122, 124; idem. 2003, pp. 20-21; B. Weiss 1966, p. 32; D. Barton 2002, loc. cit.; G. Jackson 2007, p. 370; M. Beliles and S. McDowell 1992, p. 88; I. Cornelison 1895, pp. 41 ff., 58 ff.

29. B.F. Morris 2007, pp. 73-74.

30. H. Lefler 1956, p. 16; D. Barton 2002, pp.78-79; C.Galloway 2005, p. 91; M. Beliles and S. McDowell 1992, pp. 81-82.

31. John Locke quoted in B.F. Morris 2007, pp. 123 ff.

32. E. Hazard 1792, vol. 2, p. 612; D. Barton 2002, p.78; C. Galloway 2005, p. 55; M. Beliles and S. McDowell 1992, pp. 87-88; I. Cornelison 1895, pp. 61 ff.; B.F. Morris 2007, pp. 91-93.

33. D. Barton 2002, pp. 77, 79; G. DeMar 1995, pp. 58-59, 69.

34. B. Trumbull 1797, pp. 528-533; A. Leaming and J. Spicer 1758, "Preface;" B.F. Morris 1864, pp. 83, 88, 105-107, 109; B. Weiss 1966, p. 34; D. Barton 2002, pp. 78-80; G. DeMar 1997, vol. 1, pp. 124-127; I. Cornelison 1895, pp. 68 ff.

35. *Journals of the Continental Congress* 1914, vol. 23, p. 574; J. Butler 1990, pp. 93-94; D. Barton 2002, pp. 103,108.

36. B.F. Morris 2007, p. 252 ff; G. DeMar 1997, p. 127; idem. 2003, pp. 51-52; D. Kupelian 2005, p. 41; M. Beliles and D. Anderson 2005, p. 59.

37. As quoted by D. Barton 2002, pp. 12, 133 ff.; O. Guinness 2001, p. 125; G. Jackson 2006, p. 371; N. Gingrich 2006a, p. 13.

38. Resolution of the Massachusetts Provincial Congress, 1774, cited in G. Bancroft 1838, vol. 2, p. 229; W. Federer 2004, p. 11.

39. J. Adams 1850, vol. 10, p. 45.

40. C.L. Thompson n.d., p. 99; M. Beliles and S. McDowell 1992, pp. 148-149.

41. B.F. Morris 1864, pp. 249, 262, 264-265; D. Ramsey 1813, p. 103; D. Dorchester 1888, pp. 563-564; D. Brewer 1905, p. 26; M. Berman 2006, p. 249; G. DeMar 1995, pp. 92, 114; idem. 1997, vol. 1, pp. 128-129; J.F. Kennedy 1964, p. 99; B. Weiss 1966; D. Barton 2002, pp. 8, 21, 100, 341; idem. 1992, pp. 49, 97-98; N. Gingrich 2006a, p. 20; S. Kennedy 2007, p. 218; J. Eidsmoe 2005, pp. 362-363. On the linkage of faith and the republic, John Quincy Adams (D. Barton 2002, p. 169) asserts:

> From the day of the Declaration, the people of the North American Union and of its constituent states were associated bodies of civilized men and Christians. . . . They were bound by the laws of God which they all, and by the law of the Gospel, which they nearly all, acknowledged as the rules of their conduct. The Declaration of Independence cast off the shackles of this dependency. The United States of America were no longer colonies. They were an independent nation of Christians.

42. Sources cited, loc. cit. On deliberations leading to adoption of the First Amendment, see M. Malbin 1978, passim; E. Gaustad 1993, pp. 156-158; D. Brewer 1996, pp. 20-21; J. Eidsmoe 2005, pp. 375-376, 834 ff. The Virginia "Statute of Religious Liberty," dated January 16, 1786, similarly acknowledges that "the Almighty God hath created the mind free, and manifested His supreme will that free it shall remain by making it altogether insusceptible of restraint . . ."

43. Thomas Jefferson cited in N. Gingrich 2008, p. 69.

44. T. Eastland 2005, p. 90; D. Kupelian 2005, p. 41; A. Sears and C. Osten 2005, pp. 127-129; N. Gingrich 2006b, p. 47; D. Barton 1992, pp. 37-38; idem. 2002, pp. 41, 92-94, 100-102; M. Beliles and D. Anderson 2005, p. 58; F. Church 2007, pp. 131-132; E. Gaustad 1993, pp. 116-117; M. Beliles and S. McDowell 1992, pp.141-143; I. Cornelison 1895, pp. 111 ff.; B.F. Morris 2007, pp. 245 ff., 330-331; B.F. Morris 2007, p. 376; G. DeMar 2003, p. 49.

45. Both documents quoted in D. Barton 2002, p. 109; W. Malloy 1968, vol.1, p. 586.

46. Congressional resolution cited in W. Hudson 1970, pp. 28-29; C. Galloway 2005, pp. 116-118; B.F. Morris 2007, pp. 660 ff.; R. Cord 1988, pp. 51-52.

47. B.F. Morris 2007, pp. 323 ff.

48. G. Washington 1940 quoted by J. Fitzpatrick 1931-1944, vol. 35, p. 416; D. Barton 2002, p. 324; F. Church 2007, pp. 103-104.

49. B. Weiss 1966, p. 51; E. Gaustad 1993, p. 79; D. Barton 2002, pp. 114-116; G. DeMar 1997, vol. 1, pp. 137-138; N. Gingrich 2006a, p.15; idem. 2006b, p. 49; M. Beliles and D. Anderson 2005, pp. 57-58; G. DeMar 1997, vol. 1, pp.137-138; B.F. Morris 2007, pp. 326 -330. Washington's 1789 request for a national day of prayer, made on the same day that Congress approved the final wording of the First Amendment, makes clear that the framers of that amendment did not believe that the two were in legal contradiction – as they came with a concurrent call of Congress for a public prayer service.

50. B. Weiss 1966, p. 53.

51. George Washington quoted in J. Richardson 1899, vol. 1, p. 220; O. Guinness 2001, p. 13; D. Barton 1992, p. 245; A. Stokes and L. Pfeffer 1964, p. 87; N. Cunningham 1987, p. 225; J.F. Kennedy 1964, pp. 101-102; G. DeMar 1995, pp. 134, 150, 203-204; B. Weiss

1966, p. 54; D. Barton 2002, p. 184; E. Gaustad 1993, p. 78; B.F. Morris 2007, pp. 599 ff. John Adams and James Madison likewise issued proclamations convening national days of prayer acknowledging the existence of a Supreme Being.

52. J. Eidsmoe 2005, pp. 117-118; N. Gingrich 2006b, p. 49; D. Barton 1992, pp. 114-115; F. Church 2007, pp. 60-64; C. Galloway 2005, p. 137; M. Beliles and S. McDowell 1992, p. 7; G. DeMar 2003, p. 53.

53. G. Washington 1932, vol. 30, p. 432;W. Federer 2003, pp. 175-176; M. Beliles and D. Anderson 2005, p. 61; D. Barton 2002, p. 319; J. Eidsmoe 2005, p. 119.

54. John Marshall quoted in G. Jackson 2007, p. 365.

55. G. Washington 1796, p. l; idem. 1930-1932, vol. 30, p. 32; J. Richardson 1899, vol. 1, p. 64; S. Huntington 2004b, p. 84; D. Barton 2002, p. 113; idem. 2007, pp. 10-11; N. Gingrich 2006, p. 19; W. Federer 2003, pp. 190; F. Church 2007, pp. 68-69; W. Miller 1985, p.244; M. Beliles and S. McDowell 1992, p. 179; B.F. Morris 2007, pp. 558-559.

56. John Adams quoted in W. Federer 2004, pp. 36-37; M. Beliles and S. McDowell 1992, p. 178.

57. John Adams 1850, p. 229; quoted in J. Howe 1966, pp. 185, 384; W. Federer 2003, p. 19; D. Limbaugh 2000, p. 1; S. Huntington 2004b, pp. 84,104, 115; N. Gingrich 2006a, p. 19; idem. 2006b, p. 50; W. Federer 2003, p. 181; O. Guinness 1993, p. 347; M. Beliles and D. Anderson 2005, pp. 2, 62, 119; J. Eidsmoe 2005, pp. 273, 292, 381; D. Barton 2007, p. 9; F. Church 2007, pp. 119-120; B.F. Morris 2007, pp. 680 ff.

58. John Adams quoted in E. Gaustad 1993, p. 89; G. Jackson 2006, p. 371.

59. John Adams. "Address to the Military," cited in C. Adams 1850-1856, vol. 9, p. 229; N. Gingrich 2006a, p. 12.

60. John Adams quoted in O. Guinness 2001, p. 147; B. Weiss 1966, p. 57.

61. John Adams quoted in C. Adams 1850-1856, vol. 9, p. 636; J. Eidsmoe 2005, p. 294; W. Federer 2003, pp. 18-21; idem. 2004, p. 63; N. Gingrich 2006a, p. 20; J. Meacham 2006, p. 28.

62. N. Gingrich 2006a, p. 92.

63. T. Jefferson 1904, vol. 14, p. 385; F. Church 2007, p. 295; E. Gaustad 1993, p. 108.

64. E. Gaustad 1993, pp. 100-103; C.G. Singer 1964, pp. 37 ff.; see also "Thomas Jefferson, Virginia Statute for Establishing Religious Freedom," 1786, in E. Gaustad 1993, pp. 149 ff.; D. Barton 2002, p. 207.

65. Thomas Jefferson quoted in W. Linn 1834, p. 265.

66. T. Jefferson 1904, vol. 16, p. 291.

67. Thomas Jefferson quoted in P. Wood 2003, p.172; M. Beliles and D. Anderson 2005, pp. 65-67, 70; J. Eidsmoe 2005, p. 235. E. Gaustad 1993, p. 41; W. Miller 1985, pp. 51-52.

68. Thomas Jefferson 1794, p. 237; W. Federer 2004, loc. cit.; D. Barton 1992, p. 176; idem. 2002, pp. 292; F. Church 2007, p. 283.

69. Thomas Jefferson 1782, vol. 18; quoted in P. Ford 1894, vol. 3, p. 267; W. Federer 1994, p. 323; idem. 2004, pp. 14-15, 69-70; N. Gingrich 2006a, p. 42; M. Beliles and D. Anderson 2005, p. 114, 143-144; J. Eidsmoe 2005, pp. 227, 235; M. Novak 2004, p. xxii, xxix.

70. B. Weiss 1966, p. 62;. James Madison quoted in O. Guinness 1993, pp. 348-349; J. Eidsmoe 2005, pp. 93 ff., 100; N. Gingrich 2006a, p.108; F. Church 2007, pp. 308-309. See also James Madison, "Memorial and Remonstrance, 1785," in E. Gaustad 1993, pp. 141-149. (Likewise see *The Federalist Papers*: 1982, no. 51, p. 262.) Madison's academic regimen at

Princeton reportedly was rigorous and included training in American patriotism, Lockean liberalism, and Scottish "moral sense" philosophy.

71. James Madison in "Federalist No. 51," quoted in O. Guinness 1993, pp. 348-349; J. Meacham 2006, p. 94; W. Miller 1985, p. 115; M. Beliles and S. McDowell 1992, p. 188.

72. James Madison quoted in M. Beliles and D. Anderson 2005, p. 61; M. Beliles and S. McDowell 1992, pp. 178-179; J. Eidsmoe 2005, p. 369.

73. James Madison quoted in O. Guinness 1993, pp. 226, 269; B. Weiss 1966, p. 62.

74. Sources cited, loc. cit.. Echoing Madison's assertion that "to suppose that any form of government will secure liberty or happiness without any form of virtue is a chimeric idea," de Tocqueville stated in *Democracy in America* (1945, vol 1. p. 318): "Despotism may govern without faith, but liberty cannot."

75. Benjamin Franklin quoted in J. Madison 1911, vol. 1, pp. 451-452; B. Weiss 1966, p. 37-38; G. DeMar 1995, pp. 198-200; idem. 2003, p. 83; D. Barton 2002, p.111; idem. 1992, pp. 217-218; N. Gingrich 2006a, pp. 13, 26; R. Dornan and C. Vedlic 1986, p. 27; M. Beliles and D. Anderson 2005, pp. 27, 123; J. Eidsmoe 2005, pp. 12-13; J. Davis 1984, p. 6; M. Novak 2004, pp. 147-148; J. Meacham 2006, pp. 88-89; C. Galloway 2005, p.125; W. Miller 1985, p. 110; M. Beliles and S. McDowell 1992, p. 172; I. Cornelison 1895, pp. 93, 209; B.F. Morris 2007, pp. 298-300; R. Cord 1988, pp.24-25.

76. Benjamin Franklin quoted in F. Dexter 1901, vol. 3, p. 387; E. Gaustad 1993, p. 65; N. Gingrich 2006a, p. 13; idem. 2006b, p. 23; J. Meacham 2006, p. 89.

77. Benjamin Franklin quoted in W. Federer 2004, p. 69.

78. John Jay quoted in D. Barton 2002, p. 165.

79. J. Jay 1890, vol. 4, p. 393; D. Barton 1992, pp. 35, 78.

80. Alexander Hamilton quoted in N. Schachner 1946, pp. 38, 430; W. Federer 2004, pp. 16-17.

81. O. Guinness 2001, pp. 80, 144.

82. Thomas Paine quoted in A. Sears and C. Osten 2005, p.128.

83. W. Federer 2004, p. 13; A. Schmidt 1997, p. 182; M. Beliles and D. Anderson 2005, p. 57; J. Eidsmoe 2005, p. 117; M. Beliles and S. McDowell 1992, pp. 174-175.

84. As related in W. Federer 2003, p. 49; B. Weiss 1966, pp. 53 ff.

88. From M. Noll 2002, pp. 162-163.

85. John Adams and Thomas Jefferson quoted by E. Gaustad 1993, p. 137.

86. P. Schaff 1889, p. 40; G. DeMar 1995, pp. 63-65, 82, 150-152; idem. 2003, pp. 31-34, 75; E. Gaustad 1993, p. 44; D. Barton 2002, p. 42; J. Eidsmoe 2005, pp. 359-360; W. Miller 1985, pp. 107-112; M. Beliles and S. McDowell 1992, p. 180; I. Cornelison 1895, p. 92; T. Hall 1930, p. 164. On this phenomenon, nineteenth century church historian Phillip Schaff writes: "The absence of the names of God and Christ in a purely political and legal document no more proves denial or irreverence than the absence of those names in a mathematical treatise or the statutes of a bank or railroad corporation. The term "Holiness" does not make the Pope any more holy than he is. . . . the Book of Esther and Song of Solomon are undoubtedly productions of devout worshipers of Jehovah; yet the name of God does not occur once in them."

87. D. Kupelian 2005, p. 41; N. Gingrich 2006a, p. 10; D. Brewer 1996, pp. 17, 19; C. Galloway 2005, pp. 109-l11; W. Miller 1985, p. 212; M. Beliles and S. McDowell 1992, p. 181; J. O'Neill 1949, p. 193; R. Cord 1988, p. 4. The Anglicans were established in Virginia, New York, Maryland, South Carolina, North Carolina, and Georgia. The Congregationalists were established in Massachusetts, Connecticut, and New Hampshire.

88. From M. Noll 2002, pp. 162-163.

89. U.S. Congress 1785, pp. 99-100; G. DeMar 1995, pp. 65-66, 78; idem. 2003, pp. 23-24; E. Gaustad 1993, p. 114; D. Barton 2002, pp. 40, 331-332; idem. 1992, pp. 23-24, 143; D. Kupelian 2005, p. 41; D. Brewer 1996, pp. 3, 19, 20; C. Galloway 2005, pp. 103-105, 109-111; B.F. Morris 2007, pp. 269 ff., 280 ff. The Massachusetts Constitution, Chapter VI, Article 1, similarly stipulated that all persons elected to state offices or to the legislature must "make and subscribe the following declaration. viz. 'I, ———, do declare that I believe in the Christian religion and have firm persuasion of its truth.'" The First Amendment to the North Carolina Constitution, in turn, read in part: "That no person who shall deny the being of God or the truth of the Christian religion, or the divine authority of either the Old or New Testaments, or who shall hold religious principles incompatible with the freedom and safety of the State, shall be capable of holding any office or place of trust or profit in the civil department within this State." For synopses of the various states' early declarations and constitutional provisions respecting religion, see G. DeMar 1997, vol. 1, pp. 162-163, 186-188; E. Gaustad 1993, pp. 159-174.

90. U.S. Congress 1785, p. 81; William Penn quoted in G. Jackson 2007, p. 370; G. DeMar 1995, pp. 73-74, 81; idem. 2003, p. 29; I. Cornelison 1895, pp. 99 ff.; B.F. Morris 2007, pp. 107 ff.

91. G. DeMar 1995, pp. 68-69, 72; idem. 2003, pp. 26-28; E. Gaustad 1993, pp. 114-115; D. Barton 2002, pp. 40, 331-332; B.F. Morris 2007, pp. 271-274, 277.

92. U.S. Congress 1785, p. 138; G. DeMar 1995, pp. 66, 68, 71-73; idem. 2003, pp. 27-28; E. Gaustad 1993, loc. cit.; C. Galloway 2005, pp. 104-105; W. Miller 1985, pp. 19-20.

93. B.F. Morris 2007, pp. 278 ff.; G. DeMar 2003, pp. 24-25.

94. E. Gaustad 1993, pp. 115, 159 ff.

95. B.F. Morris 1864, p. 235; D. Brewer 1996, p. 20; G. DeMar 1995, pp. 66-67; C. Galloway 2005, pp. 103-104; I. Cornelison 1895, p. 99.

96. B.Weiss 1966, pp. 162-163; A. de Tocqueville 1945, vol. 1, p. 305; W. Federer 2003, pp. 52 ff; B.F. Morris 2007, pp. 281 ff.

97. Abraham Lincoln quoted in M. Adams 1976, p. 25; M. Beliles and S. McDowell 1992, p. 179.

98. Abraham Lincoln quoted in J. Richardson 1899, vol. 4, p. 164; G. DeMar 1995, p. 217; ibid. 1997, vol. 1, pp. 138-139; B. Weiss 1966, p. 92.

99. Abraham Lincoln quoted in R. Bassler 1953, vol. 6, pp. 155-156; G. DeMar 1995, p. 205; idem. 2003, pp. 56, 79.

100. Abraham Lincoln quoted in J.B. McClure 1896, pp. 185-186; J. Hill 1920, p. 330; D. Barton: 1892, p. 259.

101. Abraham Lincoln 1953, vol. 4, pp. 270-271; quoted in M. Noll 2002, pp. 430-431.

102. President Lincoln calling for a "National State of Fasting" on March 30, 1963 citing the *Bible,* Psalm. 33:12; J. Richardson 1899, vol. 6, p, 164; W. Berns 2001, p. 89.

103. A. Lincoln 1853, p. 542; C. McCartney 1949, p. 35; W. Federer 2003, p. 123.

104. B. Weiss 1966, p. 243; N. Gingrich 2006a, pp. 20, 22; idem. 2006b, p. 48; W. Berns 2001, p. 98. See also J. Meacham 2006, p. 114.

105. I. Cornelison 1895, p. 318.

106. James McPherson quoted in M. Noll 2002, p. 16.

107. L. Ingraham 2003, pp. 136-137; N. Gingrich 2006a, pp. 10, 14; J. Butler 1990, pp. 292-293; D. Brewer 1994, p. 64; J. Meacham 2006, p. 123; M. Noll 2002, loc. cit. Other verses in "The Battle Hymn of the Republic" include:

> Mine eyes have seen the glory of the coming of the Lord;
> He is trampling out the vintage where the grapes of wrath are stored;
> He hath loosed the fateful lightning of His terrible swift sword;
> His truth is marching on
> I have seen Him in the watch-fires of a hundred circling camps;
> They have builded Him an altar in the evening dews and damps;
> I have read His righteous sentence by the dim and flaring lamps;
> His day is marching on.
> I have read a fiery gospel writ in burnished rows of steel;
> "As ye deal with my contemners, so with you my grace shall deal;"
> Let the Hero, born of woman, crush the serpent with His heel;
> Since God is marching on.
>
> —Julia Ward Howe

108. Grover Cleveland quoted in W. Federer 2004, p. 113.
109. B. Weiss 1966, p. 125.
110. W. Wilson 1966, vol. 23, p. 12; G. DeMar 1995, p. 3; idem. 2003, p. 8.
111. Woodrow Wilson quoted in S. Dawson 1988, p. I-17.
112. Franklin Roosevelt quoted in G. Sivan 1973, p. 198.
113. G. DeMar 1995, p. 2; J. Meacham 2006, pp. 169-170.
114. President Truman quoted in R. Wuthnow 1988, p. 66; O. Guinness 1993, p. 385; G. DeMar loc. cit.; idem. 2003, p. 8.
115. Harry Truman quoted in S. Dawson 1988, p. 5:4.
116. From President Kennedy's Inaugural Address, January 20, 1961, and inscribed beneath the "Eternal Flame" at his grave site in Arlington National Cemetery as quoted in W. Federer 2004, p. 19; N. Gingrich 2006a, pp. 124, 129; W. Federer 2004, p. 129. President Kennedy's Inaugural Address concluded:

> With a good conscience our only sure reward, with history the final judge of our deeds, let us go forth to lead the land we love, asking His blessing and His help, but knowing that here on earth, God's work must truly be our own.

118. John Kennedy quoted in W. Federer 2004, p. 130.
119. George W. Bush quoted in W. Federer 2004, p. 72.
120. S. Dawson 1988, p. I-12; G. DeMar 2003, p. 8; R. Hutcheson 1988, p. 1.
121. Ronald Reagan quoted in W. Federer 2004, pp. 56, 61, 77.
122. Ronald Reagan, Ecumenical Prayer Breakfast, Reunion Arena, Dallas, quoted in W. Federer 2004, p. 56.
123. B.F. Morris 1864, pp. 317, 320-321, 323, 328; D. Barton 1992, pp. 132-133, 144, 155, 158; idem. 2002, p. 30; M. Beliles and S. McDowell 1992, p. 7.
124. B.F. Morris 1864, p. 328; M. Beliles and D. Anderson 2005, p. 59.
125. S. Huntington 2004, p. 98.
126. See *Church of the Holy Trinity v. United States*, 143 U.S. 457, 465, 470-471; (1892); D. Barton 2002, pp. 52 ff.; idem. 1992, pp. 136, 166; W. Federer 2003, p. 87; idem. 2004, pp. 67-69; O. Guinness 1993, pp. 231-233; N. Gingrich 2006a, p. 8; M. Beliles and D. Anderson 2005, pp. 59-60; J. Meacham 2006, p. 144; G. DeMar 2003, pp. 10-11. Related decisions include:

*Updegraph v. the Commonwealth*, Supreme Court of Pennsylvania (1824);
*The People v. Ruggles*, Supreme Court of New York (1811);
*Commonwealth v. Abner Kneeland*, Supreme Court of Massachusetts (1824);
*The Commonwealth v. Sharpless,* Supreme Court of Pennsylvania (1815);
*Vidal v. Girard's Executors*, United States Supreme Court (1844);
*Church of the Holy Trinity v. the United States*, United States Supreme Court (1892);
*Zorach v. Clauson*, United States Supreme Court (1952);
*Abington Township v. Schempp*, United States Supreme Court (1963); and
*Crockett v. Sorenson*, U.S. District Court of West Virginia (1983)

127. *Church of the Holy Trinity v. U.S.*, 143 U.S. 457, 469 (1892); D. Barton 2002, pp. 49-52, 326; D. Brewer 1996, pp. 70-71.

128. *Updegraph v. the Commonwealth*, 11 Serg and R., 393, 399, 402-403, 406-407 (Supp Ct. Penn. 1824); D. Barton 2002, pp. 52-54, 325.

129. *United States vs. Macintosh*, 283, U.S. 625 (1930; cited in N. McFarland 1995, p. J-1; S. Huntington 2004b, p. 98; G. DeMar 1995, pp. 9 ff., 118; idem. 2003, p. 55; N. Gingrich 2006a, pp. 84-85; S. Dawson 1988, p. 5-4b. Supreme Court Justice David Joseph Brewer (1837-1910 would similarly write: "The American nation, from its first settlement at Jamestown to this hour, is based upon and permeated by the principles of the *Bible*.

130. *Zorach v. Clausen*, 343 U.S. 306, 314;W. Miller 1985, p. 132; N. Gingrich 2006a, p. 8, idem. 2007b, p. 70; G. DeMar 1995, p. 12; M. Beliles and D. Anderson 2005, p. 98; W. Federer 2004, p. 69; M. Beliles and S. McDowell 1992, p. 184; R. Cord 1988, pp. 170 ff. Justice Douglas added: "When the state encourages religious instruction, or cooperates with religious authorities by adjusting the schedule of public events to sectarian needs, it follows the best of our traditions. For it then respects the religious nature of our people and accommodates the public service to their spiritual needs." Writing the minority opinion in *McGowan v. Maryland* 366 U.S. 430, 562-562 (1961), he continued: "The institutions of our society are founded on the belief that there is an authority that is higher than the authority of the State; that there is a moral law which the state is powerless to alter, which government must respect."

131. S. Huntington 2004b, pp. 80, 98; also quoted by J. Black 1994, p. 253; N. Gingrich 2006a, pp. 85-86; S. Dawson 1988, p. 5-4b.

132. *Church of the Holy Trinity v. United States*, 1892, at 465-468, cited in D. Barton 2002, pp. 50-51.

133. M. Beliles and D. Anderson 2005, p. 60.

134. Patrick Henry quoted in S. Dawson 1988, p. 9:6; D. Barton 1992, p. 25.

135. Justice David Brewer quoted in N. Gingrich 2006a, p. 84.

136. D. Barton 1992, pp. 28-29, 54-55.

137. B.F. Morris 2007, pp. 397 ff; D. Barton 1992, pp. 31-32.

138. Thomas Jefferson quoted in J. Richardson 1907, vol. 1, pp. 379–380; C. Rice 1964, p. 63, A. de Tocqueville 1945, vol. 1, p. 316; S. Huntington 2004a, pp. 83-85; G. DeMar 1995, pp. 147, 152-154.

139. J.Q. Adams 1874, vol. 1, p. 268; D. Barton 2002, p. 119; A. Schmidt 1955, p. 182; O. Guinness 1993, p. 52; O. Guinness 1993, p. 84; W. Hudson 1970, p. 33  It was in this spirit also that "In God We Trust" became the national motto in 1956; that Congress instructed the President to proclaim a "National Day of Prayer" annually; that the "National

Prayer Breakfast" movement was born, and that the Post Office cancelled stamps with the slogan: "Pray for Peace" in this same era.

140. Sources cited, loc. cit.; D. Barton 1992, p. 104; M. Beliles and D. Anderson 2005, p. 84; S. Kennedy 2007, pp. 53-54; G. DeMar 2003, pp. 58, 67.

141. Sources cited, loc. cit.

142. B. Weiss 1966, p. 155.

143. B.F. Morris 1864, p. 219; A. Stokes and L. Pfeffer 1964, pp. 102-103, 568-570; S. Huntington 2004b, pp. 104-105; G. DeMar 1995, pp. 116 ff., 119, 121 ff., 125-126, 161; idem. 1997, vol. 1, pp. 128-129; idem. 2003, pp. 52-54, 59; B. Weiss 1966, p. 229; D. Barton 2002, pp. 102-103, 108, 119; idem. 1992, pp. 100-107; D. Kupelian 2005, p. 41; B. Goldberg 2005, p. 235; N. Gingrich 2006a, p. 79; O. Guinness 1993, p. 84; M. Beliles and S. McDowell 1992, pp.176-177.

144. Sources cited, loc. cit.; D. Barton 1992, pp. 100-104; A. Sears and C. Osten 2005, p. 127; R. Cord 1988, pp. 23, 53 ff.

145. Sources cited, loc. cit.; P. Hamburger 2002, p. 126; W. Federer 2003, pp. 45-46, 48; G. DeMar 1995, pp. 45-46; idem. 2003, pp. 55-56; B.F. Morris 2007, pp. 367 ff.; R. Cord 1988, p. 141.

146. Sources cited, loc. cit.

147. G. DeMar 1995, pp. 122-123, 126, 161; idem. 2003, pp. 58-59; B. Weiss 1966, p. 227; G. Jackson 2006, pp. 47-48.

148. Sources cited, loc. cit.

149. B. Weiss 1966, pp. 221-222; N. Gingrich 2006a, pp. 31-32, 81, 82. On a wall in the Cox Corridor in the House Wing of the Capitol, as noted, is carved the line from *America the Beautiful*: "America! God shed his grace on thee, and crown thy good with brotherhood, from sea to shining sea!" Also at the east entrance to the Senate chambers are inscribed the words: *Annuit Coeptis* — Latin for: "God has favored our undertakings." The words "In God we trust" also adorn the Senate's southern entrance.

150. Sources cited, loc. cit.; B. Weiss 1966, p. 225; J. Eidsmoe 2005, p. 114; G. DeMar 2003, pp. 56-57.

151. John Adams quoted in B. Weiss 1966, p. 231; N. Gingrich 2006a, p. 114.

152. G. DeMar 1995, p. 125; idem. 2003, p. 58; B. Weiss 1966, p. 234; N. Gingrich 2006a, p. 99.

153. G. DeMar 1995, pp. 126-127, 195-196; idem. 2003, p. 73; N. Gingrich 2006a, p. 87.

154. B. Weiss 1966, p. 236; N. Gingrich 2006a, pp. 38-39, 130. As well as the invocations:

"In God we trust;" and "May Heaven to this union continue its beneficence."

155. G. DeMar 1995, pp. 125-126; idem. 2003, pp. 58-59; B. Weiss 1966, p. 242; N. Gingrich 2006a, p. 124.

156. E. Gaustad 1993, pp. 49-50; G. DeMar 1995, p. 126; idem. 2003, p. 59; N. Gingrich 2006, pp. 42, 45; J. Eidsmoe 2005, p. 367.

157. B. Weiss 1966, p. 249.

158. G. DeMar 1995, pp. 124-125; idem. 2003, p. 58; D. Barton 2002, p. 101; idem. 1992, p. 100; B.F. Morris 2007, pp. 260-261.

159. B. Weiss 1966, pp. 253-254.

160. J. Jay 1893, vol. 4, p. 491; J.Q. Adams 1837, p. 17; J. Adams 1850, vol. 9, p. 121, vol. 10, pp. 45-46; C. Singer 1981, pp. 325-326; G. DeMar 1995, pp.128, 198; D. Barton 2002, pp. 127-128.

161. *Bible,* Proverbs 14:34; S. Adams 1907, vol. 3, p. 286; D. Kupelian 2005, p. 176.

162. Alexis de Tocqueville 1851, vol. 1, p. 337; idem. 1945, vol. 1, p. 303; also quoted in D. Barton 2002, p. 121; idem. 2007, p. 4; W. Berns 2001, pp. 43, 72; J. Butler 1990, p. 289; G. DeMar 2003, p. 9.

163. Quotations cited in W. Federer 2004, pp. 23, 67-77.

164. See B. Franklin 1927, passim.

165. T. Jefferson 1894, vol. 3, p. 267.

166. Alexander Hamilton quoted in K. Fournier 1993, vol. 2, no. 2, p. 7.

167. B. Rush 1798, p. 8.

168. Patrick Henry quoted in W. Federer 2004, p. 76.

169. S. Adams 1880, p. 34.

170. Calvin Coolidge address to the "Holy Name Society," Washington D.C., in C. Coolidge 1926, pp. 103-112.

171. President Harry S. Truman quoted in T.S. Settel 1967, p. 28.

172. President Reagan quoted in G. DeMar 1995, p. 19.

173. George Bush, "Third State of the Union Address," January 28, 2003, quoted in W. Federer 2004, p. 49.

## Chapter Two

1. C.G. Singer 1964, pp. 24-25; A. Lieven 2004, p. 94; J. O'Neill 1949, p. 22.

2. A. Schlesinger 1998, p. 34; S. Huntington 2004b, pp. 40-41, 59-64, 68-70; C.L. Thompson n.d., pp. 13, 243.

3. N. Gingrich 2006a, p. 10.

4. S. Rutherford 1982, pp. 1, 6-7; J. Eidsmoe 2005, pp. 24, 28; E. Gaustad 1993, p. 111. Melding the religious mix of America was a dynamic process. Whereas in 1776, the two largest denominations in America were the Congregationalists and the Episcopalians, for instance, a mere fifty years later, the two largest denominations were the Baptists and the Methodists. Roman Catholics likewise came in large numbers, while simultaneously the nation's frontiers would spawn new religious groupings even as it rearranged the loyalties of old ones. The process was not without its growing pains, however. In the constitutional ratification process in New Hampshire, for instance, a delegate urged rejection of the document on the pretext that it could create a circumstance wherein "a Turk, a Jew, a Roman Catholic, and what is worst of all, a Universalist may become President of the United States (!)" (quoted in M. Borden 1984, p. 16; E. Gaustad 1993, p. 113.)

5. J. Eidsmoe 2005, pp. 24-25.

6. Locke, a Puritan by background, founded his social contract theory on Samuel Rutherford's *Lex Rex* (See S. Rutherford 1982, passim); J. Eidsmoe 2005, pp. 24-25.

7. J. Eidsmoe 2005, pp. 24-25, 62, 401; M. Belisles and S.McDowell 1992, p. 141; B.F. Morris 2007, pp.127 ff. The U.S. Declaration was modeled after the Mecklenburg Declaration, proclaimed by citizens of Mecklenburg, North Carolina, a year earlier, in 1775, which took as its slogan: "Rebellion against tyrants is obedience to God!"

8. J. Madison 1785, p. 309; J. Eidsmoe 2005, pp. 102-104.

9. P. Schaff 1961, p. 72.

10. Alexis de Tocqueville quoted in S. Huntington 2004, pp. 59-63, 67-69; C.L. Thompson n.d., p. 163.
11. Edmund Burke quoted at books.google.com/books?isbn=0887386083; See also M. Noll 2002, pp. 269 ff.; T. Hall 1930, pp. 49 ff.
12. F.J. Grund 1968, pp. 355-356; W. Williams 2002, p. 30.
13. President Clinton quoted in S. Huntington 2004b, p. 70.
14. *Bible,* John 18:36.
15. *Bible,* Matthew 22:21; Mark 12: 17.
16. G.W. Truett 1920, p. 95.
17. See U.S. Congress 1834a, vol. 1, p. 451; M. Malbin 1981, pp. 3 ff.; D. Barton 2000, pp. 4-5.
18. *Everson v. Board of Education,* 330 U.S. 1, 15 (1970).
19. M. Malbin 1981, p. 2.
20. Thomas Paine quoted in F. Church 2007, p. 47; K. Armstrong 2000, p. 82; J. Meacham 2006, pp. 8-9; W. Miller 1985, p. 243; M. Noll 2002, pp. 143 ff.
21. C.G. Singer 1964, pp. 25-26; D. Barton 1992, pp. 198-199; N. Gingrich 2006a, pp. 100-101; M. Beliles and S.McDowell 1992, p. 127.
22. From S. Wiatt 1809, pp. 97-99.
23. John Locke quoted in W. Hudson 1970, p. xxv; C.G. Singer 1964, pp. 25-26, 31-33; K. Armstrong 2000, pp. 81-82.
24. J. Eidsmoe 2005, p. 363; K. Armstrong 2000, pp. 82-83.
25. *Bible*, Romans 2: 14-15.
26. See T. Jefferson 1984, pp. 34-30; quoted in *International Herald Tribune* April 6, 2007, p. 4; A. Sears and C. Osten 2005, pp. 132-133; D. Barton 2002, p. 100; F. Church 2007, p. 241; J. Meacham 2006, pp. 11-12; W. Miller 1985, pp. 53-54, 103-104.
27. T. Jefferson 1782, p. 152; D. Holmes 2006, p. 81; S. Kennedy 2007, pp. 220-221; D. Dreisbach 2002, p. 18.
28. George Washington quoted in J. Beacham 2006, pp. 18-19.
29. J. Meacham 2006, p. 75.
30. On this, see G. Amos 1989, pp. 2-3; D. Barton 2002, pp. 218-219; J. Eidsmoe 2005, pp. 60-61.
31. J. Locke 1959, ch. 1, p. 29.
32. See R. Matthews 1984, chapter 1, passim; B. Bailyn 1982, pp. vi-vii; G. Amos 1989, pp. 46, 92-93.
33. G. Amos 1989, pp. 44-45, 86; D. Barton 2002, p. 218.
34. J. Locke 1959, ch. 1, p. 1; J. Eidsmoe 2005, pp. 219-220.
35. J. Locke 1958, ch. 52, sec. 227.
36. See W. Blackstone 1771, vol.1, pp. 61-62; D. Barton 1992, p. 199; W. Federer 2003, p. 185; D. Barton 2002, p. 218; J. Eidsmoe 2005, pp. 60-62, 252. On this equation of the "Law of Nature" and the "Law of God," Locke (1772, Book 2, p. 285) said:

> The Law of Nature stands as an eternal rule to all men, legislators as well as others. The rules that they make for other men's actions must . . . be conformable to the Law of Nature, *i.e.*, to the will of God. . . . Laws human must be made according to the general Laws of Nature and without contradiction to any law of Scripture; otherwise they are ill-made.

37. J. Locke 1986, p. 75.

38. J. Locke 1986, p. 76, n. 1; W. Federer 2003, p. 185.

39. J. Locke 1958, ch. 31, secs. 13, 23; J. Calvin 1981, ch. 2, pp. 663-664; G. Amos 1989, pp. 58-62. In Calvin's words (loc. cit.): "The moral law . . . is the true and eternal rule of righteousness prescribed to men of all nations and of all times who would frame their lives agreeable to the will of God. . . . Now it is evident that the law of God which we call moral is nothing less than the testimony of the Natural Law, and of that conscience which God has engraven upon the minds of men; the whole of equity of which we now speak is prescribed in it."

40. See J. Locke 1956, passim; G. Amos 1989, p. 144.

41. John Calvin quoted in S. Ahlstrom 1972, p. 366.

42. John Locke quoted in V. Hall 1979, p. 64; G. Amos 1989, pp 128-131; J. Eidsmoe 2005, pp. 61-62, 356, 366; F. Church 2007, pp. 234-235; M. Beliles and S. McDowell 1992, p. 204.

43. W. Blackstone 1771, vol. 1, pp. 39, 41-42; D. Barton 1992, pp. 52, 56, 197; idem. 2002, pp. 216-221; J. Eidsmoe 2005, pp. 56-60, 331.

44. Ibid. at vol. 1, pp. 41-42; D. Barton 1992, loc. cit.

45. D. Barton 1992, pp. 197-200; V. Hall 1979, pp. 140-146; J. Eidsmoe 2005, p. 58.

46. J. Eidsmoe 2005, p. 58.

47. R. Walton 1984, p. 358; D. Barton 2002, p. 100.

48. G. Bancroft 1859, vol. 5, p. 24; J. Eidsmoe 2005, pp. 54-56, 350.

49. C. Montesquieu 1802, vol. 1, pp. 81, 125-126; D. Barton 1992, pp. 198-199; idem. 2002, pp. 214-216.

50. Benjamin Franklin quoted in J. Madison 1840, vol. 2, p. 984; idem. 1911, vol. 1, p. 451; D. Barton 2002, p. 213.

51. See J. Eismoe 1987, pp. 51-53; D. Lutz 1988, p. 141; idem. 1984, pp. 189-197; S. McDowell and M. Beliles 1989, p. 186; D. Barton 1992, p. 201; W. Federer 2003, pp. 184-185; D. Barton 2002, pp. 213-214. Of a total of more than 15,000 representative documents analyzed, some 3,154 quotes were selected and documented. Montesquieu clearly led with 8.3 percent of the quotes, followed closely by Blackstone at 7.9 percent, with Locke a surprising distant third at 2.9 percent.

52. D. Lutz loc. cit.; J. Eidsmoe 2005, pp. 51-53.

53. Reverend Lyman Beecher quoted in B.F. Morris 2007, p. 783.

54. Noah Webster quoted in V. Hall 1976, p. 21.

55. D. Barton 1992, pp. 219-220; R. Dornan and C. Vedlik 1986, pp. 27, 70-71; G. DeMar 1997, vol. 1, pp. 75, 14, 47, 68, 91, 113, 115-116, 170; M. Beliles and S. McDowell 1992, pp. 20, 188-191. See also *Bible*, Revelation 19: 15 and 17:14, and I Timothy 6: 15 wherein Jesus is called "King of kings and Lord of lords."

56. *Bible,* Matthew 22:21; Mark 12: 17.

57. *Bible*, Exodus 18, 25-26.

58. See also *Bible*, I Timothy 3, passim.

59. Rufus King and James Wilson quoted in R. King 1900, vol. 6, p. 276; M. Beliles and D. Anderson 2005, pp. 99-100.

60. George Washington quoted in M. Beliles and D. Anderson 2005, p. 101.

61. J. Locke 1956, ch. 56, sec. 99.

62. R. Palmer 1964, vol. 1, p. 223.

63. J. Eidsmoe 2005, pp. 366-369. The scriptural basis for such doctrine the Founders founded was embedded in Romans 13, Daniel 2, I Peter 3, I Samuel 8, II Kings 14, and Deuteronomy 16.
64. J. Locke 1956, vol. 13, sec. 241; G. Amos 1989, pp. 146-147; J. Eidsmoe 2005, pp. 372-373.
65. G. Amos 1989 pp. 148-150.
66. As delineated in M. Beliles and D. Anderson 2005, pp. 124-125, 128-129; M. Beliles and S. McDowell 1992, pp. 186-188; G. DeMar 1997, vol. 1. pp. 147-149; idem. 2001, vol. 3, pp. 100, 178.
67. Verses cited in M. Beliles and D. Anderson 2005, p, 203; G. DeMar 1997, vol. 1, pp. 200-201; F. Church 2007, p. 147.
68. *Church of the Holy Trinity v. United States*, 143 U.S. 457, 465, 170-471 (1892); D. Barton 1992, p. 83; G. DeMar 1997, vol.1, p. 135.
69. C. Columbus 1991, pp. 178-179, 182-183; D. Barton 1992, p. 84; idem. 2002, p. 76; J. Black 1993, p. 239.
70. E. Hazard 1792, vol. 1, pp. 50-51; D. Barton 1992, p. 84; I. Cornelison 1895, pp. 6 ff.
71. H. Lefler 1956, p. 16; D. Barton 1992, p. 86.
72. E. Hazard 1792, vol. 2, p. 612.
73. D. Barton 1992, p. 87.
74. "Mayflower Compact" cited in D. Barton 1992, p. 85; I. Cornelison 1895, pp. 23 ff.
75. F. Coker 1942, pp. 18-19; D. Barton 1992, loc. cit.
76. W. McDonald 1909, p. 32; D. Barton 1992, p. 86; I. Cornelison 1895, pp. 74 ff.
77. State of Connecticut 1822, p. 2; D. Barton 1992, p. 88; I. Cornelison 1895, pp. 44 ff.
78. E. Hazard 1792, vol. 1, p. 463; D. Barton 1992, loc. cit.; 41 ff.; I. Cornelison 1895, pp. 44 ff.
79. W. McDonald 1909, p. 46; H. Commager 1948, p. 26; D. Barton 1992, loc. cit.
80. P. Mode 1921, p. 163; T. Clarkson 1813, vol. 1, p. 287.
81. C. Adams 1850, vol. 2, pp. 6-7.
82. P. Ford 1892, vol. 8, p. 294, vol. 10, p. 68; G. Amos 1989, pp. 8-9, 11.
83. R. Frothingham 1872, p. 458.
84. C. Strout 1974, p. 59.
85. Both documents quoted in D. Barton 2002, p. 109; W. Malloy 1968, vol.1, p. 586.
86. B.F. Morris 1864, p. 326; D. Barton 1992, pp. 111-112; G. DeMar 2003, p. 75.
87. U.S. Congress 1834b, vol. 1, p. 25; A. Sears and C. Osten 2005, p. 127.
88. U.S. Congress 1834b, vol. 1, p. 29; D. Barton 1992, pp. 112-113.
89. S. Adams 1968, vol 4, pp. 52, 201, 385, 407; D. Holmes 2006, p. 146; D. Barton 2002, p. 333; J. Eidsmoe 2005, pp. 247, 255; B.F. Morris 2007, pp. 143-144.
90. Samuel Adams quoted in W. Federer 2003, p. 27; idem. 2004, p. 69.
91. George Washington quoted in O. Guinness 2001, p. 13; M. Gerson 2007, p. 12; John Marshall quoted in G. Jackson 2007, p. 365; A. Stokes and L. Pfeffer 1964, p. 87; N. Cunningham 1987, p. 225; J.F. Kennedy 1964, pp. 101-102; G. DeMar 1995, pp. 134, 150, 203-204; B. Weiss 1966, p. 54; D. Barton 2002, p. 184; D. Holmes 2006, pp. 59 ff.; J. Eidsmoe 2005, pp. 132, 136; B.F. Morris 2007, pp. 199 ff., 599, 607. John Adams and James Madison also issued proclamations convening national days of prayer acknowledging the existence of a Supreme Being.

92. G. Washington 1932, vol. 11, p. 343; D. Barton 1992, p. 95; J. Eidsmoe 2005, p. 121; M. Beliles and S. McDowell 1992, pp. 153 ff., 158; B.F. Morris 2007, pp. 348 ff.
93. G. Washington 1932, vol. 5, p. 245; A. Sears and C. Osten 2005, p. 127; D. Holmes 2006, p. 68; W. Federer 2003, pp. 121-122; D. Barton 2002, p. 102; J. Eidsmoe 2005, p. 116; F. Church 2007, pp. 57-60; J. Meacham 2006, p. 77; B.F. Morris 2007, pp. 338 ff., 343 ff.
94. H. Halley 1965, p. 18; D. Barton 1992, p. 113.
95. G. Washington 1838, vol. 15, p. 55; J. Eidsmoe 2005, p. 120; P. Boller 1963, pp. 68 ff.
96. R. Cord 1988, pp. 58, 62.
97. George Washington quoted in H. Halley 1965, p. 18.
98. George Washington, "First Inaugural Address," quoted in D. Barton 2002, p. 334; B.F. Morris 2007, pp. 644-645.
99. J. Meacham 2006, pp. 17-18; J. Eidsmoe 2005, p. 277; E. Gaustad 1993, pp. 88-89; B.F. Morris 2007, pp. 146 ff., 680 ff., 771-772.
100. John Adams 1850, vol. 10, pp. 45-46; idem. 1962, vol. 3, pp. 233-234; quoted in W. Federer 2003, p. 18; D. Barton 2002, p. 128.
101. F. Church 2007, pp. 162-163.
102. John Adams quoted in E. Gaustad 1993, p. 89; G. Jackson 2006, p. 371; D. Holmes 2006, pp. 77-78.
103. J. Adams 1961, vol. 3, p. 234; D. Barton 1992, p. 123.
104. J. Adams 1854, vol. 9, p. 229; D. Marsh 1970, p. 51.
105. N. Gingrich 2006, p. 92.
106. T. Jefferson 1857, vol. 1, p. 545; idem. 1904, vol. 14, p. 385; idem. 1983, p. 365; quoted in F. Church 2007, pp. 295, 430; D. Holmes 2006, p. 81; D. Barton 2002, p. 144; J. Eidsmoe 2005, pp. 92, 246; E. Gaustad 1993, p. 108; J. O'Neill 1949, pp. 6, 239; B.F. Morris 2007, pp. 167 ff., 600.
107. T. Jefferson 1857, vol. 1, p. 545; quoted in J. Meacham 2006, p. 11; J. O'Neill 1949, p. 6.
108. M. Beliles and D. Anderson 2005, p. 71; E. Gaustad 1993, p. 41.
109. Thomas Jefferson quoted in W.Whitman 1948, p. 91; M. Beliles and S. McDowell 1992, p. 178.
110. E. Gaustad 1993, p. 102; C. Singer 1964, pp. 37 ff. See also "Thomas Jefferson, "Virginia Statute for Establishing Religious Freedom, 1786," in E. Gaustad 1993, pp. 149-181; D. Barton 2002, p. 207; D. Holmes 2006, pp. 83-84.
111. Thomas Jefferson quoted in W. Linn 1834, p. 265.
112. Thomas Jefferson quoted in W. Linn 1834, loc. cit; R. Maxfield 1981-1983, p. 495.
113. Cf. D. Boorstin 1948, p. 32; C.G. Singer. 1964, pp. 38-40; J. Eidsmoe 2005, pp. 231-232.
114. T. Jefferson 1983, pp. 39-40, 347; J. Eidsmoe 2005, pp. 224-226; E. Gaustad 1993, p. 104.
115. Thomas Jefferson quoted in F. Church 2007, p. 443.
116. J. Eidsmoe 2005, p. 226.
117. G. DeMar 1997, vol. 1, pp. 187-188.
118. J. Madison 1973, vol. 8, pp. 299, 304; D. Barton 1992, pp. 119-120; B.F. Morris 2007, pp. 188-190.
119. B. Weiss 1966, p. 62; James Madison quoted in O. Guinness 1993, pp. 348-349; N. Gingrich 2006a, p.108; T. LaHaye 1987, p. 127. See also James Madison. "Memorial and

Remonstrance, 1985," in E. Gaustad 1993, pp. 141-149; J. Meacham 2006, loc. cit. (Likewise see J. Madison 1982, no. 51, p. 262.)

120. B.F. Morris 2007, p. 190.

121. J.Q. Adams 1837, pp. 5-6; D. Barton 1992, pp. 125, 151; B. Weiss 1966, pp. 67-68; F. Church 2007, p. 374; B.F. Morris 2007, pp. 215-220.

122. Benjamin Franklin quoted in G. DeMar 195, pp. 198-200; D. Barton 2002, p. 111; idem. 1992, pp. 108-110; N. Gingrich 2006a, pp. 13, 26; J. Eidsmoe 2005, p. 200, 205-206, 208; E. Gaustad 1993, p. 61; J. Meacham 2006, p. 8; W. Miller 1985, p. 241; B.F. Morris 2007, pp. 157 ff.

123. Benjamin Franklin quoted in J. Eidsmoe 2005, p. 213.

124. Benjamin Franklin quoted in P. Marshall and D. Manuel 1977, p. 370, n. 10.

125. B. Franklin 1945, p. 783; J. Eidsmoe 2005, p. 210; J. Meacham 2006, p. 21.

126. B. Franklin 1916, pp. 147-149; J. Eidsmoe 2005, p. 198.

127. J. Eidsmoe 2005, p. 209.

128. J. Orr 1934, p. 211; M.E Bradford 1982, pp. viii-ix; J. Eidsmoe 2005, pp. 44, 195.

129. B. Franklin 1840, vol. 10, pp. 281-282.

130. John Jay quoted in D. Barton 2002, p. 165; D. Holmes 2006, pp. 157, 160; J. Eidsmoe 2005, p. 164; B.F. Morris 2007, pp. 182-187, 799-800.

131. J. Jay 1890, vol. 4, p. 393; D. Barton 1992, pp. 35, 78, 119, 152; F. Church 2007, p. 331.

132. John Jay quoted in D. Barton 2002, p. 12.

133. A. Hamilton 1985, p. 511; J. Eidsmoe 2005, p. 157.

134. J. Eidsmoe 2005, pp. 160-161; F. Church 2007, pp. 277-278.

135. N. Schachner 1961, p. 430; J. Eidsmoe 2005, p. 145.

136. B. Rush 1798, p. 8; W. Federer 2004, pp. 74-75; M. Noll 2002, pp. 51, 65; B.F. Morris 2007, p. 173.

137. Benjamin Rush quoted in D. Barton 2002, p. 349.

138. J. Eidsmoe 2005, p. 313; B.F. Morris 2007, pp. 145-146, 600.

139. Patrick Henry's will cited in M. Tyler 1898/1966, p. 395; J. Eidsmoe 2005, p. 315.

140. S. Dawson 1988, p. I-5; W. Wirt 1818, p. 402; D. Barton 1992, pp. 118-119, 158; M. Beliles and S. McDowell 1992, p. 184; B.F. Morris 2007, pp. 178-179.

141. Patrick Henry quoted in W. Federer 2004, p. 76.

142. George Mason quoted in D. Barton 2002, p. 12; B.F. Morris 2007, pp. 169-171.

143. Roger Sherman quoted in L. Boutell 1896, pp. 272-273; W. Federer 2003, p. 63; J. Eidsmoe 2005, p. 317.

144. J. Eidsmoe 2005, p. 321.

145. J. Dickinson 1801, vol. 1, pp. 111-112.

146. N. Webster 1832, pp. 273-274, 300; quoted in V. Hall 1979, p. 255; D. Barton 1992, p. 125; M. Beliles and D. Anderson 2005, p. 102; M.Beliles and S. McDowell 1992, p. 192.

147. N. Webster 1832, p. 309; W. Federer 2003, p.193; G. DeMar 1997, vol. 1, p. 4.

148. James Madison quoted in W. Federer 194, p. 677, n. 9; M. Beliles and D. Anderson 2005, p. 61.

149. D. Webster 1853, vol. 1, p. 22; D. Barton 1992, p. 134; B.F. Morris 2007, pp. 232 ff.

150. Daniel Webster quoted in W. Federer 2003, p. 199.

151. Thomas Paine quoted in P. Foner 1945, vol. 1, p. 72; O. Guinness 1993, pp. 51-52.

## Notes

152. Thomas Paine quoted in A. Sears and C. Osten 2005, p. 128; D. Holmes 2006, pp. 39 ff.

153. M. Bradford 1982, pp. iv-ix; J. Eidsmoe 2005, pp. 41-44, 339-342; T. Hall 1930, p. 171; S. Dawson 1988, p. I-8. Two-thirds of the signers of the Declaration of Independence were nominally Episcopalians. Of the 55 Americans who drafted the Constitution, 49 were Protestant, as follows:

* 25 were Episcopalians (Anglicans);
* 19 were Calvinists;
* 2 were Methodists;
* 2 were Roman Catholics;
* 1 was a Lutheran.

There were also 3 Quaker serving as members.

154. W. Berns 2001, p. 135.
155. Alexis de Tocqueville quoted in M. Beliles and D. Anderson 2005, p. 102.
156. M. Beliles and S. McDowell 1992, p. 6.
157. On this, see G. Amos 1989 pp. 158-168.
158. W. Hudson 1970, pp. xxxii-xxxiii.
159. J. Marshall 2006, vol. 12, p. 278; D. Holmes 2006, p. 134; J. Eidsmoe 2005, loc. cit.
160. Reverend John Winthrop quoted in W. Hudson 1970, pp. 23-23.
161. David Ramsey quoted in W. Hudson 1970, pp. 62-63.
162. Alexis de Tocqueville 1841, vol. 1, p. 332.
163. Alexis de Tocqueville quoted in N. Gingrich 2006a, p. 108.
164. Francois Guizot and James Russell Lowell quoted in D. Marsh 1970, p. 51; D. Barton 1992, pp. 220, 268.
165. Benjamin Franklin quoted in D. Barton 1992, p. 229.
166. T. LaHaye 1987, p. 201.
167. John Adams quoted in F. Church 2007, p. 428; J. Eidsmoe 2005, p. 85.
168. S. Johnson 1755, "Providence;" J. Eidsmoe 2005, pp. 85-86; M. Beliles and S. McDowell 1992, p. 6.
169. D. Holmes 2006, p. 134; J. Eidsmoe 2005, loc. cit.
170. J. Adams 1850, vol. 10, p. 45; D. Barton 2007, p. 4; D. Holmes 2006, pp. 73, 78.
171. Cited in M. Borden 1984, p. 16; E. Gaustad 1993, p. 113.
172. Alexander Hamilton quoted in I. Cornelison 1895, p. 204; B.F. Morris 2007, pp. 296-297; G. DeMar 1995, pp. 80, 83, 85; idem. 2003, p. 31; P. Senn. "Religion, Politics, and the American Constitution," (September 21, 2006) at www.ishss.uva.nl/Lectures/ 0601 Faith AndState/210906%20Lecture%20Report.pdf.
173. D. Holmes 2006, p. 71; J. Eidsmore 2005, p. 39; F. Church 2007, p. 228. A "Deist" believes in a remote God who does not intervene in the natural order. A "Theist" believes in an omnipresent god who actively interacts in the affairs of humankind.
174. On this, see D. Holmes 2006, pp. 73 ff.
175. A. de Tocqueville 1945, vol. 1, pp. 303, 314-315.
176. C.G. Singer 1964, pp. 32 ff.; E. Gaustad 1993, p. 104.
177. *Bible*, John: 15; Matthew 28: 19; I Timothy 2:5; Matthew 27:46; K. Armstrong 1993, p. 77; idem. 2000, p. 69.
178. D. Holmes 2006, pp. 73 ff; K. Armstrong 1993, pp. 81-94, 105-110.

250                                     *Notes*

179. *Bible,* Matthew 28: 19; I John 5:7; II Corinthians 13:13; John 1:1; Jude 20-21; D. Holmes 2006, pp. 73, 90.
180. G. Fuller 2003, pp. 146-147; K. Armstrong 1993, pp. 144-151.
181. D. Holmes 2006, pp. 74-76; K. Armstrong 1993, pp. 82, 108-119, 129.This proclamation differed somewhat in its wording from what today is known as the –"Nicene Creed"– which was actually composed at the "Council of Constantinople" in 381 A.D.
182. R. Errico quoted in G. Heck 2007, p. 200.
183. N. Hatch 1989, p. 227.
184. S. Wiatt 1809, pp. 97-99.
185. J. Butler 1990, pp. 219-220; P. Hamburger 2002, pp. 113 ff., 147 ff.; D. Dreisbach 2002, pp. 18-19; E. Gaustad 1993, p. 45.
186. Timothy Dwight and William Linn quoted in D. Dreisbach 2002, loc.cit.; E. Gaustad 1993, pp. 50, 98-99. (Thus Jefferson would refer to the contemporary clergy as the "*irritabile vatum*" (the "irritable tribe of priests").The story is told of a matriarch in Quincy, Massachusetts, hometown of Jefferson's political opponent John Adams, who, concerned that her family *Bible* would be imminently torched upon the election of Jefferson, went to a prominent local citizen who supported Jefferson asking him to safeguard her *Bible*. The gentlemen graciously agreed, but asked somewhat incredulously: "But why me, of all people?" To which the lady responded: "Because no one would think of looking for a *Bible* in the home of a Democrat (!)"
187. President Kennedy quoted in W. Hudson 1970, pp. 148-149.
188. President Bush quoted in G. Müller-Fahrenholz 2007, p. 9.
189. *Bible*, II Corinthians 3:17.

## CHAPTER THREE

1. Much of this analysis is founded upon the superb book by David Barton (1992) bearing the same name as documented in the footnotes and cited in the bibliography.
2. M. Beliles and D. Anderson 2005, p. 45.
3. D. Barton 2002, p. 21; C. Galloway 2005, pp. 127-128.
4. I. Cornelison 1895, pp. 94 ff.
5. B. Franklin 1905-1907, vol. 9, p. 702; M. Beliles and D. Anderson 2005, p. 55.
6. James Madison quoted in W. Skousen, p. 5, n. 3.
7. Alexander Hamilton quoted in W. Federer 1994, p. 273; M. Beliles and D. Anderson 2005, p. 55.
8. George Washington quoted in B.F. Morris 2007, pp. 304 ff.
9. George Washington quoted in B.F. Morris 2007, p. 305.
10. E. Gaustad 1993, p. 44; J. Meacham 2006, p. 100; C. Galloway 2005, p. 128.
11. Lord G. K. Chesterfield quoted at www.lawcf.org/CMS/ uploads/358/documents/ Final-22.02.07.pdf.
12. D. Kupelian 2005, p. 216.
13. J. Black 1994, pp. 30-33.
14. D. Barton 2002, p. 12; D. Kupelian 2005, p. 42.

15. J. Storey 1833, pp. 702-703; idem. 1851b, pp. 593-594; idem. 1986, p. 316; quoted in R. Cord 1982, p. 13; M. Beliles and S. McDowell 1992, p. 182; I. Cornelison 1895, pp. 95, 207-208; J. O'Neill 1949, pp. 63-64, 208; B.F. Morris 2007, pp. 307-309; D. Kupelian 2005, p. 44; G. DeMar 1997, vol. 1, p. 1; idem. 2003, pp. 36, 63; D. Barton 2002, p. 34; J. Eidsmoe 2005, p. 377. Supreme Court Justice William Rehnquist, citing Justice Joseph Story's *Commentary on the Constitution of the United States*, in writing the dissenting opinion in *Wallace v. Jaffrey*, (1985). "United States Not Founded on Absolute Church-State Separation," at: www.belcherfoundation.org/wallace_v_jaffrey_dissent.htm.

16. D. Barton 2000, p. 4; J. Leo 2001, p. 183.

17. U.S. Congress 1834a, vol. 1, pp. 439-951, June 5-September 25, 1789, and pp. 757-759, August 15, 1789, in particular; D. Barton 2000, p. 5; idem. 2007, p. 6; M. Beliles and D. Anderson 2005, p. 62.

18. U.S. Senate 1820 (September 3, 1789), p. 70; U.S. Congress loc. cit.; D. Barton 2007, pp. 6-7; R. Cord 1988, pp. 5-7.

19. U.S. Congress 1834a, vol. 1, p. 451 (June 8, 1789), pp. 757-759 (August 15, 1789); D. Barton 2000, p. 5; idem. 2007, p. 7. R. Bork 2003, p. 289; O. Guinness 1993, pp. 213-214; J. Eidsmoe 2005, pp. 106-107; D. Dreisbach 2002, p. 88; E. Gaustad 1993, pp. 51-52. Indeed, much of the early language relating to the free exercise of religion derived from James Madison's success in shaping Article XVI of George Mason's draft of "Virginia's Declaration of Rights" of 1776, which then became a foundation for shaping both the Declaration of Independence and the Constitution.

20. D. Barton 2000, loc. cit.; idem. 2007, loc. cit; C. Galloway 2005, p. 128.

21. F. Ames 1809, p. 134; D. Barton 2000, pp. 7-8.

22. F. Ames 1809, pp. 134-135; D. Barton 2000, loc. cit.; idem. 1992, p. 1; G. Jackson 2007, p. 45.

23. B. Rush 1798, pp. 1,112; D. Barton 2000, loc. cit.; idem. 2007, p. 8.

24. N. Webster 1832, p. 339; D. Barton 2000, p. 7; idem. 2007, p. 9.

25. President John Adams in a letter to the First Brigade of the Third Division of the Militia of Massachusetts, October 11, 1798, replicated in C. Adams 1850-1856, vol. 9, p. 229; D. Barton 2000, p. 7; idem. 2007, p. 9;W. Federer 2004, p. 37.

26. D. Barton 2007, p. 9.

27. G. Washington 1796, pp. 22-23; D. Barton 2000, pp. 8-9; idem. 2007, pp. 10-11; D. Dreisbach 2002, pp. 84-85.

28. D. Barton 2000, p. 9; idem. 2007, p. 7.

29. Danbury Baptist Association 1801, p. 1; D. Barton 2000, loc. cit.; G. Jackson 2006, pp. 366 ff.; P. Hamburger 2002, pp. 3, 155 ff.; A. Sears and C. Osten 2005, pp. 211-216; E. Gaustad 1993, pp. 45-46.

30. T. Jefferson 1904, vol. 16, pp. 281-282; quoted in D. Barton 2007, pp. 12-13; P. Hamburger 2002, "Frontispiece;" M. Beliles and D. Anderson 2005, p. 173; J. Eidsmoe 2005, pp. 237 ff., 242-243; D. Dreisbach 2002, pp. 1 ff., 17 ff., 71-82, 87, 255 ff.; F. Church 2007, pp. 264-266; J. Meacham 2006, pp. 104-105; W. Miller 1985, pp 132-133; R. Cord 1988, pp. 114 ff..It must be noted that Thomas Jefferson was not the first to employ the "separation of church and state" metaphor. It was also frequently invoked by the sixteenth century Anglican cleric Thomas Hooker, radical colonial separatist Roger Williams, and the Scottish schoolmaster James Burgh, whose writings Jefferson frequently consulted.

31. T. Jefferson 1830, vol. 4, pp. 103-104; idem. 1905, vol. 9, pp. 428-430; D. Barton 2002, p. 25; J. Whitehead 1977, p. 89; J. Eidsmoe 2005, pp. 243-244; D. Dreisbach 2002, pp. 55, 59-62; M. Beliles and S. McDowell 1992, p. 183; R. Cord 1988, pp. 14, 40.

32. Thomas Jefferson quoted in J. Richardson 1907, vol. 1, pp. 379-380; J. Whitehead 1977, loc. cit.; D. Dreisbach 2002, pp. 63-64, 67-68; G. DeMar 2003, p. 66.

33. Thomas Jefferson quoted in S. Padover 1939, pp. 83-85.

34. Thomas Jefferson quoted in S. Padover 1939, pp. 97-98, 100-101.

35. T. Jefferson 1904, vol. 16, pp. 281-282; D. Barton 2000, loc. cit.; idem. 2007, pp. 12-13; W. Berns 2006, p. 157; A. Sears and C. Osten 2005, pp. 131-132, 211; D. Kupelian 2005, pp. 53-57; G. Jackson 2007, p. 340; M. Malbin 1978, pp. 33 ff.; M. Beliles and D. Anderson 2005, pp. 174-179; D. Dreisbach 2002, pp. 21-23; F. Church 2007, p. 270; J. O'Neill 1949, pp. 110 ff.

36. M. Malbin 1978, pp. 15; G. DeMar 2003, pp. 66-67.

37. See T. Jefferson 1984, 34-30; quoted in *International Herald Tribune* April 6, 2007, p. 4; A. Sears and C. Osten 2005, pp. 132-133; D. Barton 2002, p. 100.

38. N. Gingrich 2006b, pp. 51-52.

39. *Bible*, John 18:36; idem. Matthew 22:21; P. Hamburger 2002, pp. 22, 24, 351-352, 410-411.

40. M. Luther quoted in P. Hamburger 2002, 22, 29, 76-78, 81-88, passim, 91 ff, 102.

41. P. Hamburger 2002, pp. 480 ff.

42. P. Hamburger 2002, pp. 486-489, 491-492; K. Armstrong 2000, pp. 268 ff.

43. *Reynolds v. U.S.*, 98 U.S. 145, 164 (1878); D. Barton 2002, pp. 47, 441; D. Dreisbach 2002, pp. 53, 97-100.

44. *Reynolds v. United States* (1878), 98 U.S. 145, at 163; D. Barton 2000, pp. 9-10; P. Hamburger 2002, pp. 461-462.

45. D. Barton 2000, p. 10.

46. W. Rehnquist in *Wallace v. Jeffrey*, 472 U.S. 38, 113 (1985); D. Kupelian 2005, pp. 44-45; D. Barton 2002, pp. 175, 179, 202-203.

47. Justice William Rehnquist quoted in N. Gingrich 2006b, p. 67; E. Gaustad 1993, p. 139.

48. Justice William Rehnquist dissenting in *Wallace v. Jeffrey*, 472 U.S. 38, 113 (1985); *Constitutions of the United States* 1813, p. 364; D. Barton 2002, pp. 41- 43, 440.

49. James Madison quoted in M. Andrews 1933, p. 146. On Madison's further ruminations on the topic, see also W. Miller 1985, pp. 4-7, 17-18, 20-21, 28, 34 ff., 125-126, 357-364.

50. D. Barton 2002, loc. cit.; D. Kupelian 2005, p. 44; R. Bork 2003, loc. cit. Pursuant to a Joint Resolution of Congress passed on January 25, 1988, the first Thursday of each month of May was formally designated as the "National Day of Prayer."

51. *Reynolds v. United States*, 98 U.S. 145, 164 (1878) and *Pierce v. Society of Sisters*, 268 U.S. 510, 513 (1925); D. Barton 2002, pp. 13, 435; idem. 2007, p. 7; D. Dreisbach 2002, p. 121.

52. The court decisions are extracted from D. Barton 2002, pp. 14-16, 435-436.

53. *Florey v. Souix Falls School District*, 464 F. Supp. 911 (U.S.D.C., S.D. 1979) *cert. denied*, 449 U.S. 987); D. Barton 2002, pp. 15, 435.

54. *Ohio v. Whisner*, 351 N. E. 2d 750 (Sup Ct. Ohio 1976); D. Barton 2002, loc. cit.

55. *Washegesic v. Bloomingdale Public Schools*, 813 F. Sup. 559 (W.D. Mi. S.D. 1993); *affirmed*, 33 F. 3d 679 (6$^{th}$ Cir. 1994); *cert. denied*, 63 U.S.W.L. 3786 (1985); D. Barton 2002, pp. 16, 435.
56. Court decisions extracted from D. Barton 2002, pp. 14-15, 435-436.
57. *State of Florida v. George T. Broxton*, Case No. 90-02930 CF (1$^{st}$ Jud. Cir. Ct., Walton County, Fl. 1992); *Olean Times Herald*, Monday, April l, 1992, p. A-1; D. Barton 2002, pp. 16-17, 436.
58. *Commonwealth v. Chambers* cited in D. Kupelian 2005, p. 154.
59. *Cantwell v. Connecticut* 310 U.S. 296 (1940); *New York v. Gitlow,* 268 U.S. 652 (1925); *Everson v. Board of Education*, 330 U.S. 1, 18) (1947); T. Eastland 2005, p. 85; D. Kupelian 2005, pp. 54-57; D. Barton 2000, pp. 10-11; P. Hamburger 2002, pp. 448, 454 ff.; J. O'Neill 1949, pp. 172 ff., 176, 179 ff., 189 ff.; R. Cord 1988, p.101.
60. P. Hamburger 2002, pp. 434-440; C. Warren 1926, pp. 435-449, passim.
61. *Walz v. Tax Commission*, 397 U.S., 701-703 (1970); D. Barton 2007, pp. 13-14; idem. 1992, pp. 157-158, 168-169; S. Kennedy 2007, pp. 65-67; R. Cord 1988, pp. 188 ff.
62. James Madison 1988, p. 236; M. Beliles and S. McDowell 1992, p. 189.
63. Thomas Jefferson quoted in W. Stedman 1987, p. 32; M. Beliles and S. McDowell 1992, loc. cit.; *Walz v. Tax Commission*, 397 U.S., 554, 695, 672, 716 (1970); D. Barton 1992, pp.166, 181.
64. See *Baer v. Kolmorgen*, 181 N.Y.S. 2d 230, 237 (Sup. Ct. N.Y, 1958); D. Barton 2007, p. 15.
65. Thomas Jefferson quoted in G. DeMar 1997, vol. 1, pp. 187-188.
66. *Reynolds v. United States*, 98 U.S. 145 (1878); J. Richardson 1899, vol. 1, p. 379; D. Barton 1992, p. 43; P. Hamburger 2002, p. 260.
67. G. DeMar 1997, vol. 1, pp. 187-188, 195-196.
68. D. Dreisbach 2002, p. 93; S. Carter 1993, pp. 105, 115.
69. T. Eastland 2005, p. 93.
70. T. Eastland 2005, p. 86.
71. W. Rehnquist, loc. cit; D. Kupelian 2005, pp. 55-56; O. Guinness 1993, pp. 220, 264.
72. *Everson v. Board of Education*, 330, U.S. 1, 18 (1947); M. Malbin 1978, p. 2; D. Barton 2002, loc. cit.; idem. 2000, p. 10, idem. 2007, pp. 13-14; D. Kupelian 2005, p. 47; A. Kors and H. Silverglate 1998, pp. 266-267; D. Barton 1992, pp. 42-44; P. Hamburger 2002, pp. 454 ff.; A. Sears and C. Osten 2005, pp. 22, 213; M. Beliles and D. Anderson 2005, pp. 173-174; J. O'Neill 1949, pp. 189 ff. The First Amendment "establishment clause'" application to the states was effected by the ruling's incorporation by reference to the Fourteenth Amendment, which stipulates:

> No state shall make or enforce any law which shall abridge the privileges or immunities of citizens of the United States; nor shall any state deprive any person of life, liberty, or property without due process of law; nor deny to any person the equal protection of its laws.

The protections afforded by the Fourteenth Amendment thus built upon those articulated in the Ninth Amendment of the Bill of Rights, making clear that while certain rights of citizens are explicitly constitutionally set forth, such recitals do not define the whole of citizens' rights. To wit: "The enumeration in the Constitution of certain rights shall not be construed to deny or disparage others retained by the people."

73. Justice Hugo Black quoted in D. Kupelian 2005, p. 471; P. Hamburger 2002, "Frontispiece," pp. 6 ff., 461-462; A. Sears and C. Osten 2005, pp. 212-213; D. Dreisbach 2002, pp. 100-102; J. O'Neill 1949, pp. 79 ff.; R. Cord 1988, pp. 18, 49, 109 ff.

74. Justice Wiley Rutledge quoted in J. O'Neill 1949, p. 201; R. Cord 1988, pp. 124 ff.

75. *Engel v. Vital*, 370 U.S. 421-422 (1962); D. Barton 2000, pp. 10-11; idem. 2002, pp. 155-156; A. Sears and C. Osten 2005, pp. 22-23; M. Beliles and D. Anderson 2005, p. 182; D. Barton 2002, p. 186. The voluntary non-denominational prayer in question was: "Almighty God, we acknowledge our dependence upon Thee; and beg Thy blessings upon us, our parents, our teachers, and our Country."

76. *Everson v. Board of Education,* 333 U.S. 203, 237-238 (1947); quoted in R. Cord 1988, p. 143.

77. *Zorach v. Clauson*, 312-314, quoted in D. Barton 2002, pp. 73-74; idem. 1992, pp. 77-78; W. Federer 2004, pp. 67-69; M. Beliles and S. McDowell 1992, p. 184. Indeed, even in 1963, in eliminating voluntary *Bible* reading from public schools, the U.S. Supreme Court ruled that:

> The state may not establish a "religion of secularism" in the sense of affirmatively opposing or showing hostility to religion, thus "preferring those who believe in no religion over those who do believe". . . . Refusal to permit religious exercises is thus seen not as a realization of state neutrality, but rather as the establishment of a religion of secularism.

Again in 1983, in *Crockett v. Sorenson*, the U.S. District Court of West Virginia similarly determined that:

> The First Amendment was never intended to insulate our public institutions from any mention of God, the *Bible*, or religion. For when such insulation occurs, another religion, such as secular humanism, is effectively established.

78. E. Norman 1968, p. 4.

79. *Everson v. Board of Education*, 330 U.S. 1, 18 (1947); *McCollum v. Board of Education*, 333 U.S. 203 (1947); *Wallace v. Jaffrey*, 472 U.S. 38 (1985), cited in A. Kors and H. Silverglate 1998, p. 192; D. Barton 2002, pp. 155 ff., 159 ff., 191-194; idem. 2007, p. 14; idem. 1992, pp. 11, 43-44, 142-143; P. Hamburger 2002, pp. 472-478; P. Buchanan 2002, p. 184; T. Eastland 2005, p. 94, A. Sears and C. Osten 2005, pp. 22, 214; D. Dreisbach 2002, pp. 4 ff.; J. O'Neill 1949, pp. 219 ff. In *Everson* (p. 13), the Court even conceded that: "Prior to the Fourteenth Amendment, the First Amendment did not apply as a restraint against the states."

80. *McCollum v. Board of Education*, 33 U.S. 203, 207-209 (1948); R. Cord 1988, pp. 168 ff.

81. R. Cord 1988, pp.133 ff.

82. *Abington Township v. Schempp*, 374 U.S. 203, 212, 225, 83 S. Ct. 1560, 10 L. Ed. 2d 844 (1963); W. Federer 2004, p. 67.

83. *Crocker v. Sorenson*, 568 F. Supp. 1422, 1425-1430 (W.D. Va. 1983); W. Federer 2004, loc. cit.

84. Justice William O. Douglas quoted in J. Meacham 2006, pp. 239-240; R. Cord 1988, pp. 169 ff.

85. See *Engel v. Vitale*, 370 U.S. 421-423 (1962) and *State Board of Education v. Board of Education of Netcong*, 26A.2d 21, 30 (Sup. Ct. N.J. 1970), *cert denied*, 401 U.S; A. Sears and C. Osten 2005, p. 23; J. Meacham 2006, p. 187; S. Dawson 1988, p. I-7.

86. John W. Whitehead quoted in G. DeMar 199, vol. 1, p. 196.

87. See *Engel v. Vitale*, 370 U.S. 421, 425, 430 (1962); D. Barton 1992, pp. 145-149.

88. Justice Potter Stewart quoted in *Engle v. Vitale*, 370 U.S. 421, 445 (1962); R. Cord 1988, pp. 157-159.

89. J. Meachan 2006, p. 189.

90. G. DeMar 2001, vol. 3, p. 103.

91. See *Engel v. Vitale*, 431 (1962); D. Barton 1992, p. 146.

92. See *Engel v. Vitale*, 370 U.S. 421, 436 (1962); D. Barton 1992, p. 147.

93. D. Barton 1992, loc. cit. Indeed, in a 1799 ruling made by a court far more proximate to the intent of the Founders that went federally unchallenged, the Maryland Supreme Court ruled that: "By our form of government, the Christian religion is the established religion; and all sects and denominations of Christians are placed upon equal footing." (See *Runkel v. Winemiller*, 4 Harris and McHenry 276, 288 (Sup. Ct. Md. 1799).

94. G. Washington 1932, vol. 30, p. 304.

95. J. Adams 1854, vol. 9, p. 636.

96. Thomas Jefferson quoted in H. Lockyer 1969, p. 98.

97. J. Madison 1973, vol. 8, p. 304.

98. J. Adams 1854, vol. 9, p. 229; D. Barton 1992, p. 149.

99. George Washington quoted in D. Barton 1992, p. 150.

100. See *Engel v. Vitale*, 370 U.S. 421 (1962) and *Abington v. Schempp* 374 U.S. 203 (1963), passim.

101. *Abington v. Schempp*, 374 U.S. 203, 216 (1963); D. Barton 1992, p. 150; idem. 2002, pp. 160-162, 190; A. Sears and C. Osten 2005, p. 23.

102. D. Barton 1992, pp. 149 ff.

103. *Abington v. Schempp*, 374 U.S. 203, 216 (1963).

104. See *Barron v. Baltimore*, 32 U.S. 243 (1833); D. Barton 1992, pp. 169-171; J. O'Neill 1949, p. 172; R. Cord 1988, pp. 86-89.

105. *State Board of Education v. Board of Education of Netcong*, 26A.2d 21, 36, 25-26 (Sup. Ct. N.J. 1970), *cert denied*, 401 U.S. 1013.

106. Idem. at 22,26.

107. Idem. at 22-24.

108. D. Barton 1992, pp. 155-157; idem. 2002, p. 234.

109. *Stone v. Graham*, 449 U.S. 39042 (1980); D. Barton 2000, p. 11; idem. pp. 170-175; M. Beliles and D. Anderson 2005, p. 182.

110. *Abington v. Schempp*, 374 U.S. 203 (1963) at 209; D. Barton 2002, pp. 170 ff.; idem. 2000, p. 10; idem. 2007, pp.14-16, idem. 1992, pp. 154-155; A. Schmidt 1997, p. 142; J. Black 1994, pp. 9, 11; T. Eastland 2005, p. 95; *Engel v. Vitale* (1962), 370 U.S. 421.

111. Sources cited, loc. cit; D. Barton 2000, p. 11, idem. 2007, p. 14; idem. 1992, pp. 154, 165; R. Bork 2003, loc. cit; *Stone v. Graham* 449 U.S. 39 (1980) at 42.

112. Sources cited, loc. cit

113. *Brandon v. Board of Education of Guilderland Central School District*, 487 F. Supp. 1219 (1980) *Lee v. Weisman*, 505 U.S. 577, 467, 492, 505 (1992); T. Eastland 2005, pp. 96-97; D. Barton 1992, pp. 12, 16; idem. 2002, pp. 183-190. Indeed, in *Graham v. Cen-*

*tral School District* (1985), all opening and closing prayers at school graduation ceremonies were ruled unconstitutional.

114. *Wallace v. Jaffree*, 472 U.S. 38, 48, n. 30 (1984); D. Barton 1992, pp. 163-164.
115. Idem. at 43, 44, n. 22.
116. Idem. at 41-42.
117. D. Barton 1992, p. 159.
118. Sources cited, loc. cit.; M. Beliles and D. Anderson 2005, pp.181-183.
119. D. Barton 2007, pp. 12-13.
120. Ibid.
121. *Roberts v. Madigan* cited in D. Kupelian 2005, p. 41; M. Beliles and D. Anderson 2005, p. 182.
122. D. Barton 2002, pp. 233 ff.; D. Kupelian 2005, p. 11; M. Beliles and D. Anderson 2005, pp. 187-188; *Erznozik v. City of Jacksonville,* 42 U.S. 205 (1975). For example, in conflicting cases wherein the federal courts had an active involvement:

> *The prayers of Congressional chaplains are permissible = *Chambers v. Marsh* (1982); but . . .
> *High school students are prohibited from voluntarily reading them in the *Congressional Record* on their own time = *State Board of Education v. Board of Education of Netcong* (1970).
> *Voluntary prayer in schools is forbidden = *State Board of Education v. Board of Education of Netcong* (1970), but . . .
> *Protecting children from public lewdness and nudity is not = *Erznozik v. City of Jacksonville* (1975).
> *Displays of the Ten Commandments on public property are permissible in Salt Lake City = *Anderson v. Salt Lake City Corp.* (1973); but . . .
> * Similar displays are forbidden in Grand Forks = *Stone v. Graham* (1980).
> * Nativity scenes are permitted on public property in Pawtucket, Rhode Island = Lynch v. Donnelly (1985), but . . .
> * They are prohibited in Allegheny County, Pennsylvania = *County of Allegheny v. ACLU* (1989).
> * While blasphemy in a required classroom text is sanctioned as free speech = *Grove v. Mead School District* (1985); but
> * Classroom references to God are prohibited = *Reed v. van Hoven* (1965); *State of Ohio v. Wisner* (1976).
>
> *Ad infinitum.* Indeed, the hypocritical double standards problem has become acute to the degree that the question of judicial "competence" no longer speaks exclusively to matters of jurisdiction. (On these phenomena, see D. Barton 1992, pp. 187-193, passim.)

123. D. Kupelian 2005, p. 153; "Is the Declaration of Independence Unconstitutional?" replicated on WorldDailyNet.com, November 13, 2004.
124. G. DeMar 2007, pp. 57-58.
125. S. Huntington 2004b, p. 81; P. Buchanan, loc. cit.Though the Supreme Court in 2004 dismissed the suit on a technicality, another lawsuit has now been filed.
126. D. Kupelian 2005, pp. 39-41; A. Sears and C. Osten 2005, pp. 142-144; G. DeMar 2003, pp. 72-73.
127. A. Sears and C. Osten 2005, p. 141; D. Kupelian 2005, loc. cit.

128. A. Sears and C. Osten 2005, pp. 142-143.

129. *Warsaw v. Tehachapi* cited in D. Kupelian 2005, p. 42.

130. D. Barton 1992, pp. 11-12; B. Goldberg 2005, pp. 286-287; N. Gingrich 2008, p. 167.

131. T. Jefferson 1904, pp. 331-332.

132. J. Madison 1953, vol. 11, p. 293; D. Dreisbach 2002, p. 88. Madison would add that: "Nothing has yet been offered to invalidate the doctrine that the meaning of the Constitution may well be ascertained by the legislature as well as by the judicial authority" (quoted in J. Elliot 1836, vol. 4, p. 399).

133. Alexander Hamilton quoted in D. Barton 1992, p. 224.

134. T. Jefferson 1904, vol. 10, p. 302, vol. 15, p. 213.

135. M. Beliles and D. Anderson 2005, pp. 127-128.

136. M. Beliles and D. Anderson 2005, p. 185; D. Barton 1992, pp. 160-162, 181-184; idem. 2002 237-238. Indeed, a 1977 New Jersey court (*Malnak v. Yogi*, 440 F. Supp 1285, 1287 (D.C. N.J 1997) on one occasion even ruled that atheism may be deemed a religion under the Establishment Clause.

137. D. Barton 1992, pp. 161-162, 184-185, 230-231; M. Beliles and D. Anderson 2005, p. 173.

138. *Wallace v. Jeffrey*, 472 U.S. 38, 47, n. 10. (1984); A. Sears and C. Osten 2005, p. 23; D. Barton 2002, pp. 175-179.

139. *State Board of Education v. Board of Education of Netcong*, 26A.2d 21, 30 (Sup. Ct. N.J. 1970), *cert denied*, 401 U.S. 1013.

140. D. Marsh 1970, p. 51.

141. J. Eidsmoe 2005, pp. 242-243; J. O'Neill 1949, p. 4; A. Peaslee 1950, vol. 3, p. 280; D. Barton 1992, pp. 44-46, 172-174; G. DeMar 1997, vol. 1, pp. 194-195. Certainly, it contravened the will of Jefferson expressed when he wrote: "No power over the freedom of religion . . . is delegated to the United States by the Constitution" (H. Commager 1948, p. 179) — and: "In matters of religion, I have always considered its free exercise is placed by the Constitution independent of the powers of the General Government" (J. Richardson 1899, vol. 1, p. 379)."

It is noteworthy, however, that while the words "separation of church and state" do not occur in the United States Constitution, they do appear in that of the erstwhile Soviet Union. To wit:

> Article 52. The church in the Union of Soviet Socialist Republics is separated from the state and the school from the church.

142. *Church of the Holy Trinity v. U.S.*, 143 U.S. 465, 471 (1892); D. Barton 1992, pp. 48, 57, 76.

143. D. Barton 2000, p. 11; M. Beliles and D. Anderson 2005, p. 185.

144. J. Black 1994, p. 183.

145. D. Kupelian 2005, pp. 44 ff.

146. Cato Institute 2005, p. 41.

147. S. Huntington 2004b, pp. 81-82; G. DeMar 1995, pp. 75, 161.

148. Justice Hughes quoted in D. Danelski and J. Tulchin 1973, p. 143; E. Corwin 1937, p xxiv; L. McDonald 1976, p. 32; D. Barton 1992, p. 205; M. Beliles and D. Anderson 2005, p. 139.

149. E. Corwin 1937, p. 398; D. Barton 1992, p. 207.

150. Sources cited, loc. cit.
151. Abraham Lincoln quoted in J. Richardson 1899, vol. 6, p. 9.
152. Whitaker Chamber quoted in A. Harrington 2001, p. 44; *New York Times*, June 20, 2000, p. A-22; S. Huntington 2004b, pp. 347-348; P. Buchanan 2002, pp. 184, 199; N. Gingrich 2006a, p. 8.
153. O. Guinness 1993, pp. 220, 264.
154. Ronald Reagan quoted in D. Barton 1992, pp. 17-18.
155. L. Graglia 2005, pp. 31-32.
156. Cf. *Cooper v. Allen*, 358 U.S. 1 (1958) ("the federal judiciary is supreme in the exposition of the Constitution") and the Court's interpretation of the Constitution "is the supreme law of the land"); *Brown v. Allen*, 344 U.S. 443, 540 (1953) (Justice Robert Jackson concurring opinion); quoted in L. Graglia 2005, pp. 20, 28.
157. Alexis de Tocqueville quoted in T. Eastland 2005, pp. 110-111; D. Kupelian 2005, p. 213.
158. R. Lesthaeghe 1983, p. 429; D. Kupelian 2005, p. 214.
159. T. Derekhshani 1999, p. E-12; Nietzsche quoted in D. Kupelian 2005, p. 214; Dostoevsky, Sartre, and Solzhenitsyn quoted in J. Black 2004, pp. 212, 260; O. Guinness 1993, p. 402.
160. J. Black 1994, p. 29.
161. L. Graglia 1996, pp. 293, 298.
162. S. Levinson 1989, pp. 64-65.
163. G. Weigel 2005, p. 65.
164. D. Kupelian 2005, p. 53.
165. See M. Beliles and S. McDowell 1992, pp. 261 ff.; R. Cord 1988, p. 239.
166. D. Kupelian 2005, pp. 57-58; J. Black 1994, p. 33.
167. John Adams and Daniel Webster quoted in W. Federer 2003, pp. 18, 29; John Witherspoon 1815, vol. 4, p. 95, quoted in D. Barton 2002, p. 173.
168. Harry Truman quoted in S. Dawson 1988, p. I-12; W. Federer 2003, p. 32; G. DeMar 2003, p. 70.
169. Ronald Reagan quoted in W. Federer 2003, p. 33.
170. Ronald Reagan quoted in W. Federer 2003, p. 35. See also *Crockett v. Sorenson*, 568 F. Supp. 1422, 1425-1430 (D. D. Va. 1983); W. Federer 2003, p. 38.
171. Cullen Murphy quoted in J. Leo 2001, p. 259.
172. Thucydides. *History of the Peloponnesian War*, Book 3, 105.2, quoted in F. Fukuyama 2006, p. 245.
173. Cicero. *The Republic*, Book III, Ch. 22 in Cicero 1977, vol. 16, pp. 210-211; quoted in G. Heck 2006, "Frontispiece;" A. Schmidt 1997, p. 142. A 1994 survey of 1,200 people aged fifteen to thirty five, for instance, found that the vast majority of those polled could name no more than two – moving essayist Cullen Murphy to cynically note that: "they weren't too happy about some of the others either when they found out precisely what they were."
174. *Bible*, Romans 2: 14-15.
175. *Bible,* Romans 2: 14-15; M. Luther 1958, 40:98; A. Schmidt 1997, p. 142; J. Eidsmoe 2005, p. 21.
176. A. Schmidt 1997, p.142.
177. Ibid.

178. K. Woodward 1996, p. 75; Ted Koppel quoted in A. Schmidt 1997, pp. 142-143; G. DeMar 2003, p. 76; R. Bork 1989, p. 164.

179. A. Schmidt 1997, pp. 185-186, 194; L. Ingraham 2003, p. 122.

180. Adams, Jefferson, Madison, and Kennedy all quoted in L. Ingraham 2003, pp. 128-130; See also M. Beliles and S. McDowell 1992, pp. 263-264.

181. L. Ingraham 2003, p. 126.

182. Ibid.

183. James Madison quoted in L. Ingraham 2003, p. 128.

184. J. O'Neill 1949, pp. 262 ff.

185. J. O'Neill 1949, pp. 61, 77 ff., 102, 111, 115-117; 205 ff.

186. As delineated in J. O'Neill 1949, pp. 205-207, 215-216.

187. T. Jefferson 1969, pp. 946-949; J. Madison 1953, pp. 299-306; R. Cord 1988, pp. 4-5, 20 ff., 36, 155. Jefferson requested that the "Virginia Statute of Religious Liberty of 1786" be engraved upon his tombstone as one of his noteworthy accomplishments.

188. Thomas Jefferson quoted in C. Wesley 1963, pp. 38-39; G. DeMar 2003, p. 66.

189. R. Cord 1988, pp. 38-39, 58, 115-116, 210, 215, 224, 227.

190. P. Wood 2003, p. 172; M. Beliles and D. Anderson 2005, pp. 65-67, 70; J. Eidsmoe 2005, p. 235. E. Gaustad 1993, p. 41; W. Miller 1985, pp. 51-52.

191. R. Cord 1988, pp. 23-24, 46.

192. R. Cord 1988, pp. 215-216.

193. R. Cord 1988, p. 220.

194. R. Cord 1988, p. 228.

195. J. O'Neill 1949, pp. 43 ff., 49-50.

196. Justice John Marshall quoted in R. Cord 1988, p. 232.

197. J. O'Neill 1949, pp. 55-56.

198. Thomas Jefferson 1984, p. 1475.

199. James Wilson and Oliver Wendell Holmes quoted in D. Dreisback 1987, p. xiii; G. DeMar 2003, p. 62.

200. L. Ingraham 2003, pp. 117-118.

201. S. Huntington 2004b, p. 1; quoted in A. Lieven 2004, p. 124.

202. J. Black 2004, p. 212.

## CHAPTER FOUR

1. From Nietzsche's parable in *The Gay Science* as quoted in O. Guinness 1979, p. 22.

2. Dostoevsky quoted in O. Guinness 1979, p. 24.

3. O. Guinness 1993, p. 95.

4. O. Guinness 1993, pp. 97-100, 398.

5. A. Schmidt 1997, pp. 3-4.

6. D. D'Souza 1995, p. 3.

7. *Bible*, Matthew 5:14.

8. *Bible,* Matthew 5:16.

9. J. Black 1994, p. 3.

10. J. Black 1994, pp. 13-14.

11. J. Black 1994, pp. 133-134, 139-140.

12. J. Black 1994, pp. 14, 76.

13. J. Black 1994, p. 242.

14. J. Black 1994, pp. 14-15.
15. J. Black 1994, pp. 5-7, 11-12.
16. J. Black 1994, pp. 22, 49, 181-182.
17. J. Black 1994, p. 27.
18. Ibid.
19. Amitai Etzioni quoted in J. Black 1994, p. 158.
20. J. Klein 1993, p. 30.
21. On this, see D. Moynihan 1993, pp. 17-20, and p. 19 in particular.
22. Ibid.
23. Will Durant quoted in J. Black 1994, p. 9.
24. S. Renshon 2005, p. 82.
25. J. Black 2004, pp. 19, 33, 220-221.
26. Ibid.; H. Kramer and R. Kimball 1999, p. 14.
27. On them, and the so-called "Frankfurt School" of which they were members, see R. Wiggershaus 1995, passim; T. Blankley 2005, p. 100; J. Black 1994, pp. 184-186, 220-221; M. Berman 2000, pp. 107-108.
28. Sources cited, loc. cit.
29. H. Marcuse 1972, p. 17; H. Kramer and R. Kimball 1999, loc. cit.
30. H. Marcuse 1966, p. xvii; R. Kimball 1998, p. 84.
31. H. Marcuse 1966, loc. cit.; H. Kramer and R. Kimball 2000, pp. 7-8; idem. 1999, pp. 14-15.
32. R. Kimball 1998, pp. 15-16, 18; P. Buchanan 2002, pp. 85-86; J. Black 2004, p. 212; J. Leo 2001, p. 255; L. Ingraham 2003, p. 36.
33. Sources cited, loc. cit.
34. R. Bork 2003, pp. 17-19.
35. See M. Lerner 1998, passim, quoted in J. Black 2004, pp. 343-344; H. Kramer and R. Kimball 1999, pp. 17.
36. M. Lerner 1996, p. 97; quoted in J. Bovard 1999, p. 235; J. Black 1994, p. 154.
37. A. Kors and H. Silverglate 1998, p. 68.
38. On this, see H. Marcuse 1969, pp. 81-123 passim.
39. A. Kors and H. Silverglate 1998, p. 68.
40. H. Marcuse loc. cit.; also quoted in A. Kors and H. Silverglate 1998, p. 69; D. D'Souza 1991, p.152.
41. H. Marcuse quoted in A. Kors and H. Silverglate 1998, p. 70.
42. H. Marcuse quoted in A. Kors and H. Silverglate 1998, loc. cit.
43. Ibid.
44. Alexis de Tocqueville quoted in A. Schlesinger 1998, p. 165; R. Kimball 1998, p. xii.
45. R. Rorty 1994, p. E-15; idem. 1998, p. 15; A. Schlesinger 1998, pp. 21, 151, 159 ff.
46. J. Black 1994, pp. 137-138.
47. A. Bloom 1987, p. 382.
48. Susan Haack quoted in M. Berman 2000, p. 126.
49. A. Schmidt 2007, pp. 20-21.
50. B. Goldberg 2005, p. 36.
51. Loc. cit.
52. Examples are, in part, selected from A. Schmidt 1997, pp. 90-91.
53. Abbie Hoffman and Malcolm X quoted in O. Guinness 1993, p. 97.

54. O. Guinness 1993, p. 374.
55. H. Marcuse 1969, p. 134.
56. T. Leary 1970, passim.
57. Adrian Mitchell quoted in O. Guinness 1979, p. 319.
58. O. Guinness 1979, pp. 323, 338.
59. O. Guinness 1979, p. 377; idem. 1993, pp. 369, 410.
60. John Adams quoted in O. Guinness 1993, p. 276.
61. George Mason, *Virginia Declaration of Rights*, quoted in O. Guinness 1993, p. 149.
62. O. Guinness 1993, pp. 1-6.
63. O. Guinness 1993, pp. 388-389, 399.
64. Ibid.
65. F. Wooldridge 2004, pp. 78, 138-139.
66. P. Buchanan 2002, pp. 89-90, 256-257; idem. 2006, pp. 172-173.
67. A. Schmidt 1997, pp. 85-86.
68. P. Collier and D. Horowitz 1996, pp. 245 ff., 371.
69. Ibid.
70. A. Schmidt 1997, p. 86.
71. Ibid.
72. Loc. cit.
73. A. Schmidt 1997, pp. 87-88.
74. R. Kimball 1998, p. x.
75. Ibid.
76. R. Kimball 1998, pp. 57-58.
77. V. Hanson 2003b, p. 107.
78. A. Smith 1937, p. 838.
79. R. Kimball 1998, p. xi.
80. A. Bloom 1990, p. 367.
81. Ibid.
82. R. Bork 2003, pp. 262-263; V. Hanson 2003b, p. 110.
83. Sources cited, loc. cit.
84. P. Gross and N. Levitt 1994, p. 5; R. Bork 2003, p. 265.
85. W. McGowan 2001, pp. 229-230.
86. W. McGowan 2001, p. 230.
87. Sam Fulwood quoted in W. McGowan 2001, p. 231; J. Fallows 1997, p. 107.
88. W. McGowan 2001, pp. 231-232.
89. R. Bork 2005, pp. ix, x.
90. R. Bork 2005, p. xi.
91. Ibid.
92. Cf. *Texas v. Johnson*, 491 U.S. 397 (1989). (see also *United States v. Eichman*, 496 U.S. Code 310 (1990) (flag desecration); *Shad v. Mt. Ephraim,* 452 U.S. 61 (1981) (nude dancing); *Abington School District v. Schempp*, 364 U.S. 203, 225 (1963) (school prayer); *Grutter v. Bollinger*, 539 U.S. 305 (2003) (racial discrimination in college admissions). (On the right to own rubber sex toys, see J. Leo 2001, p. 185.)
93. Cf. *Cantwell v. Connecticut*, 310 U.S. 296 (1940); R. Bork 2005, p. xii, xv, xxii-xxiii, xxvi, xxxi; L. Graglia 2005, pp. 17, 41-42, 51.

94. *Plessy v. Ferguson*, 163 U.S. 537 (1896) (permitted); *Brown v. Board of Education*, 347 U.S. 483 (1954) (prohibited); *Swann v. Charlotte-Mecklenberg Board of Education*, 402 U.S. 1 (1971) (required); L. Graglia 2005, pp. 20-22.

95. L. Graglia 2005, pp. 31-32.

96. Justice Charles Evan Hughes quoted in D. Danelski and J. Tulchin 1973, p. 143; O. Guinness 1993, p. 365; J. Eidsmoe 2005, p. 397.

97. Cf. *Cooper v. Allen*, 358 U.S. 1 (1958) ("the federal judiciary is supreme in the exposition of the Constitution"), and (the Court's interpretation of the Constitution "is the supreme law of the land"); *Brown v. Allen*, 344 U.S. 443, 540 (1953) (Justice Robert Jackson concurring opinion); quoted in L.Graglia 2005, pp. 20, 28.

98. G. Himmelfarb 1974, pp. 46-47.

99. L. Graglia 2005, p. 24.

100. L. Graglia 1985, p. 446; idem. 1996, pp. 293, 298.

101. Antonin Scalia dissenting opinion in *Board of County Commissioners, Wabaunsee County, Kansas v. Umbehr*, 518, U.S. 668, 688-689 (1996), cited in R. Bork 2005, p. xi.

102. Alexis de Tocqueville quoted in L. Graglia 2005, p. 1; T. Eastland 2005, pp. 110-111, 135.

103. G. McDowell 2005, p. 60.

104. J. Black 2004, p. 272.

105. L. Ingraham 2003, pp. 132-133.

106. J. Gibson 2005, pp. xxi-xxii, 16.

107. J. Gibson 2005, p. 165.

108. A. Schmidt 1997, p. 147; R. Bork 2003, p. 1999; T. Eastland 2005, pp. 103-104; L. Ingraham 2003, p. 6. Yet in *Cohen v. California,* 403 U.S. 15, 25 ((1971), conferring First Amendment rights on a young man who refused to remove a jacket that bore the slogan "Fuck the Draft!" in a courthouse corridor, the U.S. Supreme Court cited as a decisive consideration: "One man's vulgarity is another's lyric (!)"

109. *County of Allegheny v. ACLU*, 106 L. Ed. 2d 472, 472, 475, 541, 543 (1989); D. Barbarisi 2004, p. 1; A. Sears and C. Osten 2005, p.161; D. Barton 2002, pp. 180-183.

110. On such activities, see J. Gibson 2005, passim; A. Schmidt 1997, p. 148; O. Guinness 1993, pp. 265-266.

111. A. Sears and C. Osten 2005, p. 157.

112. Ibid.

113. A. Coulter 2006, pp. 149-150.

114. Ibid.

115. L. Chavez 1994, p. A-11; A. Schmidt 1997, pp. 147-148.

116. A. Schmidt 1997, p. 148; G. DeMar 1995, pp. 45-46.

117. J. Gibson 2005, p. xx, 29, 86-87; A. Schmidt 1997, loc. cit.; J. Leo 2001, p. 181; A. Sears and C. Osten 2005, p. 161.

118. Sources cited, loc. cit.

119. A. Schmidt 1997, p.148; J. Gibson 2006, p. xx.

120. J. Gibson 2005, pp. 4-10, 16, 86-87, 113, 159.

121. A. Sears and C. Osten 2005, pp. 168-169.

122. A. Sears and C. Osten 2005, pp. 161-162; J. Gibson 2005, p. 159.

123. Richard Thompson quoted in J. Gibson 2005, p. 144, 153, 186.

124. J. Gibson 2005, pp. 137, 164, 186.

125. J.F. Revel 1993, pp. 92-93.

126. V. Hanson 2004, p. 1; M. Malkin 2005b, p. 8.
127. Edmund Burke 1967, p. 42; idem. 1969, vol. 8, p. 138; idem. 1961, p. 203; T. Sowell 2007b, pp. 56, 60, 64.
128. All incidents related in A. Schmidt 1997, pp. 34-46, passim; V. Hanson 2003, p. 104; M. Steyn 2006, p.193.
129. Ibid. As the nineteenth century British Governor General of Sind, Sir Charles Napier affirmed in elegant multicultural fashion: "You say that it is your custom to burn widows. Very well. We also have a custom. When men burn women alive, we tie ropes around their necks and hang them until dead. You build your funeral pyre; and beside it my carpenters will build a gallows. You follow your custom, and then will follow ours!"
130. Loc. cit.
131. Loc. cit.
132. A. Schlesinger 1998, p. 133.
133. A. Schlesinger 1998, p. 135; G. Jackson 2007, p. 325.
134. S. Renshon 2005, pp. 83-84; J. Black 2004, pp.178-179.
135. Sources cited, loc. cit.; A Coulter 2002, p. 201; R. Davis 1999, pp. 1-2.
136. R. Bork 2003, p. 260.
137. R. Kimball 1998, pp. 226-227; G. Jackson 2006, pp. 321 ff. The spirit of scientific inquiry was likewise given great impetus by the 19$^{th}$ century Industrial Revolution, again largely a byproduct of Anglo-Saxon civilization – which is why, outside the orbits of U.S. humanities departments, there is a frenetic quest worldwide, including in the so-called "oppressed cultures," to acquire American science and technology.
138. R. Kimball 1998, p. 236.
139. Lord Thomas Macaulay cited by J. Black 1994, p. 246.
140. J. Black 1994, p. 122.
141. Walter Lippman quoted in O. Guinness 2001, p. 32.
142. J. Ortega y Gassett 1957, p. 76; R. Bork 2003, p. 313.
143. J. Black 1994, p. 3.
144. Arthur Schlesinger quoted in P. Brimelow 1995, p. 217; J. Black 1994, p. 5.
145. G. DeMar 1995, pp. 106-107.
146. G. DeMar 1995, pp. 161, 168-169; L. Ingraham 2003, pp. 49-50.
147. G. DeMar 1995, p. 197.
148. Ibid.
149. S. Huntington 2004b, p. 340; A. Schlesinger 1998, p. 135.
150. J. Black 2004, p. 246.
151. Bishop Fulton Sheen quoted in G. Heck 2007, p. xix; J. Black 2004, p. 247.
152. See R. Conquest 1999, passim, cited in J. Black 2004, p. 267.
153. George Santayana quoted in R. Bernstein 1994, p. 342; J. Black 2004, p. 269.
154. W. Churchill 1946, passim.
155. Winston Churchill, loc. cit.; quoted in J. Black 2004, pp. 292-293.
156. J. Black 2004, loc. cit.
157. Ibid.
158. R. Kirk 1992, passim, replicated in J. Black 2004, p. 318.
159. D. Kupelian 2005, p. 103.
160. A. Schlesinger 1998, pp. 135, 165; D. Kupelian 2005, p. 103.
161. As Friedrich Nietzsche famously observed: "One does not refute a disease, he repels it." Friedrich Nietzsche quoted in R. Kimball 1998, p. 234; F. Wooldridge 2004, p. 264.

162. D. Kennedy 1997, p. 355; S. Huntington 2004b, p. 259.

## CHAPTER FIVE

1. D. Brewer 1996, pp. 47-48.
2. K. Phillips 2006, pp. 276-277, 296-297.
3. W. Wolman 1997, pp. 57 ff., 186.
4. On this phenomenon, see K. Phillips 2006, pp. 302, 311-312, 314-315, 321, 336.
5. M. Novak 2004, p. 76.
6. M. Novak 2004, p. 51.
7. M. Novak 2004, pp. 132-133.
8. A. de Tocqueville 1969, pp. 46-47, 502.
9. Reinhold Niebuhr quoted in M. Novak 2004, pp. 165, 184.
10. S.B. Clough 1951, pp. 6-7.
11. For these reasons, the Baron Montesquieu (1949, vol 26, pp. 30-31) assessed that "the Catholic religion is most agreeable to a Monarchy, and the Protestant to a Republic;" J. Eidsmoe 2005, p. 56; M. Novak 2004, pp. 53-67.
12. M. Weber 1958, p. 35; idem. 1922, pp. 251-261; 587-588. Weber argued that devout Catholics could not go into trade because the "inevitabilities of economic life" were too far from the "Christian ideal." Only Catholics who were "lax in their ethical thinking" could take up a business. Indeed, beyond Weber, more recent demographic studies have also found that incomes of nations consistently vary — that Protestant countries most frequently have higher income levels than Catholic ones; whereas countries without religion tend to have lower incomes than those with a predominant religion. (On this, see G. Anthony 1988, p. 13).
13. K. Armstrong 2000, p. 67.
14. *Bible*, "Deuteronomy 23:19; see also Exodus 22: 25-27; A. Fanfani 2003, p. 30; G. DeMar 2001, vol. 2, pp. 154-156; C. Galloway2005, pp. 45-46.
15. *Bible*, Proverbs 22: 29.
16. *Bible*, Deuteronomy 18:8.
17. *Bible*,"Proverbs, Chapter 22, Verse 29. See also Chapter 13, Verse 22: "The wealth of the sinner is laid up for the righteous."
18. John Calvin quoted in R. Wallace 1961, p. 132; J. Davis 1984, p. 3.
19. *Bible*, Matthew 25:23; John Calvin quoted in A. Bieler 1959, p. 352'; J. Richardson 1966, pp. 44-46; J. Davis 1984, pp. 111-112.
20. M. Weber 1958, pp. 57, 111 ff., 117-118, 139, 154; R. Tawney 1960, pp. 108 ff., 253 Similar reflections of Calvinistic doctrine would soon appear in Richard Steele's seminal 17th century tract: *The Tradesman's Calling* – wherein industry and trade were championed as both expedient and meritorious. They will, he claimed, help the tradesman from "frequent and needless frequenting of taverns," and "pin him to his shop, where you may expect the presence and blessings of God." (Steele quoted in R. Tawney 1970, pp. 245-246.)
21. S. Kennedy 2007, pp. 128-129; M. Beliles and S. McDowell 1992, p. 48.
22. M. Weber quoted in A. Fanfani 2003, p. 66; see also M. Weber 1958, pp. 111 ff.; R. Tawney 1960, pp. 108 ff.; M. Beliles and S. McDowell 1992, p. 48. Fanfani (p. 18) also makes the expository point that "regardless of what spirit motivates a man, if he finds him-

self in a system which recognizes no rule limiting competition; he either competes or dies. His motive for competing may not be avarice; it may be mere survival; it may be quite noble, like providing a livelihood for his family. But it is the economic structure – permitting the employment of various kinds of political means – that determines how he must behave to obtain that livelihood. (On this, see M. Weber 1958, pp. 117-118.)

23. R. Tawney 1926, p. 194; M. Weber 1958, pp. 57, 139, 154.

24. R. Tawney 1960, p. 253; see also idem. 1926, p. 96, 203-204.

25. Sources cited, loc. cit.

26. J. Black 1994, p. 245.

27. J. Bovard 2000, p. 259.

28. Cato Institute 2005, pp. 9-10.

29. G. DeMar 2001, vol. 3, p. 234. There are also close parallels between the *Magna Carta* and the *Bible* regarding the requirement of both the king and the people to adhere verbatim to the law as expressed in Deuteronomy 17: 8-12; and the requirement that the law be clearly written and explained in Deuteronomy 27:8.

30. T. DiLorenzo 2004, pp. 53-54.

31. W.M. Billings 1975, p. 8.

32. T. DiLorenzo 2004, p. 54.

33. Captain John Smith quoted at www.christianlaw.org/index.php/articles/jamestown.html; G. Demar 2001, vol. 2, pp. 185, 195; J. Eidsmoe 2005, p. 68.

34. T. DiLorenzo 2004, p. 55.

35. T. DiLorenzo 2004, loc. cit.

36. M. Andrews 1949, p. 59.

37. M. Andrews 1949, p. 32.

38. T. DiLorenzo 2004, pp. 57-61.

39. T. DiLorenzo 2004, pp. 60-61.

40. L. Schweikert 2000, p. 38.

41. S. Adams 1907, vol. 4, p. 225; D. Barton 2002, p. 346.

42. T. DiLorenzo 2004, pp. 63-64.

43. C. Adams 1999, p. 305; T. DiLorenzo 2004, p. 68; M. Beliles and S. McDowell 1992, pp. 131-132.

44. *Bible*, Mark 12:17; D. Brewer 1996, pp. 33-34; G. DeMar 2001, vol. 2, pp. 113, 123.

45. See *Bible*, I Samuel 8, passim, and verses 11-18 in particular; J. Davis 1984, pp. 8-9.

46. John Milton quoted in C. Galloway 2005, p. 61.

47. See J. Eismoe 1987, pp. 51-53; D. Lutz 1988, p. 141; idem. 1984, pp. 189-197; S. McDowell and M. Beliles 1989, p. 186; D. Barton 1992, p. 201; W. Federer 2003, pp. 184-185; D. Barton 2002, pp. 213-214. Of a total of more than 15,000 representative documents analyzed, some 3,154 quotes were selected and documented. Montesquieu clearly led with 8.3 percent of the quotes, closely by Blackstone at 7.9 percent, with Locke a surprising distant third at 2.9 percent.

48. Theodore Motley quoted in C. Galloway 2005, pp. 78-80.

49. *Bible*, Proverbs 14:34; George Washington quoted in J. Richardson 1966, p. 148.

50. *Bible*, Deuteronomy 8:18; G. North 1987, pp. 64-65.

51. *Bible*, Genesis 1:28.

52. *Bible*, Isaiah 45:3.

53. *Bible*, Deuteronomy: 28: 2-14.

54. *Bible*, Genesis 2: 11-12.
55. On this, see also Bible, I Kings 20, 1-5; Strong's Concordance as related in G. North 1979, pp. 4-6; idem. 1987, pp. 80-81. Similar comparisons of cherished objects to gold and silver may be found in Psalm 119:72; Proverbs 3: 14; 8:10, 18, 19; 16:16; II Kings 12:13; Revelations 21: 18 and elsewhere in the *Bible*.
56. *Bible*, Matthew 12:28; G. DeMar 1997, vol. 1, pp. 147 ff.; J. Black 1994, p. 121.
57. *Bible*, 1 Samuel 8: 19-22; G. DeMar 1997, vol. 1. pp. 115-116.
58. *Bible,* Matthew 22:21: Mark 12: 17; G. DeMar 1997, vol. 1, p. 114.
59. J. Richardson 1966, pp. 71, 75.
60. R.J. Rashdooney 1973, p. 282; M. Beliles and D. Anderson 2005, p. 165; M. Beliles and S. McDowell 1992, pp. 212-214.
61. *Bible*, Romans 13:7; G. DeMar 2001, vol. 2, p. 131.
62. *Bible*, Deuteronomy 21: 17; idem. I Timothy 5: 3-4;G. DeMar 1997, vol. 1, pp. 29, 50; J. Davis 1984, p. 31; M. Beliles and S. McDowell 1992, pp. 214-215.
63. T. DiLorenzo 2004, pp. 70-71.
64. James Madison quoted in J. Madison et al 1988, p. 236; M. Beliles and S. McDowell 1992, loc. cit.
65. Thomas Jefferson quoted in W. Stedman 1987, p. 32; M. Beliles and S. McDowell 1992, loc. cit.
66. J. Eidsmoe 2005, p. 387.
67. M. Friedman 1993, pp. 6,11.
68. George Washington cited in J. Bovard 1999, p. 10; H. Browne 1995, p. 38.
69. John Adams quoted in J. Bovard 1999, loc. cit.
70. James Madison quoted in G. Heck 2007, p. 46.
71. Thomas Jefferson quoted in G. Heck 2007, loc. cit.
72. Thomas Jefferson quoted in J. Davis 1984, p. 53; G. Heck 2007, p. 89; C. Carson 1981, p. 346; T. Rose 1996, p. 73.
73. Thomas Jefferson quoted in J. Black 1994, p. 63.
74. Ibid.
75. C. Adams 1993, p. 192.
76. J. Makin and N. Ornstein 1994, pp. 6, 265, 284, 303; R. Samuelson 1994, p. 41.
77. On this, see L. Silk 1996, p. 38.
78. See T. Brokaw 2000, passim.
79. P. Drucker 1969, p. 198.
80. See P. Ford 1904, vol. 8, p. 481; A. Wildavsky and C. Webber 1986, p. 370; P. Peterson 1993, pp. 43, 223-224.
81. Sources cited, loc. cit.
82. Ibid.
83. *Bible,* "Proverbs," 13:22. See also Ecclesiastes 18:33: "Be not made a beggar by banqueting on borrowing;" and II Corinthians 12:14: "Children should not save up for their parents but the parents for their children."
84. T. DiLorenzo 2004, pp. 6, 63.
85. Thomas Jefferson quoted in T. DiLorenzo 2004, pp 65-69.
86. On this, see W. McDougall 2004, pp. 202 ff.; T. DiLorenzo 2004, pp. 65-69.
87. J. Eidsmoe 2005, p. 387.
88. T. DiLorenzo 2004, pp. 70-71; J. Eidsmoe 2005, loc. cit.; M. Beliles and S. McDowell 1992, pp. 212-214.

89. W. Williams 2007c, p. 9.
90. T. DiLorenzo 2004, pp. 81-82.
91. Source cited, loc. cit.
92. M. Beliles and S. McDowell 1992, pp. 189-190.
93. M. Beliles and D. Anderson 2005, pp. 128-129.
94. M. Beliles and D. Anderson 2005, p. 152.
95. James Madison quoted in M. Beliles and D. Anderson 2005, p. 153.
96. T. Norton 1950, p. 188.
97. Thomas Jefferson quoted in M. Beliles and D. Anderson 2005, p. 159.
98. M. Beliles and D. Anderson 2005, pp. 152-153.
99. *U.S. v. Butler*, 297 U.S.1 (1936); M. Beliles and D. Anderson 2005, pp. 160 ff.
100. *Bible,* Matthew 22:21: Mark 12: 17; G. DeMar 1997, vol. 1, p. 114; idem. 2001, vol. 2, p. 113.

## Chapter Six

1. Will and Ariel Durant in *The Lessons of History*, cited at www.uga.edu/ihe/ perspectives/perpect/0102.
2. H.G. Wells in *The Outline of History*, cited at www.classicreader.com/author.php/aut.
3. Franklin Roosevelt, the "Four Freedoms," cited at www.americanrhetoric.com/speeches/fdrthe fourfreedoms.html; home.att.net/-jrhsc/fdr.html.
4. Henry David Thoreau quoted in L. Peter 1977; cited at www.quotationspage.com/quotes/Henry_David_Thoreau.
5. Victor Hugo quoted in C. Galloway 2005, p. 169.
6. Cf. *State Board of Education v. Board of Education of Netcong*, 26A.2d, 21, 22 (Sup. Ct. N.J. 1970, *cert. denied*, 401 U.S. 1013.
7. Abraham Lincoln quoted in M. Beliles and S. McDowell 1992, p. 95.
8. G. DeMar 2003, p. 39.
9. M. Friedman 1962, pp. 3-4.
10. L. Thurow 1996, p. 287.
11. On this, see R. Reich 1991, pp. 264-265.
12. J.M. Keynes 1980. quoted at www.j-bradford-delong.net/Economists/keynes.html; G. Heck, 2007, p. 144.
13. Samuel Adams quoted in V. Hall 1979, p. xiv; M. Beliles and S. McDowell 1992, p. 113.
14. Samuel Adams quoted in R. Flood 1976, p. 45; M. Beliles and S. McDowell 1992, pp. 128-129.
15. D. Kupelian 2005, p. 156.
16. D. Kupelian 2005, p. 164; G. DeMar 2001, vol. 3, pp. 245-248; B.F. Morris 2007, pp. 174 ff.; *Bible*, Deuteronomy 6:5-7, as well as Ephesians 6:4: "And, ye fathers, provoke not your children to wrath; but bring them up in the nurture and admonition of the Lord."
17. *Bible*, Hosea 4:6.
18. *Bible*, Proverbs 1: 5-7.
19. *Bible*, Proverbs 22:6.

20. Quotes from G. DeMar 2001, vol. 3, pp. 245 ff. B.F. Morris 2007, pp. 171 ff.; D. Barton 2002, pp. 252 ff.
21. G. Washington 1796, pp. 22-23; B.F. Morris 2007, p. 643.
22. J. Sparks 1832, vol. 3, p. 483; D. Barton 2002, p. 153.
23. E. Beardsley 1866, pp. 141-142.
24. W. Wells 1865, vol. 3, p. 327.
25. B. Rush 1798, p. 8; A. Schmidt 1997, p. 179; D. Barton 2002, p. 153.
26. I. Cornelison 1895, pp. 243-244.
27. Thomas Jefferson quoted in W. Berns 2001, pp. 64-65; B.F. Morris 2007, pp. 96 ff.
28. James Madison quoted in W. Berns 2001, p. 79.
29. D. Barton 2002, p. 163; J.Q. Adams 1850, p. 34.
30. N. Webster 1967, "Preface," p. 12.
31. N. Webster 1832, p. 339; idem. 1967, p. 22; D. Barton 1992, pp. 126-127; M. Beliles and S. McDowell 1992, p. 106.
32. Benjamin Franklin quoted in M. Beliles and S. McDowell 1992, p. 93.
33. F. Ames 1809, p. 434; B.F. Morris 2007, pp. 176-177.
34. B. Rush 1798, p. 112.
35. W. McGuffey 1848, "Preface," p. 5; W. Berns 2001, p. 68; W. Federer 2004, pp. 39-40.
36. *Bible*. Hosea 4:6.
37. State of Connecticut 1822, pp. 90-92, quoted in D. Barton 2002, p. 80; H.G. Good 1956, p. 41; J. Eidsmoe 2005, p. 28; C. Galloway 2005, pp. 150-151; M. Beliles and S. McDowell 1992, p. 104.
38. E. Kendall 1809, vol. 1, pp. 270-271; D. Barton 2002, p. 81; C. Galloway 2005, pp. 154 ff.
39. C. Galloway 2005, pp. 147-148.
40. H.G. Good 1956, pp. 3, 10, 13.
41. H.G. Good 1956, p. 31; G. DeMar 2003, p. 40.
42. W. Federer 2003, p. 26; J. Eidsmoe 2005, p. 28; M. Beliles and S. McDowell 1992, pp. 105-107.
43. Sources cited, loc. cit.
44. W. Channing 1879, lesson 93, pp. 284-286; W. Federer 2004, p. 41; W. Berns 2001, p. 68; M. Beliles and S. McDowell 1992, p. 108; G. DeMar 2003, p. 81.
45. *The Charter and Statutes of the College of William and Mary in Virginia, 1736*, p. 3, cited in R. Walton 1984, p. 356; D. Barton 2002, p. 82; D. Brewer 1996, p. 18; G. DeMar 1995, p. 98.
46. C. Galloway 2005, p.164; G. DeMar 2003, p. 42.
47. C. Galloway 2005, p. 167.
48. B. Pierce 1883, "Appendix, " p. 5; *The Laws of Harvard College, 1790*, pp. 7-8, cited in P. Mode 1921, pp. 74-75; D. Barton 2002, p. 81; G. DeMar 1995, pp. 102-103; idem. 1997, vol. 3, p. 273; idem. 2003, pp. 43-44; idem. 2007, pp. 75-76; D. Kupelian 2005, p. 156; C.L. Thompson n.d., pp. 136-137, 145; C. Galloway 2005, pp. 157-158; M. Beliles and S. McDowell 1992, pp. 109-110; B.F. Morris 2007, pp. 98 -100. A century and a half later, the rules had changed little, with *The Laws of Harvard College, 1790* reading :

> All persons of whatever degree forever residing at the College, and all undergraduates . . . shall constantly and seasonably attend the worship of God in the chapel, morning and evening. . . . All the scholars shall at sunset in the evening

preceding the Lord's Day lay aside all their diversions and ... it is enjoined upon every scholar carefully to apply himself to the duties of religion on said day.

49. C. Galloway 2005, p. 166.

50. J. Eidsmoe 2005, p. 261,

51. P. Mode 1921, p. 109; D. Barton 1992, p. 91; C. Galloway 2005, pp. 161-163; M. Beliles and S. McDowell 1992, p. 111; B.F. Morris 2007, pp. 100 ff.; G. DeMar 2003, p. 45-46.

52. W. Ringenberg 2006, p. 38; F. Dexter 1916, p. 27; A. Goldman 1991, p. 17; H.G. Good 1956, p. 61; G. DeMar 1995, pp. 98-99, 103-107; D. Barton 2002, p. 82.

53. *The Laws of the College of New Jersey, 1794,* pp. 28-29, cited in D. Barton 2002, p. 83; M. Beliles and S. McDowell 1992, p. 111.

54. J. Eidsmoe 2005, p. 83; C. Galloway 2005, p. 158; M. Beliles and S. McDowell 1992, p. 119; B.F. Morris 2007, pp. 152 ff. For the first century of its existence, three-sevenths of all Harvard graduates likewise became ministers.

55. Columbia University 1785, pp. 5-8; W. Federer 2003, p. 114; D. Barton 2002, p. 84; G. DeMar 1995, pp. 106-107; idem. 2003, pp. 46-47; idem. 2007, pp. 24-25; J. Eidsmoe 2005, p. 22; F. Monaghan 1972, p. 26; C. Galloway 2005, pp. 163-164.

56. F. Monaghan 1972, p. 26; J. Eidsmoe 2005, p. 165.

57. J. Black 2004, pp. xiii-xiv.

58. College of William and Mary 1736, p. 3; T. Jefferson 1884, vol. 15, p. 156; D. Barton 2002, p. 82; G. DeMar 1995, pp. 107-108; idem. 2003, p. 47; C. Galloway 2005, pp. 158-161.

59. Rutgers University 1965, p. 2; D. Barton 2002, p. 84; M. Beliles and S. McDowell 1992, loc. cit.

60. S. McDowell and M. Beliles 1989, p. 109; D. Holmes 2006, pp. 15-16; D. Barton 2002, pp. 84-85; E.P. Cubberly 1919, p. 204.

61. G. DeMar 1995, pp. 106-107; J. Black 2004, pp. xiii-xiv.

62. H.G. Good 1956, p. 87.

63. G. Washington 1932, vol. 15, p. 55; D. Barton 2002, p. 85.

64. Sources cited, loc. cit.

65. John Adams quoted in C. Thomas 2007b, p. 28.

66. Washington, Jay, and Madison all quoted in H.G. Good 1956, pp. 91-93. Benjamin Rush, a primary signer of the U.S. *Declaration of Independence*, would similarly observe:

> To conform the principles, morals, and manners of our citizens to our republican forms of government, it is absolutely necessary that knowledge of every kind should be disseminated throughout every part of the United States.

67. O. Guinness 1993, p. 228.

68. John Adams quoted in E. Sandoz 1984, p. 67.

69. M. Malbin 1978, pp. 14-15; G. DeMar 1995, pp. 154-155; E. Gaustad 1993, pp. 116-117; D. Barton 2002, p. 41; A. Schmidt 1997, p. 175. On Continental Congress deliberations leading to enacting of the Northwest Ordinance, see E. Gaustad 1993, pp. 151-156.

70. D. Barton 2002, pp. 41-42.

71. E. Gaustad 1993, p. 116.

72. O. Guinness 1993, p. 228.

73. S. Steinberg 1981, p. 54; S. Huntington 2004b, p. 134; S. Renson 2005, p. 57; W. Berns 2001, passim.

74. Ronald Reagan quoted in J. Black 2004, p. 13.
75. J. Black 1994, pp. 76-77.
76. J. Black 2004, p. 108.
77. Ibid.
78. J. Black 2004, p.103.
79. Cf. C. Iserbyt 1999, passim; J. Black 2004, pp. xiv, 83ff.
80. Charlotte Iserbyt quoted in J. Black 2004, p. 86.
81. Theodore Sizer quoted in J. Black 2004, p. 88.
82. J. Dewey 1997, pp. 77-80; P. Schafly 1995, p. 33. This is the same NEA, it must be borne in mind, that promoted in Fairfax, Virginia the merits of homosexual lifestyle and has a "Gay and Lesbian Caucus" defining its agenda. Among resolutions passed at its annual conventions have been calls that homosexuality be incorporated into K-12 sex education, that school prayers be banned, and that preschools establish "diversity" programs.
83. Catherine Barrett quoted in C. Iserbyt, 1999, see entire work, passim.
84. Charles Pierce quoted in G. DeMar 2001, vol. 3, p. 248; J. Black 2004, p. 50.
85. H. Browne 1995, pp. 112-113; J. Black 2004, pp. 86-88; P. Buchanan 2002, pp. 57 ff.
86. R. Bork 2003, pp. 300-302.
87. R. Bork 2003, pp. 302-303.
88. Ibid.
89. National Center for History in the Schools 1994, p. 47; R. Bork 2003, pp. 254-255.
90. L. Cheney 1994, p. A-22; R. Bork 2003, p. 255.
91. R. Bork 2003, loc. cit.
92. R. Bork 2003, p. 259.
93. J. Black 2004, p. 163.
94. J. Black 2004, pp. 105-106.
95. T. Sowell. March 2003, p. 1.
96. J. Black 2004, pp. 106, 123.
97. James Coleman quoted in J. Davis 1984, p. 35.
98. On this, see L. Dobbs. September 15, 2003, p. 40; U.S. Department of Education 1983, pp.1 ff.; J. Bovard 1999, p. 132.
99. Sources cited, loc. cit.
100. U.S. Department of Education, September 1990, pp. 1 ff.
101. M. Friedman 1993, p. 2.
102. PISA educational statistics cited in W. Williams 2007, p. 15.
103. R. Bernstein 1994, pp. 198-199.
104. J. Martinez. August 15, 2007, p. 1.
105. J. Eidsmoe 2005, p. 380.
106. J. Eidsmoe 2005, p. 381.
107. C.Thomas. July 14, 2004, p. 10.
108. *Human Events*, 2006, p. 3; P. Buchanan 2006, p. 40.
109. W. Williams December 26, 2002, p. 1.
110. See T. Sowell 1994, p. 21; L. Perelman 1990, passim; T. Geier 1994, p. 17.
111. G. Trowbridge and M. Hornbeck 2007, p. 1.
112. State Exhibit 1989, passim.
113. Ibid.
114. A. Carnevale 1998, p. 129.

115. M. Whitman 1998, p. 183; R. Mundell 1998, p. 197; L. Dobbs 2006, p. 158.
116. M. Whitman 1998, p. 139.
117. L. Dobbs 2006, p. 161.
118. L. Dobbs 2006, p. 158.
119. Ibid.
120. L. Dobbs 2006, pp. 158-159.
121. L. Dobbs 2006, p. 171.
122. L. Dobbs 2006, p. 157.
123. Albert Shanker quoted in W. Bennett 1994, p. 89; L. Dobbs 2006, p. 167.
124. Thomas Jefferson quoted in W. Williams, December 10, 2008, p. 21.

## Epilogue

1. Ralph Waldo Emerson quoted in J. Richardson 1966, p. 169.
2. Justice Rehnquist writing in *Wallace v. Jeffrey*, 472 U.S. 38, 113 (1985); *Lemon v. Kurtzman*, 403 U.S. 602, 612 (1971); D. Barton 2002, pp. 41- 43, 440; D. Dreisbach 2002, p. 124.
3. Aristotle 1984, vol. 2, pp. 2334-2335.
4. D. Dreisbach 2002, p. 2, 113-114.
5. Robert Frost quoted at www.americanpoems.com/poets/robertfrost/12057.
6. Justice Black in *Wallace v. Jeffrey*, 472 U.S. (1985), quoted in D. Dreisbach 2002, pp. 7, 102-103, 128. See also Justice Black in *McCollum v. Board of Education* (1948) and *Engle v. Vitale* (1962).
7. Justice Frankfurter concurring in *Tiller v. Atlantic Coast Railroad Co.*, 318 U.S. 54, 68 (1943); D. Dreisbach 2002, pp. 115–116 128, 242.
8. Justice Stanley Reed in *McCollum v. Board of Education*, 333 U.S. 247 (1948); D. Dreisbach 2002, p. 104.
9. Justice Holmes quoted in *Hyde v. United States*, 225 U.S. 347, 391 (1912); D. Dreisbach 2002, p. 106.
10. D. Dreisbach 2002, p. 105.
11. W. Miller 1985, p. 340.
12. J. Farah."Hannibal is Inside the Gates," May 11, 2004, at World NetDaily.com.
13. Lord Thomas Macauley quoted in J. Black 1994, p. 246.
14. J. Farah 2004, loc. cit.
15. Daniel Webster quoted at quotes.liberty-tree.com/quotes_by/daniel+webster.
16. J. Farah 2004, loc. cit.
17. G. Washington quoted by J. Fitzpatrick 1931-1944, vol. 35, p. 416; D. Barton 2002, p. 324; F. Church 2007, pp. 103-104.
18. Franklin Roosevelt quoted in M. Gerson 2007, pp. 11, 100.
19. Howard Dean quoted in M. Gerson 2007, p. 12.
20. William Jennings Bryan quoted in M. Gerson 2007, loc cit.
21. Bible, Jeremiah 9:23-24, the Prophet Jeremiah as related in J. Black 1994, p. 249.
22. Bible, Ezekiel 389: 21, the Prophet Ezekiel as related in J. Black 1994, loc. cit.
23. C. Galloway 2005, pp. 3-5, 20.

24. J. Lukacs 1993, pp. 272 ff.; J. Black 1994, p. 259.
25. D. Halberstam 1992, p. 16; J. Black 1994, p. 260.
26. J. Black 1994, p. 247.
27. Samuel Huntington quoted in A. Lieven 2004, p. 124.
28. Rousseau quoted in C. Galloway 2005, p. 10.
29. R. Bork 2003, pp. 3-4.
30. T. DiLorenzo 2004, p. 179.
31. Ronald Reagan quoted at www.govtrack.us/congress/record.xpd?id=110s20080521-15& person 400272; L. Kudlow 2007, p. 2.
32. T. Jeffrey, July 30, 2008, p. 26; Tax Foundation 2008, p. 1; G. Heck 2007, p. 50; H. Browne 1995, pp. 2-4, 51-52. This 47 percent represents a combination of federal, state, local, and FICA taxes, both personal and corporate, capitalized into price. The FICA tax alone has risen from a combined 2 percent employee rate in 1935 to 15.35 percent today.
33. Sources cited. loc. cit.
34. John Grigg cited in J. Green 1982, p. 83.
35. J. Madison cited in C. Adams 1993, pp. 365 ff., 465; 28; T. DiLorenzo 2004, pp. 81-82.
35. Thomas Jefferson quoted in G. Heck 2007, loc. cit.
37. Thomas Paine. *Common Sense* (1776), as quoted in C. Adams 1993, pp. 276 (cited), 448.
38. Montesquieu, *Spirit of Laws*, vol. 1, ch. 8, quoted in C. Adams 1993, pp. 474, 476.
39. Voltaire quoted in T. Rose 1996, p. 85.
40. J. Madison quoted in C. Adams 1993, p. 365.
41. George Bernard Shaw quoted at www.quotatio.com/s/shaw-george-bernard-quotes.html.
42. J. Black 1994, p. 122.
43. Timothy Dwight quoted in E. Tuveson 1968, p. 105.
44. J. Strong 1893, p. 354.
45. Herman Melville quoted in E. Tuveson 1968, pp. 156-157.
46. J. Meacham 2009, p. 4.
47. J. Black 1994, pp. 250-251.

## Appendix A

1. John Stuart Mill quoted in G. Himmelfarb 1974, pp. 46-47.
2. John Winthrop quoted in R. Bellah 1975, p. 14.
3. R. Palmer 1964, vol. 1, p. 223.
4. John Adams quoted in E. Tuveson 1968, pp. 20-21, 102.
5. A. Schlesinger 1998, p. 142; P. Buchanan 2002, p. 145.
6. G. DeMar 2003, p. 8.
7. C. Prestowitz 2005, pp. 256-257.
8. Ronald Reagan quoted at www.heritage.org/Research/GovernmentReform/hl988.cfm.
9. C. Edwards February 2, 2004, p. 2.
10. On this, see D. Osbourne and C. T. Gaebler 1993, pp. 215 ff.

11. Congressional Budget Office 2008, pp. 1 ff.
12. Alan Greenspan quoted in N. Gingrich 2008, p. 139.
13. R. Rahn. July 11, 2004, p. 1.
14. P. Merrill 2004, p. 2; J. Leonard, pp. 1, 2, 22.
15. D. D'Souza 1991, p. 249.
16. D. D'Souza 1991, p. 250.
17. C. Prestowitz 2005, p. 133.
18. Ibid.
19. E. Kendall 1809, vol. 1, pp. 270-271; D. Barton 2002, p. 81.
20. A. Schlesinger 1998, p. 146.
21. L. Dobbs 2006, p. 168.

# Appendix B

1. Cf. E. Wolfe 2003, p. 1; B. Stein and P. DeMuth 2008, p. 147.
2. Sources cited, loc. cit.
3. See J. Schumpeter 1950 pp. 82 ff.
4. Cf. P. Schiff 2007, Chapter 6, passim.
5. P. Schiff 2007, pp. 118 ff.
6. P. Schiff 2007, p. 119.
7. P. Schiff 2007, pp. 126 ff.
8. P. Schiff 2007, p. 121.
9. P. Schiff 2007, pp. 124-126.
10. H. Browne 1995, p. 47.
11. T. DiLorenzo 2007, p. 179.
12. Ronald Reagan quoted in L. Kudlow 2007, p. 2.
13. T. Jones 2008, p. 1. Three years ago, Senator John McCain of Arizona similarly sought to regulatorily rein in such real estate mortgage market excess but again to no avail.
14. Ibid.
15. Loc. cit.
16. W. Wolman 1997, p. 186.
17. W. Wolman 1997, p. 142.
18. W. Wolman 1997, pp. 143, 186.
19. W. Wolman 1997, pp. 142, 143, 186.
20. J. Bradley 2006, pp. 281-295; A. Zolberg 2006, pp. 435-436.

# BIBLIOGRAPHY

Adams, C. *For Good and Evil: the Impact of Taxes on the Course of Civilization* (New York: 1993/1999)
Adams, J. *The Works of John Adams*, C. Adams ed., 10 vols. (Boston: 1850/1865)
—— *Diary and Autobiography of John Adams*, L. Butterfield ed. (Cambridge: 1961-1962)
—— *A Defense of the Constitutions of Government of the United States of America* (New York: 1971)
Adams, J.Q. *Address Delivered at the Request of the Committee of Arrangements for Celebrating the Anniversary of Independence at the City of Washington on the Fourth of July, 1821, Upon the Occasion of Reading the Declaration of Independence* (Cambridge: 1821)
—— *An Oration Delivered Before the Inhabitants of the Town of Newburyport at their Request on the Sixty-First Anniversary of the Declaration of Independence* (Newburyport: 1837)
—— *Letters of John Quincy Adams to His Son on the Bible and Its Teachings* (Auburn: 1850)
—— *Memoirs of John Quincy Adams* (Philadelphia: 1874)
Adams, M. *America Is Too Young to Die* (New York: 1976)
Adams, S. *The Writings of Samuel Adams*, H. Cushing ed. (New York: 1907/1968)
Addison, J. "A Letter from Italy to the Right Honorable Charles Lord Halifax in the Year MDCCI," in *A Collection of English Poems, 1660-1800*, R. Crane ed. (New York: 1932)
Adler, M. "The Mayflower Compact," in *Annals of America* (Chicago: 1968), vol.1
Ahlstrom, S. *A Religious History of the American People* (New Haven: 1972)
Ames, F. *Works of Fisher Ames* (Boston: 1809)
Amos, G. *Defending the Declaration: How the Bible and Christianity Influenced the Writing of the Declaration of Independence* (Charlottesville: 1989)
Andrews, M. *Virginia: the Old Dominion* (Richmond: 1949)
Anthony, G. *Biblical Economics* (Charlottesville VA: 1988)
Aristotle. *The Complete Works of Aristotle*, J. Barnes ed. (Princeton: 1984)
Armstrong, K. *A History of God* (New York: 1993)
—— *The Battle for God: a History of Fundamentalism* (New York: 2000)
Bailyn, B. *The Ideological Origins of the American Revolution* (Cambridge: 1982)
Bancroft, G. *History of the Colonization of the United States* (Boston: 1837 et seq.), vols.1-6
Barbarisi, D. "After Last Year's Flap, City Hall's 2004 Display is Decidedly Tamer," *Providence Journal* (Providence: December 14: 2004)

Barton, D. *The Myth of Separation* (Aledo TX: 1992)
────── *The Foundations of American Government* (Aledo TX: 2000)
────── *Original Intent: the Courts the Constitution, and Religion*. (Aledo TX: 2002)
────── *Separation of Church and State: What the Founders Meant* (Aledo TX: 2007)
Beardsley, E. *Life and Times of William Samuel Johnson* (Boston: 1886)
Beliles M. and Anderson D. *Contending for the Constitution: Recalling the Christian Influence on the Writing of the Constitution and the Biblical Basis of American Law and Liberty* (Charlottesville: 2005)
Beliles M. and McDowell, A. *America's Providential History* (Charlottesville: 1992)
Bellah, R. *The Broken Covenant* (Chicago: 1975).
Bennett, W. *Index of Leading Cultural Indicators* (New York: 1994)
────── *America; the Last Best Hope* (Nashville: 2006)
Berman, M. *The Twilight of American Culture* (New York: 2000)
────── *Dark Ages America*. (New York: 2006)
Berns, W. *Making Patriots* (Chicago: 2001)
Bernstein, R. *Dictatorship of Virtue: Multiculturalism and the Battle for America's Future* (New York: 1994)
*Bible*, "King James" version (U.S.A: 1975)
Bieler, A. *La Pensée Éonomique et Sociale de Calvin* (Geneva:1959)
Billings, W.M. ed. "George Percy's Account of the Voyage to Virginia and the Colony's First Days," in *The Old Dominion in the Seventeenth Century: A Documentary History of Virginia, 1606-1689* (Chapel Hill NC: 1975)
Black, J. *When Nations Die* (Wheaton IL: 1994)
────── *Freefall of the American University* (Nashville: 2004)
Blackstone, W. *Commentaries on the Law of England* (Philadelphia: 1771)
Blankley, T. *The West's Last Chance* (Washington: 2005)
────── "Where is the Heir Apparent to Ronald Reagan?" *Conservative Chronicle*, Washington: September 26, 2007
Bloom, A. *The Closing of the American Mind* (New York: 1987)
────── "The Democratization of the University," in *Giants and Dwarfs: Essays 1960-1990* (New York: 1990)
Boller, P. *George Washington and Religion* (Dallas: 1963)
Boorstin, D. *The Lost World of Thomas Jefferson* (New York: 1948)
Borden, M. *Jews, Turks, and Infidels* (Chapel Hill NC: 1984)
Bork, R. *The Tempting of America: the Political Seduction of the Law* (New York: 1989)
────── *Slouching Toward Gomorrah* (New York: 2003)
────── "Introduction," in R. Bork ed. *A Country I Do Not Recognize* (Stanford: 2005)
Boutell, L. *The Life of Roger Sherman* (Chicago: 1896)
Bovard, J. *The Fair Trade Fraud* (New York: 1991)
────── *Freedom in Chains* (New York: 1999)

―――― *Lost Rights: the Destruction of American Liberty* (New York: 2000)
―――― *Attention Deficit Democracy* (New York: 2005)
Bradford, M.E. *A Worthy Company: Brief Lives of the Framers of the Constitution* (New Hampshire: 1982)
Bradley, J. *Flags of Our Fathers* (New York: 2006)
Brewer, D. *The United States: a Christian Nation* (Philadelphia: 1905/ Smyrna GA: 1996)
Brimelow, P. *Alien Nation.* (New York: 1995)
―――― Milton Friedman, Soothsayer," *Hoover Digest*, 1998, vol. 2 at www.hoover.stanford.edu/publications/digest/982/friedman3.html
―――― "In Memoriam: Ronald W. Reagan," *VDARE*, June 5, 2004@www.vdare.com.
Brokaw, T. *The Greatest Generation* (New York: 2000)
Brookhiser, R. *The Way of the Wasp* (New York: 1991)
Browne, H. *Why Government Doesn't Work* (New York: 1995)
Brydon, G. *Virginia's Mother Church and the Conditions Under Which It Grew*, (Richmond: 1947-1952)
Buchanan, P. *The Death of the West* (New York: 2002)
―――― *State of Emergency: the Third World Invasion and Conquest of America* (New York: 2006)
――――. "America Is Now An Auto Graveyard," *Conservative Chronicle*, February 28, 2007
――――. "Free Trade and Funny Math," *Conservative Chronicle*, March 7, 2007
―――― "Katrina Nation," *Conservative Chronicle*, Washington: March 12, 2008
Burke, E. "Speech on Moving Resolutions for Conciliation with the Colonies," in R. Hoffman and P. Levack, eds. *Burke's Politics* (New York: 1949)
―――― *Speeches and Letters on American Affairs* (New York: 1961)
―――― *Reflections on the Revolution in France* (New York: 1967)
―――― *The Correspondence of Edmund Burke* (Chicago: 1969)
Butler, J. *Awash in a Sea of Faith* (Cambridge: 1990)
Campbell, C. "Our Semi-Pagan Forebears," *Atlantic Constitution*, June 19, 1994
Campbell, N. *Patrick Henry: Patriot and Statesman* (Old Greenwich CN: 1975)
Carnevale, A. "Investing in Education and Training for Higher Growth," in J. Jasinowski ed. *The Rising Tide* (New York: 1998)
Carson, C. "Economy in Government," *The Freeman*, June, 1981
Carter, S. *The Culture of Disbelief: How American Law and Politics Trivialize Religious Devotion* (New York: 1993)
Cato Institute. *Cato Handbook on Policy* (Washington: 2005)
Channing, W. "Religion: the Only Basis of Society," in W. McGuffey. *McGuffey's Fifth Eclectic Reader* (New York: 1879)
Chavez, L. "Aztec Idols, Yes; Mary and Jesus, No," *USA Today*, December 7, 1994
Cheney, L. "The End of History," *Wall Street Journal*, October 20, 1994
Church, F. *So Help Me God: The Founding Fathers and the First Great Battle Over Church and State* (New York: 2007)
Churchill, W. "The Iron Curtain Speech: 1946," National Center for Public Policy

Research at www.nationalcenter.org/ChurchillIronCurtain.html
Cicero. *Cicero in Twenty-Eight Volumes*, G.P. Gould ed. (Cambridge/London: 1977)
Clarkson, T. *Memoirs of the Private and Public Life of William Penn* (London: 1813)
Clough, S.B. *The Rise and Fall of Civilization* (Westport: 1951)
Coker, F. ed. *Democracy. Liberty, and Property: Readings in the American Political Tradition* (New York: 1942)
Collier, P. and Horowitz, D. *Destructive Generation: Second Thoughts About the '60s* (New York: 1996)
College of William and Mary. *The Charter and Statutes of the College of William and Mary in Virginia* (Williamsburg VA: 1736)
Columbus, C. *Christopher Columbus's Book of Prophecies: Reproduction of the Original Manuscript with English Translation*, K. Brigham tr. (Ft. Lauderdale: 1991)
Commager, H. *Documents of American History* (New York: 1958)
Congressional Budget Office (*Preliminary Analysis of the President's Budget Request Proposal* (Washington: March 3:2008)
Conquest, R. "Liberals and Totalitarianism," in Kramer H. and Kimball R. *The Betrayal of Liberalism: How the Disciples of Freedom and Equality Helped Foster the Illiberal Politics of Coercion and Control* (Chicago: 1999)
*Constitutions of the Several States Composing the Union* (Boston: 1785)
*Constitutions of the United States of America with the Latest Amendments* (Trenton: 1813)
Coolidge, C. *Foundations of the Republic - Speeches and Addresses* (New York: 1926)
Coper, D. *The Death of the Family* (New York: 1970)
Cord, R. *Separation of Church and State: Historical Fact and Current Fiction* (Grand Rapids: 1988)
Cornelison, I. *The Relation of Religion to Civil Government in the United States of America* (New York: 1895/1970)
Corwin, E. *The Constitution and What It Means Today* (Princeton: 1937)
——— "Curbing the Court," *The Annals of the National Academy of Political and Social Science*, vol. 185, May, 1936
Coulter, A. *Godless: the Church of Liberalism* (New York: 2006)
——— *Slander* (New York: 2002)
——— "Barack Obama: Lucifer is My Homeboy," *Conservative Chronicle*, Washington: October 1, 2008
Cubberly, E.P. *Public Education in the United States* (Boston; 1919)
Cunningham, N. *In Pursuit of Reason: the Life of Thomas Jefferson* (Baton Rouge: 1987)
Daniel-Rops, H. *Daily Life in the Time of Jesus* (New York: 1962)
Danelski, D. and Tulchin, J. eds. *The Autobiographical Notes of Charles Evans Hughes* (Cambridge: 1973)
Dartmouth College. *The Charter of Dartmouth College* (Dresden: 1779)

Davis, J. *Your Wealth in God's Hands* (Phillipsburg NJ: 1984)
Davis, R. "Al–Gor(e)ing Blacks Again," National Center for Public Policy Research, October, 1999 at www.nationalcenter.org/P21NVDavisVote1099.html
Dawson, H. ed. *The Federalist* (New York: 1890)
Dawson, S. *God's Providence in American History* (Rancho Cordova CA: 1988)
DeMar, G. *America's Christian History: the Untold Story* (Atlanta: 1995)
——— *God and Government,* 3 vols. (Atlanta: vol 1: 1997; vols. 2 and 3: 2001)
——— *America's Christian Heritage* (Nashville: 2003)
Derekhshani, T. "At God's Funeral, Biographer Describes 'Killers' of the Deity," *Arizona Republic*, August 29, 1999
Dexter, F. ed. *The Literary Diary of Ezra Stiles* (New York: 1901)
Dewey, J. "My Pedagogic Creed," *The School Journal*, vol. 54, no. 3, January 16, 1997
DiBacco. T. "Simple Creed Sums Up Basics," *Washington Times*, October 1, 2001
Dickinson, J. *The Political Writings of John Dickinson* (Wilmington: 1801)
DiLorenzo, T. *How Capitalism Saved America* (New York: 2004)
Dobbs, L. "Still Failing the Grade," *U.S. News and World Report*, September 15, 2003
——— *War On the Middle Class* (Washington: 2006)
Dorchester, D. *Christianity in America* (New York: 1888)
Dornan, R. and Vedlic, C. *Judicial Supremacy: The Supreme Court on Trial* (Massachusetts: 1986)
Dreisbach, D. *Real Threat and Mere Shadow: Religious Liberty and the First Amendment* (Westchester IL: 1987)
——— *Thomas Jefferson and the Wall of Separation Between Church and State* (New York: 2002)
Drucker, P. *The New Society* (New York: 1949)
——— *The Age of Discontinuity* (London: 1969)
——— *The New Realities* (New York: 1989)
D'Souza, D. *Illiberal Education: the Politics of Race and Sex on Campus* (New York: 1991)
——— *The End of Racism: Principles for a Multiracial Society* (New York: 1995)
Ducat, C. and Chase, W. *Constitutional Interpretation* (St. Paul: 1983)
Eastland, T. "A Court Tilting Against Religious Liberty," in R. Bork ed. *A Country I Do Not Recognize* (Stanford: 2005)
Edwards, C. "The Era of Big Government," *Cato Institute*, Washington: February 2, 2004
——— "Downsizing the Federal Government," *Cato Institute*, Washington: June 2, 2004
Eidsmoe, J. *Christianity and the Constitution* (Grand Rapids: 1987/2005)
Elliot, J. ed. *The Debates in Several State Conventions on the Adoption of the Federal Constitution* (Washington: 1836)
Fallows, J. *Breaking the News: How the Media Undermine Democracy* (New York: 1997)
Fanfani, A. *Catholicism, Protestantism, and Capitalism* (Norfolk: 2003)

*The Federalist Papers* (New York: 1982)

Federer, W. *America's God and Country Encyclopedia of Quotations* (St. Louis: 1994)

────── *The Ten Commandments and their Influence on American Law* (St. Louis: 2003)

────── *3 Secular Reasons Why America Should Be Under God*. (St. Louis: 2004)

────── *Backfired* (St. Louis:2005)

Ferguson, N. *The Rise and Demise of the British World Order and the Lessons for Global Power* (New York: 2003)

Fitzpatrick, J. ed. *The Writings of Washington* (Washington: 1932)

Flood, R. *Men Who Shaped America* (Chicago: 1976)

Foner, P. ed. "Thomas Paine. 'The American Crisis,'" in *The Complete Writings of Thomas Paine* (New York: 1945)

Fopp, R. "Herbert Marcuse. 'Repressive Tolerance' and His Critics," Borderland E-Mail Journal," vol.6, no. 1, at www.borderlands.net.au/vol6no1_ 2007/fopp_marcuse.htm

Ford, P. ed. *The Writings of Thomas Jefferson*, 10 vols. (New York: 1892)

Foster, M. and Swanson, M. *The American Covenant* (Plymouth: 1992)

Fox, J. and Sandler, S. *Bringing Religion Into International Relations* (New York: 2004)

Franklin, B. The Works of Benjamin Franklin, J. Sparks ed. (Boston: 1840)

────── *The Writings of Benjamin Franklin*, A.H. Smith ed. (New York (1905-1907)

────── *Autobiography* (Garden City NY: 1916)

────── *Maxims and Morals of Benjamin Franklin*, W. Pfaff ed. (New Orleans: 1927)

────── *Franklin's Autobiographical Writings*, C. Van Doren ed. (New York: 1945)

Freeman, C. *The Closing of the Western Mind* (New York: 2002)

Friedman, M. *Capitalism and Freedom* (Chicago: 1962)

──────"Fiscal Responsibility, *Newsweek,* August 7, 1967

────── "The Limitations of Tax Limitation," *Policy Review*, Summer, 1978

────── *Why Government Is The Problem* (Stanford: 1993)

Frost, R. *Collected Poems of Robert Frost* (New York: 1930)

Fournier, K. *In Defense of Liberty* (Virginia Beach: 1993)

Frothingham, R. *Rise of the Republic of the United States* (Boston: 1872)

Fukuyama, F. *The End of History and the Last Man* (New York: 2006)

──────. *Ameriea at the Crossroads* (New Haven: 2007)

Galloway, C. *Christianity and the American Commonwealth* (Powders Springs GA 2005)

Gaustad, E. *Neither King nor Prelate: Religion and the New Nation: 1776-1826* (Grand Rapids: 1993)

Geier, T. "World Math Champs: U.S. Teens," *U.S. News and World Report*, August 1, 1994

Gerson, M. *Heroic Conservatism* (New York: 2007)

Gibson, J. *The War on Christmas* (New York: 2005)
Gingrich, N. *Rediscovering God in America: Reflections on the Role of Faith in Our Nation's History and Future* (Nashville: 2006a)
────── *Winning the Future* (Washington: 2006b)
────── *Real Change: From the World that Fails to the World that Works* (Washington: 2008)
Goldberg, B. "Networks Need a Reality Check," *Wall Street Journal,* February 13, 1996
────── *Bias: a CBS Insider Exposes How the Media Distort the News* (Washington: 2002)
────── *Arrogance: Rescuing America from the Media Elite* (New York: 2003)
────── *100 People Who Are Screwing Up America.* (New York: 2005)
Goldman, A. *The Search for God at Harvard* (New York: 1991)
Good, H.G. *A History of American Education* (New York: 1956)
Graglia, L. "Judicial Review on the Basis of 'Regime Principles': a Prescription for Government by Judges," *South Texas Law Journal* (1985), vol. 6, no. 3
────── "It's Not Constitutionalism, It's Judicial Activism," *Harvard Journal of Law and Public Policy*, Winter, 1996
────── "Constitutional Law without the Constitution: the Supreme Court's Remaking of America," in R. Bork ed. *A Country I Do Not Recognize* (Stanford: 2005)
Gross, P. and Levitt, N. *Higher Superstition: the Academic Left and Its Quarrels with Science* (Baltimore: 1994)
Green, J. *The Book of Political Quotations* (London: 1982)
Guinness, O. *The Death of Dust (*Downers Grove, IL: 1979)
────── *The American Hour* (New York: 1993)
────── *The Great Experiment: Faith and Freedom in America* (Colorado Springs: 2001)
Hall, T. *The Religious Background of American Culture* (Boston: 1930)
Hall, V. *The Christian History of the United States of America* (San Francisco: 1960/1979)
────── *The Christian History of the American Revolution* (New York: 1976)
Halley, H. *Halley's Bible Handbook* (Grand Rapids; 1965)
Halberstam, D. *The Next Century* (New York: 1992)
Hamburger, P. *Separation of Church and State* (Cambridge: 2002)
Hamilton, A. *Selected Writings and Speeches of Alexander Hamilton*, M. Frisch ed. (Washington: 1985)
Hanson, V. "Bomb Texas," *Commentary*. January 16, 2003a
────── *Mexifornia*. New York: 2003b\2007
────── "Brace Yourself," *National Review Online*, at www.nationalreview.com/script/printpage.p?ref=hanson/hanson200409022149.asp, September 2, 2004
Haraszti, Z. *John Adams and the Prophets of Progress* (Cambridge: 1952)
Harrington, A. "The New Anti-Civilization," *Chronicles*, June 2001
Hatch, N. *The Democratization of American Christianity* (New Haven: 1989)
Hazard, E. ed. *Historical Collections: Consisting of State Papers and other Authen-*

tic Documents: Intended as Materials for An History of the United States of America (Philadelphia: 1792)
Heck, G. *Building Prosperity: Why Ronald Reagan and the Founding Fathers Were Right on the Economy* (Lanham: 2007a)
—— *When Worlds Collide* (Lanham: 2007b)
—— *The Eclipse of the American Century* (Lanham: 2008)
Hill, J. *Abraham Lincoln: Man of God* (New York: 1920)
Himmelfarb, G. *On Liberty and Liberalism: the Case of John Stuart Mill* (New York: 1974)
Holmes, D. *The Faiths of the Founding Fathers* (Oxford: 2006)
Howe, J. *The Changing Political Thought of John Adams* (Princeton: 1966)
Hudson, W. ed. *Nationalism and Religion in America* (New York: 1970)
*Human Events.* "$16,344 per Student, But Only 12 Percent Read Proficiently," March 20, 2006
Huntington, S. *American Politics: the Promise of Disharmony* (Cambridge MA, 1961)
—— "The Clash of Civilizations, *Foreign Affairs*, Summer 1993, vol. 72, no. 3
—— "The Erosion of American National Affairs," *Foreign Affairs*, vol. 76, no. 5, September- October, 1997
—— *The Clash of Civilizations and Remaking of the World Order* (New York: 2003)
—— "The Hispanic Challenge," *Foreign Policy,* March-April, 2004a
—— *Who Are We? The Challenges to America's National Identity* (New York: 2004-b)
—— "Dead Souls: the Denationalization of the American Elite," *National Interest*, Spring, 2004c, no. 75
Hurst, L. "The First Immigrant," *Toronto Star*, October 12, 1991
Hutcheson, R. *God in the White House: How Religion Changed the Modern Presidency* (New York: 1988)
Ingraham, L. *Shut Up and Sing! How Elites from Hollywood, Politics, and the UN Are Subverting America* (Washington: 2003)
Iserbyt, C. *The Deliberate Dumbing Down of America (*Ravenna: 1999)
International Monetary Fund ("IMF"), IMF Center," "EconEd Online," at www.imf.org/external/np/exr/center/econed/index.html
Jackson, G. *Conservative Comebacks to Liberal Lies* (Ramsey NJ: 2006/2007)
Jacobs, J. *Dark Age Ahead* (New York: 2005)
Janssens, A. ed. *The Rise and Decline of the Male Breadwinner Family* (Cambridge: 1998)
Jay, J. *The Correspondence and Public Papers of John Jay,* H. Johnson, ed. (New York: 1893)
Jefferson, T. *Notes on the State of Virginia* (New York: 1782/Philadelphia: 1794)
—— *Memoir, Correspondence, and Miscellanies, the Papers of Thomas Jefferson*, T.R. Jefferson ed. (Boston: 1830)
—— *The Writings of Thomas Jefferson*, H.A. Washington ed. (New York: 1857)
—— *The Writings of Thomas Jefferson*, P. Ford ed. ( New York: 1894)

―――― *The Writings of Thomas Jefferson*, A. Bergh ed. (Washington: 1904)
―――― *Jefferson's Writings*, Monticello ed. (Washington: 1905)
―――― *The Complete Jefferson*, S. Padover ed. (New York: 1969)
―――― *Extracts from the Gospel* (Princeton: 1983)
―――― *Writings. Autobiography* (New York: 1984)
Jeffrey, T. "How Much Bigger Can Our Government Get?" *Conservative Chronicle*: Washington, July 30, 2008
―――― "Send Your Children to D.C. Public School, Obama," *Conservative Chronicle*, November 19, 2008
Johnson, S. *Dictionary of the English Language* (London: 1755/ New York: 1967)
Jones, T. "Saddest Thing About This Mess: Congress Had a Chance to Stop It," *Investor's Business,* Daily September 26, 2008
*Journals of the Continental Congress* (Washington: 1914)
Kendall, E. *Kendall's Travels* (New York: 1809)
Kennedy, D. "Can We Still Afford to Be a Nation of Immigrants?" *Atlantic Monthly*, vol. 278, November, 1996
―――― "Culture Wars: the Sources and Uses of Enmity in American History," in *Enemy Images in American History* (Providence: 1997)
Kennedy, J. F. *A Nation of Immigrants* (New York: 1964)
Kennedy, P. *The Rise and Fall of the Great Powers* (New York: 1987)
Kennedy, S. *God and Country: America in Red and Blue* (Waco: 2007)
Keynes, J.M. *The General Theory of Employment, Interest, and Money* (New York: 1980)
Kimball, R. *Tenured Radicals* (Chicago: 1998)
King, R. *The Life and Correspondence of Rufus King*, C. King ed. (New York: 1900)
Kirk, R. "Renewing a Shaken Culture,' *Heritage Foundation*, Lecture 434, December 11, 1992.
Klein, J. "How About a Swift Kick?" *Newsweek*, July 26, 1993
Kors, A. and Silverglate, H. *The Shadow University: the Betrayal of Liberty on America's Campuses* (New York: 1998)
Kramer, H. and Kimball, R. *The Betrayal of Liberalism* (Chicago: 1999)
―――― "The Betrayal of Liberalism," in *The New Criterion*, 2000, at www.newcriterion.com:81/ constant/books/betrayal/betrayintro
Kudlow, L. "The Big Easy's Billion Dollar Boondagle," *Conservative Chronicle*, September 12, 2007
Kupelian, D. *The Marketing of Evil* (Nashville: 2005)
LaHaye, T. *Faith of Our Founding Fathers* (Brentwood TN: 1987)
Lane, H. *Liberty! Cry Liberty!* (Boston: 1939)
Leaming, A. and Spicer, J. eds. *The Grants, Concessions, and Original Constitutions of the Province of New Jersey* (Philadelphia: 1758)
Leary, T. *The Politics of Ecstasy* (New York: 1970)
Lefler, H. ed. *North Carolina History* (Chapel Hill: 1956)
Leo, J. *Two Steps Ahead of the Thought Police (*New York: 1994)
―――― *Incorrect Thoughts: Notes on Our Wayward Culture* (New Brunswick:

2001)

Leonard, J. *How Structural Costs Imposed on U.S. Manufacturers Harm Workers and Threaten Competitiveness*, NAM (Washington: 2004)

Lerner, M. *America as a Civilization*. (New York: 1957)

——— *The Politics of Meaning* (New York: 1996)

——— "Marcuse at 100," *Tikkun*. September-October, 1998

Lesthaeghe, R. "A Century of Cultural and Demographic Change in Western Europe: an Exploration of Underlying Dimensions," *Population and Development Review*, Fall, 1983

Levinson, S. *Constitutional Faith* (Princeton: 1989)

Lieven, A. *America Right or Wrong* (Oxford: 2005)

Lilla, M. *The Stillborn God* (New York: 2007)

Limbaugh, D. "On a Mission for Marriage," *Creators Syndicate*, September 7, 2000

——— Genuine American Hero, General Petraeus," in *Conservative Chronicle*, Washington: September 19, 2007

Lincoln, A. *The Collected Works of Abraham Lincoln*, R. Basler ed. (New Brunswick NJ: 1953)

Linn, W. *The Life of Thomas Jefferson* (Ithaca NY: 1834)

Locke, J. *The Reasonableness of Christianity*, I.T. Ramsey ed. (Stanford: 1958)

——— *An Essay Concerning Human Understanding*, A. Fraser ed. (New York: 1959)

——— *The Second Treatise of Government* (New York: 1986)

Lockyer, H. *Last Words of Saints and Sinners* (Grand Rapids: 1969)

Lukacs, J. *The End of the Twentieth Century and the End of the Modern Age* (New York: 1993)

Luther, M. "Against the Heavenly Prophets in the Matter of Images and Sacraments, *Luther's Works*, Ehrling, B. tr. and Bergendorf, C. ed. ( Philadelphia: 1958)

Lutz, D. "The Relative Influence of European Writers in Late Eighteenth Century American on American Political Thought," *American Political Science Review* (1984), vol. 189

——— *The Origins of American Constitutionalism* (Baton Rouge: 1982)

Madison, J. *A Memorial and Remonstrance Presented to the General Assembly of the State of Virginia* (Massachusetts: 1785)

——— *The Papers of James Madison*, H. Gilpin ed. (Washington: 1840)

——— *The Papers of James Madison*, R. Rutland ed. (Chicago: 1911)

——— *The Complete Madison*, S. Padover ed. (New York: 1953)

——— "Federalist No. 51," in *The Federalist Papers* (New York: 1982)

Madison, J., Hamilton A., and Jay, J. *The Federalist Papers* (New York: 1988)

Makin, J. and Ornstein, N. *Debt and Taxes*. New York: 1994

Malbin, M. *Religion and Politics: the Intentions of the Authors of the First Amendment* (Washington: 1978/1981)

———*Invasion* (Washington: 2002)

Malloy, W. *Treaties, Conventions, International Acts, Protocols, and Agreements*

*between the United States of America and Other Powers, 1776-1909* (New York: 1968)
Marcuse, H. *Eros and Civilization: a Philosophical Inquiry Into Freud* (Boston:1966)
—————— "Repressive Tolerance," in R. Wolff et al, eds. *A Critique of Pure Tolerance* (Boston: 1969a)
—————— *A Critique of Pure Tolerance* (London: 1969b)
—————— *Counter-Revolution and Revolt* (New York: 1972)
Marsden, G. *Fundamentalism and American Culture* (Oxford: 2006)
Marsh, D. *Unto the Generations* (Buena Park, CA: 1970)
Marshall, J. *The Papers of John Marshall*, Charles Hobson ed. (Chapel Hill: 2006)
Marshall, P. and Manuel, D. *The Light and the Glory* (New York: 1977)
Martinez, J. "More that Half of State's Juniors Fail Math, Writing, in New High School Test," *Detroit News*, August 15, 2007
Matthews, R. *The Radical Politics of Thomas Jefferson* (Lawrence KAN: 1984)
Maxfield, R. et al. *The Real Thomas Jefferson* (Washington 1981-1983)
McCartney. C. *Lincoln and the Bible* (New York: 1949)
McDonald, L. *We Hold These Truths* (Long Beach, CA: 1976)
McDonald, W. ed. *Documentary Source Book of American History, 1606-1889*, (New York: 1909)
McDougall, W. *Promised Land, Crusader State* (New York: 1997)
—————— ed. *Freedom Just Around the Corner* (New York: 2004)
McDowell," G. "The Perverse Paradox of Privacy," in R. Bork ed. *A Country I Do Not Recognize* (Stanford: 2005)
McDowell, S. and Beliles, M. *America's Providential History* (Charlottesville: 1989)
McFarland, N. "A July 4 Meditation on the Faith of the Founders: One Nation Under God," *Orange County Register*, July 2, 1995
McGowan, W. *Coloring the News: How Crusading for Diversity Has Corrupted American Journalism* (San Francisco: 2001)
—————— *Coloring the News: How Political Correctness Has Corrupted American Journalism* (New York: 2003)
McGuffey, W. *McGuffey's Eclectic Third Reader* (Cincinnati: 1848)
McClure, J. ed. *Abraham Lincoln's Stories and Speeches* (Chicago: 1896)
Meacham, J. *American Gospel: God, the Founding Fathers, and the Making of a Nation* (New York: 2006)
—————— "The Editor's Desk," *Newsweek*, January 5, 2009
Mead, W. *Special Providence* (New York: 2001)
—————— *God and Gold: Britain and America and the Making of the Modern World* (New York: 2007)
Merrill, P. "Testimony Before the House Budget Committee" (Washington: July 22, 2004)
Miller, J. *Sam Adams: Pioneer in Propaganda* (Stanford: 1960)
Miller, W. *The First Liberty: Religion and the American Republic* (New York: 1986)

Mode, P. *Sourcebook and Biographical Guide for American Church History* (Menasha WI: 1921/ Powder Springs GA: 2007)
Modern Library. *The Federalist: A Commentary on the Constitution of the United States* (New York: 1937)
Monaghan, F. *John Jay: Defender of Liberty* (Indianapolis: 1972)
Montesquieu, C. *The Spirit of Laws* ((Philadelphia 1802/New York 1949)
Morris. B.F. *The Christian Life and Character of the Civil Institutions of the United States* (Philadelphia: 1864)
Moynihan, D. "Defining Deviancy Down," *American Spectator*, vol. 17, Winter 1993
Mundell, R. "A Pro-Growth Fiscal System," in J. Jasinowski ed. *The Rising Tide* (New York: 1998)
National Center for History in the Schools. *National Standards for United States History: Exploring the American Experience, Grades 5-12* (Los Angeles: 1994)
Noll, M. *Eerdmans' Handbook to Christianity in America* (Grand Rapids: 1983)
―――― *America's God: From Jonathan Edwards to Abraham Lincoln* (New York: 2002)
North, G. *An Introduction to Christian Economics* (Durham NC: 1979)
―――― *The Dominion Covenant* (Tyler TX: 1987)
Norman, E.R. *The Conscience of the State in North America* (London: 1968)
Norton, T. *Undermining the Constitution: a History of Lawless Government* (New York: 1950)
Novak, M. *The Universal Hunger for Liberty* (New York: 2004)
O'Neill, J.M. *Religion and Education Under the Constitution* (New York: 1949)
Orr, J. *English Deism: Its Roots and Its Fruits* (Grand Rapids: 1934)
Ortega y Gassettt, J. *The Revolt of the Masses* (New York: 1957)
Osbourne, D. and Gaebler, T. *Reinventing Government* (New York: 1993)
Padover, S. ed. *Democracy by Thomas Jefferson* (New York: 1939)
―――― *Jefferson* (New York: 1942)
―――― *The Complete Jefferson* (New York: 1943)
―――― *The Mind of Alexander Hamilton* (New York: 1958)
Palmer, R. *The Age of Democratic Revolution: a Political History of Europe and America, 1760-1800* (Princeton: 1964)
Peabody, S. ed. *American Patriotism: Speeches, Letters, and Other Papers Which Illustrate the Foundation, Development, and Preservation of the United States of America* (New York: 1880)
Peaslee, A. *Constitutions of Nations* (Concord NH: 1950)
Perelman, L. "The Acanemia Deception," *Hudson Institute,* Alexandria: 1990
Peterson, P. *Facing Up* (New York: 1993)
―――― *Running on Empty* (New York: 2004)
Phillips, K. *American Theocracy* (New York: 2006)
Pierce, B. *A History of Harvard University* (Cambridge: 1833)
Prestowitz, C. *Three Billion New Capitalists: the Great Shift of Wealth and Power to the East* (New York: 2005)

Rahn, R. "Regulatory Therapy," *Washington Times,* Washington: July 11, 2004
Rashdooney, R.J. *The Institutes of Biblical Law* (Vallecito CA: 1973)
Rehnquist, W. "United States Not Founded on Absolute Church-State Separation," 1985, at www.belcherfoundation.org/wallace_v_jaffrey_dissent.htm
Reich, R. *Tales of a New America* (New York: 1987)
—— *The Work of Nations* (New York: 1991)
Renshon, S. *Dual Citizens in America* (Washington: July, 2000)
—— *Dual Citizenship and American National Identity*, Center for Immigration Studies, Paper 20, Washington, October, 2001
—— *The 50% American.* (Washington: 2005)
Revel, J.F. *Democracy Against Itself.* R. Kaplan tr. (New York: 1993)
Rice, C. *The Supreme Court and Public Prayer: the Need for Restraint* (New York: 1964)
Richard, C. *The Founders and the Classics: Greece, Rome, and the American Enlightenment* (Cambridge: 1994)
—— *Greeks and Romans Bearing Gifts* (Lanham: 2008)
Richardson, J. *A Compilation of the Messages and Papers of the Presidents, 1789-1897* (Washington: 1899/1907)
Richardson, J. *Christian Economics* (Atlanta: 1966)
Ringenberg, W. *The Christian College: a History of Protestant Higher Education in America* (Grand Rapids: 2006)
Root. I. *Speeches of Oliver Cromwell* (London: 1989)
Rorty, R. "The Unpatriotic Academy," *New York Times*, February 13, 1994
——*Achieving Our Country: Leftist Thought in Twentieth Century America* (Cambridge: 1998)
Rose, T. *Economics: Principles and Policy from a Christian Perspective* (Mercer PA: 1996)
Rowland, K. *The Life of George Mason* (New York: 1892)
Rush, B. *Essays: Literary, Moral, and Philosophical* (Philadelphia: 1779/1798)
—— *Letters of Benjamin Rush* (Princeton: 1951)
Rutgers University. *Rutgers Fact Book of 1965* (New Jersey: 1965)
Rutland, R. Ed. *The Papers of James Madison* (Chicago: 1962)
Rutherford, S. *Lex Rex, or The Law and the Prince* (Harrisonburg VA: 1982)
Safire, W. ed. *Lend Me Your Ears – Great Speeches in History* (New York: 1992)
Samuelson, R."The Budget: Back to the Future," *Newsweek,* February 14, 1994
—— "We Don't Need Guest Workers," *Washington Post*, March 22, 2006
Sandoz, E. "Power and Spirit in the Founding," *This World*, no. 9, Fall, 1984
Schachner, N. *Alexander Hamilton* (New York: 1961)
Schaff, P. *Church and State in the United States* (New York: 1889)
Schafly, P. "If NEA Delegates Get Their Way," *Washington Times*, weekly edition, August 7-13, 1995
—— "To College Students: Don't Major in English," *Conservative Chronicle,* Washington: October 10, 2007
Schiff, P. *Crash Proof* (Hoboken: 2007)
Schlesinger, A. "When Ethnic Studies are Un-American," *Wall Street Journal*,

April 23, 1990
——— *The Disuniting of America: Reflections on a Multicultural Society* (New York: 1998)
Schmidt, A. *The Menace of Multiculturalism: Trojan Horse in America* (Westport: 1997)
Schumpeter, J. *Capitalism, Socialism, and Democracy* (New York: 1950)
Schweikert, L. *The Entrepreneurial Venture: a History of Business in the United States* (New York: 2000)
Sears, A. and Osten, C. *The ACLU vs. America* (Nashville: 2005)
Senn, W. "Religion, Politics, and the American Constitution," *Conservative Chronicle,* Washington, September 21, 2006
Settel, T.S. et al. *The Quotable Harry Truman* (New York: 1967)
Silk, L. *Making Capitalism Work* (New York: 1996)
Singer, C.G.. *A Theological Interpretation of American History* (Phillipsburg (NJ: 1964)
Singer, M. and Bracken, P. "Don't Blame the U.S," *New York Times Magazine*, November, 1976
Skousen, W. *The Miracle of America* (Salt Lake City: 1981)
——— *The Making of America* (Washington: 1985)
Smith, A. *An Inquiry Into the Nature and Causes of the Wealth of Nations* (New York: 1937)
Smith, R. "The American Creed and American Identity: the Limits of Liberal Citizenship in the United States," *Western Political Quarterly*, 1987, vol. 41
Smith. S.F. "America," *The Hymnal of the Protestant Episcopal Church* (New York: 1940)
Sowell, T. "The New Racism on Campus," *Fortune*, February 13, 1989
——— "The Road to Hell Is Paved With Good Intentions," *Forbes*, January 17, 1994
——— *Migrations and Cultures: a World View* (New York: 1996)
——— *A Conflict of Visions* (New York: 2002)
——— "Artificial Stupidity," *Creators Syndicate*, March 26, 2003
——— "A Dose of Economic Reality," *Conservative Chronicle,* Washington: July 1, 2003
——— "The New 'Yellow Peril," *Conservative Chronicle*, January 17, 2007a.
——— *A Conflict of Visions* (New York: 2007b)
Sparks, J. *The Life of Gouverneur Morris* (Boston: 1832)
State Exhibit: Window to Future Jobs," *Detroit Business* (April 10, 1989)
State of Connecticut. *The Code of 1650: Being a Compilation of the Earliest Laws and Orders of the General Court of Connecticut* (Hartford: 1822)
Stedman, W. *Our Ageless Constitution* (Asheboro NC: 1987)
Steyn, M. *America Alone* (Washington: 2006)
Stein, B. and DeMuth, P. *How to Ruin the United States of America* (Carlsbad: 2008)
Steinberg, S. *The Ethnic Myth: Race, Ethnicity, and Class in America* (New York: 1981)

Stokes, A. and Pfeffer, L. *Church and State in the United States* (New York: 1964)
Storey, J. *Commentaries on the Constitution of the United States* (Boston: 1833)
——— *Life and Letters of Joseph Storey*, W. Storey ed. (Boston: 1851a)
——— *Commentaries on the Constitution of the United States* (Boston: 1851b)
——— *A Familiar Exposition of the Constitution of the United States* (Lake Bluff IL: 1986)
Strong, H. *The New Era, or The Coming Kingdom* (New York: 1893)
Strout, C. *The New Heavens and the New Earth* (New York: 1974)
Tawney, R. *Religion and the Rise of Capitalism* (New York: 1926/London: 1960)
Tax Foundation. "America Celebrates Tax Freedom Day, (Washington: March 28, 2008)
Taylor, R. ed. *The Papers of John Adams* (Cambridge: 1977)
Tocqueville, A. de. *Democracy in America* (Garden City NY: 1851/New York: 1945/1969)
Thomas, C. "Feds Should Drop Out of Education," *Conservative Chronicle*, July 14, 2004
——— "England May End Up Just History," *Lansing State Journal*, September 3, 2007a
——— "Colleges Are Cheating Their Students," *Conservative Chronicle,* Washington: September 8, 2007b.
Thompson, C.L. *The Religious Foundations of America: a Study in National Origins* (New York n.d.)
Thurow, L. *The Zero Sum Society* (New York: 1980)
——— *The Zero Sum Solution* (New York: 1985)
——— *Head-to-Head (*New York: 1992)
——— *The Future of Capitalism (*New York: 1996)
Trowbridge, G. and Hornbeck, M. "CEOs to Governors: Schools Don't Make the Grade," *Detroit News*, July 22, 2007
Truett, G.W. *The Inspiration of Ideas* (Grand Rapids: 1950)
Trumbull, B. *A Complete History of Connecticut, Civil and Ecclesiastical, from the Emigration of its First Planters from England* (Hartford: 1797)
Tuveson, E. *Redeemer Nation* (Chicago: 1968)
Tyler, M. *Patrick Henry* (New York: 1898/1966)
U.S. Congress. *The Constitutions of the Several Independent States of America* (Boston: 1785)
——— *Debates and Proceedings in the Congress of the United States* (Washington: 1834a)
——— *Annals of Congress, 1789-1791* (Washington: 1834b)
——— *Journals of the Continental Congress* (Washington; 1904-1937)
U.S. Department of Education. "A Nation at Risk," a Report of the National Commission on Excellence in Education, Washington: D.C., 1983
——— "The Nation's Report Card," National Assessment of Educational Progress (NAEP), September, 1990
U.S. Senate. *Journal of the First Session of the Senate of the United States of America, Begun and Held at the City of New York, March 4, 1789* (Washington:

1820)

Wallace, R. *Calvin's Doctrine of the Christian Life* (Grand Rapids: 1961)

Walton, R. *Biblical Principles of Importance to Godly Christians* (New Hampshire: 1984)

Warren, C. "The 'New Liberty' Under the Fourteenth Amendment," *Harvard Law Review*, vol. 39, (Cambridge: 1926)

Washington, G. *Address of George Washington, President of the United States* (Baltimore: 1796)

———— *The Writings of Washington*, Jared Sparks ed. (Boston: 1838)

———— *The Writings of Washington*, J. Fitzpatrick ed. (Washington: (1930-1932)

Weber, M. *The Sociology of Religion* (Boston: 1922/1963)

———— *The Protestant Ethic and the Spirit of Capitalism* (New York: 1958)

Webster, D. *The Works of Daniel Webster* (Boston: 1853)

Webster, N. *History of the United States* (New Haven: 1832)

———— *American Dictionary of the English Language, 1828* (San Francisco: 1967)

Weigel, G. *The Cube and the Cathedral* (New York: 2005)

Weiss, B. *God in America's History* (South Pasadena CA: 1966)

Wells, W. *The Life and Public Service of Samuel Adams* (Boston: 1865)

Wesley, C. *To Pray or Not to Pray!* (Washington: 1963)

Whitehead, J. *The Separation Illusion* (Milford MI: 1977)

Whitman, M. "Trade and Growth: Restoring the Virtuous Circle," in J. Jasinowski ed. *The Rising Tide* (New York: 1998)

Whitman, W. *A Christian History of the American Republic; a Textbook for Secondary Schools* (Boston; 1948)

Wiggershaus, R. *The Frankfurt School, Its History, Theories, and Political Significance* (Cambridge: 1995)

Wiatt, S. *Wiatt's Impartial Selection of Hymns and Spiritual Songs* (Philadelphia: 1809)

Wildavsky, A. and Weber, C. *A History of Taxation and Expenditure in the Western World* (New York:1986)

Will, G. "TARP and ADD," *Newsweek*, December 1, 2008

Williams, W. "Improve Education: Fire the Experts," *Creators Syndicate*, August 26, 2002

———— "Threats to the Rule of Law," *Conservative Chronicle,* Washington: June 12, 2002

———— "Fiddling While Rome Burns, *Conservative Chronicle*, December 26, 2002

———— "The Morality of Markets," *Conservative Chronicle,* Washington: May 7, 2003

———— "Economics 101," *Conservative Chronicle,* Washington: August 11, 2004

———— "Income Inequality," *Conservative Chronicle,* Washington: September 8, 2004

———— "Academic Cesspools," *Conservative Chronicle,* Washington: October 8, 2007a

———— "Academic Cesspools: Part II," *Conservative Chronicle,* Washington: November 14, 2007b

——— "Academic Slums: U.S. 33rd and 27th," *Conservative Chronicle,* Washington: December 8, 2007c
——— "Ignorance Reigns Supreme in Civics," *Conservative Chronicle*, Washington, December 10, 2008
Wilson, W. *The Papers of Woodrow Wilson*, A. Link ed. (Princeton: 1966)
Wirt, W. *The Life and Character of Patrick Henry* (Philadelphia: 1818)
Witherspoon, J. *The Works of John Witherspoon* (Edinburgh: 1815)
Wolfe, E. "The Wealth Divide: The Growing Gap in the United States Between the Rich and the Rest," *Multinational Monitor*, vol. 24, no. 5 (May 2003, @ multinationalmonitor/org/mm2003/03may/may03.interviewswolfe.html
Wolman, W. *The Triumph of Capital and the Betrayal of Work* (New York: 1997)
Wood, P. *Diversity; the Invention of a Concept* (San Francisco: 2003)
Woodward, K. "Hymns, Hers, and Theirs," *Newsweek*, February 12, 1996
Wooldridge, F. *Immigration's Unarmed Invasion* (Bloomington: 2004)
Wuthnow, R. *The Restructuring of American Religion* (Princeton: 1988)
Zolberg, A. *A Nation By Design* (New York: 2006)

# Index

*Abington Township v. Schempp*, 81
academia and political correctness, 114–15
ACLU (American Civil Liberties Union), 86–88, 119–22
Adams, John: ancient cultural influences on, xiii, xvii–xviii; on Christianity, 9, 11, 29, 40, 50, 58–59; on Constitution, 71; on covenants, 196; death of, 18; on education, 172; on government, xiii, 13–14, 83, 112, 153, 172–73; inauguration of, 17; on manifest destiny, xviii; on separation of powers, xv; so-called Deist, 51, 52; on tyranny, xvii
Adams, John Quincy: on Christianity, 10, 29, 236n41; on education, 166–67; inauguration of, 17; on manifest destiny, xxi; so-called Deist, 53–54
Adams, Samuel: on Christianity, 10, 30; on day of thanksgiving, 12, 13; on education, 164–65, 166; on government, 144; on manifest destiny, xviii–x; on righteousness, 29
*Aeneid,* x
affluence and taxation, 198
*The Age of Discontinuity,* 154
*The Age of Reason,* 37
Alabama, 85, 87
*Allegheny v. ACLU*, 120
*America,* ix–xx
American Civil Liberties Union (ACLU), 86–88, 119–22
American Indians, 97, 98
America's Creed, 34–36
Ames, Fisher, 70–71, 167
ancient cultures, xv–xvii, 3–4, 187, 189, 191, 234n93
Apollo Project, xx–xxi
Aristotle, 185–86
Athanasian Creed, 61–62
atheism, 81, 90, 96

*Baer v. Kolmorgen*, 79

bankers, 221–24, 227–29
barbarism, 125–26, 186–88
Barrett, Catherine, 175
*Barron v. Baltimore,* 84
"The Battle Hymn of the Republic," 21, 240n107
"The Beauties of Predestination," 62
Beecher, Lyman, 42
*Bible:* banning of, 91, 250n186, 254–55n77; covenants in, xi, 196; distribution of, 9; economic model in, 144–49; education and, 70–71, 83, 85, 86, 162, 165–73; federal building inscriptions, 27–28; Founders' views on, 41–45; governing precepts in, 22, 47–48, 99; Lincoln on, 21; Locke on, 39–40; prophets' words, 144, 188; Ten Commandments, 84–85, 93–96. *See also* Christianity
Bill of Rights: founders' vision of religion in, 22, 67–72; Fourteenth Amendment, 78, 83, 254n72; Tenth Amendment, 18, 150–51; Warren on, 24. *See also* Constitution; First Amendment
Black, Hugo, 36–37, 80, 82, 186
Blackstone, William, 40–41
Bloom, Alan, 109–10
*Brandon v. Board of Education,* 85
Brewer, David, 25
Brinsley, John, 168
Brokaw, Tom, 154
Bryan, William Jennings, 188
building inscriptions, 27–28, 242n149
*Building Prosperity,* xxi–xxii
bureaucratic programs, 202
Burke, Edmund, 35
Bush, George W., xiv, 22, 31, 63
business. *See* economics

Caesar, Julius, xv–xvi

Calvinism, 34, 138–44
capital gains tax, 207–8
capitalistic greed, 219–20
capital surplus, 136–38
Capitol building, 27
Carter, Jimmy, 22
censorship, 115
challenges for America's survival, 188–92
Chambers, Whittaker, 91
change, age of, 191–92
Channing, William Ellery, 169
charters of colonies, 6–9, 49–50
Chavez, Linda, 121
checks and balances, 93
Chesterfield, Lord, 69
Chesterton, G.K., xi
Christianity: denominations, 18, 56, 58–59, 239n88, 244n4, 249n153; faith of nation's leaders, 20–24, 30–31; Jesus as prophet, 61; Protestant culture, 33–36; statistics, 92; Supreme Court and, 24–25. *See also* God; religion; separation of church and state
Christmas symbols, 119–23
Churchill, Winston, 127–28
*Church of the Holy Trinity v. U.S.,* 89
CIA headquarters, 28
Cicero, xv, 95
"city on a hill" sermon, xix, 7, 57, 102
civic illiteracy, 179
civil governance, 146, 147
civilization war, 105
Civil Rights Act, 125
Clark, William, xv–xxi
classic history: ancient cultures, xv–xvi, 3–4, 187, 191, 234n93; cultural dissolutions, 189; Founders and, xii–xviii
classics in academia, 114
Cleveland, Grover, 21

Clinton, Bill, 36
*The Closing of the American Mind,* 109–10
Coleman, James, 178
College of William and Mary, 169, 171
colleges, 169–71
colonial leadership, 142–43
colonial nations and exploitation, 4
colonists and God, 5–11
Columbia University, 169, 171
Columbus, Christopher, 5, 24, 49
Commager, Henry, xiii
Commission on National Security, 180
common sense doctrine, 81–82
communal leadership, 142–43
communism, 4–5, 128
community covenant, 221–24, 226
Congress, 22–23
*Congressional Record,* 84
Connecticut, Fundamental Orders of, 7, 24, 50
Conquest, Robert, 128
*A Consolation for Our Grammar Schooles,* 168
Constitution: courts' disregard for, 98–99; education and, 163; government functions permitted by, 199; precepts founded on, 47–48; religion and, 18, 25, 34–35, 59, 67–72, 238–39n86. *See also* Bill of Rights
Constitutional Convention, xvii–xix
constitutions of colonies, 18–20, 25
consumption taxes, 207
Coolidge, Calvin, 30–31
corporate taxation reform, 211
corporate tax myth, 197–98
cost benefit analyses, 209
costs of government functions, 203–4
counter-culturalism: agenda of, 109–10; cancer of, 105–7; Christmas symbols and, 119–23; deconstructing old order, 101–5; Marcuse and, xxii, 106–9, 111; moral view of America and, 126–30; political correctness, 112–19; rule of law and, 110–12; societal impact of, 123–26; as threat to America, 187–88
*Counter-Revolution and Revolt,* 106
covenants, 34, 145, 195–97, 221–24, 226, 228–29. *See also* New Economic Contract with America
*Crocker v. Sorenson,* 81
Cromwell, Oliver, x
cultural diversity and values, 124–26
cultural relativism, 103
cures, 226–29
currency, 26, 27
curriculum, mandatory, 216

Dale, Sir Thomas, 142–43
Danbury Baptist Association, 72–76, 75–76, 89, 186
Dark Ages, 138–42
day of fasting, 20
day of prayer, 26–27, 73, 237n49, 237n51, 242n139
day of thanksgiving, 12, 13, 20
Dean, Howard, 188
debt, government, 153–54, 189–91, 201–5
Declaration of Independence: God invoked in, 5, 26, 96; Natural and Divine Laws as basis for, 46; as social contract, 153, 196; Supreme Court on, 24–25; unalienable rights and, 11–12
"defining deviancy down," 105–7
Deism, 37–39, 50–59, 62–63
Delaware, 19
democracy and classics, xv
democratic capitalism, 150–51

de Montesquieu, Baron, 190–91
Descartes, René, 37
de Tocqueville, Alexis: on freedom, 109, 135; on judiciary, 118–19; on religion and America, xi, xii, xiv, xx, 5, 20, 29, 57–58, 60, 135
deviancy, 105–7
Dewey, John, 175
Dickinson, John, xvi, 9
diligence in *Bible,* 149
diversity and political correctness, 114
divine being. *See* Christianity; God; religion
dominion covenant, 145
Douglas, William O., 23, 81–82, 241–42n130
Drucker, Peter, 154
D'Souza, Dinesh, 102
Duffield, George, xix
Durant, Ariel, 161
Durant, Will, 4, 161
Durkheim constant, 104
Dwight, Timothy, 191

*The Eclipse of the American Century,* xx
economics: bankers, 221–24, 227–29; *Bible* model, 144–49; fiscal responsibility, 198–206; myths, 197–98; New Economic Contract with America, 199–206; profit motive, 133–44; quest for remedy, 154–60
education: contemporary challenges, 174–82; contract with America, 214–17; federal spending on, 180; foreign and U.S. students, 181–82, 183, 215; founders' vision and, 164–73; importance of, 161–64; jobs and, 182–84; reform measures, 181–82; religion and, 76–77, 81–87, 120–22, 165–73; teachers'

unions, 184, 216–17; teaching history, 216; technology and, 183–84
Edwards, Chris, 203
Emerson, Ralph Waldo, 185, 191–92
employee stock ownership programs (ESOP), 205–6
*The End of the Twentieth Century,* 189
*Engel v. Vitale,* 80
Enterprise America Authority, 228–29
*Equality of Educational Opportunity,* 178
*Eros and Civilization,* 106
*Essay Concerning Human Understanding,* 39
Establishment Clause, 70, 74–75, 78–79, 98, 123
Etzioni, Amitai, 104
*Everson v. Board of Education,* 36–37, 78, 80, 186
Ezekiel (Prophet), 188

failure of federalism, 220–24, 227–29
family's role, 148–49
Fannie May, 222–23, 227, 228
fear of churches, 74
federal government functions, 156–60, 203–4
federalism, failure of, 220–24, 227–29
Federalist Papers, xv, 15, 88, 153, 156
federal spending, 157–60, 180, 214. *See also* taxation
Ferguson, Niall, x
financial accounting, 203–4
financial bailouts, 227–29
"financialization," 227–29
financial triplets, 222–23

First Amendment: Establishment Clause, 70, 74–75, 78–79, 98, 123; founders' intent, 5–6, 36–37, 67–72; Free Exercise Clause, 70, 75, 78–79, 98; Supreme Court interpretations, 36–37, 75–81, 186
fiscal responsibility, 198–206
foreign and U.S. student comparisons, 181–82, 183, 215
founding fathers: ancient cultural influences on, xii–xviii; Calvinistic model and, 142–44; defined, xxii–xxiii; Deist mythology and, 37–39, 50–59, 62–63; education and, 164–73; on God, 9–11, 13–18, 57, 59, 68; ideological underpinnings, 150–54; manifest destiny and, xviii–xxiii; religion and, vii–x, 3–5, 18–20, 30, 36–50, 67–72, 97–99, 164–73. *See also* Constitution; Declaration of Independence; separation of church and state; *specific founders*
Four Freedoms speech, 188
Fourteenth Amendment, 78, 83, 254n72
Frankfurter, Justice Felix, 186
Franklin, Benjamin: ancient cultural influences on, xiv, xviii, xvii; on education, 167; on money, 140; on religion, 16, 30, 167; so-called Deist, 54; on taxation, 154
Freddie Mac, 222–23, 227, 228
Free Exercise Clause, 70, 75, 78–79, 98
Friedman, Milton, 152, 162, 178–79
fund accounting, 203
Fundamental Orders of Connecticut, 7, 24, 50

general welfare spending, 156–60
George III, King, 155
Georgia constitution, 19
Gettysburg address, 11, 29
Ginnie Mae, 222–23, 228
Ginsberg, Ruth Bader, 90
global trade, 211–12
God: colonists and, 5–11; death of, 101–5; Founding Fathers on, 9–11, 13–18, 57, 59, 68; inaugural addresses invoking, 17, 21–22, 63, 192; reigning supreme over Republic, 25–31. *See also* Bible; Christianity; religion
God, Law of, 39–42, 46, 94–96, 245n36, 245n39
gold, 145–46
government bureaucracy, 224–25
Graglia, Lino, 93, 118
Greenspan, Alan, 207
Grigg, John, 190
gross domestic products (GDP), 199–206
Grund, F.J., 35
Guinness, Os, 111

Haack, Susan, 110
Haiman, Bob, 116
Halberstam, David, 189
Hamilton, Alexander: ancient cultural influences on, xv; on capitalism, 150; compared to Caesar, xvi; on God, 9, 16–17, 68; on government debt, 153–54; on judiciary, 88; on liberty, 30; so-called Deist, 55
Hanson, Victor David, 123
Harrison, William Henry, 17
Hart-Rudman Commission on National Security, 180
Harvard College, 169–70
health care portability, 213–14
Henry, Patrick, 11, 25, 30, 55
high school dropout rate, 179

historical revisionism, 103
history, teaching of, 216
*History of the Peloponnesian War,* 94–95
Hodges, Luther, 197
Holmes, Oliver Wendell, 99, 186
home ownership, 221–24, 226
hornbook, 168
House of Representatives, 22–23
Hudson Institute, 181
*Hudson vs. Macmillan,* 92
Hughes, Charles Evans, 118
Hugo, Victor, 162
Huntington, Samuel, x, 189

illiteracy, civic, 179
inaugural addresses, 17, 21–22, 63, 153, 192, 240n116
investments, 136–37
Iron Curtain speech, 127–28
Iserbyt, Catherine, 175
Islamic Ethics, 141–42

Jackson, Andrew, 17
Jackson, Robert, 80
Jamestown settlement, 142–43
Jay, John, xvii, 10, 16, 29, 54–55, 172
Jefferson, Thomas: on America's virtuousness, xix; ancient cultural influences on, xiii–xv; on Constitution, 99; on Constitutional Convention, xvii; Danbury Baptist Association and, 72–74, 75–76, 89, 186; death of, 18; on debt, 154–55, 190; Deism and, 37–38, 52–53, 62–63; on education, 166, 172, 184; on federal functions, 151, 156–57; on government, 78–79, 83, 150, 151, 153–54; inauguration of, 17; on judiciary, 88; on religion, 14–15, 30, 38, 50, 97–98; on seal of nation, xii, 26; on tyranny, xvi–xvii; on unalienable rights, 11–12
Jefferson Memorial, 28
Jeremiah (Prophet), 188
Jesus. *See* Christianity; God
job training tax credits, 213
Johnson, William Samuel, 166
journalism. *See* media
judicial system: counter-culturalism and, 116–19; founders' views on, 88; modern interpretations by, 90–93; power of, 88–90; Ten Commandments and, 93–96. *See also* Supreme Court; *specific cases*

K-12 challenges, 174–82
Kennedy, John F., xviii, xx–xxi, 22, 63, 192, 240n116
Kentucky laws, 84–85
Keynes, John Maynard, 163
King, Rufus, 46
King's College, 171
Kirk, Russell, 129
Klein, Joe, 104
knowledge as resource, 163–64

Law of Nature and Law of God, 39–42, 46, 94–96, 245n36, 245n39
Lee, Charles, xviii
Lee, Richard Henry, 11
the "left," 68–69. *See also* counter-culturalism; "New Left" dogma
legacies, 155
legislature, 22–23, 199–200, 224–25
Lerner, Michael, 107
Levinson, Stanford, 93
Lewis, Meriwether, xx–xxi
"The Liberal Christ Gives an Interview," 111
Library of Congress, 27–28

Lincoln, Abraham, xx, 11, 20–21, 29, 91, 162
Lincoln Memorial, 28
Lippman, Walter, 126
literacy, 179–80, 216
Locke, John, xi, 34, 37–40, 46, 153
Longfellow, Henry Wadsworth, 133–34
Lukacs, John, 189
Luther, Martin, 74
*Lynch v. Donnelly*, 120

Macaulay, Lord Thomas, 126, 187
Madison, James: ancient cultural influences on, xiv; on Constitutional Convention, xvii–xviii; on education, 166, 172; on federal functions, 157; on God, 15–16, 68; on government, 35, 78, 83, 151, 153; inauguration of, 17; on judiciary, 88; on religion, 83, 97–98, 166; on separation of church and state, 76; so-called Deist, 53; on taxation, 156, 191
Magna Carta, 142, 199, 265n29
malpractice suits, 214
manifest destiny, xviii–xxiii
*Manifesto of a Passionate Moderate,* 110
Marcuse, Herbert, xxii, 106–9, 111
market-based solutions, 204, 205–6, 228–29
Marshall, John, 6, 13, 84
Maryland, 19, 49, 255n93
Mason, George, 10, 41, 55, 112, 234n17
Massachusetts: charter, 6–7; constitution, 8, 19, 25, 196, 239n89; God invoked by colonists in, 50; legislature, 19–20; Winthrop on, 7
Massachusetts Provincial Congress, 11
May, Henry, 171

Mayflower Compact, 6–7, 24, 49, 57
*McCollum v. Board of Education,* 81, 90
McGuffey, William, 167
*McGuffey's Readers,* 169
media, 116
medieval Europe, 138–42
Melville, Herman, 191
middle class taxation, 206–7
Mill, John Stuart, 118, 162, 195–96
Mitchell, Adrian, 111
Monroe, James, 17, 53
Montesquieu of France, Baron, 41
Moore, Roy, 87
moral exemplar, demise of, 126–30
moral relativism, 103–5
Morris, Gouverneur, 11, 165
Morton, John, 10
Motley, Theodore, 145

National Assessment of Educational Progress (NAEP), 183
National Education Association (NEA), 175
*Nation at Risk* report, 178
Nature, Law of, 39–42, 46, 94–96, 245n36, 245n39
NEA (National Education Association), 175
New Economic Contract with America, 199–206
New England Confederation, 7
*New England Primer,* 168
*A New Guide to the English Tongue,* 168
New Hampshire, 25, 50
New Hampshire Province, 7
New Jersey, 20, 84, 85
"New Left" dogma, 106–7
*New Politic,* 140
*The Next Century,* 189
Nicaea, proclamation at, 61

Niebuhr, Reinhold, 136
9/11, xix
Norman, E.R., 81
North Carolina, 8, 19, 49, 239n89
Northwest Ordinance, 12, 74, 76, 173

oaths of office, 26–27
O'Connor, Sandra Day, 92
Ortega y Gasset, José, 126
outsourcing of jobs, 198, 212

Paine, Thomas, xii, 10, 17, 37, 56, 190
Parable of the Talents, 140
paradigms, 158–60, 200
Penn, William, xviii, 19, 50
Pennsylvania, 8, 19, 24
Pierce, Charles, 176
Pinckney, Charles, 10
Pledge of Allegiance, 27, 87
Plutarch, 4
political correctness, 103, 105–6, 112–19
politics, modern, 68–69, 188, 224–25
portable health care, 213–14
postage stamps, 27
Powell, Colin, xxi
Poynter Institute for Media Studies, 116
pragmatic education, 216
prayer in schools, 82. *See also Wallace v. Jaffrey*
Preamble to the Constitution, 47
precious metals, 145–46
presidential oaths of office, 26
Princeton University, 169, 170–71
private property system, 143
private sector marketplace, 134–36, 142, 204, 205–6
Proclamation at Nicaea, 61
proficiency testing, 216
profit motive, 133–44, 151–52

property rights, 143
Protestant culture, 33–36
Protestant Ethic, 141–42
*The Protestant Ethic and the Spirit of Capitalism,* 139
"Providence" as term, 58
public competition, 204, 205–6
public funds for religious purposes, 97
public schools, 172–73, 183
Puritans, 33–36, 235n23

Rahn, Richard, 209
rainy day funds, 202
Raleigh, Walter, 24
Ramsay, David, 57
rankings of students, 179
Reagan, Ronald: on bureaucratic programs, 202; on divine destiny, x; on God, 22, 31; on the Great Society, 189; on student prayer, 91–92; on Ten Commandments, 94
real estate market, 221–24, 226
recessions, 220, 221, 222
recovery bonds, 228–29
Reed, Stanley, 186
regulation, 142, 152, 190, 208–10
Rehnquist, William, 75–76, 79, 91, 185–86
religion: Deism mythology, 37–39, 50–59, 62–63; education and, 76–77, 81–87, 120–22, 165–73; fear of churches, 74; of founders, ix–xii, 3–5, 18–20, 30, 36–50, 67–72, 97–99, 164–73; prayer in schools, 82. *See also Bible*; Christianity; God; separation of church and state
"Religion: the Only Basis of Society," 169
religious expression, court rulings on, 76–77
Renaissance, 4

Republican democracy, redefined, 127
republican government, xiv–xv
research and development tax credits, 213
Revel, Jean-François, 123
Revolutionary War armistice, 12
*Reynolds v. United States*, 75, 79
Rhode Island charter, 8
Rome (ancient), xv–xvi, 187, 189, 191, 234n93
Roosevelt, Franklin, 22, 161–62, 188, 197
Rorty, Richard, 109
Rousseau, Jean-Jacques, x, 3, 189
Rush, Benjamin, 30, 55, 71, 166, 167
Russell, James Lowell, xviii
Rutgers University, 169, 171
Rutledge, Wiley, 80

sales tax, 207
Samuel (Prophet), 144
savings, 136–37
Scalia, Antonin, 118
Schlesinger, Arthur, 127, 196–97
Scholastic Aptitude Tests, 176–77
*School District of Abington Township v. Schempp*, 83
Scriptures. *See* Bible
seal of United States, 26, 28–29
*Second Treatise of Government*, 40, 46
self-determination, 46
separation of church and state: mending or dividing wall, 185–86; myth of, 67–72; not in Constitution, 117, 122–23; scriptural model, 147; Supreme Court rulings on, 36–37; underpinnings of, 72–75, 252n30. *See also* First Amendment
separation of powers, xv

Shadegg, John, 199
Shanker, Albert, 184
Shaw, George Bernard, 191
Sheen, Fulton, 128
Sherman, Roger, 55–56
*Ship of State,* 133–34
silver as money, 145–46
the sixties, 101–2, 105–8
slavery, 124
Smith, Adam, 114–15, 136
Smith, Captain John, 142
Smith, Samuel Francis, xix–xx
social compact theory, 34
social contracts, 195–97
South Carolina, 8, 19
Soviet Union, 4–5
Sowell, Thomas, 177, 181
special interest appropriation earmarks, 210
Stamp Act, xiv, 144
stamps (postage), mottos on, 27
*State Board of Education v. Board of Education of Netcong*, 89
states' rights/power, 73, 83, 150–51. *See also specific states*
states' rulings on religion, 84–86
Stewart, Potter, 82
*Stone v. Graham,* 84–85
Story, Joseph, 69–70
Strong, Josiah, xi–xii, 191
sub-prime mortgages, 223–24
sunset clauses, 202–3, 210
Supreme Court, 23–26, 36–37, 69, 75–81. *See also specific cases*
Supreme Court building, 28
survival issues for America, 188–92
Synod of New England Churches, 8

Tawney, R.H., 141
taxation: capital gains, 207–8; colonists and, 144; corporate, 197–98; cost of, 160; credit establishment, 213; education

and, 167–68; founders on, 155–56; government size and, 152–54; of middle class, 206–7; national debt and, 189–91; reducing, 214; regulation and, 142; scriptural model, 148–49; territorial, 211–12. *See also* federal spending
teachers' unions, 184, 216–17
technology and education, 183–84
Ten Commandments, 84–85, 93–96
Tenth Amendment, 18, 150–51
territorial taxation, 211–12
testing (educational), 176–77, 181, 216
thanksgiving, day of, 12, 13, 20
Thompson, Myron, 87
Thompson, Richard, 123
Thoreau, Henry David, 162
Thucydides, 94–95
Tiananmen Square, 125
*Tiller v. Atlantic Coast Railroad Co.*, 186
tithe, 144, 200
tolerance, 108
Tomb of the Unknown Soldier, 29
Trinitarian conundrum, 58–63
Truett, George W., 36
Truman, Harry, 22, 31
Tyler, John, 17
tyranny, xvi–xvii, 167

unalienable rights and, 11–12
Unitarianism, 60
*Updegraph v. the Commonwealth,* 23
*U.S. v. Butler,* 157–58
usury, 138–39

Van Buren, Martin, 17
Vietnam War, 107
Virgil, x, 18
Virginia, 24, 112
Voltaire, 191

*Wallace v. Jaffrey*, 75, 85, 89, 185
*Waltz v. Tax Commission,* 78
Warren, Earl, 23–24
*Warsaw v. Tehachapi*, 87
Washington, George: on education and religion, 165, 172; on God, 9, 17, 46, 68; on government, 83, 152–53; inauguration of, 12, 13, 17; on morality, 71–72, 145, 187–88; on religious freedom, 38; so-called Deist, 51–52
Washington monument, 28
*Wealth of Nations,* 136
Weber, Max, 139, 140
Webster, Daniel, 27, 56, 187
Webster, Noah, 42, 56, 71, 166–67
Wells, H.G., 161
westward expansion, xx–xxi
White, Timothy, 62
Wilhelm II, xi
Williams, Walter, 180
Wilson, James, 46, 99
Wilson, Woodrow, 21–22
Winthrop, John, ix, xix, 7, 57, 102, 196
Wolfe, Edward, 219
Wolman, William, 134, 227–29
the "Word," 60–61

Yale College, 169, 170

*Zorach v. Clauson,* 23, 80–82, 241–42n130, 254–55n77